MANAGEMENT INFORMATION SYSTEMS
Best Practices and Applications in Business

SECOND EDITION

T.A. ADIKESAVAN

Management Consultant (IT)
and
Visiting Faculty
University of Madras, Chennai

PHI Learning Private Limited

Delhi-110092

2014

₹ 395.00

MANAGEMENT INFORMATION SYSTEMS: Best Practices and Applications in Business
Second Edition
T.A. Adikesavan

ISBN-978-81-203-4896-7

The export rights of this book are vested solely with the publisher.

Second Printing (Second Edition)   ⋯   ⋯   **August, 2014**

Published by Asoke K. Ghosh, PHI Learning Private Limited, Rimjhim House, 111, Patparganj Industrial Estate, Delhi-110092 and Printed by Rajkamal Electric Press, Plot No. 2, Phase IV, HSIDC, Kundli-131028, Sonepat, Haryana.

To
my beloved son
Dr. T.A. GOPINATH
and my father
T. AYYASAMY
who was a humble agriculturist

CONTENTS

Preface   *xix*

Acronyms/Abbreviations   *xxv*

Chapter 1   **MIS/INFORMATION TECHNOLOGY (IT): Leveraging Modern
            Business and Management**   **1–41**

Chapter Quest   *1*
1.1   Knowledge Era   *2*
      1.1.1   Three Dimensions of Modern Business   *2*
      1.1.2   Focus of IT in Business   *3*
      1.1.3   Potential Contributions of IT to Business   *3*
1.2   Business Functions   *7*
1.3   Management Functions   *7*
1.4   Challenges Faced by Business in Knowledge Economy   *7*
1.5   Business as Glass Box (Three Dimensions of Business)   *8*
1.6   Business: Line and Support Functions   *9*
      1.6.1   Line Functions   *10*
      1.6.2   Support Functions (Staff Functions)   *12*
1.7   Modern Management Functions   *14*
      1.7.1   Three Levels of Management   *14*
      1.7.2   Responsibilities of Top Management   *14*
      1.7.3   Modern Managerial Functions   *15*
1.8   Information Technology   *20*
      1.8.1   Information Systems   *21*
      1.8.2   Communication Systems   *21*
      1.8.3   Modern Communication Technology   *21*
1.9   Tactical IT Applications in Business   *21*
      1.9.1   What are Tactical IT Applications?   *22*
      1.9.2   Tactical IT Applications   *22*
1.10 Strategic IT Applications   *22*
      1.10.1   What are Strategic IT Applications?   *23*
      1.10.2   Strategic IT Applications   *23*

v

1.11 Enormity of the Business Processes and their Interaction with IT   23
    1.11.1 Logical Interface between Business, IT Applications and
            the Computer Database   24
1.12 Interaction between Business and IT   25
1.13 Need for Integrated Business Applications (IBA)   26
    1.13.1 Disintegrated Information Systems/IT Applications   26
    1.13.2 Drawbacks of Disintegrated Information Systems   27
    1.13.3 Attributes of Integrated Business Applications (IBA/ERP)   27
    1.13.4 Advantages of IBA/ERP   27
1.14 Constituents of IT Applications in Business   28
1.15 Business and Its Environments   29
1.16 Information Technology Makes Businesses More Competitive   29
1.17 Business: Physical Processes   32
1.18 Information Technology: Leveraging the Business   33
Sum Up   40

Chapter 2 **DECISION MAKING IN BUSINESS (Data, Information,
Knowledge and Wisdom)**   42–56
Chapter Quest   42
2.1 Introduction   42
2.2 Data   43
    2.2.1 Data Processing   43
2.3 Information   44
2.4 Knowledge   48
2.5 Knowledge Base of the Business   48
2.6 Wisdom   49
2.7 Decisions   49
2.8 Action   49
2.9 Feedback   49
2.10 Business, Managers and Decisions   50
2.11 Business Entities and Events   50
2.12 Entities   51
2.13 Events   51
2.14 Logical Database   52
2.15 Data Types   52
2.16 Management Information—A Super Resource   52
    2.16.1 Management Information and Business Knowledge as
            Business Resources   52
    2.16.2 Management Information and Business Knowledge
            (Super Resources) Help Manage Other Resources More
            Profitably   53
2.17 Characteristics of Business Decisions   55
2.18 Information Resource Management   55
Sum Up   56

Chapter 3   **CONSTITUENTS OF IT APPLICATIONS IN BUSINESS**   **57–66**

Chapter Quest   57
3.1   Introduction   *58*
3.2   People   *58*
        3.2.1   People Outside the Organization   *58*
        3.2.2   Service Providers/Vendors   *59*
        3.2.3   Criteria for the Selection of Service Providers   *61*
3.3   People Within the Organization   *61*
        3.3.1   Top Management's Responsibilities   *62*
        3.3.2   Responsibilities of the Functional Managers and
                  Department Heads   *63*
        3.3.3   Business Operational Users (Transaction Processors)   *65*
        3.3.4   Business Processes   *65*
3.4   Data/Information   *65*
3.5   Computer Software   *66*
3.6   Computers and Network Infrastructure   *66*
Sum Up   *66*

Chapter 4   **INFORMATION TECHNOLOGY: Tactical Applications
in Business**   **67–96**

Chapter Quest   67
4.1   Introduction   *68*
4.2   Batch Data Processing System
        (Electronic Data Processing—EDP)   *68*
        4.2.1   Advantages of Batch Data Processing   *69*
        4.2.2   Limitations of Batch Data Processing   *70*
4.3   On Line Transaction Processing System (OLTPS)   *70*
        4.3.1   System Flowchart Indicating OLTPS Pertaining to
                  Purchase Function (Macro Level)   *71*
        4.3.2   System Flowchart Indicating OLTPS Pertaining to Sales
                  Function (Macro Level)   *72*
        4.3.3   Advantages of OLTPS   *74*
4.4   Management Information Systems (MIS)   *75*
        4.4.1   Illustrative Examples of MIS   *75*
        4.4.2   Advantages of MIS   *76*
4.5   Office Automation Systems (OAS)   *76*
4.6   Business Intelligence (BI) Executive Information System (EIS)
        and Enterprise Information System   *80*
        4.6.1   Sources and Types of Information Associated with EIS/BI   *80*
        4.6.2   Characteristics/Attributes of Effective EIS   *81*
        4.6.3   Examples of EIS   *82*
        4.6.4   Business Intelligence (BI)   *82*
4.7   Knowledge Management System (KMS)   *82*
        4.7.1   Categories of Business Knowledge   *84*
        4.7.2   Knowledge Based Management (KBM)   *85*
        4.7.3   Advantages of KMS   *85*

4.8   Geographic Information System (GIS)   *85*
4.9   On Line Analytical Processing System (OLAPS)   *86*
4.10   On Line Complex Processing System   *87*
4.11   Workflow Management Systems   *87*
4.12   Groupware Applications/Group Decisions   *88*
4.13   Web Publishing (Website on Internet)   *88*
4.14   Case Study—Dataflow Diagram   *89*
4.15   Case Study: Evolution of IT Applications in
        Business   *91*
Sum Up   *96*

Chapter 5   **BUSINESS TECHNOLOGY: Strategic IT Applications
             in Business**   **97–161**

Chapter Quest   *97*
5.1   Introduction   *98*
5.2   Integrated Business Applications (IBA/ERP)   *98*
        5.2.1   Introduction   *98*
        5.2.2   Logical Structure of IBA/ERP in Business   *98*
        5.2.3   What IBA/ERP Does to the Business?   *98*
        5.2.4   Business Processes Automated Through IBA/ERP   *99*
        5.2.5   IBA Software Packages (IBASP)   *103*
5.3   Supply Chain Integrated Business Applications (SC-IBA)   *103*
        5.3.1   Introduction   *103*
        5.3.2   Supply Chain Entities   *103*
        5.3.3   Logical Structure of Supply Chain Integrated IBA   *103*
        5.3.4   IT Applications Associated with SC-IBA   *103*
        5.3.5   Privacy and Security Concerns   *106*
        5.3.6   Benefits of Supply Chain Integrated Applications   *106*
        5.3.7   SC-IBASP (SC–IBA Software Package)   *107*
5.4   Sales Force Automation (SFA) System   *107*
5.5   Customer Relationship Management (CRM)   *108*
        5.5.1   Introduction   *108*
        5.5.2   CRM Objectives   *108*
        5.5.3   CRM in Knowledge Economy   *109*
        5.5.4   Components of CRM System   *109*
        5.5.5   CRM Applications in Business   *109*
5.6   E-business   *112*
        5.6.1   Benefits of E-business   *113*
        5.6.2   Benefits of E-business to the People/Customers   *115*
        5.6.3   E-business Application Software   *115*
        5.6.4   E-business IT Infrastructure   *115*
        5.6.5   E-business Challenges   *118*
        5.6.6   E-business Strategy   *118*
        5.6.7   Wrong Notions of E-business   *121*
        5.6.8   E-business Models   *122*

5.6.9   E-Business Life Cycle   *126*

5.6.10   E-business—Management Concerns   *129*

5.6.11   Advertising E-business (Conventional Methods)   *130*

5.6.12   E-marketing   *130*

5.6.13   E-business/E-marketing—View Points   *139*

5.6.14   Internet Applications Standards   *142*

5.6.15   Internet Communication Standards (TCP/IP)   *145*

5.6.16   E-business in India   *145*

5.7   Logistics and Goods in Transit Tracking Systems   *147*

     5.7.1   Global Positioning System (GPS)   *147*

5.8   Product Development Life Cycle (PDLC) Management System   *148*

5.9   Data Warehouse and Data Mining   *148*

     5.9.1   Data Warehouse   *149*

     5.9.2   Business Usage-based Classification of Data (Files/Database)   *149*

     5.9.3   Advantages of Data Warehouse   *150*

     5.9.4   Components of Data Warehouse System   *150*

     5.9.5   Data Mining   *151*

     5.9.6   Models Used in Data Mining   *152*

     5.9.7   Advantages of Data Mining to Business   *152*

5.10   Decision Support Systems   *153*

     5.10.1   Components of DSS   *153*

     5.10.2   Benefits of DSS to Business   *155*

5.11   Expert System   *155*

5.12   Case Studies (Part 1)   *156*

     5.12.1   Materials Purchases and Suppliers' Bills Payable System   *156*

     5.12.2   Retrospective Price Increases   *157*

     5.12.3   Retrospective Revision of Taxes   *158*

     5.12.4   Extension of Vehicles Warranty Period   *158*

     5.12.5   Vehicles to Reach the Markets Quicker   *159*

5.13   Case Studies (Part 2)   *159*

     5.13.1   Integration of Business Functions   *159*

     5.13.2   Executive Information Systems (EIS)   *160*

Sum Up   *161*

Chapter 6   INFORMATION TECHNOLOGY APPLICATIONS IN MANAGEMENT FUNCTIONS   162–176

Chapter Quest   *162*

6.1   Introduction   *163*

6.2   Selection of Business, Setting Objectives and Framing Policies   *163*

     6.2.1   IT Support in Selection and Setting Business Objectives and Policies   *163*

6.3   Establishing Systems and Procedures (Business Process Manuals)   *164*

     6.3.1   IT Support in Establishing Systems, Procedures   *164*

6.4 Planning *164*
  6.4.1 Strategic Planning *164*
  6.4.2 Tactical Planning *165*
6.5 Organizing *167*
  6.5.1 Organization Structure *167*
6.6 Staffing (HR Positions and Recruitment) *168*
6.7 Coordination/Collaboration (Integration) *169*
  6.7.1 Work Groups Applications/KMS *169*
  6.7.2 Workflow Management and E-Approvals *169*
  6.7.3 Networked Organization Structure *170*
  6.7.4 Integrated Business Applications *170*
6.8 Communication *170*
6.9 Control *171*
  6.9.1 Budget Control (Targets vs. Actual) *171*
  6.9.2 Functional Controls *172*
6.10 Compliance Management *172*
6.11 Risk Management *172*
6.12 Decision Making *173*
6.13 Innovation *173*
6.14 IT Strategy *174*
6.15 Relationship Management *174*
6.16 Knowledge Management *175*
6.17 Case Study: Performance Appraisal through Responsibility Accounting System *175*
Sum Up *176*

Chapter 7 PRACTICAL APPROACH FOR MANAGERS IN IDENTIFYING RIGHT IT APPLICATIONS

Chapter Quest *177*
7.1 Introduction *177*
7.2 Potential Benefits of IT and Associative Applications *178*
7.3 Steps Involved in Identifying Right IT Applications for each Department/Business Function *178*
7.4 Indicative List of CSFs and KRA *180*
  7.4.1 Marketing *180*
  7.4.2 Production *181*
  7.4.3 Procurement/Materials Management *181*
  7.4.4 Finance *182*
  7.4.5 Personnel (HR) *183*
Sum Up *183*

Chapter 8 **DESIGN AND IMPLEMENTATION OF INTEGRATED BUSINESS APPLICATION SOFTWARE PACKAGE (IBASP) FOR BUSINESS: Software Development Life Cycle Activities—SDLC (Waterfall Method)**   **184–228**

Chapter Quest   *184*

8.1   Introduction   *185*

8.2   Requirement Analysis, Systems Analysis and Requirement Specifications   *187*

     8.2.1   'As is' Study of Existing Business and Requirement Analysis   *187*

     8.2.2   Systems Analysis/Business Process Engineering   *190*

     8.2.3   Feasibility Analysis   *193*

     8.2.4   Logical Database   *194*

     8.2.5   Requirement Specifications/'To Be' Processes Documentation   *194*

8.3   IT Infrastructure Design, Project Costing and Implementation Schedule   *196*

     8.3.1   Infrastructure Design   *196*

     8.3.2   Software (IBASP) Development Efforts Estimation   *197*

     8.3.3   IBASP Development Cost Estimation   *200*

     8.3.4   Metrics and Measures   *201*

     8.3.5   Project Approval   *202*

8.4   System Design and System Specifications   *202*

     8.4.1   Data Flow Diagram   *203*

     8.4.2   System Design   *203*

     8.4.3   System Flowchart   *204*

     8.4.4   System Specifications   *204*

     8.4.5   Systems Audit Requirements   *207*

     8.4.6   Software Engineering—Quality Assurance   *208*

8.5   Programming and Testing   *208*

     8.5.1   Program Specifications   *208*

     8.5.2   Program Flowcharts   *209*

     8.5.3   Programming   *209*

     8.5.4   Program 'Walk-thru'   *210*

     8.5.5   Program Compilation and Unit Testing   *210*

     8.5.6   Application Package (IBASP) Integration Testing and Moving to 'Base Line'   *211*

8.6   User Training, Installation of Computer Resources and IBASP Implementation   *211*

     8.6.1   Business Users Training   *212*

     8.6.2   Acquisition and Installation of Computer Resources   *213*

     8.6.3   Data Conversion/Data Migration   *213*

     8.6.4   Implementation of New IBASP   *213*

     8.6.5   User Manuals/On line Help   *215*

     8.6.6   Intimation to Managers and Business Associates   *215*

     8.6.7   IBASP Implementation–Feedback   *216*

8.7   IBASP—Documentation and Maintenance   *216*
    8.7.1   System Documentation   *217*
    8.7.2   IBASP System Reliability   *217*
    8.7.3   IBASP Project—Metrics and Measures   *218*
    8.7.4   Post-implementation Audit   *218*
    8.7.5   Data Backup   *219*
    8.7.6   Software Updates and Upgrades   *219*
    8.7.7   Configuration Management   *220*
    8.7.8   Managing Computer Resources (Network Support)   *221*
8.8   Life Cycle Support Activities   *221*
    8.8.1   Procurement of Computers   *221*
    8.8.2   Procurement of Software   *221*
8.9   Systems Audit   *222*
8.10   End User Methodology   *222*
    8.10.1   Benefits   *222*
    8.10.2   Drawbacks   *222*
8.11   Ready to Use Application Packages AND/ERP   *223*
    8.11.1   Circumstances When ERP Software is Chosen   *223*
    8.11.2   Merits of ERP Packages   *223*
    8.11.3   Demerits of ERP Packages   *223*
8.12   IBASP Development—Outsourcing   *224*
    8.12.1   Benefits   *224*
    8.12.2   Disadvantages   *224*
    8.12.3   When Not to Outsource   *225*
8.13   Customized IBASP (Developed In-house or Outsourced)   *225*
    8.13.1   Merits   *225*
    8.13.2   Demerits   *225*
8.14   Rapid Application Development (RAD)   *226*
8.15   Joint Application Development (JAD)   *226*
8.16   Waterfall Method   *226*
8.17   Software for Small/Medium Business   *227*
8.18   Program Testing-Other Methods   *228*
Sum Up   *228*

Chapter 9   **IT APPLICATIONS' INTEGRITY, AUDIT AND CONTROL AND ATTRIBUTES OF IDEAL IT APPLICATIONS IN BUSINESS**   **229–248**
Chapter Quest   *229*
9.1   Business Expectations of IT   *230*
9.2   Characteristics and Attributes of Ideal IT Applications in Business (20 Points Approach)   *230*
9.3   Integrity of IT Applications   *233*
9.4   Information Systems Audit and Control   *235*
9.5   IT Management Controls   *236*
    9.5.1   Top Management Control   *236*
    9.5.2   Information Technology Services Division (ITSD): Management Control   *237*
    9.5.3   General Controls to be Followed by ITSD   *237*

9.6   IT Applications/Systems Integrity Controls   *238*
        9.6.1   Authenticity Control   *238*
        9.6.2   Accuracy Control   *238*
        9.6.3   Integrity Control   *239*
        9.6.4   Completeness Control   *240*
        9.6.5   Redundancy Control   *240*
        9.6.6   Data Security Control   *240*
        9.6.7   Existence Control   *241*
        9.6.8   IT Assets Safeguarding Control   *241*
        9.6.9   Effectiveness Control   *241*
        9.6.10 Efficiency Control   *242*
        9.6.11 Testing Control   *242*
        9.6.12 Documentation Control   *242*
        9.6.13 Preventive Control   *242*
        9.6.14 Detective Control   *243*
        9.6.15 Corrective Control   *243*
        9.6.16 System Controls   *243*
        9.6.17 System Audit Controls   *244*
        9.6.18 Quality Assurance   *244*
9.7   Case Studies   *244*
        9.7.1   Data Integrity Controls Established in Materials Purchase and
                Supplier Bills Payable System   *244*
        9.7.2   Employee Fraud   *246*
        9.7.3   Manager's Unethical Practice   *247*
Sum Up   *248*

Chapter 10   **SECURITY OF IT RESOURCES INCLUDING BUSINESS DATA
             AND INFORMATION**   **249–259**

Chapter Quest   *249*
10.1   Introduction—Need for Data Security?   *249*
10.2   Security Issues Concerning IT Applications in Business   *250*
10.3   Security Techniques   *250*
        10.3.1   Data Encryption   *250*
        10.3.2   Cryptography   *250*
        10.3.3   Encryption Program Logic   *251*
10.4   Symmetric Cryptography   *251*
        10.4.1   Symmetric Encryption Method (Ensuring Message Security)   *252*
10.5   Asymmetric Cryptography (Ensuring Confidentiality
       and Authentication)   *252*
        10.5.1   Key Pairs Used to Provide Confidentiality   *253*
        10.5.2   Key Pairs Used to Provide Authenticity   *253*
        10.5.3   Key Pairs Used to Provide Authenticity
                 and Confidentiality   *253*
        10.5.4   Combining of Symmetric and Asymmetric Cryptography   *254*
10.6   Digital Envelope   *254*
10.7   Hashing   *254*

10.8   Digital Signature   *254*
    10.8.1   Digital Certificate/Digital ID   *255*
10.9   Certification Authority   *255*
10.10   Good Encryption/Authentication Practices   *255*
10.11   Firewalls   *256*
10.12   Software Piracy/Security   *257*
10.13   Internet (Information) Robbery   *257*
10.14   Cyber-Crimes   *257*
10.15   Hacking   *258*
10.16   Cyber Theft   *258*
10.17   Consumer Privacy Issues   *259*
Sum Up   *259*

Chapter 11   **COMPUTERS: Structure, Networks and Architectures**   260–283
Chapter Quest   *260*
11.1   Logical Structure of Computer
    (John Von Neumann Architecture)   *261*
11.2   Central Processing Unit (CPU)   *261*
    11.2.1   Complex Instruction Set Computers (CISC Processor)   *262*
    11.2.2   Reduced Instruction Set Computers (RISC Processor)   *262*
11.3   System Bus/Channel   *263*
    11.3.1   Other Ratings Used for the Processors   *263*
    11.3.2   Computer Instructions   *263*
11.4   Computer Main Memory (DRAM)   *263*
11.5   CACHE Memory   *264*
    11.5.1   Special Memory Units   *265*
11.6   Data Storage (Multimedia) Devices   *265*
11.7   Input (Multimedia) Devices   *267*
11.8   Output (Multimedia) Devices   *270*
11.9   Networking Hardware   *272*
    11.9.1   Network Interface Cards (NIC)   *272*
    11.9.2   Modems   *272*
    11.9.3   Structured Cabling   *272*
    11.9.4   Hubs/Switches/Routers/Gateways/Bridges   *273*
    11.9.5   Computer Network—Mediums   *273*
    11.9.6   Mobile Devices   *274*
    11.9.7   Wireless LANs   *274*
    11.9.8   Power Supply—Generators and UPS   *274*
11.10   Criteria for the Selection of Computer Hardware   *274*
11.11   Computer Architecture   *276*
    11.11.1 Proprietary Systems/Main Frame Computers   *276*
    11.11.2 Open Systems/Client Server Architecture   *277*
11.12   Network Architecture   *278*
11.13   Generations of Computers   *282*
Sum Up   *282*

Chapter 12 **COMPUTER SOFTWARE, CASE TOOLS AND GOOD PROGRAMMING PRACTICES** 284–305

Chapter Quest **284**
12.1 Introduction **285**
12.2 Classification of Software **285**
12.3 Interface Layers Between Users and the Hardware **286**
12.4 Operating Systems (O/S) **286**
12.5 Other System Softwares **288**
12.6 Networking Operating System (NOS) **289**
12.7 Programming Languages **289**
  12.7.1 Types of Programming Languages **290**
12.8 Application Software **291**
  12.8.1 Integrated Business Application Software Package (IBASP) **291**
  12.8.2 General Purpose/Utility Software Packages **291**
  12.8.3 Utility Programs **292**
  12.8.4 General Purpose Application Packages **292**
  12.8.5 Application Specific Software Packages (ASP) **292**
  12.8.6 ERP Packages **293**
12.9 Office Automation Software **293**
12.10 Front End Tools **293**
12.11 Batching of Programs (JCL) **293**
12.12 Principles of Good Programming **293**
12.13 Computer Aided Software Engineering (CASE) **295**
  12.13.1 Advantages of CASE **296**
  12.13.2 CASE Tools **297**
12.14 Computer Virus **298**
12.15 Software and Hardware Interface **299**
12.16 Procurement of Software—Criteria for the Selection of Software **300**
12.17 Application Architecture/Platforms **302**
12.18 Case Study—Distributed Computing **305**
Sum Up **305**

Chapter 13 **DATA AND DATABASE MANAGEMENT SYSTEMS** 306–329

Chapter Quest **306**
13.1 Introduction **307**
13.2 Data Processing **307**
13.3 Database, Data Dictionary and Data Structures **308**
13.4 Data Storage Devices, File Organization and Access Methods **310**
13.5 Logical Structure of Database **314**
13.6 Steps Involved in the Creation of DBMS **315**
13.7 Entity/Event Relationship Diagrams **315**
13.8 Rules for Deciding Record Structures **316**
13.9 DBMS: Files/Records/Data Management Functions **318**

13.10 Functions and Advantages of DBMS/RDBMS   *318*
13.11 DBMS Implementation Methodologies   *320*
13.12 Data Administration/Database Administrator   *322*
13.13 Structured Query Language (SQL)   *323*
13.14 Data Backup and Restoration   *323*
13.15 Data Warehouse and Data Mining   *324*
13.16 Advantages of Database to the Business   *324*
13.17 Data Concurrency   *324*
13.18 Methods of Collecting Data   *325*
13.19 Data Independence   *325*
13.20 Case Study—Data Management   *326*
Sum Up   *329*

Chapter 14 **SYSTEM THEORY AND INFORMATION SYSTEMS**   **330–333**

Chapter Quest   *330*
14.1 Introduction   *330*
14.2 Comparisons of Three Known Systems   *331*
14.3 What the Systems Theory Advocates?   *331*
14.4 Two Way Approach Leading to Better Understanding
       of a System   *332*
14.5 How IT Applications Relate to Systems Theory   *332*
14.6 Systems Theory Concepts   *333*
14.7 Logical Components of Information Systems   *333*
Sum Up   *333*

Chapter 15 **INFORMATION TECHNOLOGY SERVICES DIVISION (ITSD):**
Functions and Responsibilities   **334–343**

Chapter Quest   *334*
15.1 Introduction   *335*
15.2 Mission   *335*
15.3 Focus   *335*
15.4 Role/Functions of ITSD   *336*
15.5 Business Organization   *336*
15.6 ITSD—Typical Organization Structure   *337*
15.7 ITSD—Responsibilities of Technical Functions   *337*
15.8 ISO Standards for Software Engineering   *341*
15.9 Information Technology Infrastructure Library (ITIL)   *342*
15.10 Chief Digital Officer (CDO)   *342*
       15.10.1 What CDOs need to be?   *342*
Sum Up   *343*

Chapter 16 **IT APPLICATIONS IN SELECT SERVICE INDUSTRIES (Banks, Hospitals and Hotels) AND E-GOVERNANCE** 344–360

Chapter Quest **344**
16.1 Banks **344**
    16.1.1 Core Banking Solutions (CBS) **345**
    16.1.2 Internet Banking (Online Banking) **346**
    16.1.3 POS (Point of Sales) Devices—ATM/Debit Cards/ Credit Cards/E-Wallet **346**
    16.1.4 ATM Services **347**
    16.1.5 Mobile Banking **348**
    16.1.6 Branchless Banking (Bank and Non Bank Based) **348**
    16.1.7 Payment Services/ECS **349**
    16.1.8 Online Trading **349**
    16.1.9 Impact of Information Technology on Banking Services **350**
    16.1.10 Other IT Applications at Banks **350**
16.2 Hospitals **350**
    16.2.1 Websites **351**
    16.2.2 Hospital Portals **351**
    16.2.3 Patients' Clinical Information System **351**
    16.2.4 In-patients Billing Systems **352**
    16.2.5 Hospital Beds and Operation Theatres Allocation/Occupancy Monitoring Systems **352**
    16.2.6 Hospital Pharmacy Management Systems **353**
    16.2.7 Medical Insurance Claims for In-patients **353**
    16.2.8 Issue of Discharge Summaries for In-patients **353**
    16.2.9 Quality Rating for the Hospitals **353**
    16.2.10 Other IT Applications **354**
16.3 Hotels and Resorts (Property Management) **354**
    16.3.1 Hotels and Resorts—Internet Portal **354**
    16.3.2 Guest Billing Systems **355**
    16.3.3 Guests Tour and Travel Planning System **355**
    16.3.4 Restaurant Reservation, Ordering of Food and Billing **355**
    16.3.5 Hotel Room Reservation and Occupancy Monitoring Systems **356**
    16.3.6 CRM for Hotels and Resorts **356**
    16.3.7 Other IT Applications **356**
16.4 E-Governance in India **356**
    16.4.1 Introduction **356**
    16.4.2 Tamil Nadu State Government (TNSG) **357**
    16.4.3 E-governance Infrastructure **357**
    16.4.4 TNSG E-governance Mission **357**
    16.4.5 E-governance Objectives **358**
    16.4.6 Services Offered by ALL Government Departments (of TNSG) **358**
    16.4.7 Department SPECIFIC E-governance Services (Select Departments) **358**
Sum Up **360**

Chapter 17 **INFORMATION TECHNOLOGY: Genuine Concerns for Humanity** 361–370

Chapter Quest *361*
17.1 Introduction *361*
17.2 Social Concerns—Favourable Contributions *362*
17.3 Social Concerns—Adverse Contributions *363*
17.4 Privacy Concerns *364*
17.5 Health Concerns *365*
17.6 Ethical Issues *366*
17.7 E-Fraud/Cyber Crimes *367*
17.8 Cyber Terrorism *368*
17.9 Dos' and Don'ts for Information Technology/Internet Users *369*
Sum Up *370*

Chapter 18 **BUSINESS TECHNOLOGY MANAGEMENT** 371–387

Chapter Quest *371*
18.1 Introduction *371*
18.2 Twelve Perspectives of Business Strategy *372*
    18.2.1 Business as a Battlefield *372*
    18.2.2 Business as a Chain of Marketing Operations *373*
    18.2.3 Business as a Repository of Resources *374*
    18.2.4 Business as a Series of Decision Making Processes *375*
    18.2.5 Business as a System Influenced by its Environments *375*
    18.2.6 Business as a Continually Learning Organization *376*
    18.2.7 Business as Creating Win-Win Relationship with Diverse Human Entities *378*
    18.2.8 Business as a Conglomeration of Management Functions *378*
    18.2.9 Business as Value Creation for Customers *380*
    18.2.10 Business as an Adopter of Right IT Strategies *382*
    18.2.11 Business as an Establishment Focussing on Risks *382*
    18.2.12 Business as System Involving Measures, Metrics and Analytics *382*
18.3 Business Technology (BT) *383*
18.4 Business Technology Management (BTM) *383*
18.5 Building Blocks of BTM *383*
    18.5.1 Business Processes *383*
    18.5.2 Organization *384*
    18.5.3 Information *384*
    18.5.4 Technology *385*
18.6 BTM Capabilities *385*
18.7 BTM Maturity Model *385*
18.8 Capability Maturity Model (CMM) *385*
Sum Up *387*

Index 389–396

PREFACE

Information Technology (IT)

In the early 1970s, II generation computers capable of performing just one task at a time were used in business for processing large volumes of data in one go. The impact of such applications was so profound that the computer technology itself was referred by the name of the application, viz. EDP (electronic data processing).

By the end of the 1970s, III generation computers capable of performing multiple tasks concurrently (multi user systems) were used in business. EDP, OLTP (on-line transaction processing) and MIS (management information systems) became the applications of computers in business. The technology was referred as MIS as it was the most rewarding application to business and its managers. No one imagined at that time that the technology would grow to the extent of what we witness today.

Even today, the names like EDP and MIS are being used to refer the technology in some organizations and educational institutions.

In subsequent years, the technology was also referred as MRP (material requirement planning), IIS (integrated information systems), ERP (enterprise resource planning), and IBA (integrated business applications).

Today, since the computer technology and communication technology have seamlessly merged into a single mosaic of vast space, such space is referred as Information Technology (IT).

Further, as the Technology is aimed at bringing strategic benefits to business, the whole concept is termed as 'Business Technology', E-business being an important segment of it.

Best IT Practices

Technology by itself could not bring all benefits to business. Instead, right IT practices leading to implementation of IT applications decide their success. Such practices are taken as one of the subject matter for this book.

IT Applications

Today, IT offers hundreds of solutions/applications for any type of business. It is necessary to have a good knowledge of all such applications. This book discusses all possible

IT applications today, to enable the readers in understanding the scope and benefits of individual applications and their relevance to their respective businesses.

What is in This Book?

This book packs necessary and sufficient knowledge of the business processes, modern management functions, Information Technology, and best IT practices and applications including software engineering to enable discerning readers in becoming experts in the subject.

This book is unique as it presents an integrated view of all the above entities and responsibilities of people in delivering ideal IT applications in business.

The focus of this book is business and its management and how the business could be made more efficient and effective using the technology. The technology is looked at from the business perspective of business process automation, collaboration, integration, decision support, knowledge accumulation and dissemination, global reach for the business, efficient customer relationships, and so on.

Modern concepts such as 'Business Technology' which bring strategic advantages to business and E-business are discussed exhaustively.

This book would enable business managers to play a proactive role in implementing right IT applications in their respective businesses.

Practical IT applications related to all line and support functions and management functions are described with live examples, tables, diagrams and case studies. This would help business managers in identifying more appropriate IT applications in their work environments.

All readers would be rewarded by way of getting a better insight into the business and its management, good knowledge of IT and vast benefits it brings to the business.

For some readers this could serve as a textbook and for others a reference book. Prior knowledge of IT is not mandatory for the readers of this book.

Why This Book?

This book combines Technology, and business management very exhaustively. Computers are being used in business organizations very extensively today. But if we ask the employees, managers, customers and other people associated with the business, they will always enumerate the problems encountered in the computerized business processes. This book is to help eliminate such problems.

I have more than three decades of experience in implementing highly successful IT applications in big manufacturing industries. I have witnessed huge mismatch of knowledge possessed by the business managers of the technology and the software professionals of the business and its management. I have been educating these entities in overcoming such shortfalls. Such education, I feel, is essential for implementing right and reliable IT applications in business. This is the main motivation for writing this book.

I have also 12 years of experience in teaching the subject to MBA students belonging to different colleges affiliated to University of Madras and found the students gaining very good knowledge of the subject which is an added motivation for me to write this book.

A wide variety of IT applications in business, best IT practices and the human efforts involved in implementing highly reliable and successful applications are stressed throughout this book because it is finally the human efforts that make a beauty out of the beast of this technology/computers.

Target Groups

Graduates in any discipline and the students pursuing MBA/PGDBM/MCA programmes:

- Both graduates and students would get an integrated view of the business operations, modern management functions and IT applications which has become the third essential dimension of modern business.
- The role of MIS (management information systems) in enhancing the knowledge of the managers and the decision making processes are explained with practical case studies.
- The fundamentals of computer hardware, software, data and database management concepts are explained thoroughly so that the readers having no prior exposure to them also would gain good knowledge of the technology in a short time.
- This book will equip them well in facing their examinations and subsequently turn this group into successful business/systems analysts capable of exploiting the technology at optimal levels.
- Ten great contributions of IT to business and the attributes of ideal IT applications are also summed up.

Business managers and the functional heads

- Business managers and functional heads will become fully aware of all IT applications that could leverage their business and make it more competitive. Since both tactical and strategic applications are discussed in detail with their scope, merits and limitations, the managers could choose and implement right IT solutions for their respective business functions.
- This book also describes the functions of modern management and the technology support for such management functions.
- Five major constituents of IT applications in business, viz. business processes, people, data, computer hardware and software and how these resources need to be acquired and managed in implementing ideal IT applications in business are also explained so as to enable them to realize the importance of all five entities.
- The roles and responsibilities of the managers in identifying right IT applications, development/acquisition of quality software and implementing successful IT applications are also stressed.
- The process and the need for integrating all business functions/entities are explained with practical examples so as to make them understand the importance of business communication, coordination and collaboration.

Top management

- Top management will be able to appreciate the technology very objectively in terms of the benefits they bring to the business, both tactical and strategic and the ways by which the technology leverages today's business to make it more competitive. They could visualize the ways by which IT could make their business more efficient and its management highly effective.

- Essentials of 'Business Technology Management' (BTM) and E-business are discussed very exhaustively.

- The strategic IT applications (Business Technology) discussed in detail would enable them get associated while implementing such applications in their business.

- All the ways by which the IT resources could be acquired and managed successfully, with relative merits and demerits, are highlighted clearly so as to enable top management in formulating right IT strategies and taking right decisions while acquiring such resources.

- The roles and responsibilities of technical personnel have also been discussed in detail so as to enable top management in establishing right IT services division within the organization.

System auditors and IT applications quality assurance functions

- The attributes of ideal IT applications in business are explained so as to enable systems auditors and software quality engineers in taking appropriate and right steps in achieving the same.

- System security and integrity controls discussed elaborately in this book would enable them incorporating the same in all IT applications.

IT professionals, project managers and software engineers

- Software engineering activities involved in the design and implementation of integrated business applications software are discussed in such great detail that this book would serve as a reference manual for them.

- IT professionals would clearly be able to understand the business processes and modern management functions and be aware of what the business expects from IT. They would learn all the ways of delivering highly reliable and ideal IT applications to business.

- The need for security of IT resources and integrity of business data/information and the ways by which the same could be achieved are also discussed to enable them implementing high quality applications in any business organization they work for.

- Various computer and IT application architectures are also discussed so as to enable this group in identifying right architectures for a given business environment.

Book's Reach

The book covers the MBA syllabus (IT/MIS/EDP) of University of Madras in particular and other universities in general. The students would gain highly focused knowledge through this book. This book would also be useful for students pursuing PGDBM and allied programmes at leading business schools.

The book packs such vast knowledge that it can be used as a reference book by business managers, top management, software engineers, system auditors, software quality assurance personnel, and so on in India and abroad. The libraries of the business organizations and software companies can also stack this book to help their employees and managers get a good grasp of the subject.

There are a number of books on business and its management and also books on IT and MIS. This book is unique as it is written by an IT practitioner who has been implementing successful IT applications in big business organizations for more than three decades.

This book imparts vast practical knowledge of the subject using real business examples.

How the Book is Organized?

There are 18 chapters in the book, each having a chapter quest (synopsis) at the beginning to guide the readers navigating through the respective chapters. Each chapter concludes with a summary at the end.

Case studies, examples, diagrams and live business scenario are provided profusely in this book such that the readers would get a realistic feel of the subject in all chapters.

Acknowledgements

I have gained vast knowledge of the subject through experience, hundreds of books, periodicals, technical journals, seminars, product brochures, and so on. Though it is not possible to acknowledge all such sources, I am indebted to all of them.

I have shared my vast experience and knowledge through this book with a fond hope that the business organizations and the target readers would exploit this technology more effectively and profitably.

T.A. ADIKESAVAN

ACRONYMS/ABBREVIATIONS

2G	Second generation wireless technology
3G	Third generation wireless technology
4G	Fourth generation wireless technology
ASCII	American standard code for information interchange
ASP	Application service providers
ATM	Automated teller machine
B2B	Business to business
B2C	Business to customers
BI	Business intelligence
BIT	Binary digit
BOM	Bill of materials
BPA	Business process automation
BPO	Business process outsourcing
BT/BTM	Business technology management
BYTE	String of eight bits
CASE	Computer aided software engineering
CAT	Computer aided training
CBS	Core banking solutions
CBT	Computer based training
CD	Compact disks
CDO	Chief digital officer
CDMA	Code division multiple access
CISC	Complex instruction set computers
CMM	Capability maturity model
COBOL	Common business oriented language
CPU	Central processing unit
CP/M	Control program/microprocessor
CRM	Customer relationship management
CSF	Critical success factors
DAT	Digital audio tapes
DBMS	Database management systems

DFD	Data flow diagram
DM	Data mining
DNS	Domain name system
DRAM	Dynamic random access memory
DSS	Decision support system
DTP	Desk top publishing
DVD	Digital video disks
DW	Data warehouse

EBCDIC	Extended binary coded decimal interchange code
ECS	Electronic clearing system
EDP	Electronic data processing
EIA	Enterprise integrated applications
EIS	Executive information system
EPROM	Erasable programmable read only memory
ERP	Enterprise resource planning packages
ES	Expert system

FLOPS	Floating point operations per second
FMS	File management system
Fortran	Formula transmission (Language)
FTP	File transfer protocol

GB	Giga bytes
GDSS	Group decision support system
GIS	Geographic information system
GIT	Goods in transit
GPRS	General packet radio service
GSM	Global system for mobile communication
GUI	Graphic user interface

HLD	High level design
HPO	High performance organization
HTML	Hypertext markup language
HTTP	Hypertext transport protocol

IT	Information technology
IBA	Integrated business applications
IBASP	Integrated business applications software package
IGSP	Internet gateway service providers
IMSP	Infrastructure maintenance service provider
ISP	Internet service provider
ISO	International standards organization
ITD	Information technology division
ITES	IT enabled services
ITIL	Information technology infrastructure library
ITSD	Information technology services division
IV GL	Fourth generation languages

JAD	Joint application development
JCL	Job control language
JIT	Just-in-time (inventory)
KB	Kilo bytes
KMS	Knowledge management system
KRA	Key result areas
LAN	Local area network
LCD	Liquid crystal display
LLD	Low level design
MAN	Metropolitan area network
MB	Mega bytes
MBE	Management by exceptions
MBO	Management by objectives
MI	Management information
MIPS	Million instructions per second
MIS	Management information system
MRP	Material requirement planning
MTBF	Mean time between failures
NAP	Network access point
NDA	Non disclosure agreement
NSP	Network service provider
NFS	Network file system
NOS	Networking operating system
OAS	Office automation systems
OCR	Optical character recognition
OLAPS	Online analytical processing system
OLCPS	Online complex processing system
OLTPS	Online transaction processing system
OS	Operating systems
OSI	Open system interconnection
PC DOS	Personal computer Disk operating system
PDLC	Product development life cycle
PGSP	Payment gateway service provider
PL1	Programming language-1
PMS	Project management system
POP	Post office protocol
POS	Point of sales
PROM	Programmable read only memory
R&D	Research and development
RAD	Rapid application development
RDBMS	Relational database management system

RISC	Reduced instruction set computer
ROI	Return on investment
ROM	Read only memory
RTI	Right to information act
SC IBA	Supply chain integrated business applications
SDLC	Software development life cycle
SDSP	Software development service providers
SSL	Secured socket layer
SFA	Sales force automation
SFTP	Secured file transfer protocol
SIM	Subscriber identity module
SMTP	Simple mail transfer protocol
SMTP	Simple message transfer protocol
SNMP	Simple network management protocol
SQL	Structured query language
TCP/IP	Transmission control protocol/Internet protocol
TDMA	Time division multiple access
TLS	Transport layer security
TPS	Transactions per second
UPS	Uninterrupted power supply
URL	Uniform resource locator
URM	Unit record machines
USB	Universal serial bus
VCD	Video compact disk
VDU	Video display unit
VPN	Virtual private network
WP	Word processing
WAN	Wide area network
Wi-Fi	Wireless fidelity
WiMax	Wireless max
WMS	Workflow management system

CHAPTER

1

MIS/
INFORMATION TECHNOLOGY (IT)
Leveraging Modern Business and
Management

Chapter Quest

The following questions would guide the readers in navigating through this chapter:

1. Why Information Technology (IT) is considered to be the third essential dimension of today's business?
2. What needs to be the focus of the management while exploiting IT?
3. What potential (ten) benefits IT offers to the business?
4. What are the challenges being faced by business in the knowledge era?
5. What are the business operations performed by line and support functions in a manufacturing organization?
6. What are modern management functions?
7. What is the enormity of the business processes and how IT applications get superimposed on thousands of such business processes?
8. What are tactical IT applications in business?
9. What are strategic IT applications in business?
10. How the physical business gets truly reflected in electronic form in the computer database?
11. How IT applications get integrated with the business and its management?

12. What is meant by integrated business applications (IBA) and the need for the same?
13. What are the ways by which the technology makes the business more competitive?
14. What are the key factors by which the business gets leveraged by IT?

After finishing this chapter, the readers would have clear answers for these questions.

1.1 KNOWLEDGE ERA

After having passed through agricultural, capital and industrialization based economies, the human race is right now passing through 'knowledge economy'.

People around the globe are being continuously exposed to worldwide knowledge of newer, better and cheaper products, facilities and services which would improve the quality of their daily life. Computers, Internet, mobile phones, and so on are making them more knowledgeable and enabling them to take wiser decisions. What is learnt by one or a few individuals is made known to the world instantly (e.g., consumers' bad experience with a product or service is made known to everyone) through social networks. People, anywhere they are on the globe, always keep in touch with their families, relatives and friends not only through voice but even with video talks.

In 'knowledge economy', business and its management could be successful only if they know about their markets, innovative and cheaper products, more capable competitors, power retailers, highly demanding customers, their fast changing preferences and the technologies impacting the business. Knowledge is reckoned as a competing force today. Computers and the Internet are also making the customers and competitors more knowledgeable. Hence, the business and the management need to become much more knowledgeable and continually learning organizations.

Business today needs to resort to best business practices. Integration of business operations including the supply chain, knowledge accumulation and dissemination across entire enterprise and efficient customer relations and response management systems are to be in place. Business management and decision making have become too complex, though the actions need to be taken fast.

In addition to making the managers more knowledgeable, (IT) consisting of computers and communication systems bring many tactical and strategic advantages to business, thereby making it more competitive. IT leverages the business far greater than the efforts and investments made in it.

1.1.1 Three Dimensions of Modern Business

Modern business has three dimensions:

1. Efficient **business operations** which are highly responsive to customer expectations and fast in reaching the markets.
2. Effective **management** relying on right business knowledge that leads to optimal utilization of its resources and opportunities.
3. **Information technology** applications that bring competitive edge to the business.

These three dimensions, however, are being dynamically altered by the markets, retailers, customers, supply chains, governments, competitors, innovations and newer technologies.

IT/Internet is breaking the constraints posed by political, geographic, socio-economic, cultural and linguistic boundaries.

IT is bringing remarkable efficiency (speed of operations) to the business by integrating all business functions including supply chain and admirable effectiveness (optimal utilization of the resources) through good planning, coordination and control of all business operations.

Today's businesses need to become high performance organizations (HPOs) capable of tackling market and supply chain dynamics. It needs to have matching capabilities in the form of business process automation and integration, business intelligence, sharing of business knowledge among all decision makers, innovativeness and managerial decisiveness.

Managers need to be empowered and need to become aggressive, collaborative and cooperative knowledge workers. The process of knowledge acquisition, accumulation and dissemination needs to make the business a continuously learning organization. The opportunities and threats need to be anticipated and acted upon fast.

1.1.2 Focus of IT in Business

The focus of IT should be to achieve:

- Result oriented, customer focused, cost conscious, committed, collaborative and innovative management.
- Integration of all business operations including supply chain, leading to close coordination and collective decision making.
- Business growth by exploiting the opportunities around the globe.
- Good and quick decision making based on sound knowledge of the business.
- Transparency in all its operations and accountability for all managers.
- Realistic reporting of its operations and business outcomes.
- Producing right products and placing them at right place and at right time so that they could be liquidated at the earliest.

1.1.3 Potential Contributions of IT to Business

Potential (ten) contributions of IT to today's business elicited below have made the technology the third essential dimension of modern business (business operations and management functions being the other two dimensions).

All IT applications discussed in this book exploit one or more of these potentials. If we visualize the business as a grid made up of hundreds of business operations on the X-axis and fourteen modern management functions on the Y-axis, one or more IT applications discussed in this book would sit on each cell of such grid, thus making IT the third dimension of today's business.

1. **Business process automation (BPA):** Information Technology automates most of repetitive, time-consuming, monotonous and error-prone data associative business

activities/processes, thereby freeing the human resources to undertake more profitable/innovative tasks. BPA mostly would mean any of the following five processes:

(i) *Structured/programmable decisions.* Structured decisions in business are possible provided that:

- All factors (data) associated with a decision are known.
- Such factors are either quantifiable or be stated in definite terms.
- It is possible to establish relationships among all such factors leading to a decision (like rule or formula or model).
- Action to be taken on such decision outcome is pre-stated and clear.

Structured decisions could be automated through computer programs and hence are also called programmable decisions.

A business involves thousands of structured/programmable decisions being made in daily operations, like offering definite discounts based on sales quantities, charging definite interest on investments, repayment schedules based on the terms of the loans taken, assessing vendor quality based on quantum of rejections, taxes and duties to be levied based on statutory laws, employee salary based on attendance and scales of pay, computing profit margin, ROI and financial ratios, and so on.

Programmable decisions incorporated in the computer software lead to automatic compliance of business rules with no deviation or exception and also allow people with less experience and skills to handle the business operations.

(ii) *Transaction processing and printing of business documents.* A business is associated with a large number of entities (like suppliers, customers and so on) and events (buying, payments, selling, collections and so on) through which business resources get committed or realised. Such events get recorded through the documents like purchase orders, payment vouchers, sales invoices, receipts for collections, expense vouchers and so on. There are thousands of transactions taking place daily under each such event. IT enables capturing, processing, printing and storing of all business transactions/documents as and when they occur, fast and accurate.

Because of this, the business operations get speeded up and become more efficient and accurate. The data associated with these events also get added up to the computer database which is used for subsequent analysis and review (management information).

Since all business events are captured as and when they occur by the IT applications, the database reflects the true status of physical business in real time.

(iii) *Bookkeeping—books of accounts, registers and ledgers.* Computers maintain all statutory, operational and control records in electronic form like books of accounts, assets registers, stock ledgers, day books, general ledgers, attendance registers, statement of accounts, tax returns, and so on very accurately.

(iv) *Business computations.* All types of business computations, simple, like interest and salary computations and complex like statistical analyses, quantitative techniques (like linear programming), mathematical models, material requirement planning, production planning, capacity planning, and so on involving extensive computations and iterations are automated and completed very fast and accurately.

(v) *Large volume printing.*   Large volume printing like employee pay slips, statement of accounts to be sent to external entities, dividend warrants, daybooks and ledgers, etc. are accomplished fast and with great ease.

In addition to this, BPA would also include automation of data associative business processes listed under Section 1.17. IT makes the business processes more efficient (fast), accurate and saves tremendous manual efforts (effectiveness).

2. **Storing large volumes of business data and accessing the same fast:**   Business organizations generate large volumes of transactions (of all business events) on a daily basis, resulting in the accumulation of huge volumes of business data. Such transactions also get posted on to the respective business entities (like suppliers, customers, materials, banks and so on) to reflect true business status of all entities. Computers are capable of storing huge volumes of business data (covering all entities and events) and accessing and updating the same very fast. This capability in the form of computer database helps business to know what is happening in business anytime (electronic memory).

In addition to operational data mentioned above, historical data is also accumulated over longer periods of time in order to understand what had happened in the past and also in making business forecasts and discoveries (like Data warehouse, Data mining and Decision support systems discussed in Chapter 5).

In addition to business data, it is also possible to store and access multimedia files/contents (documents, texts, pictures, images, audio, video, graphs, animation, etc.) through the computers (like knowledge management systems discussed in Chapter 4).

3. **Enhances business knowledge/intelligence:**   Real time IT applications capture data related to all business events and entities and store them in a single database, to reflect (like a mirror) the true status of the physical business in electronic form at any moment. Such data is easily converted into meaningful management information to make the managers of all business functions highly knowledgeable of what is happening in business.

In addition, it enables sharing of such business information/knowledge across all functions and managers. Management information system (MIS), Executive information system (EIS), Business intelligence (BI), Knowledge management system (KMS), Decision support system (DSS), Data mining, and Customer relationship management (CRM) are the applications (discussed in Chapters 4 and 5) that help managers in enhancing their knowledge of the business and the markets.

4. **Integration of business functions/operations:**   Business organizations have a number of business functions, each having their own individual operational plans which are in line with organizational goals. IT enables the operations of all business functions, pending tasks, bottlenecks, fixes for the problems and accomplishments get integrated/made known to others through a common database shareable by all managers in the organization.

Such integration leads to closer coordination, collaboration, collective decision making and good planning by the managers. This synchronizes and integrates the efforts of individual functions in to one single business entity in achieving common business objectives. This also leads to unity of purpose among all business functions. Integration is achieved within and with the supply chain entities situated external to the business organization.

Integrated business applications (IBA) and Supply chain integrated business applications SC-IBA offer great benefits to the business (discussed in Sections 5.1 and 5.2).

5. **Establishes efficient electronic relationships with all business entities:** IT by virtue of Internet enabled business applications (like IBA, SC-IBA, web sites, e-mail, e-business, Internet portals, etc.) supported by efficient communication systems enable highly effective and mutually beneficial electronic relationships to be established among the investors, employees, managers, top management, suppliers, logistics service providers, market channels, sales force, retailers, regulating/government agencies, customers and the general public.

All these entities are able to freely and effortlessly exchange/communicate their plans, aspirations and expectations, unconstrained by the geographic distances and political boundaries, all the time. Electronic relationships make the business highly efficient and effective and also reduce the operational costs considerably. E-business and its advantages are discussed in Chapters 5 and 16.

6. **Shrinks physical business space:** By virtue of one single database for the entire business and efficient Internet for sharing of business information around the world, even multinational operations are made to look like a local business for its operations and management. Physical infrastructure required to run the business gets reduced considerably. Managers sitting at home or any place or on the move could still (mobile computing) manage the business as if they are sitting in their office.

People sitting in the comforts of their homes can buy and do what they want without having to travel to do it. Branchless banking, e-commerce, Internet portals, etc. are such benefits derived by this facility.

7. **Global reach for the business:** IT (Internet) enables the products and services being offered and required by any business to be made known to the world at large instantly and with negligible costs. This has enabled global reach for the business, both for buying and selling.

8. **Convergence/multimedia:** Today's computers handle data, text, documents, pictures, images, animation, audio, and video of any standard or format and the communication devices carry them very fast through Internet. In addition to conventional data processing, IT enables processing of multimedia files also. All types of multimedia devices (like camera, microphone, speaker, LCD projectors, TV) also get connected to the computers and the Internet. Information technology encompasses human entertainment also in the process.

9. **Miniaturization and decreasing costs:** Since computers and communication devices are becoming very small in size, the mobility/portability factors of these devices themselves offer great benefits to business, more particularly the sales force

and field personnel. In addition to miniaturization, the costs of these devices are also coming down rapidly due to the scales of economy (higher sales volumes and global markets) and large scale R&D efforts put in by all such players in IT arena.

A pen-like device (pen drive) can store the business data of an entire organization and can be carried anywhere. A button size camera can capture any type of images in business and send the same around the world instantly using Internet.

No other technology today is offering the products and services which are becoming continuously cheaper and at the same time with increasing capabilities and benefits.

10. **User-friendly interfaces and potent applications:** Last but not least, other important factors that contributed to the phenomenal growth of computers and IT applications in business are their highly user friendly/simplified human interface and availability of thousands of easy to use application software which bring immense benefits to the business.

And also, any electronic device can just be connected to computers today and be used instantly (plug and play devices) because of the pre-established standards made available for such interfaces. Any application software can also be loaded on to the computers and used immediately because of easy user interface incorporated in the software.

All IT applications discussed in this book exploit one or more of these ten potential benefits of the technology.

Attributes of ideal IT applications are also discussed in Chapter 9.

1.2 BUSINESS FUNCTIONS

All business functions working together offer products/services that add value to the customers for which they are willing to pay. The line and support functions of a typical manufacturing business are listed in Section 1.6.

All business operations/processes associated with these functions need to be performed with perfect coordination and collaboration not only within the organization but also with the external entities like suppliers, market channels, customers, and so on.

1.3 MANAGEMENT FUNCTIONS

Modern managerial functions of today's business are listed in Section 1.7.3. Information technology offering direct and supportive solutions to the management functions (management support systems) are discussed in Chapter 6. IT applications make management tasks simpler and enable managers with lesser experience to shoulder the responsibilities of senior management.

1.4 CHALLENGES FACED BY BUSINESS IN KNOWLEDGE ECONOMY

Challenges faced by the businesses in knowledge economy are unique as indicated:

1. **'Pull market' strategy:** Customers have become highly knowledgeable and demanding. The competition is fierce and all businesses target the purses of the same consumers. The business needs to pull information related to customer needs and expectations, product preferences, competing products, etc. from the markets continuously so as to offer better products and services ahead of competition.

2. **Innovative business processes, products and services:** Product life spans are shrinking and the business needs to offer innovative and cheaper products to its customers on a continual basis. Production processes need to be improved either to reduce costs or to enhance products' worth (better value addition) to the customers. R&D and value engineering need to be focused on achieving this. Managers need to be engaged in creative thinking and product enhancement tasks leaving the tasks that could be automated to the computers.

3. **Right IT strategy:** Information technology has become the third essential dimension of today's business. In many businesses, it sits in the driving seat of business. The management needs to very clearly state its strategy with respect to the use of IT and implement right applications that bring tactical and strategic advantages to the business. IT needs to be reckoned as strategic tool and should contribute to the success of the business. The emerging concepts of Business Technology and its management in this regard are discussed in Chapter 18. Responsibilities for this are to be fixed, with a right manager within the organization, with right authority. This book greatly would guide the top management in evolving right IT strategies for their business.

4. **Knowledge based/learning organizations:** Business needs to learn from its past and create a knowledge base from such learning. The knowledge base needs to reflect the experience gained/lessons learnt by all managers. The accumulation and dissemination of such knowledge needs to happen on a continual basis. Managers need to be made committed and accountable in creating such knowledge base (highly valuable resource as discussed in section 2.16.2.).

Knowledge based organizations would enable the managers at operational levels to take decisions which hitherto are done by higher levels of management. Knowledge has to be made an organizational resource (why reinvent the wheel).

5. **Transparency in business processes, accounting and reporting:** Business needs to be sufficiently transparent to its managers, stakeholders and the general public. Accurate accounting and profit reporting systems should be in place.

6. **Social and environmental responsibilities:** Business organizations need to be responsible to its environments and the society. Funding social welfare schemes, environment protection, pollution control, educational services, and so on need to be given due consideration.

1.5 BUSINESS AS GLASS BOX (Three Dimensions of Business)

Modern business can be considered as a glass box, its three dimensions being efficient business operations, effective management functions and information technology applications, as depicted in **Figure 1.1**.

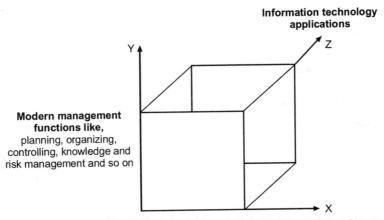

FIGURE 1.1 Three dimensions of modern business.

It is the responsibility of the managers and employees in the organization to fill the box, with right value addition processes benefiting customers, efficient business operations, optimal deployment of organizational resources, constant drive for cost reduction, responsiveness to customer needs, right information technology applications, and so on.

The business (glass box) also needs to be filled with knowledge workers and result oriented/committed managers.

The box does not exist in isolation but is surrounded by the markets influenced by socio-economic, political and competitive environments. People within the business need to have good perception of all that happens outside the organization (see through the glass box).

Being a glass box, the external world would be constantly watching as to what is happening inside the business. The business reputation, brand image, etc. would suffer if any thing bad is noticed from outside. At the same time, right things happening inside the box will also be seen and appreciated by one and all, leading to better business reputation and brand image.

1.6 BUSINESS: Line and Support Functions

The objectives of a business are to offer its customers the products/services for which they are willing to pay, keep the customers satisfied, enhance the customer base and thus chart organic growth for the business.

Business deploys **seven** resources (7M), viz. men, materials, machinery, money, minutes (time), managers and management information in achieving the business objectives. Tactful deployment and utilization of these resources measure the effectiveness of the business. The speed with which the business operations are performed decides its efficiency.

A business involves line and support functions as listed below. Depending on the type and size of business, these business functions could even be more or less. Under each business function, important sub functions are also listed in order to reveal the enormity of the business operations.

1.6.1 Line Functions

The line functions of a business are as follows:

1. **Sourcing of inputs and vendor development:** There are businesses wherein the identification of right sources for inputs alone, decides the success of the business. Inputs could be raw materials, plant and machinery, consumables such as power, water, packing materials, etc. finished/semi finished products and a variety of other services.

   Successful sourcing involves deciding, right and new vendors, quality specifications for all inputs, right prices (value engineering), prompt and consistent deliveries (vendor reliability), shortest lead time, cheapest transportation costs, and so on.

2. **Purchasing:** Material requirement planning (MRP) means identifying right materials, quantities, costs and delivery schedules in consultation with production and marketing functions. MRP is mandatory for purchasing.

   Purchasing involves events such as calling for quotations from rightly identified vendors, getting quotations from vendors, vendor evaluation in terms of price, quality and reliability, negotiations with the vendors, preparation and forwarding the purchase orders, follow-up on delivery schedules, cash flow planning for the purchases (commitments), vendor reliability evaluation, and so on.

3. **Quality control of inputs:** It involves establishing quality standards (drawings and specifications) for all inputs, identifying right quality assurance techniques to be implemented at the vendor premises, establishing norms for conducting quality control tests (e.g., sampling techniques), inspection of input materials, rejection of defective materials, return of rejected materials, acceptance of good materials, vendor quality rating, and so on.

4. **Materials management:** It involves receiving the materials as per the delivery schedules, acknowledging materials/services received, accounting of inspected/good stocks in stores, maintenance of stock ledgers, physical accommodation of stocks, safeguarding the stocks, issue of materials to production, valuation of issues, inventory management (minimum stock levels, economic order quantities, surplus/ obsolete stocks, etc.), stock valuation, minimizing inventory carrying costs and so on.

5. **Production planning and scheduling:** Based on the sales plan and already existing finished stocks, production planning is done for a week or month in advance. Production planning logically leads to MRP based on the bill of materials (BOM). It also involves planning the working capital, capacity utilization of production resources and manpower planning.

Scheduling identifies the weekly/daily/shift wise production targets based on the availability of raw materials, product mix, existing capacities of plant and machinery, available manpower, quality control infrastructure, and so on. Based on the production schedule, the materials are drawn from the stores.

6. **Production and production control:** Actual production involves drawing of materials from stores, optimal utilization of the production resources, deployment of men and machinery in production processes, control on work-in-progress (WIP stocks), product costing, maintaining production history (so as to track product complaints later), assessing capacity utilization, and so on.

7. **Quality assurance and control—finished products:** This function involves implementing quality assurance techniques, inspection of production processes, quality control on work-in-progress and finished products as per quality control norms/sampling techniques, quality rejections, analyzing reasons for rejections, rectification of defects, costing of rejections, and so on.

8. **Product packaging:** Products of different quantities and qualities are put in different and right packing or containers. Packing should display all information about the products. In addition to protecting the products from damage and deterioration, packing also needs to add value (like reusable jars) to the customers. Associative processes are similar to production and production planning.

9. **Finished stock inventory:** This activity would involve maintaining finished stocks ledger indicating receipts and issues of stocks, safe custody/insurance cover for stocks, stock verification, accounting for damaged stocks, finished stock valuation, inventory control, and so on at all stock points.

10. **Logistics and warehousing:** Moving right quantities of products at right time and to right place, identifying cheaper modes of transport and routes with least lead time, tracking goods in transit, insurance cover for the goods in transit, costing of logistics including warehousing, payments to logistics service providers, etc. are the activities to be performed under this function.

11. **Wholesalers and distributors:** Wholesalers and distributors are extended profit centres of the business. Stock accounting for all products, sales planning, monitoring of product dispatches and goods in transit (GIT), actual sales, accounts receivables, managing defective/damaged stocks and commissions payable, etc. are the activities to be performed by this function at all such locations.

12. **Retailers:** All activities referred above are also to be performed for all the retailers. In addition to this, competitor stocks and sales, display locations (shelves) and space, feedback obtained from retailers, etc. are to be managed at all retail outlets.

13. **Customers:** Business organizations need to know their customers very precisely in terms of their preferences, loyalty, buying power, demography, buying experiences (how they are treated at points of sales), customer satisfaction, products performance and complaints, and so on. Customer relationship management and customer feedback systems are to be given top priority.

14. **Sales and marketing:** Sales forecast, preparation of marketing budgets, booking customer orders, product dispatches, sales invoicing, sales realization, sales promotion activities and advertisements, fixing sales force responsibilities, sales force automation, assessment of product strength and weakness in the market, customer feedback analysis, sales analysis, assessing market potential and the market share, and so on are the activities to be performed by this function.

In knowledge based economy, product innovation, expanding existing customer base, cost reduction, customer relations management and establishing efficient customer response systems, and so on are to be prioritized.

15. **E-business:** The IT applications implemented within the organization and extended to the supply chain need to make use of Internet, Intranet, Extranet, mobile computing, E-mail, web sites, e-business, and so on. Right IT strategies and infrastructure are to be planned and implemented in deriving these benefits.

16. **Exports and imports:** Exploring international markets for both buying and selling of products and services, compliance to import/export regulations and procedures, foreign trade barriers, foreign exchange regulations, trading of imported products, and so on need careful evaluation and management.

17. **After-sales service/customer support:** After-sales follow-up with the customers, registering new customers, feedback from the customers, warranty claims, redressing customer complaints, post-sale services like annual maintenance contracts until the life time of the products, call centres, rectification of product defects, product improvement/buyback, managing service and call centers, etc. are the activities to be performed under this function.

18. **Repairs and maintenance:** Plant and machinery (assets) management, replacement decisions, breakdown maintenance, maintaining history of breakdowns, repairs management and costing, preventive maintenance, replacement planning, etc. are the operations to be undertaken under this function.

19. **Product development:** Product development life cycle (PDLC) management in the stages of identification of customer preferences, product development, production engineering, launch of new products, test marketing, managing market growth, value engineering, identification of more durable and cheaper inputs, improved production processes (process engineering), enhancement of product performance, improved product presentation, and so on are to be carried out under this function.

1.6.2 Support Functions (Staff Functions)

1. **Finance:** Capital planning, decisions on debt/equity ratio, identifying cheaper sources for capital, acquisition of right funds at right time, servicing of debts at right time, investment decisions, banking and treasury operations, cash-flow planning based on the business plans (long term and short term), budgeting for all

business functions, budget controls, assets management, cost control, financial accounting and profit reporting, debtors and creditors management, auditing, responsibility/commitment accounting, expenditure control, managing financial risks, compliance management, delegation of power, and so on are the activities to be performed under finance function.

2. **Human resources management:** Establishing right job specifications/responsibilities for all positions in the organization, creation of organization structure (approved positions), establishing span of control and reporting relationships, recruitment, attendance and leave management, salary administration with recoveries and statutory deductions, HR compliance management, performance appraisal, salary increments, promotions, transfers, separation, retirement, disciplinary/legal actions, employee welfare, industrial relations, improving employee morale, job enrichment/enlargement, training, career planning, etc. are the activities to be performed under this function.

3. **Information technology services division (ITSD):** This function needs to map right and emerging technology solutions on to the business so as to make the business derive maximum benefits from the technology. This also involves identification and implementation of ideal/integrated business applications for the entire business using Internet.

The responsibilities of IT division are discussed in Chapter 15. Software development methodologies, quality and integrity of IT applications, systems audit, attributes of ideal applications in business, business technology management etc. are discussed in Chapters 8, 9 and 18.

4. **Legal proceedings, statutory compliances and risk management:** Initiation of legal action against unlawful entities and events, follow-up on legal proceedings pending in various courts of law, court verdicts, etc. need to be taken care by legal function.

Statutory and regulatory laws, rules and procedures that are to be complied with, fixing the responsibilities for the same and follow-up on actual compliance are also to be done by this function.

Identification of all types of risks, covering all insurable risks, risk mitigation procedures and risk management are to be taken care through appropriate risk management systems by this function.

5. **Office management/administration:** Organization's estate/assets management, security of the office and factory premises, housekeeping, office infrastructure, office equipment repairs and maintenance, office administration, postal and courier services, telephones and other communication systems, electricity, air conditioning, travel, hospitality, employee entertainment and leisure time activities, and so on are to be managed by this function.

6. **Company law and investor management:** Formation of the company, appointment of board of directors, conducting board meetings, managing shareholder accounts, dividend payments, issue of bonus and rights shares, statutory compliance with regard to the companies act, registrar of companies, SEBI and stock exchanges, investor relations, and so on are to be managed effectively.

7. **Corporate-social responsibility:** Social responsibility of the business to the nation and its people, public relations, trade relations, trade unions, corporate governance, transparency in business operations, truthful reporting of the operating results, safeguarding stakeholders' interests, pollution control, environment safety and so on are the functions to be taken care by this function.

IT applications related to all the above line and support functions are discussed in Chapters 4 and 5 (as tactical and strategic IT applications).

1.7 MODERN MANAGEMENT FUNCTIONS

Managers are intellectual resources in a business who manage all other resources judiciously and profitably. Management functions are discussed briefly here, to enable the readers in understanding the role of IT in management functions discussed in Chapter 6.

1.7.1 Three Levels of Management

There are three levels of management in business, viz. top, middle and operational, each having distinctively different roles and responsibilities.

1. **Top management:** Top management is responsible for establishing and running the business itself, achieving business goals and strategic management. Additional responsibilities of the top management are discussed in Section 1.7.2.

2. **Middle level management:** They are responsible for tactful management of available resources including working capital, and getting optimal returns on investments (operating profits).

3. **Operations management:** They are responsible for daily business operations including events management and transactions processing, quality control, efficiency of business operations, cost control, customer services, and so on.

1.7.2 Responsibilities of Top Management

Top management needs to establish the structural framework for business and clearly state the following objects:

1. **Vision:** It is what is foreseen as an opportunity with a strong conviction that it could be achieved. The vision reflects aspirations and ambitions for the business itself, its customers, employees, stakeholders, society and the country in general in long run.

2. **Mission:** It gives physical structure to vision. The mission of the business states the purpose of the business, like what type of products or services, whether to compete on price or quality, market share/leadership, intended paths in fulfilling the vision, and so on.

3. **Objectives:** The objectives of the business refer to step-by-step approach in reaching the mission in definite time frame like one or two years. This states the end results or the targets that will be achieved by business with respect to time, like paying dividends to the shareholders, reaching 50% market share, 100% product reliability, and so on.

4. **Strategy:** The business strategy refers to knowledge based management plans devised in order to realize the business' vision, mission and objectives. The strategy has greater relevance to the external (socio-economic) business environments. Business strategy is to decide the scope of the business and the ways of running it. It refers to choosing the paths of growth, market share, where and when to set up the business, technology to be used, investment outlay, source of funds, debt-equity ratio, top management personnel, time to reach the markets, and so on.

5. **Business policies:** These prescribe executive framework for the managers in the form of rules, regulations, guidelines, decision making processes, organization structure, delegation of power, span of control, and so on, within which the managers themselves can perform.

Management policies evolve from the strategies and are necessary for creation and operation of the business. They set the direction and boundaries for all employees and managers.

6. **Business process manuals (best business practices):** Business process manuals are function oriented directives that elaborately and explicitly state at micro levels, as to how the operations/processes need to be performed under each business function and all sub functions under it. They clearly state as to what, how, when, who, where and the methods by which all business activities need to be performed. They are very exhaustive and incorporate the best business practices. Most such processes do get automated through IT applications. The procedure manuals would also be updated regularly to incorporate improved/better business practices (business process re-engineering).

The business procedure manuals need to be made available to all managers in the organization and this has been discussed under KMS in Section 4.7.

7. **Delegation of power:** It is the management directive which clearly states the levels of the management/managers who are authorized to commit organizational resources necessary for running the business and their limiting powers in doing so. This is aimed at establishing good financial and management control in business organizations.

1.7.3 Modern Managerial Functions

In addition to the responsibilities of the top management discussed above, managers at all levels need to perform the managerial functions discussed below in varying degrees, depending on the type of the business and the levels of management.

The role of information technology in management functions are discussed in Chapter 6, which are also called management support systems (MSS).

1. **Planning:** It is the process of forward thinking, before committing business resources as to what, when, how much and where they are to be deployed in achieving the business objectives. Planning is mandatory for all business operations and precedes all other management functions.

Planning by the top management could cover periods as long as three to five years. For middle management, the planning periods could be a few months or a year. For operational management, it could be a few weeks or months. Business plans, targets, budgets, etc. are planning activities.

Setting business objectives, and formulating business strategies, policies and procedures for achieving the objectives are long-term planning functions.

   (i) *Strategic plans.* These are designed to meet an organization's broad goals, such as market leadership, establishing new business, expanding existing markets, creating newer markets, newer products and services, growth plans both organic and inorganic, acquiring new business and so on. The data/ information associated with these decisions are mostly unstructured, not readily available and remain external to the organization.

   (ii) *Business plans.* It is a formal document containing the business targets, in terms of investments, cash flows, sales volumes and turnover, organization structure, expenditure, profit, and so on for a year or more. It would also contain the description of the firm's business (goods or services), market analysis, market share, financial projections, and so on. It is the blue print for the business's success and a guide for all managers in setting up their functional goals.

   (iii) *Tactical plans.* These plans involve judicious deployment of organizational resources in achieving the business objectives. Tactical planning involves shorter time periods and is generally carried out by middle level management/ functional heads. Budgeting in terms of business incomes, all types of expenses, cost of capital, capacity utilization, sales volumes, inventory costs, fixed expenses, administrative overheads, and so on for all business functions constitute tactical plans. IT applications greatly help management in tactical planning.

   (iv) *Operational plans.* These are associated with the completion of business processes on a day-to-day basis involving procurement, production, sales, payments, collections, and so on (events/transaction management). Speed of the business operations (efficiency), quality of the products and services offered and deploying least working capital (effectiveness) are the main focus for operations management.

2. **Organizing:** It refers to the activities leading to mobilization of business resources and services both within and outside the organization and engaging them in establishing and running the business. It is the process of getting things done as per the plans. It is also a process of engaging human resources (organization structure) who would work in unison and structured way in achieving the business objectives.

(i) *Organizing to get the things done.*   External to the business, organizing is the process of getting approvals from regulating agencies/governments, establishing the vendors, vendor development, mobilising the capital, acquiring production infrastructure, appointment of marketing channels and the retailers and integration of all these entities.

Organizing also mean establishing formal relationships among different human entities so that the business is run and managed through such entities. It also involves identifying right human resources and engaging them in achieving business objectives. This is called staffing. Staffing could be to create a new organization or to fill the vacancies in an existing organization.

(ii) *Organization structure.*   Within the business, organizing is the process of identifying all job responsibilities, creation of right job specifications, assigning authority, establishing reporting relationships, fixing responsibilities, establishing accountability and allocation of work.

The management must match the organization structure to its goals. The organization structure could be hierarchical, functional, matrix (combination of hierarchical and functional) or networked.

Networked organization structures are gaining prominence now, where versatile human skills (from different business functions) are networked together to achieve a specific task. The network of people work in unison in completing the task. A network has a leader and members having necessary and varying skills required for completing the task in time. The network is dismantled once the assigned task is completed.

Organization structure creates a set of requirements (job specifications) for each position within the organization. This may include educational qualifications, experience, personal capabilities to deliver end results, decision making skills, knowledge of the business, leadership qualities and so on.

3. **Staffing:**   This is a process of matching the skill sets of people who are to join the organization with the job specifications and offering them right compensation. It involves recruitment and retention of human resources. It also involves assessing existing workforce and recruiting to fill vacancies.

Each person in the organization needs to know his responsibilities clearly, and explicitly understand the parameters on which his performance is measured (accountability). People need to have right skills demanded by the position and should have the potential to undertake higher responsibilities.

4. **Coordination/collaboration (integration):**   Collaboration is a management process through which people interact with one another in achieving harmony of individual and group efforts aimed at achieving organizational goals. In the process, the organization's overall capability (synergy) becomes more than the sum total of individual's capabilities. This can be achieved only through collaboration and coordination.

Coordination relates to all business/support functions whose operations/processes are synchronized with one another in achieving the business objectives.

Good collaboration and coordination seamlessly merge (integrate) individual efforts into the organizational synergy aimed at achieving business excellence.

5. **Leading:** This involves directing, guiding, motivating, rewarding and training the people to make them perform more effectively and efficiently. Establishing cordial employee relationships, convincing them of their responsibilities, motivation and earning willing participation are the essence of good leadership.

Good leaders could motivate the employees far more than all other motivational factors combined together. Leaders need to be dealers of hope.

6. **Controlling:** This is the most important management function which ensures that all business resources are deployed properly and adequately and also yield commensurate returns.

What we cannot measure, we cannot manage. Controlling involves setting targets on various business performance yardsticks (like ROI, sales volumes, capacity utilization, cost of production and so on) for all employees and the managers and measuring their actual performance, so as to assess their performances in time.

Control takes many forms at the functional levels, like cost control, production control, inventory control, quality control, and so on.

7. **Communicating:** This is the process by which people's ideas, thoughts, instructions, orders, commands, acceptances, refusals and so on, are transmitted to others enabling them to take right action at right time. This encompasses all management and business functions. Communication can take place from top management to all others at lower levels (vertical communication), across all business functions (horizontal communication) and with the external business entities (external communication).

Communications need to be explicit, timely, and devoid of ambiguity, misinterpretation and misunderstanding. It needs to have proof of acceptance/acknowledgement to eliminate the chances for its denial/repudiation later.

What are communicated could be data, business information, decisions, business knowledge, charts, graphs, images, instructions, audio, video, and so on. The mediums for communication could be oral (face-to-face), telephones, letters, e-mail, SMS, tele-conference, electronic files, video conference and so on.

IT has brought revolutionary changes to business communications (affordability) and eliminated the constraints posed by geographical and political boundaries and different time zones.

8. **Decision making:** The decisions are to be taken by all managers and the people involved in daily business operations. Most of the operational decisions in the business are structured as discussed in Section 1.1.3.1. Such structured decisions could be incorporated in the computer software as programmed decisions.

On the contrary, there are a number of other decisions that are unstructured which means that the four conditions stated in Section 1.1.3.1 are not met. For example, the sales forecast is an unstructured decision.

Good decisions take the business from its present state to the most preferred state.

Decision makers need to have sufficient knowledge and good perception of the business. There needs to be good MIS (Management Information System) that enables the managers in clearly perceiving what is happening in business and make them knowledgeable.

Decision making involves:

- Good knowledge of the business and its environments
- Clear perception of business problems
- Creativity and imagination
- Excellence or task orientation
- Codes of ethics
- Identification of all decision alternatives
- Deciding the best alternative
- Implementation of a decision
- Assessment of decision outcome (feedback).

Wherever the decisions are unstructured, the managers' wisdom (intelligence, intuition and ability to infer), experience, risk taking abilities and decision support systems (discussed in Section 5.10) influence their decision making.

9. **Compliance with statutory rules and regulations:** Business organizations need to comply with local, national and international laws related to the business, statutory rules and regulations related to taxes, tariffs, customers, employees, investors, public safety, pollution, product quality, product pricing, monopolistic and restrictive trade practices, and so on. All business functions and the managers need to comply with such rules and regulations without fail since violations, if any, could lead to penalty, prosecution, punishment and bad reputation.

There needs to be exhaustive 'Compliance management manual' for the entire organization and also for respective business functions covering all the issues mentioned above. It should identify all the rules and regulations that are to be complied with, managers responsible for each of them, procedures to be followed for their compliance and so on. There needs to be a system to monitor all compliances, and non compliances, if any, need to be reported to the top management. Clearly stated responsibilities for all employees and the managers in this regard are to be explicitly stated in the manual.

10. **Risk management:** Business organizations are always exposed to a variety of business risks, some of them very serious, like product obsolescence, shifting customer loyalty, cheaper/substitute products, stoppage of work, fire, floods, earthquake, new political/tax regimes, and import/export curbs, financial risks like operating losses, non-availability of working capital, bad debtors and credit squeeze and public risks like destruction to public property, accidents, pollution, threat to human lives, and so on.

Management needs to have necessary strategies to mitigate all possible risks so that the business is least impacted by any such risks. Insurable risks are to be covered by appropriate insurance policies.

Risk management involves identification of all types of risks in business, risk mitigation procedures and risk management in the event of their occurrence.

There needs to be exhaustive 'Risk management manual' for the entire organization covering all business functions with clearly stated responsibilities for all its employees and the managers.

11. **Evolve IT strategy:** We have seen that IT has evolved into an essential third dimension of any business today. There need to be clearly stated IT strategies in place to get the best leverage from it. IT should be deployed to gain competitive edge in the marketplace.

Top management need to identify/formulate right IT strategy for their business and beware of:

- Various ways by which IT leverages the business today.
- How a business could gain competitive edge using IT.
- Tactical and strategic IT applications used in business.
- Various alternatives of acquiring and managing the IT resources.
- Efforts to be put in by the business managers in implementing right, reliable and quality IT applications.
- Attributes of ideal IT applications in business and so on.

By virtue of this, the top management will be able to adopt right IT strategy for their respective business. Today's business need to gain Business Technology leadership, discussed in Chapter 18.

12. **Relationships management:** Business organizations today need to establish and manage good and mutually rewarding (win-win) relationships with the customers, retailers, market channels, logistics operators, employees, managers, vendors, various service providers, investors, banks, governments, regulating agencies and general public. Management needs to set right strategies and establish supporting organization structure in maintaining beneficial relationship with all these entities.

13. **Knowledge management:** We have seen that today's business needs to be knowledge based organization and its managers the knowledge workers. Knowledge of the customers, their buying behaviours and product preferences, competing products, market dynamics, cheaper inputs, better production processes, cost reduction techniques, innovative products/services are essential parts of the knowledge economy.

Such knowledge, being possessed by individual managers and employees needs to be pooled into the organizational know-how, to be exploited by all employees and managers. It is the responsibility of the management to ensure that the knowledge possessed by the individuals is channeled into organizational know-how/asset. Knowledge management systems which can immensely benefit the business in this regard are discussed in Section 4.7.

14. **Innovation:** Managers and employees should devote their time and efforts in identifying innovative products and services, more efficient business processes including marketing, cheaper and better inputs, newer production technologies, innovative sales promotions and so on. Knowledge and innovation need to complement each other.

1.8 INFORMATION TECHNOLOGY

Information technology is an amalgam of two revolutionary technologies, viz. Computer technology (computer systems engaged in business process automation that produce right business information in real time) and Communication technology (that delivers business information to right person at right place).

1.8.1   Information Systems

Information systems have been in vogue ever since the human race came into existence. For example, a baby's cry is a sort of information communicated to the mother to act. Mother rightly interprets the baby's cry and perceives possible reasons in its context (like hunger or pain or fear). She applies her mind/wisdom to identify possible causes and makes a decision.

Applied to business, information systems help managers in perceiving the business situation/problem better. The business could be put on the right track only if the managers are knowledgeable enough and wise in taking right decisions at right time.

1.8.2   Communication Systems

When the human race started living in groups across different villages, they still were communicating the information that were of mutual interests to them.

For example, one group communicated the incoming danger to other groups by beating the drums. Depending on the number of beats, they communicated different information at different occasions.

Today we have computer based wired, wireless and satellite communication systems which enable people around the world to communicate round the clock with no constraints whatsoever. Communication technology today, seamlessly integrates all the mediums such as voice, text, data, pictures, graphics, images, audio, video and so on (convergence/multimedia). This has revolutionized the way the human race could acquire, accumulate and share knowledge with great ease and least efforts.

1.8.3   Modern Communication Technology

Internet has evolved into universal standards for connecting (networking), computers, communication devices, variety of communication mediums, operating systems, wide variety of applications software, mobile devices, and so on. Any entity complying with such standards can get connected to Internet (world-wide-web). These standards are being managed by technical experts in different countries independent of political and military interventions.

Information/knowledge around the world are being stored in thousands of computers (servers) and shared by millions of people (clients). Internet is further discussed in Section 5.6.4.

1.9   TACTICAL IT APPLICATIONS IN BUSINESS

IT applications in business can be classified as tactical and strategic based on certain attributes.

1.9.1 What are Tactical IT Applications?

The tactical IT applications have the following attributes:

1. They help in tactical management (optimal utilization) of all business resources which leads to organizational effectiveness. Managers are able to manage the business with least efforts, leading to managerial effectiveness.
2. They automate most of the business processes and speed up the business operations. This enhances organizational efficiency and its responsiveness to dynamic market situations.
3. Organizational and statutory rules and regulations get embedded in the software resulting in automatic compliance of the same with no deviations.
4. All types and sizes of business use these applications and the application software required for this purpose is easily available or can be developed fast.
5. These applications are mandatory for all types and sizes of the business today and any business cannot be run without them.
6. They do not impact/alter the existing business structures (like organization structure, reporting relationships, market channels, etc.) either within or outside the organization.
7. Though these applications support the business processes and the management functions to a large extent, they do not sit in the driver's seat of the business.

1.9.2 Tactical IT Applications

Tactical IT applications that are discussed in this book are.

1. Batch data processing/electronic data processing (EDP)
2. On line transaction processing systems (OLTPS)
3. Management information systems (MIS)
4. Office automation systems (OAS)
5. Business intelligence (BI)/Executive information systems (EIS)
6. Knowledge management systems (KMS)
7. Geographic information systems (GIS)
8. On line analytical processing systems (OLAPS)
9. On line complex processing systems (OLCPS)
10. Workflow management systems (WMS)
11. Groupware applications
12. Web publishing (web sites on Internet).

Individual tactical applications are discussed in Chapter 4.

1.10 STRATEGIC IT APPLICATIONS

As the name implies, these IT applications bring strategic benefits to business and they require exhaustive planning, great efforts and careful evaluation and implementation.

1.10.1 What are Strategic IT Applications?

1. These applications bring strategic advantages to business like reaching out to new customers, expanding the markets, supply chain integration, discovering newer customer behaviour, newer market channels, and so on. These applications make the technology sit in the driving seat of the business.
2. These applications would make structural changes to the organization structure including the supply chain. IT applications become an integral and inseparable part of the business.
3. Careful evaluation, long time planning and great efforts need to be made by management, business functions and IT professionals in implementing right type of applications based on the type and size of the business.
4. Investments in IT infrastructures are higher and the IT resources are to be made highly reliable.

1.10.2 Strategic IT Applications

1. Integrated business applications (IBA/ERP)
2. Supply chain IBA/ERP (SC-IBA/ERP)
3. Sales force automation systems (SFA)
4. Customer relationship management systems (CRM)
5. E-business and Internet enabled applications
6. Logistics and goods tracking systems
7. Product development life cycle management systems (PDLC)
8. Data warehouse and data mining
9. Decision support system (DSS)
10. Expert system (ES)

Individual strategic IT applications are discussed in detail in Chapter 5.

In addition to these applications, applications related to management functions (management support systems) are discussed in Chapter 6.

1.11 ENORMITY OF THE BUSINESS PROCESSES AND THEIR INTERACTION WITH IT

Figure 1.2 illustrates how 26 business operations mentioned in Section 1.6, and hundreds of sub operations under them and 14 management functions mentioned in Section 1.7.3, mapped together lead to thousands of business activities. How these business activities actually are performed by individual organizations are called the business processes. IT applications support thousands of such business processes and lead to organizational and managerial effectiveness and efficiency.

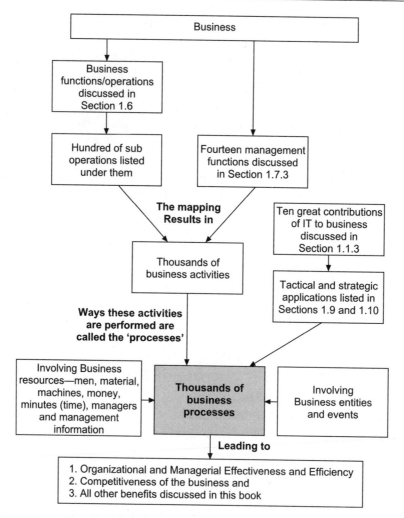

FIGURE 1.2 Mapping of IT applications on to business processes.

All benefits of IT to business are derived by mapping 10 great benefits of IT discussed in Section 1.1.3, on to the business processes.

Figure 1.2 summarizes business operations, management functions and IT applications discussed so far in this chapter.

1.11.1 Logical Interface between Business, IT Applications and the Computer Database

Figure 1.3 is self-explanatory and depicts how the physical business gets morphed into the computer database that reflects true physical status of the business in digital form in electronic mediums (computer database). Stages A to E mentioned in the diagram are discussed in Chapter 13.

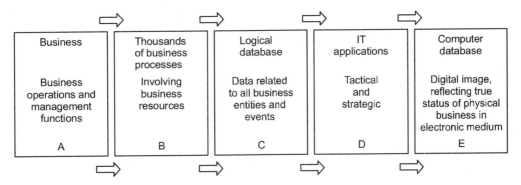

FIGURE 1.3   Morphing of physical business in to computer database.

When the computer database (E) reflects true/real status of the physical business (A) in digital form with no variance (for example, stock as shown in the database is same as physical stocks at the stores) at any given moment, such system is called the real time information system.

1.12   INTERACTION BETWEEN BUSINESS AND IT

Figure 1.4 depicts the road map of the subjects discussed in this book indicating the chapters where respective topics are discussed.

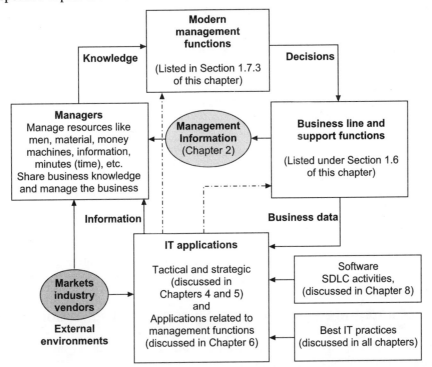

FIGURE 1.4   Interaction between business, management and IT applications.

Figure 1.4 shows,

- The interaction between the business and the IT applications.
- Flow of data into IT applications and management information to the management,
- Decision making processes of modern management functions.
- Computer software.
- Best IT practices and so on.

1.13 NEED FOR INTEGRATED BUSINESS APPLICATIONS (IBA)

A business involves interaction among diverse business functions/departments, the managers and the supply chain entities spread across distant geographic locations all working towards achieving common business objectives. All their operations need to be integrated in order to gain closer coordination and collaboration. Integration of business functions is a natural/logical requirement of any business.

However, the technology is able to offer such facility only for last ten years, thanks to Internet which enables connecting the business spread around distant geographical locations, powerful computers (servers/main frame computers) capable of automating the business processes of hundreds of business users (concurrent tasks), large data storage devices (hard disks) and efficient database management systems (RDBMS).

For example,

1. Declining sales continuously for a few weeks need to send timely signals to business functions concerned so as to speed up sales promotion efforts, slowing down production, arranging additional cash flow, deferring purchase of inputs, and so on.
2. Delivery schedules contained in the purchase orders need to be used for monitoring timely receipt of raw materials, planning for timely inspection of incoming materials, cash flow planning for making timely payments to the suppliers, stock accounting, and so on.
3. Orders received from customers and the dealers need to be used for planning production, timely inspection of finished products, product despatches, logistics, cash-flow estimation, and so on.

IT applications/information systems need to integrate all business functions and make them look like one single/integrated entity in achieving the organizational goals. This brings enormous synergy into the organization.

No functions could claim exclusive ownership for the organizational information. Ownership, update and access rights of business information for all managers need to be clearly stated and approved by the management.

1.13.1 Disintegrated Information Systems/IT Applications

Disintegrated information systems create islands of information in an organization that are not easily shared among all business functions. The reasons could be the following:

1. Applications are implemented at different geographical locations (like different manufacturing and marketing sites) which maintain independent computer resources and databases which are not networked with one another.
2. Applications in the same location are implemented on different computers which are not networked or databases/application software which are not compatible to one another (different IT platforms).
3. Applications that do not make use of a DBMS but performing data/file management tasks independently which make sharing of information more difficult.

1.13.2 Drawbacks of Disintegrated Information Systems

1. Individual business functions like procurement, production, marketing, etc. give priority to the functional goals (because of over enthusiasm or to play safe or due to organizational politics) instead of the organizational objectives. This leads to non-sharing of a function's information with other functions or passing false information.
2. Great benefits being offered by IBA/ERP are lost by the business.

Please refer case study discussed in Section 5.13.1.

1.13.3 Attributes of Integrated Business Applications (IBA/ERP)

1. IBA automates the business processes as discussed in Sections 1.1.3 and 1.17 of the entire business.
2. IBA implements the applications like EDP, OLTPS, OLAPS, OLCPS, MIS, EIS, Business intelligence, etc. for all business functions.
3. IBA is implemented using powerful computers (mainframe or servers) which can process the requests of all business users simultaneously.
4. IBA makes use of one single and common database for all IT applications involving huge data storage capacities and efficient RDBMS (relational data base management system).
5. IBA is implemented on the computer which connects all functional users including the supply chain entities stationed across all geographic locations both within and outside the country through Internet (Extranet).
6. The IBA processes are performed by a single software package (IBASP/ERP) for the entire business with a common, simple and standard menu driven user interface for all functions.

1.13.4 Advantages of IBA/ERP

1. **Integration:** IBA integrates all business functions and brings in transparency in business operations by capturing data related to all operations in one common database and making the same information shareable among all functions. This leads to unified planning, organizing and completion of business operations faster.

For example, when purchase orders are released to buy raw materials, they mean different things to different functions, e.g. quality control function of when, how and what to inspect, production to do production planning, materials management to plan where to store and stock accounting, finance function to arrange cash flow, and so on. This automatically enables them planning and organizing their respective operations with no further communications from others. When raw materials are received, all associated business operations get completed fast.

Any thing bad happening in business is also noticed fast and acted upon by business functions concerned. The functional responsibilities get integrated as one single entity in achieving the business objectives. This eventually enables networked groups in taking decisions collectively (group decision support system).

2. **Coordination and collaboration:** Since real time information is made available to all business functions, it enables close coordination, collaboration and collective decision making among managers/employees of all functions. The business processes get completed fast since pending activities/bottlenecks are automatically made known to business functions concerned. This helps respective business functions to know what they need to do and to plan, organize and complete their tasks fast.

3. **Consistency:** Since the MIS for all business/management functions are extracted from the common database, it results in consistency in information reporting, decision making and knowledge sharing. This creates unity of purpose among all managers and employees.

4. **Common user interface:** IBA provides common user friendly interface (menu and sub menus options) for performing thousands of business processes. The entire business' operations get performed through simple menu options which mimic functional/departmental processes/operations. The users need not be technology savvy. Employees shifted from one department to the other would still feel conversant with IBA.

5. **Real time information:** Since all business operations are performed using IBA, the business data gets captured into the database in real time. This enables the database to reflect true image of the business any time. Thus, MIS obtained through IBA makes the managers to know exactly what is happening in business currently.

6. **Creates knowledge based organization:** Since all managers know what is happening in their and other functions, they become knowledgeable about bottlenecks, delays, reasons for delays, fixes for the problems, and so on. Such applications lead to knowledge based organizations/knowledge workers.

1.14 CONSTITUENTS OF IT APPLICATIONS IN BUSINESS

The five main constituents of IT applications in business are:

- Business processes
- People

- Computer hardware
- Software
- Data

These entities are discussed in Chapters 3, 11, 12 and 13. The quality, reliability, usefulness, effectiveness and efficiency of the IT applications solely depend on these five constituents.

1.15 BUSINESS AND ITS ENVIRONMENTS

There is always a regular flow of data/information/knowledge from the business organization to its environments and vice versa, as illustrated in **Figure 1.5**.

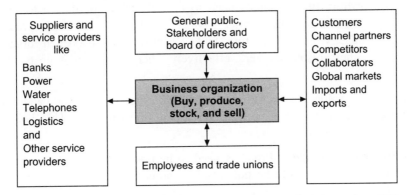

FIGURE 1.5 Interaction between business and external entities.

1.16 INFORMATION TECHNOLOGY MAKES BUSINESSES MORE COMPETITIVE

Competitiveness of businesses depends on **5 internal factors**, viz. products' utility and quality, price/affordability, products positioning/placement, promotional efforts including advertisements and products presentation/packing.

Competitiveness is also influenced by **7 external factors**, viz. the competitors, bargaining power of the suppliers of inputs, buying power of the customers, new products entering the markets, substitute/complementary products, customer loyalty/retention and customer complaints and their reprisal mechanisms.

The contributions of IT towards these factors are discussed herein.

1. **Products utility and quality:** In knowledge based economy, the customers' knowledge of the products available in the markets and their utility is high. The markets are highly competitive since too many players are offering too many products.

Social networking sites also compare and contrast the products available in the markets on various attributes. Customers are also highly demanding and their preferences are changing fast.

The business organizations now need to adopt 'pull marketing' strategies wherein the merits of the products offered by the business, customer priorities/preferences, buying power, product complaints, competitor offerings, etc. are assessed on a continual basis using a variety of data acquisition systems like direct customer feedback, web sites, channels, and sales force feedback and so on. Organizations need to build extensive knowledgebase (KMS) of their customers' needs and brainstorm on all possibilities of enhancing products utility to its customers. Company's historic sales data need also to be analyzed in identifying customer profiles and the attributes of products bought by such profiles.

Based on this, the business organizations need to do right value addition to their products to keep their customers satisfied all the time.

2. **Price/affordability:** Products need to be affordable for the customers and also challenge the competition on price front. IT applications like MIS, product costing, value chain/activity based costing, budget controls and so on help organizations in managing their resources very effectively, thereby reducing costs of their end products.

For example, the value chain costing would identify the costs of value addition activities for which the customers would be willing (or not willing) to pay. This could eliminate superficial costs very effectively.

3. **Positioning/placement:** Products need to be positioned at right place and at right time such that they could be liquidated at the earliest.

For example products to be positioned for *sale for a week at all retail outlets* can be decided based on:

● Weekly sales for the last three years obtained from the data warehouse (MIS) for all retail outlets.

● Current year weekly sales targets (obtained from MIS).

● Stocks available at each point of sales (obtained from SC-IBA).

● Stocks of competing products (sales force/channel feedback) and so on.

Marketing managers can take cognizance of other unstructured parameters affecting/ influencing the sales at each point of sales and position the products accordingly.

4. **Promotion/advertisement:** It refers to all marketing efforts including advertisement aimed at increasing the sales. It would include advertisements, discounts/ offers, sales campaigns, door to door canvassing, customer meets, telemarketing, credit sales, and so on. All promotional activities involve costs and such costs need to justify consequential increase in sales revenues.

Appropriately designed MIS to compare promotional costs with consequential increase in sales turnover would provide a good understanding of all promotional activities and also the most profitable ones.

Data warehouse and data mining applications discussed in Sections 5.9 would help identifying the profiles of more prospective/target customers (out of total customer population) and the most effective sales campaigns. Promotional efforts aimed at more prospective customers assure better returns on promotional expenses.

5. **Product presentation and packing:** Some customers prefer the products they buy to be seen and evaluated before making purchase decisions. Samples of products are made available to the customers for this purpose. Product presentation is very crucial and need to be done in innovative ways so as to influence purchase decisions. Products need to be presented in attractive containers and packs which may also have definite utility/reuse values for the customers. Instructions on how to use the products, procedure for registering the customers and complaints, etc. are to be made available along with the products. Various issues discussed under paragraph 1 above are also applicable in deciding the methods of how the products are to be packed and presented.

6. **Competitors:** Markets are influenced by competitors and the scales of economy they enjoy. Most of the data associated with these entities are unstructured and need to be acquired from external sources. Business organizations could capture markets/ competitors' information like total industrial volumes, market shares, financial ratios of their business operations, installed capacities, capacity utilization, business plans, production processes, etc. from their annual reports, web sites and various other industrial sources and media.

Such information needs to be included as part of EIS and KMS so as to enable the business managers taking collaborative decisions on all such issues before adopting a matching strategy challenging the competition.

7. **Bargaining power of the suppliers of inputs:** Business organizations need to create exhaustive database of all their suppliers, all materials supplied by them, the prices, data required to perform value engineering (costing) on all inputs, history of all inputs bought and their prices, total sales turnover of each supplier and market shares of their buyers, alternative sources for inputs, development of new vendors, costs of own production, rate of inflation in last few years and so on will enable the business to have more effective/win-win bargaining power with the vendors. Applications like MIS, KMS, OLCPS, data warehouse, etc. are very useful applications in this regard.

8. **Buying power of the customers:** Most of the data associated with these entities are unstructured. Sales forecasts for the industry as a whole, competitor strategies and sales targets, cost of living indices, inflation, recession, GDP growths and various other economic indicators are to be reckoned as part of knowledge management systems and be made available to the managers and economists in taking appropriate action in this regard. Organizations need to capture such information from the markets to take cognizance of the same.

It is also possible to build complex models as indicated in Section 5.9.6 for this purpose.

9. **New products entering the markets:** Information related to new products, prices, product characteristics, customer preferences, customer loyalty, and so on needs to be collected from external sources. Sources for such unstructured data are Internet, Industry publications, channels' feedback, product brochures and so on. Such data need to be stored as part of KMS discussed in Section 4.7. Managers responsible for making decisions in these aspects need to interact with one another and take collective decisions on such issues even if it involves certain risks.

10. **Substitute/complementary products:** Same processes as discussed above are applicable for this factor also.

11. **Customer loyalty/retention:** In the competitive market environments, retaining existing customers is less costly than acquiring new customers.

Businesses need to know their customers better through various feedback systems designed for the purpose. Customers' data residing in the computer database need to be effectively utilized for establishing closer customer relations and enhancing customer loyalty.

Applications like CRM help identifying more profitable and loyal customers and Data mining applications help identifying customer profiles very accurately. Such profiles, if mapped on to total population, could help identify more prospective customers. IT applications enable the business to be more responsive to customer interactions and expectations.

12. **Customer complaints and their redressal:** Most of consumer durable products are covered by warranty and costs of such claims are also included in product costing. In some countries, the products are replaced or taken back when the customers return the products for some reason or other. Customers need to be treated politely as the brand loyalty is influenced by these factors more than the products and their prices.

The reasons for product returns, customer expectations, product failures, etc. are to be captured and analyzed for this purpose. R&D functions need to improve the quality of the products thereby reducing such complaints. All customers touch points are to be integrated and used effectively in redressing customers complaints.

1.17 BUSINESS: PHYSICAL PROCESSES

A business performs thousands of processes involving:

- Inward flow of materials, products and services
- Internal flow of materials and services
- Value addition activities (production)
- Outward flow of products and services (to the markets)
- Decision making
- Management functions associated with the above
- Deployment of organizational resources
- Flow of data/information (of business entities and events) across all functions

- Processing of data and converting them into information
- Accumulation and dissipation of business knowledge
- Flow of instructions, commands, acceptance, denials, etc. across all business functions and so on.

Business process automation means automation of data associative processes of all above processes in addition to what we have already discussed in Section 1.1.3.

1.18 INFORMATION TECHNOLOGY: Leveraging the Business

Information technology leverages the business to a great extent compared to the costs and the efforts involved in implementing them. These applications bring immense benefits to the business. And more importantly the costs and efforts associated with IT applications are always declining while their benefits are always increasing.

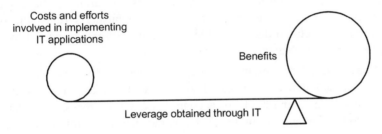

FIGURE 1.6 IT leveraging the business.

Numerous benefits brought by IT applications to the business are discussed in the following chapters. However, the key benefits of IT applications to business are summarized below to present a consolidated view and to have one point reference for the convenience of the managers and readers.

1. **Enhances the quality and structure of business processes:** IT applications make business processes highly structured and error free. Each process gets defined in terms of what to do, where to do, how to do, when to do, who to do and so on. Best business practices also get embedded through IT applications. IT eliminates manual efforts which are unstructured, error-prone, time-consuming and monotonous, very appreciably.

2. **Speeds up the business processes (efficiency):** IT applications speed up the data associative processes and make them more efficient (faster). IT applications could measure the time delays in completing all business events and this enables fixing responsibilities (accountability) on employees for completing the events faster. This makes the business more efficient, e.g., products reach the markets faster, debtors are collected earlier, materials arrive in time, and so on. Efficient business operations also lead to highly responsive organizations. The managers are able to take decisions faster.

3. **Effective management:** IT applications help organizations in optimal utilization of business resources since all resources get measured and controlled (through MIS) all the time leading to cost reduction, cheaper products, minimum working capital and better ROI. The managers are able to manage the business with least efforts and time and their time could be spent more usefully on creative thinking and innovation.

4. **Business data management:** Database management systems (DBMS) enable large volumes of business data (of all entities and events) to be captured, stored, updated and accessed by the business fast and easy. It delivers the most important resource, viz. the MIS to its managers, to manage all other business resources very effectively. Variety of patterns, trends and predictions could be obtained from current and historic data. Fourth generation languages like SQL (structured query language) allow managers in retrieving critical business information from the database using simple English like commands.

5. **Business documents/transactions become accurate:** The business documents and transactions created through IT applications are accurate as the computations and programmed decisions are made based on the business rules, the organizational policies and structured decision tables. The business gets respected by its customers, suppliers, market channels and others.

6. **EDP/batch data processing:** Large volumes of business data/transactions put together as a batch are processed and converted into useful information (MIS), statements, ledgers and books of accounts in one go. Processing of large volumes of data becomes fast and accurate. This was the first and foremost use of computers in business. Market survey, customer feedback analysis, etc. provide fairly good market information through these applications.

7. **Online transaction processing systems (OLTPS):** The business documents/ transactions get processed and printed as and when the business events take place. Preparation of business documents becomes easy, fast and accurate. Data associated with the business events get captured in the computer database and also get posted against respective entities (material stock, cash balance, debtors, creditors and so on.). OLTPS enable real time MIS to be extracted from the computer database. All types and sizes of business extensively use OLTPS. OLTPS are mandatory for real time information systems and MIS.

8. **Real time information:** Real time information system is explained in Section 1.11.1. The OLTP applications enable business data stored in the computer database to be true electronic image of the physical business. This allows real time information to be made available to all managers in knowing the current business situation and taking right decisions at right time.

9. **Programmed decisions:** All decisions which are rule based and involve structured data (most of the business decisions fall under this clause) are programmed through application software. This saves the decision making efforts, expertise and time of the functional users. This also reduces the skill levels of the people to be engaged in business operations. Programmed decisions ensure strict compliance to organizational rules and regulations.

10. **Large scale printing in business:**   Business needs to do large volumes of printing of documents and statements for statutory or bookkeeping (to create proofs of occurrence) purposes. Printing of all business documents and statements (of high volumes, varying sizes and any number of copies) using pre-printed stationery with multiple colors are made easy. IT has greatly improved the aesthetics and readability of business documents and statements. Large volume printing of business documents, statements, reports, ledgers, registers, books of accounts, etc. have become fast and accurate.

11. **Effective business communication:**   Internet and integrated business applications (IBA) implemented using Internet can easily be accessed by all business functions situated around the world and also by its managers who are travelling (mobile computing) using Intranet. The supply chain entities can also be connected to such network (extranet). Business communication among all employees, managers and the supply chain entities stationed anywhere in the world have become easy and cost effective.

12. **Automation of bookkeeping/ledgers:**   A business needs to maintain a number of registers/ledgers/books of accounts, etc. to create proof of occurrence, to exercise management control and to enable subsequent audits on all business entities and events. Computers very effectively, reliably and accurately automate all such tasks.

13. **Improved business perception/knowledge:**   Data related to all business entities and events are processed and converted into useful management information. Even complex business information is converted into simple formats/charts/graphs in colours which are easily perceivable/discernible by the managers. In addition to internal information which are mostly structured, vast external unstructured information (like customer behaviour, competing products, supply chain activities, socio political factors influencing the business, etc.) are also made available to the managers as business intelligence. This enhances business perception/knowledge of the managers at all levels.

14. **Integration of business functions:**   IT applications integrate all business functions and the supply chain including the retail outlets, thus enabling good and effective coordination, collaboration and collective decision making among all business managers and the employees. This also leads to better management control on all business entities and events.

15. **Decision support systems (DSS):**   DSS aid managers in taking action in decision situations which are complex and involve unstructured data. Business data pertaining to earlier years (historic data) get converted into data warehouse. By applying statistical techniques on the historic data it is possible to make business forecasts like sales forecast, inflationary trends of raw material costs, etc. Such Decision support systems are useful in strategic planning.

16. **E-business:**   E-business enables all business operations/processes to be performed electronically using e-mail, e-commerce, e-recruitment, e-procurement, Intranet, Extranet and so on. E-business enables doing business in virtual form, without having to invest on the physical infrastructure (dot com companies). E-business enables the business operations of even multinational companies to be managed as if it is a local business.

17. **Mobile/pervasive computing:** Mobile (anywhere/pervasive) computing enables managers to manage the business from anywhere, while on tour or sitting at home. IBA, Internet, note book computers, mobile phones and wireless (3G) devices make the mobile computing highly effective in business.

18. **Customer relationship management (CRM):** CRM helps business organizations in building closer customer relations and gaining loyal and new customers. The sales and customer database held within the business contain rich information about all the customers, their product preferences and their buying behaviour. Such information is used in understanding customers better and establishing closer and profitable customer relations. CRM is the new and potential opportunity for the customer focused industries.

19. **Data warehouse:** IT applications store data associated with current business operations in an operational database. The data related to the completed events (historic data) are removed from the operational data base and added to data warehouse. IT enables in creating, managing and accessing huge data warehouse fast and easy. The business organizations now use the data warehouse to gain more insight into business and to adopt new strategies. Management information in the form of multidimensional views, graphs, charts, geographical interpolation, statistical analysis, modelling, etc. can be obtained from the data warehouse to learn precisely what had happened in the business in immediate past. This overcomes the human limitations in perceiving and understanding complex data.

20. **Data mining:** It is the process of extracting highly valuable, previously unknown but potentially useful business information from the data warehouse (historic data). It enables detection of relevant and useful business patterns from historic data. Complex decision models and statistical packages are available for data mining applications to extract such potential/valuable hidden information.

21. **Office automation:** Thanks to IT, all of office administration and management functions are automated with least efforts today. Office automation is also an important factor for the exponential growth of computers in business. Hundreds of application software that cater to office automation requirements and which are highly user friendly are also available as ready to use packages. The people involved in these activities are able to learn and use these software in a day or two. Thanks to knowledge workers, the offices today function very efficiently and effectively.

22. **Business process automation:** Business operations/activities of all line and support functions are extensively automated and integrated through IT applications. Management of business operations/functions have been simplified and made faster to a great extent today. Employees are saved from monotonous, repetitive and time-consuming tasks and are free to do creative works.

23. **Ease of management:** The management functions with exceptions like strategic planning and unstructured decisions, are also simplified to a great extent through a number of IT applications including real time MIS. The expertise/skill levels required in managing the business have greatly been reduced by IT applications. Managers with lesser experience are able to take up the responsibilities of senior

management. Because of this, the organization structures are becoming flatter (as envisaged by Peter Drucker, a management expert two decades back).

24. **Management information system (MIS):** Managers get right business information in real time which enables taking right decisions at right time. MIS truly reflects what had happened, what is happening and what is likely to happen in the business. This makes the managers highly knowledgeable. Human limitations in perceiving complex business data have overly been simplified by a number of analytical tools (statistical software packages) made available to today's business.

25. **Management by objectives:** If anything is to be managed effectively in business, the associative performances need to be measured accurately. Fortunately most of the business performance yardsticks are quantifiable and measurable (like sales quantities. sales turnover, cost of production, marketing costs, employee costs, inventory carrying cost, capacity utilization, specific consumption, administrative overheads, ROI and so on). Management could set quantitative targets (objectives) for all managers in terms of such yardsticks which are agreeable by them. Such targets become individual manager's objectives (MBO). The actual performances could then be measured and compared with the objectives. This makes the managers more responsible and accountable for the business outcomes. In the process, the business becomes a high performance organization (HPO). Please refer case study discussed in Section 6.17.

26. **Management by exception:** It is nearly impossible for the managers to manage all business events and the entities very closely (one to one) because of their huge volumes. Instead, they can closely/effectively manage the business exceptions. For example, stores manager can do ABC analysis on material stock values and select high value items and closely monitor only those stocks (e.g., 80% of inventory costs could be made up of 20% of materials). It is possible to identify any number of business exceptions in this process (like products making losses, regions where the market share is falling, machines that breakdown more frequently and so on.) and take timely action on such exceptions.

27. **Good management control:** Since information related to all business entities and events are available in electronic form and business performance yardsticks are quantifiable, IT helps managers in effectively controlling business entities and events. MIS is an effective tool in the hands of the managers in controlling the business. They could extract any type of control information to ensure that the business operations are managed well. Next to OLTPS, management control is yet another great use of IT in business.

28. **Learning organization:** The managers (and the employees) gain good knowledge of the business by virtue of their experience, decisions taken earlier and the decision outcomes from them. IT enables the organizations to convert such knowledge into the organizational knowledge and make it shareable among others and new managers. In the process, the organization becomes a knowledge based/learning organization. The people in business become knowledge workers. As managers who join the organization get access to such valuable knowledge, they become

knowledgeable instantly and their valuable time and efforts in learning them afresh are saved.

29. **Knowledge (multimedia) management systems:** Knowledge management systems allow accumulation and dissemination of organizational knowledge among all its employees and managers. The knowledge could be in the form of structured data, descriptive text, diagrams, graphs, pictures, audio, video, and so on. Backed by right knowledge management systems (KMS), the business could acquire the knowledge possessed by all its managers including senior management. Such knowledge become intellectual assets of the business.

30. **Enhances coordination and collaboration (integration):** In addition to conventional telephones, today's technology allows various forms of communications like, e-mail, voice mail, file transfer, SMS, mobile phones, video conference, teleconference, voice over internet and so on in business. Integrated business applications also reflect the true status of physical business (in the computer database) which is accessed and shared by all employees and the managers. This allows people to communicate business events/activities (completed, pending, bottlenecks and so on) with one another from any part of the world, resulting in closer coordination and collaboration.

31. **Networked organization structure:** IT supports networked organization structure, where a network of people work together in achieving a common objective or completing a specific project. The group needs to work in close coordination/ collaboration in completing the task fast. The activities pending, who to do what, reasons for bottlenecks, solutions for problems etc., need to be shared among them instantly. IT applications like KMS and Group Decision Support Systems enable exchange of ideas, knowledge, responsi-bilities, and so on with one another very effectively. It enables the network in completing the task fast and successfully.

32. **Best business practices:** IT applications enable implementation of best business practices (efficient and effective way of conducting/running business) by incorporat-ing the same in application software which ensure automatic compliance of the same without exceptions. This enhances the brand image and reputation of the business. The business process manuals (ISO certified processes) for all business functions are also made available to all employees through KMS.

33. **Data security and confidentiality:** It is possible to ensure security and confidentiality of the business data, information, and business documents either stored in the computers or communicated through the networks. Data encryption (cryptography) and decryption technologies ensure that the business data/ information always remain secured and confidential. In addition, IT applications also ensure data/system security through user identification and passwords assigned to all employees and allowing only authenticated employees to perform business operations preassigned to them. User identifications are also captured in the computers along with the business transactions to establish accountability on people who are engaged in such processes.

34. **Paperless office:** By virtue of extensive business process automation, all business information and documents get stored in electronic form in a centralized database.

Such information and documents are also shared by all employees, managers and the external entities in electronic form. Even management approvals are given in electronic forms. This has greatly reduced the flow of physical papers going around the organization and also saved the manual efforts involved in filing and retrieval of papers. Physical infrastructures required for storing huge volumes of documents are also saved in the process.

35. **Scalability of business processes:** Automated business processes allow business organizations to easily scale up to higher business volumes either arising out of, seasonal sales or adding newer products to its merchandise or extending its business to new geographies. The business can also expand its operations to other countries. In such situations, the business could easily scale up to higher volume just by adding more computer resources for the purpose.

36. **High performance organization (HPO):** Information technology makes the business processes highly structured, systematic, dynamic and efficient. This makes organizations to be highly responsive to its customers, markets and the supply chain. The business processes get easily modified or adjusted or improved to incorporate the changes taking place in its environments. In the process, the business becomes a high performance organization.

37. **Managerial effectiveness and creative thinking:** The managers need not chase the information and waste their time, as MIS is readily made available to them all the time. Managing by exceptions and by objectives has also enhanced managerial effectiveness. The mangers now can devote their time and efforts in creative thinking which eventually would make the business an innovative organization (innovative products, services and business processes).

38. **Ensure strict compliance to rules and regulations:** Management policies, organizational rules, best business practices, statutory regulations, etc. when once get embedded in the application software, IT applications ensure automatic compliance to all such provisions all the time without deviation or exception. Top management is relieved of their anxiety of whether the organizational rules and regulations are followed or not.

39. **End user computing:** All business functions and their managers are called 'end users' of IT applications. End users used to depend on the computer professionals (software engineers) for the development of application software for automating number of departmental activities.

As the personal computers have become affordable and number of user friendly application software development tools are made available (e.g., electronic spread sheet, data base management systems, 4 GL programming languages, etc.), the end users themselves started developing the application software required for their respective departments. End users developed applications meet the business requirements fully since they are developed by the business users with right business domain knowledge.

40. **Websites and search engines:** There are thousands of computers (websites) around the world where information related to vast variety of subjects are stored in them.

Thanks to the search engines, such vast information is easily located, accessed and used by all managers in business. Information explosion and knowledge sharing are happening at unbelievable magnitudes. The search engines search all the computers around the world and inform the managers of all computers where the desired information is stored.

Business organizations have their own websites through which they publish the business objectives, products and services offered, operating results, key management personnel and so on to the investors, stakeholders and general public.

41. **Computer-based/aided learning (CBT/CAT):** Computer-based training has become very effective in business. The 'courseware' consisting of good lectures (audio and video), illustrations, text, graphs, diagrams, etc. which are stored in the computers are repeatedly accessed by the new managers and the trainees. The learning process has become more effective as the trainees can go back or forward in their own pace, until the subject is understood by them. The learning can also be interactive. This is used in corporate and management training programs extensively.

42. **User-friendly interface/GUI:** Rapid growth of IT applications in business, exponential growth of computer population and proliferation of variety of input/output devices are all made possible, only because of the simplification of human interface with the computers and all other applications. The computer users today need not be technology savvy in exploiting the potentials of IT applications in business. The business users are very comfortable with the user interfaces provided in all type of IT applications in business.

Note

As already mentioned, though the advantages summarized in above section are also discussed under various IT applications in this book, they are summed up here to enable the readers to have one source of reference of such key benefits offered by the technology to today's business.

The readers themselves would become aware of more such potential benefits when they read and understand the IT applications discussed in Chapters 4, 5, 6 and 16.

All the ways by which technology leverage the business are endless and beyond the scope of this book.

SUM UP

Through this pivotal chapter, the readers should have gained a good understanding/knowledge of:

◆ Three dimensions of modern business and the ways by which IT gets integrated with the business and management.

◆ The management issues that need to be focused by the managers while deploying IT applications in business.

◆ Key contributions (10 great benefits) the IT offers to the business which make the technology an integral/inseparable part of today's business.

◆ The challenges being faced by the modern management for which IT is offering matching solutions.

◆ Business operations associated with all line and support functions in a manufacturing business.

◆ Modern management functions in today's context.

◆ The attributes that decide the IT applications in business to be tactical and all such tactical applications being used in business.

◆ The attributes of strategic IT applications in business and all strategic applications being used in business.

◆ The enormity of the business processes and how IT applications get superimposed on thousands of business processes.

◆ The transformation of physical business into the computer database in electronic form.

◆ The interface between the technology, its applications, the business and the management functions.

◆ The advantages derived from the integrated business applications (IBA) in business.

◆ How IT applications bring competitive edge to the business.

◆ How IT leverages modern business and understand the reasons why huge investments are made in implementing IT applications in business.

2

DECISION MAKING IN BUSINESS
(Data, Information, Knowledge and Wisdom)

The following questions would guide the readers in navigating through this chapter:

1. What is the relevance of data, information and knowledge to the business and its managers?
2. What is logical database in business?
3. How does data/information become yet another important resource in business organizations and how this super resource helps managing other resources including the managers effectively?
4. What are the characteristics of business decisions? and
5. What is information resource management.

2.1 INTRODUCTION

Decision making is an everyday affair for managers, and those who make right decisions end up managing the business resources more effectively.

Let us review the decision making process through a well-known example of a patient going to the doctor and explaining the symptoms (facts) of his ailment. From the symptoms (data) presented, the doctor processes the data and converts them into clinical information, which enables him to perceive the patient's ailment.

If the symptoms explained (data presented) to him are not sufficient, the doctor asks more questions (to get additional data) and may also suggest to undergo certain clinical tests (like x-ray, blood test, etc.) to get more information.

Based on all the information on his hand and through his professional knowledge, the doctor prescribes certain treatments (decision/action). If the patient is cured, the outcome of the treatment (feedback) enhances the doctor's knowledge further. If the patient is not cured, the reasons could be insufficient data or data not perceived rightly or lack of knowledge/wisdom.

This is true for business managers too, who need to identify the business problems by simply observing bad symptoms in business or through appropriate MIS (management information systems). Managers need to prescribe cures for business problems.

In this example, we have come across entities such as data, information, knowledge, wisdom, decision/action and feedback. In this chapter we will discuss these entities with respect to business, with the help of a case study.

2.2 DATA

Data are collection of facts. Business data are collection of facts related to business entities and events. Business data as a mass are not organized or not processed and hence not capable of conveying perceivable information or meaning to the managers. However, data (facts) are the building blocks for obtaining information. Data and information are defined in Chapter 13.

Let us consider a mobile phone manufacturing company selling 15 models of its products across 20 states in India. Individual sales invoices of the company contain the sales data, viz. the model, price, name of the customer, town/city, district and state where sold, name of the retailer, date of sale, discounts offered, and so on.

The sales invoices (documents) are physically filed state-wise at the head office and also in electronic mediums in the computer database. Such vast data as such could not convey any perceivable meaning to the marketing managers even though they are facts. Hence, such data need to be processed and converted into meaningful information for the marketing managers to know the sales performance.

2.2.1 Data Processing

Data processing would involve one or more of the tasks, like sorting, summation, grouping, computing, comparing, application of rules or formula, formatting, editing, selecting, tabulating, describing, colouring, graphical presentation, and so on.

Computers are very good in processing the data and presenting the information in varied formats (graphs, tables, charts, multidimensional views, statements, colours, animation, etc.) and media so as to make it easily understandable/perceivable by the managers. Human beings have limitations in understanding multidimensional/large number of variables even if they are presented in good formats.

2.3 INFORMATION

Data compared, condensed, calculated, categorised and contextualised become information. Information is defined in Chapter 13.

Information is data processed and presented in appropriate formats which help the managers in perceiving the business situation clearly. They convey a meaning which enable them to interpret the same with reference to the business context. Managers' decision or action is based on the information they have received, their cognitive skills and also the business knowledge already possessed by them (because of experience).

Management information should equip the managers to rightly perceive what is happening in business and enhance their knowledge. Information designed for the managers is called management information and the systems that deliver them are called Management Information System (MIS).

Now let us look into the case study, where current and previous years' sales data are processed and converted into two typical formats, viz. MIS-1 and MIS-2.

There could be hundreds of MIS formats for marketing and other business functions depending on the types of decisions to be taken. MIS enables managers in knowing what is happening in business and guide them in taking right decisions. MIS is the most beneficial IT application for managers.

Let us discuss these two MIS formats and understand the attributes of ideal MIS in business. In the process, we will also discuss the ways by which MIS helps the marketing managers in enhancing their knowledge viz., company's market performance.

MIS format 1: Illustrative MIS for mobile phone company—Current year sales

Name of the State	Sales turnover ₹ 1,000's	Units sold 1,000's	Average sales realization per unit	Market share in %
Maharashtra	64,000	8	8,000	20
Uttar Pradesh	45,000	10	4,500	30
Tamil Nadu	30,000	5	6,000	15
Haryana	28,000	4	7,000	30
Gujarat	26,000	4	6,500	35
Punjab	22,500	3	7,500	20
West Bengal	20,000	5	4,000	15
Andhra Pradesh	18,000	4	4,500	20
Rajasthan	18,000	3	6,000	26
Bihar	16,000	8	2,000	10
Odisha	15,000	6	2,500	32
Karnataka	10,500	3	3,500	25
Kerala	10,000	2	5,000	12
Madhya Pradesh	9,000	3	3,000	30
Delhi	8,500	1	8,500	35
Jharkhand	6,600	2	3,300	34
Uttarakhand	4,000	1	4,000	35
Jammu & Kashmir	3,500	1	3,500	25
Arunachal Pradesh	3,000	1	3,000	24
Assam	2,600	1	2,600	15
Total for India	360,200	75	**4,802**	30

Note: Fictitious data for illustration purposes only.

Attributes of ideal MIS

Let us learn step by step activities involved in obtaining management information with reference to MIS format 1.

1. **MIS—Information contents:** It is the most challenging and rewarding responsibility for the managers in deciding what information they should get through MIS. Managers need to do this, depending on the decisions to be taken by them or knowledge to be gained or managing the business resources effectively or for interacting with other business functions/external entities. The success of MIS solely depends on what information is identified by the managers.

Information presented in MIS format 1 are:

- State-wise and all India sales of all their models
- Sales in terms of quantities and turnover
- Average sales realization per unit of their products
- The market share of the company computed from TIV (total industrial volume) obtained from external sources.

2. **Process:** Sales data for the year are summed up from individual invoices for each state (sales value and number of units sold), average realization per unit is computed by the program (sales revenue divided by number of units sold) and the market share is also computed as company sales divided by TIV. The MIS report is printed in the descending sequence of the sales turnover value (highest sales turnover in the first row and the lowest in the last row).

3. **Format:** Formatting is done for better presentation, readability, comprehension and perception. It generally involves tabulation in the form of columns and rows, report headings, sub headings, column and row headings, grouping (5 states as a group), sufficient spacing of information for clarity, punctuations, and so on. Values are given close to one another to have continuous reading of rows. Formatting is both a science and an art.

4. **Comprehension:** For better comprehension, the sales quantities and sales revenue are given in thousands with no decimals so that the managers need not comprehend unnecessarily big numbers. Important information is given in bold print.

5. **Medium:** This MIS is in print form. Generally, MIS is in video displays mediums with different formats (tables, graphs, charts, multi colours and so on). MIS could also be in electronic mediums to communicate across different locations.

6. **Enable better perception of what is happening in business:** The marketing manager perceives the markets as good or bad from top row to down as the sales turnover is diminishing (maximum 64 and minimum 2.6 millions).

Average sales realization of ₹ 4,802 per unit (for the entire country given in the bottom row) signifies the market affordability of the mobile phones in India. It is an important information signifying that the pricing of future models needs to be in this range. Market affordability in individual states varies appreciably and this can be used in market segmentation.

Market share is given for the entire country and also for each state so as to have distinct perception of the markets in individual states.

Managers can gain more knowledge of the business by making more such interpretations.

7. **Additional MIS:** This information can also be sorted in descending sequence of the 'number of units sold' so that the company can perceive the high volume states where additional sales and service outlets are to be opened.

This information can also be sorted in descending sequence of average realization per unit of the products sold so that the company can perceive premium states (segments) and the cost sensitive states.

The information can also be sorted in descending sequence of the market share to identify the states where it is a market leader and also to concentrate on the states where the market share is poor.

It is to be understood that all the issues discussed with respect to MIS-1 and MIS-2 are only indicative and not exhaustive. They have been chosen just to make the readers aware of the scope and attributes of a good MIS.

It is to be noted that management information is like daily bread for the managers, since all management functions are influenced by it. In any business, management information needs to flow freely, like that of blood flow in the human body, across all business functions horizontally and among all levels of management vertically.

8. **Limiting perception:** MIS format 1 though makes the marketing manager knowledgeable of sales performance during the year, he still does not know whether the sales performance is better or worse. To do this, the current year's sales performance should be benchmarked against targets or previous year sales. For example, MIS format 2 compares current year sales with previous year sales.

The previous year's sales performance is also included in MIS-2 format. Managers would get totally a new perception of the market performance when the sales performance is compared with the previous year sales.

1. **Comprehension:** To have better comprehension, the previous year sales performance figures are shown in italics and in bigger fonts. Certain information is printed in bold numbers.

Different colours can be used when such MIS is presented on the computer screens. It is also possible to show the adverse information in red to easily perceive adverse performance.

2. **Enabling better perception of the business:** Though MIS-1 gives the sales performance for the year, the manager cannot be sure whether the current years sales performance is good or bad. For better perception, current year sales are compared with that of the previous year.

MIS-2 also informs the manager of the states where the sales are increasing and other states where sales are declining. Different marketing strategies may have to be adopted for different states. Lot many interpretations can be made through MIS-2 which offer wider perception to the marketing managers compared to the previous format.

MIS format 2: Illustrative MIS for mobile phone company
Comparing current year sales to previous year

Name of the State	Current Year				Previous Year			
	Sales turnover ₹ 1,000's	Units sold 1,000's	Average sales realization per unit	Market share in %	Sales turnover ₹ 1,000's	Units sold 1,000's	Average sales realization per unit	Market share in %
Maharashtra	64,000	8	8,000	20	59,500	7	8,500	25
Uttar Pradesh	45,000	10	4,500	30	32,000	8	4,000	25
Tamil Nadu	30,000	5	6,000	15	33,000	6	5,500	20
Haryana	28,000	4	7,000	30	45,000	5	9,000	35
Gujarat	26,000	4	6,500	35	33,000	6	5,500	20
Punjab	22,500	3	7,500	20	24,000	4	6,000	25
West Bengal	20,000	5	4,000	15	26,000	4	4,500	30
Andhra Pradesh	18,000	4	4,500	20	25,000	5	5,000	10
Rajasthan	18,000	3	6,000	26	24,000	4	6,000	20
Bihar	16,000	8	2,000	10	27,000	9	3,000	20
Odisha	15,000	6	2,500	32	15,000	5	3,000	24
Karnataka	10,500	3	3,500	25	12,000	3	4,000	20
Kerala	10,000	2	5,000	12	12,000	2	6,000	10
Madhya Pradesh	9,000	3	3,000	30	12,000	4	3,000	20
Delhi	8,500	1	8,500	35	12,000	2	6,000	15
Jharkhand	6,600	2	3,300	34	5,000	1	5,000	30
Uttarakhand	4,000	1	4,000	35	15,000	5	3,000	35
Jammu & Kashmir	3,500	1	3,500	25	4,000	1	4,000	20
Arunachal Pradesh	3,000	1	3,000	24	5,000	2	2,500	25
Assam	2,600	1	2,600	15	6,000	2	3,000	15
Total for India	360,200	75	**4,802**	30	426,500	85	5,018	30

Note: Fictitious data compiled for illustration purposes only.

3. **Multidimensional MIS:** In addition to the previous year, comparison can also be made with the targets set for current year. Additional MIS can also be obtained model-wise or month-wise or dealer-wise.

Comparison can also be made with earlier four years (separately for sales turnover, sales volumes, average realization per unit and the market share) and such MIS can be in the form of bar charts or graphs to have better perception of the sales with respect to last four years.

In addition to absolute sales figures, it is also possible to get percentage variances (favourable or adverse) over the last four years (separately for sales turnover, sales volumes, average realization per unit and the market share) to make the information more useful.

Any number of multidimensional MIS could be obtained from the sales data depending on the needs of the decision situations and the requirements of the marketing managers.

4. **Information drill down:** The above MIS report provides information at the country level. MIS reports can be prepared for each state separately and analyzed at micro levels (like district-wise or city-wise or dealer-wise) by the marketing managers responsible for the respective states.

Going down from the summary levels to micro levels to get detailed information is called information drill down. The managers can analyze the information down to the levels of individual invoices.

2.4 KNOWLEDGE

Information rightly perceived with reference to a business situation becomes one of the sources for business knowledge. It is intuitive information gained through contextual evaluation.

Knowledge is gained not only from the MIS generated from the internal operations of the business but also from external sources (industry, peers, competitors, media, governments, Internet, and so on) and through experience.

The illustrative formats MIS-1 and MIS-2 discussed above would make the marketing managers knowledgeable of:

- The states where the company is the market leader
- The states where the company is losing the market
- The states where the company's market share is increasing or decreasing
- The states where the customers prefer the premium models, and so on.

The marketing manager can classify 20 states in the country into the following four classifications through another MIS report like states, where

- Both sales revenue and the market share are increasing.
- Sales revenue increases but the market share decreases.
- Sales revenue decreases but the market share increases.
- Both sales revenue and market share are decreasing.

Each of these market situations would lead to different decisions/actions. MIS opens up very wide avenues for gaining more knowledge and insight into the business performance.

To sum up, knowledge is true beliefs having the attributes like certainty, evidence, practicality and acceptability. It could be in the form of perceivable information, description, skills, experience, education and so on.

2.5 KNOWLEDGE BASE OF THE BUSINESS

It is not possible to retain vast information and knowledge in one's mind. However, it is possible to convert them into clear statements or charts or graphs or diagrams and store them as 'knowledge base' in the computer.

Marketing managers can make knowledge statements based on how they perceive the market in individual states (by doing SWOT analysis) and what needs to be done by the company to improve its markets. Their statements also become the organization's marketing knowledge. This can be made available to all business functions across the organization. This can also be part of the 'Knowledge Management Systems' discussed in Section 4.7.

Simply put, knowledge, in this context, means managers' preparedness to answer the questions like know-how?, know-where?, know-why?, know-what?, know-whom?, know-when? and so on of their respective business functions.

Business knowledge is a useful asset/resource that create value for the business and hence sustainable competitive edge.

2.6 WISDOM

Wisdom means deep understanding and realisation of people, things, events and situations resulting in the ability to apply perceptions, judgements and actions in line with such understanding. It also refers to the soundness of one's decisions and actions.

If a business could be run based only on information and knowledge, no managers would be needed. Wisdom refers to a person's intelligence, intuitive ability and inference skills (3i) to interpret the knowledge possessed by him to the circumstances/situations of the business and his ability (cognitive skills) in taking right decisions.

2.7 DECISIONS

Decision is a mental/intellectual outcome from an individual towards a situation but based on his knowledge and wisdom.

MIS is to be targeted in aiding clear perception, intelligent interpretation and taking wiser decisions. Business decisions are too complex in many situations and may not always result in right decisions. However, MIS helps reducing the risk of bad decisions since the decisions at least become informed decisions. Business needs to learn from bad decisions also. Outcomes from bad decisions are again reflected through MIS. MIS help getting the feedback at the earliest.

2.8 ACTION

A business decision results in an action, which influences/impacts the business processes or commits business resources. The consequences of decisions could be immediate or long drawn. Managers' decisions and their actions are controlled through their authority levels as stated in the manual of delegation of power, discussed in section 1.7.2.

2.9 FEEDBACK

By virtue of business process automation, business outcomes of new decisions are also captured in the computer systems. Business performances, prior to and following the new decisions, are compared through MIS. The feedback in the form of MIS initiates another cycle, involving data-information-knowledge-wisdom-decision-action and feedback. MIS helps in getting timely feedback on all managerial decisions. Even if the decisions are bad, early feedback obtained from MIS would enable managers to take corrective action in time to put the business on the right track at the earliest.

2.10 BUSINESS, MANAGERS AND DECISIONS

Business managers get MIS both from the business operations and external environments. By virtue of being in business, they also gain good knowledge of the business by experience. The information rightly perceived adds up to their knowledge. If the actions taken are not right, they need to take alternative actions and continue the process until the problem is solved. The decision making cycle is explained in **Figure 2.1**.

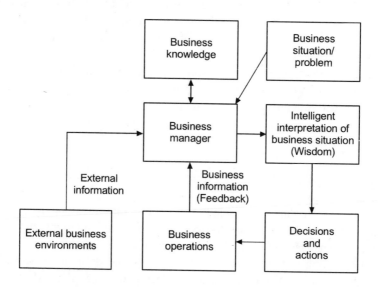

FIGURE 2.1 Flow of information in business.

2.11 BUSINESS ENTITIES AND EVENTS

A business is **associated** with a number of **entities**, both internal and external. Internal entities are employees, plant and machinery, managers, raw materials, finished products, fixed assets, cash, and so on and external entities are suppliers, customers, bankers, investors, channels of marketing, and so on. The entities remain in the (ongoing) business for ever.

The business is engaged in performing a number of **events** like purchasing, receiving materials, sales, sales collections, payments, production and so on. Under each type of event, hundreds of transactions take place every day.

Each transaction has its own life span, i.e. each has its starting and ending dates (e.g., life of a sales transaction starts on the day the product is delivered and ends once the money is collected).

A business will have 50 or so types of entities and 50 or so types of events. Each entity and event is associated with numerous data elements (facts) describing respective event or entity fully. All such data elements are captured by the IT applications on to the centralized database. Subsequently, such data are processed and converted into appropriate MIS.

Some examples of entities and events and the data elements associated with them are illustrated below, to have a good understanding of the business data. Data elements or simply called the data are the building blocks of MIS. Data is fed through the IT applications in business.

2.12 ENTITIES

Some of the entities and data elements (indicative and not exhaustive) associated with them are illustrated below.

Suppliers: Suppliers name, address, materials supplied, cost, transportation cost, taxes, lead time for material delivery, reliability, and so on.

Products: Name of the product, product description, unit of measure, price, date of manufacture, batch number, taxes payable, and so on.

Customers: Customer's name, address, products bought, customer address, and so on.

Raw materials: Name of raw material, price, quality specification, unit of measure, and so on.

Employees: Name of the employee, qualifications, experience, salary, designation, address, date of birth, and so on.

2.13 EVENTS

Some of the business events and data elements associated with them are illustrated below.

Purchase: Supplier's name, order number and date, materials ordered, quantity ordered, price, delivery schedule, taxes to be paid, and so on.

Payments: Payee's name, amount paid, instrument number, date, drawn bank, and so on.

Sales: Customer's name, products sold, quantity sold, price, taxes, payment terms, and so on.

Sales collections: Customer's name, amount collected, instrument number and date, drawn bank, and so on.

2.14 LOGICAL DATABASE

We have seen that business entities and events are always associated with numerous data elements. The data elements associated/identified with respect to all business entities and events in a business is called the logical database.

It is the responsibility of the managers of respective business functions to identify all such data elements that are required to meet operational and MIS requirements of the business. MIS helps in managing the business entities and events effectively. Logical database is also discussed in Section 13.6.

2.15 DATA TYPES

Data elements may fall into any of the data types discussed in Section 13.3. In computer parlance, data related to business entities are called the **master data** and data related to business events are called the **transaction data**.

2.16 MANAGEMENT INFORMATION—A SUPER RESOURCE

Seven business resources (7M-listed in Section 1.6) are deployed in value creation for the customers in satisfying their needs or in identifying what values need to be added. In knowledge based economy, business data, management information and organizational knowledge have become very important resources. They help managing other resources profitably.

The business resources have the following attributes:

1. Do value addition for the customers or identify what value addition to be made.
2. Make the products/services affordable to customers.
3. Involve costs in acquiring and deploying them.
4. They are to be acquired and managed effectively.

2.16.1 Management Information and Business Knowledge as Business Resources

Management information and business knowledge do possess all attributes of business resources mentioned above.

1. **Help creating right value for the customers:** A business offers products/services which carry definite 'value' for its customers. Customers today have become highly selective and demanding while buying products and services.

Market information systems guide the businesses in identifying the customers' requirements and preferences precisely (pull marketing strategy discussed in Section 1.16.1). Based on this, products are engineered to pack maximum value for the customers. Information systems enable right products to be placed at right place and at right time, thanks to supply chain integrated information systems.

Data mining applications enable mining of vast customers' database to retrieve valuable and hidden information, leading to crucial understanding of current and potential customers. Customer relationship management applications help bringing the customers closer, keeping them satisfied and enhancing customer loyalty.

2. **Information systems make the products affordable to consumers:** Markets are sensitive to the prices and the organizations need to keep production, marketing and administrative costs at minimum levels. Information systems allow meticulous cost control and cost reduction so as to offer products and services at competitive prices to consumers.

3. **Involves costs in acquiring and using management information and business knowledge:** Like other resources, the acquisition of data and processing of information and accumulation of knowledge involve costs. Costs are involved in:

   • Acquiring relevant business data, processing them through computers, extraction and distribution of MIS across the organization.

   • Buying information/knowledge/know-how from authentic external sources.

   • Engaging external consultants for obtaining information/knowledge relevant to the business.

4. **Information is to be acquired and managed effectively:** Information systems are built to give precise information of the business and making right decisions. Decision support systems (DSS) help in business forecasting (using past data and the statistical techniques). Information systems enable free flow of real time business information across all functions and all levels of management and also integrate the business.

All such systems need to be effectively exploited by the business and its managers.

In addition to meeting the criteria of organizational resource, management information and organizational knowledge also help managing other resources more profitably and hence they can also be called **the super resources**.

2.16.2 Management Information and Business Knowledge (Super Resources) Help Manage Other Resources More Profitably

Management information and business knowledge are super resources that help managing other resources profitably. Information systems make the managers more knowledgeable and enable them to deploy the resources at their disposal more judiciously and profitably.

Let us discuss how management information helps business in managing other resources effectively.

1. **Money**

   • *Cost reduction.* Information systems analyse the costs of all value addition activities (activity based costing) and help eliminate the activities that do not add value to its customers. All costs are effectively controlled through budget management and control systems.

- *Cash management.* Cash locked up in business incurs interest costs. Cash-flow management systems allow economical management of cash.

- *Liquidity.* Capital gets locked up in business in the form of debtors, inventories, non-performing assets, and so on. Management gets precise information on such entities and initiates action in order to improve liquidity.

2. **Men**

   - People in the organization need to use their skills and abilities in precisely identifying the customer needs, improving the products, reducing the costs and so on. Business process automation systems release the people from their routine activities so that they can be innovative and responsive to the above expectations.

   - Information systems enable fixing of people's responsibilities in more objective terms and measuring actual performance periodically (management by objectives). Employees and managers are made accountable. The business becomes performance oriented in the process.

3. **Materials**

   - OLTP and MIS enable good control on all materials and associated inventory carrying costs.

   - The supply chain integration systems enable the suppliers and market channels in achieving Just-in-time (JIT) inventory.

4. **Plant and machinery/equipment**

   - The information related to all plant and machinery, their capacity utilization, breakdowns, etc., which is maintained in the database, enables production planning functions in optimal utilization of these resources.

   - Information related to breakdowns and plant maintenance guides the managers in making timely repairs/replacements for existing machines and equipment.

5. **Minutes (Time):** There is a saying that 'Early bird catches the worm'. This is true for the business and its operations. Information systems attach date and time to all business events. Elapsed time for all business events thus gets measured and controlled effectively. Management also sets targets for reduction of elapsed time for key business processes (illustrated in case study in Section 5.12.5) in order to speed up them.

6. **Managers:** Managers are intellectual resources responsible for managing other resources profitably. Information systems help managing the managers very objectively. Responsibility/commitment accounting systems help setting objectives/business performance targets for all managers. Fortunately most of the business performance yardsticks in business are quantifiable and measurable. Actual performances of the managers are measured and monitored with their targets. Such systems (responsibility/commitment accounting) help managing the managers effectively (illustrated through a case study in Section 6.17).

Now the readers would be in a position to appreciate as to why management information is considered a super resource.

2.17 CHARACTERISTICS OF BUSINESS DECISIONS

- Business decisions are too complex and require indepth understanding of the situations involving business resources, entities and events, creative thinking, risk assessment, change management and managerial wisdom.
- They would impact business resources or the processes or both, and could lead to dissent with one or more human entities associated with the business.
- They are influenced by job responsibilities, interrelationship among the decision makers, levels of expertise, feasibility, personal, moral and ethical values, cognitive skills, excellence or task orientation or both, availability of time and so on.
- The decision outcomes could be known immediately or in the long run through appropriate feedback systems which in turn would lead to corrective decisions/ actions.
- Decision makers need to consider number of decision alternatives weighing the probability of success or failure of each such alternative.
- Decisions could be structured as discussed in Section 1.1.3, semi structured as discussed in Section 5.10 and unstructured.

2.18 INFORMATION RESOURCE MANAGEMENT

Information resource management involves following responsibilities:

- Identification of information needs of all business functions and managers depending on the critical success factors/key result areas of each function and managing (refer managerial functions discussed in Section 1.7.3) the business more effectively and efficiently. An effective MIS does not happen by chance.
- Identification of relevant data which either is available internally or to be acquired from external sources, associative processes and costs involved in collection and processing of such data and converting them into right, reliable and real time information.
- Transportation/communication of right information to concerned managers at right time wherever they are positioned geographically.
- Establishing procedures for co-ordination, collaboration and collective decision-making based on the information communicated to collaborative business functions.
- Be alert always in enhancing the scope and benefits of existing MIS in tune with changing business environments/scenarios and market conditions.
- Establishing responsibilities for information ownership, accuracy and access rights among all mangers.
- Establishing strict control in maintaining the confidentiality and security of critical information.

- Establishing right information resource management manual to be used and referred across entire business and so on.

Readers are requested to refer to data administration discussed in Section 13.12 in this regard.

SUM UP

After reading this chapter, readers should have,

◆ Gained good understanding of intellectual entities involved in the decision making process.

◆ Understood what is the logical database and the responsibilities of business managers in designing right logical database.

◆ Learnt the attributes by which management information is considered as yet another business resource and the reasons for it to be considered a super resource.

◆ Understood the characteristics of business decisions and information resource management.

3

CONSTITUENTS OF IT APPLICATIONS IN BUSINESS

Chapter Quest

The following questions would guide the readers in navigating through this chapter:

1. What are the five great entities that constitute IT applications in business and what are the issues related to each of these entities that need to be taken care while implementing reliable and quality IT applications?
2. Who are the people outside the business who will be interacting with the IT applications and what are their expectations in using such applications?
3. Who are various types of service providers/vendors, what value they add to the business and what are the criteria in selecting them?
4. What are the roles and responsibilities of the IT professionals in implementing ideal applications in business?
5. What are the responsibilities of the top management towards IT and establishing right business processes for successful deployment of IT applications?
6. What are the responsibilities of the functional heads and managers in getting maximum leverage from the technology? What are the step-by-step activities that need to be performed by them in identifying and implementing right IT applications in their respective business functions?
7. What are the responsibilities of the people engaged in business operations in making IT applications and data reliable?
8. How the business processes themselves contribute to the successful implementation of IT applications in business?

After finishing this chapter, the readers would have clear answers for these questions.

3.1 INTRODUCTION

If IT applications in business are considered as a circle, they actually are the congruence of five circles, viz. business processes, people, computer hardware, software and data.

The quality of IT applications implemented in business would be decided by all these five entities and the final outcome would be as bad as the weakest link in this chain. These five entities need to fit and match perfectly with one another (configuration management discussed in Section 8.7.7) with no let up. It is to be understood that each of these entities has numerous sub entities and if any one among them goes wrong, it would result in chaos in business.

How to take care of all these entities and sub entities under them is discussed throughout this book. Compliance with all the procedures/practices suggested in this book surely would enable business organizations in implementing ideal IT applications.

Of the five key entities of IT applications, three entities, viz. computer hardware, software and data are the basic components of the technology, discussed separately in Chapters 11, 12 and 13. People (human entities associated with the business) are discussed in this Chapter. Business processes are discussed in many chapters.

3.2 PEOPLE

It is an irony that it is the people who decide the success or failure of IT applications in business. Throughout this book, the responsibilities of various human entities associated with IT applications have always been highlighted.

3.2.1 People Outside the Organization

The people outside the organization are the human entities like,

- Vendors interacting through supply chain integrated business applications
- Customers interacting through e-business, CRM, post-sales services oriented applications, and so on
- Market channels interacting through supply chain integrated business applications
- Investors, bankers, regulating agencies, general public, and so on accessing the company's web site for business/finance information and other specific Internet enabled applications.

The IT applications associated with these entities are considered good, if the following features are incorporated in them:

- Applications meant for each of these external entities serve their requirements fully.
- User interface for them in using such applications is easy and friendly.
- System response time is fast/quick.

- Business resources are safeguarded against any misuse by such entities.
- Data, information and IT resources are fully secured against all external threats and frauds.
- Access rights for each of these entities are clearly stated, managed and controlled.
- Authorized entities are allowed to perform only those processes meant for them.
- Appropriate feedback systems are in place for all these entities to communicate their requirements to the business through such interface.

3.2.2 Service Providers/Vendors

ITES (IT enabled services) is also the general term used to refer to these services.

1. **ASPs (Application service providers):** ASPs make necessary investments and install IT applications along with requisite infrastructures (hardware, application software, RDBMS and Internet) for specific type of business applications and offer such services to their clients. The clients need not invest on these resources and need only to use these facilities as required in the business and pay as per usage. ASPs are emerging in ERP type of application services for small and medium business organizations who could not make big investments in such resources. Cloud computing which falls under this category is discussed in Section 12.17.5.

ASPs' offering Internet applications like e-mail, search engines, social networking, etc. free of cost fall into this category. Web portal service providers in the areas of employment, auctions, travel, hospitality, matrimonial services, etc. offering specific services either free or on chargeable basis also fall under this category.

Financial institutions offering on line trading facilities in share markets on chargeable basis for their customers also fall under ASPs.

2. **ISP's (Internet service providers):** ISPs offer last mile connectivity for the individual computers or the LAN (local area network) to the Information Super Highway, i.e. Internet. On clients' side, it could be cheaper mediums like PSTN, ISDN and microwave links and on the server side, it could be co-axial or fiber optic cables. They charge the clients based on the volumes of data passing through their hubs.

3. **NSPs (Network service providers):** NSPs are big players in Internet arena who connect ISPs to Internet backbone and charge them according to the databand widths usage. They own and operate co-axial/fiber-optic cables laid across the continents under the seas, which alone make Internet a global phenomenon.

4. **IMSP (Infrastructure maintenance service providers)/Facilities management companies:** IMSPs possess requisite expertise and skills in maintaining the computers, communication networks, support infrastructures, administration of operating systems, RDBMS and web servers and in configuration management.

They generally enter into annual maintenance contract (AMC) with their clients and ensure that IT infrastructures are up and running all the time very efficiently. This is also discussed in Section 8.7.8.

5. **ITES—back office:** The back office service providers take completed business transactions from their client companies and do the rest of the activities like data processing, MIS, database updates, data warehouse, data backup and so on. The client companies install necessary IT resources only for on-line transaction processing (front end/customer interfaced) applications like branch bank services to the customers, supermarket/retail sales counters, and so on.

These types of services are utilized by the banks, health care institutions (medical transcription), general and life insurance companies, and so on.

Many Indian companies offer such services to their clients in USA making use of 12 hours time difference with them. All transactions completed by US companies in their day time are taken up by Indian companies in their day time (when USA sleeps), for such processes. The database is updated and made ready when US companies start their business operations next day.

6. **ITES—front desk:** The front desk service providers (like call centres) provide IT enabled services that are interfaced with the customers. Customer registrations, product/service complaints, warranty services, post-sales services to the customers, and so on are done by these agencies. They interface communication infrastructure with the respective company's database for this purpose.

7. **Business process outsourcing (BPO):** Some service providers undertake to offer selective services like processing of employees payroll, managing shareholders accounts, fixed deposits management, etc. and offer end to end services in select business functional areas. The business organizations need not spend their time and efforts in such business functions. And since BPOs have requisite infrastructure and expertise for specific business applications, they are able to offer more efficient and cost-effective services to their client companies.

8. **SDSP (Software development service providers):** These agencies undertake software development works and perform all SDLC activities (discussed in Chapter 8) for their clients. These agencies (e.g., Infosys) possess high levels of technical skills of software engineering in emerging and newer technologies. They develop high quality business applications software meeting the requirements of their clients.

9. **Vendors (Software):** The software vendors sell packaged software like the operating systems, RDBMS, application specific software (like Tally), ERP packages, office automation software, CASE tools, and so on. Factors to be taken into consideration in buying such software are discussed in Section 12.16.

10. **Vendors (Hardware):** The hardware vendors sell hardware like computers, input/output devices, networking hardware, support infrastructure like power generators, UPS, and so on. Factors to be considered in buying hardware are discussed in Section 11.10.

11. **PGSP (Payment gateway service providers):** The business organizations accepting e-payments from their customers avail the services from such service providers. These service providers (e.g., Verisign) offer highly secured data communication links to the computers held at the premises of the customers, their

banks, the payee organizations and their banks. They own highly secured and proprietary data encryption/decryption technologies for this purpose. (Data encryption and decryption are discussed in Chapter 10.)

12. **Computer time share/Computer centres:**   During the 1970s, computers were very costly and even big business organizations were not able to buy their own computers. IBM, at that time, established computer centres in big cities and allowed business organizations to use the computers on time share basis. Such users paid IBM based on hours of their usage. Such models do not exist today. Instead, there are leasing companies who are making such investments on computer resources (hardware and software) and install them at their clients' premises and charge the clients lease rentals on a monthly basis.

However, the browsing centres today allow people to access Internet through their computers and charge them based on hours of such usage.

3.2.3   Criteria for the Selection of Service Providers

Business organizations need to take care of the issues listed below while selecting the service providers.

- The scope of the services needs to be described in great detail, the responsibilities of both parties and the payment terms need to be clearly stated without ambiguity and the same be documented and signed by both parties.
- A comprehensive non disclosure agreement (NDA) needs to be signed with the vendors in safeguarding the interests of the business.
- In the event of disputes, there needs to be clearly stated arbitration mechanism agreed by both parties.
- One person on both sides needs to be assigned for all interactions and all issues need to pass through them only.

Certain criteria for the selection of computer hardware and software discussed in Sections 11.10 and 12.16, respectively, are also applicable while selecting these service providers.

3.3   PEOPLE WITHIN THE ORGANIZATION

People within the organization can be grouped as follows:

1. **Technical people:**   IT services division (ITSD) in a business organization is staffed with technical personnel. The organization structure of the ITSD and the roles and responsibilities of various technical personnel are discussed in detail in Chapter 15.
2. **Business users:**   Users and managers belonging to all business functions are the beneficiaries of IT applications. IT is a powerful tool in their hands in effectively

and efficiently managing the business. The success of IT implementation in business mostly depends on the business users.

The following issues need to be addressed in getting the business users committed to all IT initiatives and applications:

- Business users generally resist changes and they need to be clearly and convincingly told of the benefits the business would derive from information technology (change management).
- Since most of the manual processes including programmable decisions are automated, the business users may feel that their importance is being lost. People need to be given higher responsibilities (job enrichment/job enlargement) to overcome such reactions.
- Since information is power, business users may tend to be reluctant or resistant in sharing the information pertaining to their functions with others. Management needs to establish the ownership/access rights for the information pertaining to all business functions and make the information shareable among all the managers, based on their roles, responsibilities and authority levels (need to know basis). Information needs to be treated as organizational resource and be allowed to flow across all functions and levels of management.
- Managers may tend to cover up certain information (sweeping under the carpet) if it is detrimental to their personal interest or career growth or expose their inadequacy and incapability. Management should play a proactive role and motivate them to perform better instead of pointing fingers at them.
- Influenced by the above factors, business users could point fingers at the IT applications and magnify even small problems encountered in the IT applications. Software engineers and IT infrastructure maintenance engineers need to design and implement reliable systems to avoid such complaints.

There are three categories of business users, viz. top management, functional heads/ managers and operational users whose expectations and responsibilities vary appreciably. The responsibilities of these three categories of business users are discussed below.

3.3.1 Top Management's Responsibilities

Top management needs to undertake the following responsibilities in order to exploit the technology fully and also in establishing right business processes:

- Create a right organization structure with clearly states responsibilities and reporting relationships for all line and staff functions.
- Put an integrated business plan in action, after consolidating the plans obtained from individual business functions. Resources need to be made available to all business functions as per the business plan.
- Establish right strategies and policies related to acquisition and deployment of IT resources and identification of right IT applications including MIS for all business functions. They need to fix the access rights for the business information and should

not allow individual functions to hold exclusive rights to it. Right MIS needs to be generated and used by all functions, in real time. No islands of information with functional ownership are to be allowed.

- Put in place the best business practices supported by good procedure manuals for all functions and ensure their compliance (also discussed in Sections 1.7.2 and 6.3).
- Appropriate and right IT applications need to be implemented for all business functions. Necessary policies towards this also need to be stated clearly.
- The business policies/rules are to be stated clearly so that the employees can make their own decisions without referring to the management.
- State the delegation of power (authority for committing the organizational resources) with limits for all levels of managers.
- Establish accountability for all managers, through appropriately selected quantifiable business targets (discussed in a case study in Section 6.17).
- Cost control needs to be inculcated among all employees, as a corporate discipline. Responsibilities need to be fixed for cost reduction as well.
- Top management needs to support all IT initiatives undertaken by the head of IT division and allocate sufficient funds for IT projects.
- Should be aware of the IT applications that bring in strategic advantages to the business and take steps in implementing the same.
- They need to fix responsibilities among all functional heads for successful imple-mentation of IT applications and managing the changes they bring to the business.
- Top management needs to create a senior position in the organization capable of formulating and implementing right strategies with respect to business technology and business technology management discussed in Chapter 18.

These activities will set right framework for the organization and enable leveraging the technology to optimal levels.

3.3.2   Responsibilities of the Functional Managers and Department Heads

The managers of all line and support functions, functional/departmental heads need to perform all six activities listed below in order to exploit the technology fully.

1. **Critical success factors (CSF)/Key result areas (KRA):** For each business function, right CSF and KRA are to be identified and stated. All employees in respective business functions need to be fully aware of this and work in conform-ation with the stated CSF/KRA. The IT applications associated with individual business functions also need to be designed in achieving this.

The CSF/KRA of individual business functions need to conform to the organizational objectives. CSF/KRA related to critical business functions, viz. materials management, production, marketing, finance and HR are discussed in Sections 7.4.1 to 7.4.5.

2. **Roles for all employees in respective business functions:** Roles and responsibilities of all employees in respective business function needs to be stated clearly. There need to be a fully and exhaustively documented business procedure manual for each business function. These documents should guide the employees in achieving the CSF/KRA stated above.

These documents also need to state the business rules, statutory regulations, organizational policies, compliance and risk management, relationship building, etc. very clearly. These procedures need to be very exhaustive and should guide the employees in daily operations.

Such procedure manuals are the prerequisites and become the basis for business process automation.

3. **Roles of functional/departmental heads:** The business procedure manuals of each business function need also to state the roles and responsibilities of all managers and heads of the departments.

The decision rules, reporting relationship and the authority levels in taking decisions and committing organizational resources are also to be stated clearly for each managerial position.

The functional/departmental heads need to ensure that the business is run as per the stated procedure manuals and without any deviations from the stated organizational policies, rules and the manual of delegation of power.

Business process automation needs to ensure that the business rules are complied fully with no exceptions.

4. **Selection of right IT applications for each business function:** The business managers should be aware of the benefits of all IT applications in business. They should be capable of choosing right applications for their respective business functions.

IT applications in business, their functions and the advantages are discussed in great detail in Chapter 4 (Tactical IT applications) and Chapter 5 (Strategic IT applications). IT applications related to management functions (management support systems) are discussed in Chapter 6.

The design of IT infrastructure, development of application software, quality of application software, efforts to be put in by the functional managers in ensuring data accuracy, security and integrity, etc. are discussed in great detail in Chapter 8 and Chapter 9.

The functional heads need to have good understanding of the technology and its applications and this book is intended to make them more knowledgeable in this regard.

5. **Identification of right MIS:** To enable taking right decisions, right MIS (format, contents and mediums) needs to be identified by individual managers (as explained in Section 2.3). Identification of right MIS is the foremost responsibility of the managers.

MIS should enable managers in clearly perceiving what is happening in business, so that they can take right decisions at right time.

Designing of right MIS requires good business knowledge, managerial skills and analytical abilities. MIS is to be designed for individual managers (MIS users), depending on their functions, responsibilities and type of decisions to be made.

6. **Guidelines to be followed by all managers**

- They should be able to control the business operations and identify business exceptions promptly. Cost reduction and efficiency of the operations need to be the focus of the IT applications including MIS. These issues are discussed in Chapter 7.
- Managers need to have highly user-friendly interface with IT applications and should know the functions and features of all applications implemented for their function/department.
- Managers should be able to collaborate and communicate with one another within and with other business functions. IT applications should enable such integration.

3.3.3 Business Operational Users (Transaction Processors)

- Majority of the IT users in business fall into this category. They are the people who feed input data into the computers and execute all automated processes. Correct data need to be entered as per the formats designed for the purpose.
- All business data need to be entered in the system as and when business events are initiated and completed (real time information systems). All business documents need to be generated only through the system.
- They should be fully trained in performing all the tasks associated with IT applications, like starting/shut down of the computers, feeding and correcting the data, completing the automated processes, generating business documents/statements, data backup/restoration, reconciliation/checking of data integrity controls, reporting hardware/software problems to concerned technical teams, and so on.
- IT applications should be designed such that the data entry efforts are kept to the minimum and all possible errors in the input data are detected and corrected promptly.
- People with little computer/technical skills should be able to interact with IT applications with ease.

3.3.4 Business Processes

The business processes are to be structured, transparent and stated clearly for successful exploitation of IT. These issues have been discussed in Sections 1.1.2, 1.7.2 and 3.3.1.

3.4 DATA/INFORMATION

- Data and information are the most important organizational resources and, if managed well, they would bring immense benefits to the business.

- Identification of all and right data elements (in the form of logical database) is an important managerial activity for the successful implementation of IT applications.
- The data and information are discussed in great detail in Chapter 13.
- Data accuracy and integrity controls that need to be implemented in IT applications are discussed in Chapter 9.

3.5 COMPUTER SOFTWARE

Computer software made up of system software and application software are discussed separately in Chapter 12.

3.6 COMPUTERS AND NETWORK INFRASTRUCTURE

Computers and network infrastructure are discussed separately in Chapter 11.

SUM UP

In this chapter, the readers should have gained good knowledge of the following:

- ◆ Five great entities associated with IT applications and the issues related to one of the entities, viz. people, in getting optimal leverage from the technology.
- ◆ All external users who will be interacting with the IT applications and their expectations.
- ◆ Various types of service providers/vendors in IT arena, what value they add to the business and the factors that need to be taken into consideration while engaging such service providers.
- ◆ The responsibilities of top management towards IT and establishing right business processes conducive to successful implementation of IT.
- ◆ The responsibilities of the functional heads towards IT and activities that need to be performed by them, in implementing successful IT applications.
- ◆ The responsibilities of all operational/business users in using IT applications.

CHAPTER

4

INFORMATION TECHNOLOGY
Tactical Applications in Business

Chapter Quest

In this chapter, the readers would easily understand the tactical IT applications mentioned below which are generally being used in all business organizations today.

1. Batch data processing/Electronic data processing (EDP)
2. On line transaction processing system (OLTPS)
3. Management information system (MIS)
4. Office automation systems (OAS)
5. Business intelligence (BI)/Executive information system (EIS)
6. Knowledge management system (KMS)
7. Geographic information system (GIS)
8. On line analytical processing system (OLAPS)
9. On line complex processing system (OLCPS)
10. Workflow management system (WMS)
11. Groupware applications/Group decisions
12. Web publishing (Web sites on Internet).

After finishing this chapter, the readers would have good understanding of all tactical applications in business and precisely be aware of,

- What these applications are?
- What are the benefits they bring to the business?

- What are the efforts that need to be put in by the employees and managers in order to make these applications highly effective?
- What are their limitations?

Two case studies are also given at the end of this chapter to enable readers understanding the 'Data Flow Diagrams' and evolution of IT applications in business.

4.1   INTRODUCTION

Tactical IT applications, as the name implies, help managing the business resources more effectively. The business processes also get more structured and efficient (faster). The attributes of tactical IT applications have been discussed in Section 1.9.1.

Business organizations today implement these applications without fail because they bring in immense benefits to the business compared to their costs. These applications have become mandatory in any type of business today.

Since some of the applications are explained with the help of system flowcharts (for better understanding), it is necessary for the readers to understand some of the flow chart symbols shown in **Figure 4.1**.

System flowcharts are explained in section 4.3.

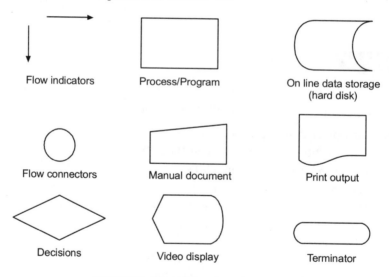

FIGURE 4.1   Flowchart symbols.

4.2   BATCH DATA PROCESSING SYSTEM (Electronic Data Processing—EDP)

During the 1970s when computers were introduced in business, EDP was the sole IT application in business. The computer technology itself was referred to as EDP as it had a profound impact on business.

Under batch data processing (EDP), the transactions (data) pertaining to a business function are bunched (batched) together for specific periods (say, a month) and processed through the computer in one go. The computer processes all transactions in one go and converts them into appropriate outputs, which could be one or more of, business documents, management information, statements or ledgers in print or electronic media and computer files.

The business processes like employee payroll, books of accounts, stock ledger, payment of dividend to shareholders, etc. are the examples of such processes which are being used even today.

Computers at that time were considered very fast (though very slow compared to today's computers) for EDP applications. However, the business organizations were exhilarated since such processes, which otherwise took many days of human efforts, got completed fast and accurate. The batch processing capabilities of the computer were considered to be a boon to business in those years. No one imagined that the computer would be put into such extensive use in business, as being done now. Evolution of IT applications in business is discussed in Section 4.15.

Computers were capable of performing only one task at a time (single user and single task systems). All business functions were sharing (by carrying the transactions to the computer room) the same computer and the processes were carried out one at a time and one after the other.

1. For example, the employees' payroll processing for a month involves batching together transactions such as employees' attendance, over time, recoveries, deductions, and so on. **Figure 4.2** depicts this process.

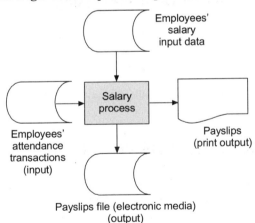

FIGURE 4.2 Batch processing of employees payroll.

2. Another example is processing of books of accounts for a month by batching all financial transactions and processing the day books and general ledger. **Figure 4.3** depicts this process.

4.2.1 Advantages of Batch Data Processing

- Very large volumes of business transactions are processed fast and accurate.
- It is highly cost effective.

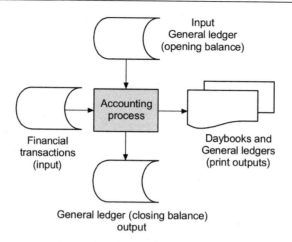

FIGURE 4.3 Batch processing of books of accounts.

- Saves enormous manual efforts which are also error-prone (to err is human).
- It automates the most cumbersome processes in business like bookkeeping, maintenance of registers and ledgers, and so on, in electronic form.
- Large volume outputs like ledgers/registers are printed with ease.
- MIS obtained through these systems is useful, though in a limited sense.

4.2.2 Limitations of Batch Data Processing

- Information obtained is not current and does not reflect the business status in real time.
- Do not support day-to-day business processes and transaction processing.

Note: As against data batching, the programs can also be batched together as discussed in section 12.11.

4.3 ON LINE TRANSACTION PROCESSING SYSTEM (OLTPS)

This is the greatest benefit the technology has brought to the business as of today. As the name implies, all business transactions (events)/documents get processed, printed and stored in the computer. Since the computer resources are always made available on line for all business functions, it gets its name 'on line transaction processing systems'.

In the early 1980s, much before the personal computer and computer networks came into existence, a number of (about 30 to 100) **dumb terminals** consisting of just monitors and keyboards, with no processor and memory, were connected to a central computer (host computer either mainframe or mini or super mini). They were referred to as multi-terminal systems. These terminals allowed a number of business users to be connected to the main computer simultaneously and process all their transactions in real time (as and when the business events occur). The operating systems had the capability to handle multi-tasking and multi-users.

The dumb terminals did not have their own processing capabilities and hence all the processes were carried out only by the host computer. Dumb terminals were only capable of accepting input data from the users and displaying outputs from the computers.

However, the technology enabled all business functions/departments to be connected to the host computers simultaneously, process all transactions and generate business documents. In addition to transactions, many other complex business processes (like material requirement planning, capacity planning, product costing and so on) were also automated through such systems. Business organizations started enjoying marvellous benefits, which continue even today.

Today, almost all business organizations, big and small, and retail outlets use OLTPS extensively. For example, sales at the supermarkets, booking of railway tickets at the counters, banking, and so on are performed through OLTPS. The only difference is, dumb terminals are replaced by personal computers having their own processor and hard disk.

Following are the examples of transactions/business documents generated through OLTPS:

- Request for quotations sent to suppliers
- Purchase orders placed with the suppliers
- Goods receipt notes (for the materials received from the suppliers)
- Materials inspection/rejection advice sent to the suppliers
- Payments to the suppliers
- Customer orders acceptance and acknowledgement
- Product despatch notes (products sent to the customers)
- Sales invoices
- Receipts for the amounts collected from the customers
- Expense vouchers, and so on.

OLTPS generates and records the business transactions necessary for the conduct of the business on line. OLTPS also automates book keeping, maintenance of registers/ledgers pertaining to business entities, creation of business documents, database updates, real-time MIS, and so on.

The system flowcharts (Figures 4.4 and 4.5) explain OLTPS related to purchase and sales functions of the business.

System flowchart is a pictorial representation of logical flow of physical business processes through computer applications/systems. It depicts inputs, process and outputs of each process and associative mediums (manual document, print output, computer file, etc.). An output from one process becomes an input to the following process.

4.3.1   System Flowchart Indicating OLTPS Pertaining to Purchase Function (Macro Level)

Processes 1, 2, 3 and 4 as indicated in **Figure 4.4** are performed by four application programs (software) written to perform these business processes on line. Application programs perform all the checks and processes as done by human beings. Links to other systems/entities are shown by dotted arrows. Since these are the logical operations involved in any purchase process, they are not explained and left to be understood by the readers.

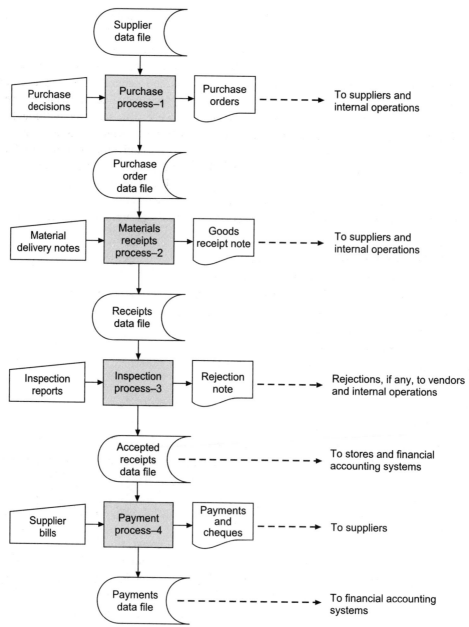

FIGURE 4.4 System flowchart—purchase function.

4.3.2 System Flowchart Indicating OLTPS Pertaining to Sales Function (Macro Level)

Processes A, B, C and D shown in **Figure 4.5** are carried out by application programs that are written for the purpose, which are carried out as and when such activities are performed by

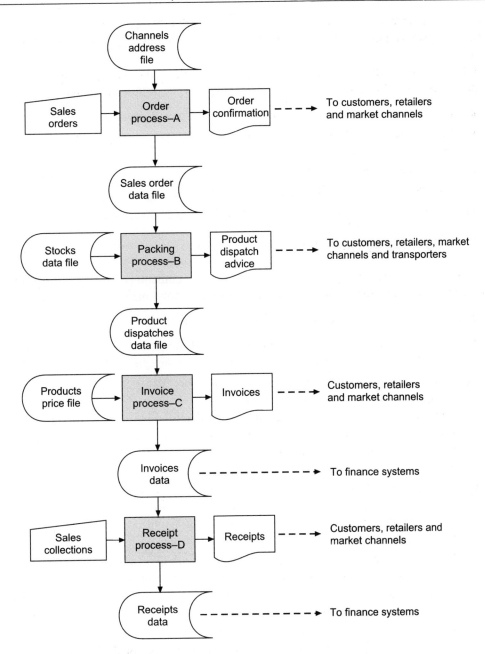

FIGURE 4.5 System flowchart—sales function.

respective business functions. Application programs perform all checks and processes as done by human beings. Links to other systems and entities are shown in dotted arrows.

If the physical business activities and OLTPS operations take place simultaneously, such systems are called real time systems. The real time systems reflect the true physical status of the business at any given time in electronic form. OLTPS are mandatory for real time information systems and have become an integral part of any business today. OLTPS provides real time MIS.

OLTPS also leads to integrated business applications discussed in Section 5.1. For example, sales invoicing done through OLTPS integrates the following business processes:

- Posts sales transactions in the books of accounts and debtors' ledgers.
- Enables taxes collected from customers to be paid promptly to the respective government agencies.
- Posts sales quantities on to the stocks.
- Provides varieties of MIS related to sales to marketing managers.

Supplement to system flow charts, Dataflow diagram is discussed in section 4.14.

4.3.3 Advantages of OLTPS

Transaction processing and preparation of business documents are major and important business activities but time-consuming and error-prone if done manually.

The following are the benefits of OLTPS to business:

- Since time-consuming activities in business get automated, they speed up (increased efficiency) the business processes. Human efforts are also saved considerably.
- Since OLTPS captures business data in real time, MIS obtained from the system is always current and up-to-date.
- The business transactions/documents automatically comply with the business rules, statutory regulations and management policies since they are incorporated in the computer software. Management is assured of such compliance with no deviation. The business documents become accurate.
- Since all structured decisions (e.g., sales discount to be given based on sales volume) are programmed in the software (programmed decisions), skill requirements of the people involved in transaction processing activities get reduced considerably. Less skilled manpower also costs less to the business.
- By virtue of the real time system enabled by OLTPS, a variety of MIS and data analysis applications can be made available to the managers automatically.
- Since all (transactions) data are captured in the main database, the information becomes an organizational resource. Managers of all business functions can have easy access to business information (on need to know basis).
- OLTPS covering all business functions integrates all business and management functions discussed in Section 5.2. This leads to close collaboration and co-ordination among them.
- Enables close follow-up on uncompleted/open transactions, making the business more responsive.
- The generation of business documents even at peak business volumes becomes smooth.

4.4 MANAGEMENT INFORMATION SYSTEMS (MIS)

Management information can be defined as the business data appropriately processed and converted into right formats to enable managers in perceiving the happenings in business better (of what has happened and what is happening) and make them knowledgeable.

MIS is a great decision tool for managers. It helps managers in taking right decisions while committing organizational resources.

MIS is aimed at managers based on their functions and decision environments. These issues have been discussed in detail in Chapter 2.

By virtue of batch processing and OLTPS, the data pertaining to all business entities and events get stored in computers in electronic form. Computers are highly capable of performing a variety of analyses (analytical applications) on such large volumes of data and extract right information, for the managers.

MIS needs to reflect the true physical status of the business at any point of time, e.g. the stocks as reflected in MIS should be the same as the physical stock held in stores at any time.

4.4.1 Illustrative Examples of MIS

MIS that can be **obtained** from the data available, both within and outside the business for important business functions, are given in **Table 4.1** to enable the readers to understand the scope of MIS in business. Such information would initiate further actions and decisions by the managers. It is to be understood that such information is obtained only through appropriately written programs (software) for the purpose.

Table 4.1 Illustrative examples of MIS

Function	*Internal data*	*External data*
Procurement	• Raw material requirements • Suppliers who are reliable • Purchase prices	• Source of supplies • Competitors' purchase prices
Stores	• Materials stock levels • Materials with minimum/surplus/obsolete stocks • Inventory carrying costs	• Inventory carrying costs of competitors • Industry norms for inventory carrying costs
Production	• Cost of production • Capacity utilization • Costs of rejections	• Industry/competitor norms for cost of production and rejections
Marketing	• Product-wise profitability • Dealers sales performance • Marketing costs • Sales turnover target versus actual	• Total industry volume • Competitors' market share
Finance	• Working capital requirements • Cost of capital • Loan repayments schedules • Financial ratios	• External sources for funds • Cost of the funds • Financial ratios—industry norms
HR	• Manpower costs • Manpower requirements	• Employee costs of the competitors

Note: MIS in a real business would be very exhaustive and too many and the above table is for illustration purposes only.

4.4.2 Advantages of MIS

- MIS is the greatest tool for managers in decision making in business. In the 1980s, the technology itself was referred to as MIS (after EDP).
- MIS enables the employees and managers become more knowledgeable of what is happening in business in real time.
- MIS helps managers in taking right decisions at right time and reduces the risk of bad decisions.
- MIS makes the business management (planning, organizing, coordination, control, and so on) more effective. It is also the Management Support System (MSS).

4.5 OFFICE AUTOMATION SYSTEMS (OAS)

Office automation is a major contributor to the proliferation of personal computers in business organizations. Office automation applications have totally revolutionized the way offices are administered and managed. Jobs of typists and stenographers were lost and instead created a new breed of office executives well versed with computers and scores of office automation applications.

OAS systems increase the productivity of white collared employees and also make them knowledge workers. Today, an employee is invariably provided with a computer, which is connected to the organizational network and also Internet.

Office automation applications are very easy to learn and are used extensively in office administration and management functions. Such application software are bought as ready to use software packages in the markets.

Some important office automation applications are discussed below.

1. **Word processing (WP):** Any person having a computer would be aware of this application. Office work predominantly involves typing and creating a variety of business documents and communiqués. WP is a simple, user-friendly and versatile software, which enables creation of a variety of office documents in electronic mediums. Generally, typing is done using computer keyboard. Word processors and non-impact printers (laser and ink-jet) have made typewriting machines obsolete.

Once the text is converted into electronic form, subsequent corrections are fast and easy as no re-typing is necessary. This increases office productivity substantially. Formats and contents of the business documents can continually be improved and stored for recurrent use (called templates).

Filing and retrieval of electronic documents (leading to paperless office) are easy and efficient compared to the physical files, papers and filing cabinets. This has also shrunk the physical office space very considerably.

Standard texts, documents and formats involved in routine correspondence, agreements, tenders, appointment letters, contracts, purchase orders, etc. running into a number of pages can be stored in the computer as referral documents and can be reproduced fast, by just keying in only those entries that change in each instance.

A common letter to be sent to a number of addressees can also be printed by merging the text with all such addresses (mail merge).

Electronic documents (files) can be stored in different electronic folders, appropriately named by the subject matter. Electronic documents can be stored for many years and retrieved fast and smooth as and when required.

A business organization can also have a central electronic document repository and retrieval system so that all employees can store and share large varieties of office documents as and when required, without having to take copies of them.

2. **Digital imaging/document management system:** Documents consisting of text, pictures, charts, graphs and diagrams in colours can also be scanned and stored in electronic form (bit map format) in the hard disk permanently. It is possible to create an electronic index of all such scanned documents, so that these documents are retrieved fast. This eliminates the need for taking physical copies of important/ legal documents and distributing them across the organization.

Confidentiality of such documents can also be maintained through appropriate passwords attached with each of the documents. Documents stored in the central computer can be accessed only by those who have such access rights. This also leads to 'paperless office'. However, it is not possible to modify these documents (because they are in 'bit map' format).

3. **Optical character recognition (OCR):** OCR is a software used in recognizing the printed text (alphabets and numbers) through scanner and conversion of the same into ASCII (American standards code for information interchange) formats. OCR systems can recognize many different fonts and sizes. Advanced OCR systems can recognize hand writing also to some extent.

When a document is scanned into the computer, it is turned into a bitmap file (dots of black and white). OCR software then analyses the bitmap and converts them into ASCII formats. Texts in ASCII formats can then be edited using word processors. It saves efforts and time involved in manual typing.

4. **Voice mail:** When a caller makes a phone call and the called person is not available to take the call, the caller can still communicate and leave the voice message in the voice mail box of the latter. The called person can access the voice mail either when he returns from his office or from any other location. Thus, the 'person to person' calls are completed successfully even if the called person is not available in his place. Both parties can not deny or disown the calls made as they get stored permanently in these machines.

5. **E-mail:** E-mail is similar to voice mail, but it is very versatile as the communication could be plain text, documents, charts, diagrams, images, picture, data, audio and video files. The Internet has grown fast and become popular mainly due to e-mail being offered free of cost over Internet. It is easy, flexible and cheaper to communicate through e-mail.

E-mail addresses are short, descriptive, easy to remember and unique across the world. People can send and receive e-mails wherever they are on the globe, provided they are connected to the Internet. It is easy to organize e-mails into convenient electronic folders.

The mobile devices, instant messaging, SMS, e-chats, and Internet telephones (voice over TCP/IP) have greatly improved the office communication around the globe.

6. **Video conferencing:** By attaching video cameras to the computers, people stationed at different locations can engage in video conferencing using the communication networks like Internet. This is a 'face-to-face' conversation in virtual form. This greatly eliminates the need for people to travel. This is very useful for interviewing people, group discussions, brainstorming among managers, and so on. Newer technologies like 3G make video conferencing fast and more effective, even through mobile phones.

7. **Digital (PowerPoint) presentation:** Computers enable digital presentations to be made using text, graphs, pictures, audio and video of high qualities. LCD projectors can be connected to computers to make the presentation on to a large screen. Large size screens make presentations more pleasant and effective. Some LCD projectors even accept inputs directly from the data storage mediums without the need for computers. This is very useful in corporate presentations, training and computer aided learning.

8. **Electronic spreadsheets:** There are many situations in office where quantitative values and descriptions are written in the tabulation sheets (consisting of number of rows and columns) and the values are summed up both horizontally (row) and vertically (columns).

This whole process is automated through the software called electronic spreadsheets. Electronic spreadsheets can have a large number of rows and columns. Individual data elements (cells) are identified through their respective row and column numbers. In addition to data, formula (in terms of other cell elements represented by their cell addresses) can also be entered into the cells. Based on the formula, it computes the value of the cell and puts the value in the cell. Data manipulation and computations can be made fast and easy using the electronic spreadsheets (Excel). They are also used in 'what if analysis?' discussed under OLAPS (Section 4.9). Some simple applications like payroll processing and financial applications for small businesses can also developed using this.

9. **Electronic diary**: A physical diary for recording the events and engagements is simulated in the form of electronic diary in the computer. In addition to marking the appointments and notes in the diary, meeting schedules, agenda and minutes of the meetings, etc. can also be recorded and followed up effectively. 'To do' activities, target dates with responsibilities, sending automatic reminders, etc. can also be carried out through electronic diaries. It is also possible to maintain address books and telephone directories in the computers. Thanks to the note book and palm top computers, the electronic diaries can also be carried anywhere by the users. Electronic diary can also be shared by a group of people engaged in a project through special purpose software called KMS (knowledge management system) discussed in Section 4.7.

10. **Office data management:** Inventory management involving office equipment, furniture and other organizational assets and office consumables (stationery, writing materials, etc.) can effectively be managed through a simple database (DBMS) designed for the purpose. Contact addresses and phone numbers of employees, suppliers, customers and external agencies can also be maintained in the computer database for quick access.

11. **Desktop publishing (DTP):** Using computers, it is possible to publish or produce print-quality books combining text, pictures, diagrams, graphs, etc. in small numbers. DTP could also produce ready to print outputs for mass printing. It involves desktop publishing software, which performs all the activities performed by publishing houses. Corporate brochures, textbooks, product publicity leaflets, etc. can be designed and printed using this software. Colour laser printers are used for this purpose.

12. **Project management:** Office management also involves projects consisting of a number of activities that need extensive planning and organizing, for example, installation of computer network in the office. Project management tools help office managers to draw PERT/CPM charts involving hundreds of discreet activities that need to be completed in order to complete the project. Each activity is identified in terms of preceding and following activities, the duration and parallel activities.

By using project management software, it is possible to identify the critical path to complete the project in the shortest time. The impact of delay in one activity, on the entire project, can also be assessed using these tools. It also allows identification of activities that need to be quickened to complete the project ahead of schedule.

13. **Digital stenography:** Computers are capable of automating the stenographer's tasks. A special purpose software builds up the link between an individual's voice/pronunciation to the actual words spoken in ASCII form through a process called voice synthesis. A person using the software needs to read out the stream of words displayed on the computer screen, loud. The software builds up voice to word vocabulary (voice synthesis) in the process. Once this is done, the computer is ready to take dictation.

As the person talks to the computer microphone, the text in ASCII form is displayed directly on the screen. This text can be edited like any other word processor document subsequently.

Variants of this software are available for the professionals such as doctors, lawyers, architects, engineers, and so on. Small mistakes encountered in dictation can be corrected manually. It is an easier and faster solution, to create the text from a person's oral dictation directly (without typing).

Affordability of personal computers, availability of versatile input and output devices and highly user-friendly software packages have made the office administration more efficient and effective.

The office automation systems (OAS) discussed so far are only indicative and not exhaustive.

4.6 BUSINESS INTELLIGENCE (BI) EXECUTIVE INFORMATION SYSTEM (EIS) AND ENTERPRISE INFORMATION SYSTEM

Business intelligence is an emerging concept which combines the outputs from various knowledge based applications discussed in this book, aimed at enhancing top management's overall perception of the business not only of its internal operations but also external environments.

Business intelligence guides top management in running the business. It offers valuable inputs to the functional heads and the top management engaged in tactical and strategic management of the business. BI is also referred to as information dash board.

Business intelligence combines seven knowledge applications, viz.,

- MIS (already discussed)
- EIS (Executive information system)/(Enterprise information system)
- OLAPS (Online analytical processing systems)
- DSS (Decision support systems)
- CRM (Customer relationship management)
- Data mining
- KMS (Knowledge management systems)

These applications are discussed in this and the following chapters. BI combines the advantages of all the applications mentioned above and supplements the manager's knowledge of the markets, customers, the competition, supply chain, and so on.

Information systems aimed at the functional heads and top management who are involved in strategic management is called EIS. This is distinctly different from MIS, which is aimed at middle management who is involved in tactical management.

However, the top management also uses MIS in a summary form to know what is happening in business and in controlling the business operations.

EIS helps assessing the organization's performance vis-a-vis the competition and the industry as a whole. The concerns of the top management are to enhance the organizational capability to handle challenges posed by dynamic business environments.

EIS is associated with internal and external information, both structured and unstructured. The information could be descriptive, quantitative, tables, graphs, pictures, audio, animation and video forms. EIS would also consist of subjective/qualitative statements derived through MIS or through other analytical methods carried out by the business analysts, statisticians, economists and chartered accountants.

4.6.1 Sources and Types of Information Associated with EIS/BI

1. **Structured information:** It is precise statements or quantitative values which enable managers to assess the business situation objectively. For example, profit earned, market share, discounts to be offered, and so on.

2. **Unstructured information:** It is not quantifiable and is subjective. For example, customer satisfaction, brand image, sales forecast, and so on.

3. **Semi structured information:** It is obtained when some form of structures are superimposed on unstructured data. For example, information related to customer satisfaction is unstructured. But a rating scale of 1 to 5 can be used to classify customer satisfaction (e.g., best, good, fair, bad and very bad) instead of the subjective rating. When customer feedback is converted into such ratings, some sort of structure is induced into it.

4. **External unstructured information:** It needs to be captured from reliable sources and be made available to the top management. Such information needs to be properly indexed and cross-referenced for ease of retrieval. For example, demand forecasts, competitors' plans, new entrants to the business, customers' preferences/profiles, and so on.

5. **External structured information:** External structured data are available from many authentic sources and the business needs to fish for such useful information from different sources. For example, competitors' sales volumes/turnover, total industrial volumes (TIV), competitors' operating results, installed capacities, and so on.

6. **Internal unstructured information:** There are many unstructured information within the organization, like manager's productivity, employee morale, sales forecast, skills, patents, product design and so on.

7. **Internal structured information:** Fortunately, most of the information generated within the organization is structured and it helps management in knowing exactly what is happening in business. Examples are cash flow, sales volumes, sales turnover, cost of production, cost of sales, profit margins, ROI, financial ratios, and so on.

4.6.2 Characteristics/Attributes of Effective EIS

1. The EIS software needs to be user-friendly and senior executives should be able to access vast information through simple menu options/short cuts.

2. The information presented, both structured and unstructured, needs to be current all the time.

3. The information needs to be presented to the top management in easily understandable formats using different colours, graphs and charts.

4. The information needs to be in a summarized form. The summary needs to be supported by micro level details. Wherever the senior executive's attention is to be drawn to a specific item, such information needs to be displayed in distinct colour (like red).

5. Business analysts need to make a detailed analysis of all business outcomes and report their findings to the top management along with EIS/BI formats.

6. Since EIS would involve confidential and business critical information, it should be protected from unauthorized access.

4.6.3   Examples of EIS

1. Financial ratios of the business compared with key competitors (about 20 ratios)
2. Critical information related to all business functions
3. Loan outstanding and repayment schedules
4. Operating results of the business compared with key competitors
5. Compliances—action taken report
6. Bad debtors and legal action taken
7. Capacity utilization
8. Capital requirements
9. Stoppage of works and the reasons for the same
10. Cash flow forecasts and short falls
11. Functional heads performance—planned versus actual
12. Installed capacities of competitors
13. Market share, TIV, and so on.

A case study related to EIS is presented in Section 5.13.2.

4.6.4   Business Intelligence (BI)

BI is integration of

1. Analytical information that is obtained from the past business data (from data warehouse).
2. New and valuable information not known earlier and hidden inside the corporate database, which is extracted through data mining.
3. Current status of the business operations (MIS from all business and support functions).
4. Structured and unstructured information from the market/external environments (EIS).
5. Business forecasts like sales forecast, impact of inflation on margins, etc. which could be obtained through definite forecast models (decision support systems).
6. Customer behaviour, impact of sales promotions and campaigns on sales, etc. obtained from customer relationship management.
7. Knowledge management systems which hold vast knowledge of the business and shared by all managers in the organization.

BI tightly integrates querying and reporting from all associated applications stated above. It enables managers to obtain "all" the information/intelligence from the organization's numerous applications and databases.

Special application software needs to be developed for EIS and BI as they may not be available as part of IBASP or ERP packages.

4.7   KNOWLEDGE MANAGEMENT SYSTEM (KMS)

Knowledge management is the process through which organisations generate value from their intellectual and knowledge based assets in order to excel in business. Business need to harness these intangible assets in productive ways.

Knowledge management system is a very interesting and highly useful application enabled by current technologies like Internet, multimedia, convergence, 3G, powerful computers and efficient RDBMS. KMS allows accumulation and dissemination of vast organizational and business knowledge among all its employees and managers.

Most of the IT applications discussed in this book are associated with structured data. KMS is not only associated with structured data, but also documents, images, designs, patents, pictures, graphs, charts, animation, audio, video, maps and so on. Knowledge in any form and medium is included in KMS.

KMS can also be Internet enabled so that knowledge accumulation and access is made possible for all entities stationed across different geographical locations.

Business knowledge possessed by an organization are so vast that it is very difficult to identify all of them in this book. However, some examples are given below to enable readers in understanding the scope/extent of such knowledge associated with a business.

- Business process/procedure manuals (best practices) for all business functions, departments and managers (migratory knowledge)
- Simple do's and don'ts pertaining to each business operation and management functions (internalization)
- Business vision, mission, objectives, growth plans, etc. (documents)
- Roles and responsibilities of all managers
- Organization structure with reporting relationships
- Business targets for each function
- Know-how possessed by managers of all functions by virtue of their experience (tacit knowledge)
- Contracts and agreements
- Management policies
- Manual of delegation of power
- Work flow diagrams
- Management circulars
- Employment rules
- Lessons learnt by employees while solving business problems (embedded knowledge)
- Progress made on key projects and bottlenecks
- Project management reports on all projects
- Minutes of management meetings with target activities and responsibilities
- Confidential assessment of external entities (vendors, distributors, banks, and so on)
- Patents, designs and specific skills (explicit knowledge)
- Fixes for problems
- Product complaints and improvements to be made
- Customer preferences
- Market trends and subjective assessment of markets by marketing functions (Externalization)

- Competitor plans
- Cost saving suggestions/techniques
- Strength and weakness of company's products (SWOT)
- Employees and managers' contact numbers, addresses, e-mail addresses, etc.
- Supply chain entities' contacts and addresses

KM is indeed a challenge for the management as how to recognize, identify, bring out, accumulate and share such valuable resource. KM also include a set of processes through which an enterprise consciously and comprehensively gathers, organizes, shares and analyses its knowledge is terms of resources, documents, people, skills and so on. KM also include a range of strategies and practices used to identify, create, represent and adoption of insights and experiences embedded in the business processes and practices.

KMS enables all employees in the organization to share and access such huge knowledge base (on right to know basis). The knowledge base is appropriately indexed in terms of business functions and business contexts. KMS makes people in the organization knowledge workers. Some more types of business knowledge are discussed in Section 18.2.6.

4.7.1   Categories of Business Knowledge

Knowledge-based organizations need to exploit two kinds of knowledge:

1. Explicit knowledge in the form of data/information and documents which are structured and stored in the computer. They are objective and rational.

2. The 'know-how' (how to do, when to do, what to do, where to do or similarly not to do, etc.) possessed by knowledge workers/managers of all business and management functions which are mostly unstructured are tacit knowledge. They are subjective and experimental. e.g., product design, patents etc.,

The goal of the knowledge management systems is to allow knowledge workers/ managers to create, organize and update business knowledge (knowledge base) so that everyone else can access the organizational knowledge. This enables the knowledge possessed by one individual to be transferred to others in the organization. Management needs to evolve necessary strategies/directives to make this operational and effective.

KMS is an effective tool in resolving the above challenges. It is capable of converting tacit knowledge into explicit knowledge in various media and forms. In business organizations, it enables accumulation, updating and dissemination of both tacit and explicit knowledge by,

- Creation and sharing of tacit knowledge gained in the past.
- Learning and accumulating new tacit knowledge in the course of running the business.
- Clearly understanding tacit knowledge through dialogues, and brainstorming.
- Sharing and applying tacit and explicit knowledge across the organization and among all managers.

4.7.2 Knowledge Based Management (KBM)

Objectives of knowledge based management are:

- Improved business and managerial performance.
- Gaining competitive advantage.
- Product/process/market innovation.
- Integration of knowledge sources.
- Continuous improvements to the business.
- Creating a knowledge based organization.

4.7.3 Advantages of KMS

1. KMS enables employees and managers joining the organization to have access to the organization's knowledge base instantly. They need not put in years of experience in acquiring the same again.
2. KMS facilitates organizational knowledge creation and learning. The creation, dissemination and application of knowledge makes the business a knowledgeable organization.
3. KMS converts the knowledge possessed by individuals into organizational assets. This could enable people of limited experience and skills to undertake responsibilities of higher positions.
4. KMS implemented through Internet/Intranet enables (formerly known as groupware) a group of people to collaborate/interact with one another in accomplishing business tasks faster. By virtue of Internet, the employees anywhere on the planet can share the organizational knowledge. KMS enables networked groups in taking decisions collectively (Group decisions).

The focus of KMS is to identify and gather business knowledge from any sources and in any form.

4.8 GEOGRAPHIC INFORMATION SYSTEM (GIS)

Geographic information systems allow superimposing of business information on to digital geographic maps to enhance human perception of the business situation (to have better understanding), across all business regions.

For example, a company's sales performance across different states in India can be mapped on to the map of India. The states where the company is losing the market share can also be shown in red to draw immediate attention of the marketing managers.

Using satellites and aerial photography (remote sensing), it is possible to generate digital maps of the states/countries/continents. These maps are superimposed with business information that could be used for a variety of analyses.

For example, FMCG (fast moving consumer goods) companies can map the consumption patterns of their products on to various states, districts and towns on the map of India. This gives a better perception of the customers' behaviour and preferences across different geographies within the country. It enables them to adopt different strategies for different geographies of their markets.

4.9 ON LINE ANALYTICAL PROCESSING SYSTEM (OLAPS)

The human mind has cognitive limitations in understanding data involving too many numbers and multiple dimensions. OLAPS allows the users to quickly analyse business information into multidimensional views in the form of tables, graphs, charts and animation.

OLAPS tools also perform trend analysis in making business forecast. They make use of statistical techniques for this purpose.

OLAPS enables users to analyse masses of sales and other business data into multi-dimensional analysis or views (e.g., region-wise, month-wise, product-wise, dealer-wise sales) to have a better perception of the business (e.g., to isolate the products that are losing the market share).

OLAPS summarizes transactions from the OLTPS or operational database or data warehouse into multidimensional views and stores them as summaries. Managers' queries on such summaries are extremely fast, because no processing needs to be done further.

OLAPS applications use analytical modelling/statistical techniques on business data. Statistical software packages [like PAS (Predictive analytic software)] are used for this purpose.

Four basic types of analytical modelling used by OLAPS applications are as follows:

1. **What if analysis:** This is generally done on business data using electronic spreadsheet software discussed in Section 4.5.8. For example, costs of all raw materials, consumption norms, conversion costs, labour costs, production overheads, marketing overheads, administrative overheads, dealer margins, profit margin and so on are stored in the electronic spreadsheet (in one column) for each product. This enables automatic computation of the selling price of end products. The increase in the material or other costs (in a column) would alter the selling price of the end product automatically.

What if analysis presents the outcomes from various alternatives in quantitative terms, so that the decision maker can look into all alternatives and take right decisions.

2. **Sensitive analysis:** This is similar to 'what if analysis', except that the value of one variable is incremented repeatedly, for example the raw material cost, to assess the impact of it on the selling price. This analysis is useful when the input costs are highly fluctuating. The values are incremented in small amounts to assess their sensitivity on the end result (selling price). If input costs are too sensitive to the selling prices of the end products, different marketing strategies need to be adopted.

3. **Goal seeking analysis:** This is also similar to 'what if analysis' with a difference that it works backward. For example when end product prices are reduced and if the profit margins are still to be maintained, it suggests what needs to be the costs of inputs.

4. **Optimization analysis:** Instead of setting specific target values for each decision variable, the objective is to find the optimum value for all variables, given certain constraints. This is done through linear programming. Special purpose software packages (LP packages) are used for this analysis.

OLAPS have evolved into DSS (decision support system), which is discussed in detail in Section 5.10.

4.10 ON LINE COMPLEX PROCESSING SYSTEM

OLCPS applications do very extensive data processing, do more complex computations and involve too many programmed decisions and computations back and forth (iterations). They create new files and access and update a number of files in the database before accomplishing the task.

For example, when a business decides the product mix and production volumes, OLCPS computes requirements of all inputs and other raw materials (material requirement planning) required/to be procured for the purpose. This system makes use of the bill of materials (BOM) for this.

The IBA/ERP packages, which integrate the processes of all business functions using a common database, also perform such complex processes.

For example, when a material is received from the vendor, IBA prints an acknowledgment to be sent to the vendor, notifies the quality control department to initiate inspection/testing process, updates the stock, notifies the cash-flow requirements to finance, informs the production manager of product availability and posts the supplied quantities on to the purchase orders. Thus, for one reported activity (called a long transaction), many computer files are updated, many new records are added in the database and number of tasks are accomplished.

Most of the complex processing are incorporated in IBA/ERP.

4.11 WORKFLOW MANAGEMENT SYSTEMS

When a number of distinctive activities involving clerical, physical, managerial and professional works are to be performed in accomplishing a given business task (like, assembling a car, producing a batch of medicine, new product launch, etc.) and each activity lasts a few hours or days, workflow management systems are used.

Workflow management system is the process by which business activities are streamlined, automated wherever possible, associated documents/decisions are moved electronically from one person to the other and approvals are given in electronic form. It also enables generation of MIS indicating the bottlenecks in the processes.

For example, when an insurance claim is received at the insurance company, a series of steps like verification of documents, approvals, intimation, disbursements, etc. are to be performed before the claim is settled. Workflow systems are capable of handling large volumes of work-related activities and allow close scrutiny of each activity.

In production floors, workflow system lists all the activities to be performed in chronological/logical order, like input materials to be used, quality procedures to be adopted, and so on until a new product is delivered. Actual tasks completed are also recorded in terms of people, time, materials and machine. It also helps managing the support infrastructure.

Workflow automation improves the operational efficiency and reduces costs and paper work. It enables better control and results in improved coordination. This can also be part of knowledge management systems discussed in Section 4.7.

4.12 GROUPWARE APPLICATIONS/GROUP DECISIONS

As computer networks (LAN) came into use, a group of people (networked organization structure) were able to share the computer resources, exchange business information and access and update a common database pertaining to their business operations. They were able to freely communicate with one another of their responsibilities, accomplishments and bottlenecks in their business activities. Special purpose groupware (software) was used for the purpose. Groupware applications were fore runners of IBA and KMS.

Today's technology, like IBA/ERP packages, Knowledge management systems and Internet enable such collaboration among many groups more effectively with much wider scope. Group Decision Support Systems (GDSS) also make use of this.

4.13 WEB PUBLISHING (WEBSITE ON INTERNET)

Most of the business organizations today have their own websites and their website addresses are made known to all employees, suppliers, market-channels, investors, regulating agencies, banks and the general public. The website has become the company's global electronic noticeboard. The companies post lot of information related to the business on their websites, like

- Company's objectives and growth plan
- Promoters and shareholding patterns
- Senior executives and their functions
- Products and services offered
- Collaboration and services required
- Operating results
- Career opportunities
- Investor information
- Contact addresses and phone numbers for key executives, and so on

In India it is mandatory to post the operating results on to their websites for private limited companies.

This is the most economical and effective way of publishing the organizational information for the people within and outside the organization.

4.14   CASE STUDY—DATAFLOW DIAGRAM

Dataflow diagram is a pictorial representation of the flow of business data indicating its origin, destinations, associative business processes and finally its storage (data sink).The dataflow diagram (Figure 4.6) depicts the dataflow related to procurement, materials management, quality control, finance and production functions at macro level. Abbreviations and symbols used in the diagram are clarified at the bottom.

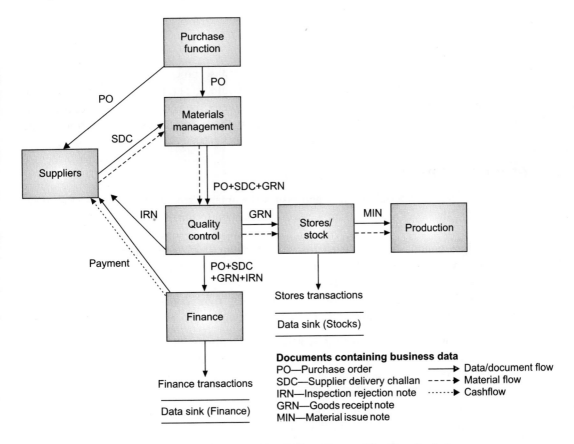

FIGURE 4.6   Dataflow depicting flow of business data.

If computers are not used in business, all business documents (mentioned in the diagram) are created by concerned business functions manually and copies of such documents are sent to other business functions. These documents would contain the data like, the names of the suppliers, materials and the quantities ordered, supplied, received, rejected, and accepted, dates and time of these events, costs, taxes and so on. These documents serve as proof of occurrence and also enable subsequent tasks to be initiated/performed by concerned business functions.

Activities performed by concerned functions are:

- Creation of business documents (multiple copies).
- Sending the documents to other functions.
- Materials management.
- Preparation of books of accounts.
- Preparation of stock ledgers.
- Extraction of management information for planning and controlling these processes.
- Making payments to the suppliers and so on.

Data sink (Finance)

Figure 4.6 shows the financial records generated in purchase processes only. Similarly, sales processes and expenses accounting processes also would generate financial records. All financial records are processed to get the books of accounts, i.e. Day books, General ledger, P&L accounts and Balance sheet. If done manually these processes are laborious, time consuming and error prone.

Data sink (Stores)

Figure 4.6 also shows material receipts and issues documents stored at the stores. Based on these documents, the stock ledger is processed. Stock monitoring is done using 'kardex/bin' cards.

Stock ledger would show for each material, opening stock with value, receipts for the month and their value, issues for the month and their value and the closing stock with value (weighted average cost or highest cost).

If done manually, these processes are laborious, time consuming and error prone. Benefits brought by various IT applications in these business processes are illustrated below.

1. **Impact of EDP (computer application) in the above business processes (1970's):**
   All processes are still performed manually as indicated in Figure 4.6 shown above except the books of accounts and stores/stock ledgers which are processed through computers (EDP) as explained below.

   The manual records kept at the finance and stores functions, as shown in the diagram, are entered into the computer (data entry) and converted into electronic transactions. The electronic transactions batched together are processed using the computers through EDP application. The financial transactions are processed accurately and converted into the books of accounts viz., day books, general ledger, P&L and balance sheet. The stores transactions are processed accurately and converted into stores ledger very accurately.

2. **Impact of OLTP and MIS (computer applications) in the above functions (1980's):** All business documents indicated in Figure 4.6 are generated through computers using the computer resources made available all the time (on line transaction processing). These documents and associated data also get stored in the computers and enable such data to be accessed by concerned functions without the

need for paper documents. The documents and the payments sent to suppliers are, still physical (paper) documents. However the database reflects true status of physical business events like purchase, materials management, quality control and finance activities in electronic media (MIS).

However, data pertaining to these business activities used to be scattered in different files/computers which can only be accessed by respective functions since no database management systems (DBMS) were deployed initially.

3. **Impact of Integrated business applications (1990's):** In addition to automating above business processes, a common database maintained for entire business, reflects true status of physical purchase, materials management, quality control and finance activities in electronic media which are easily shared by the rest of the organization (business data/information becomes an organizational resource).

   E-business (Internet) today integrates the business functions of entire organization wherever they are situated on the globe.

4. **Impact of supply chain integrated applications (e-business):** In addition to automating these business processes, the computer resources are also shared by the suppliers (Internet enabled supply chain integration). The documents and the payments sent to the suppliers are also in electronic mediums (e-documents and e-payments).

4.15 CASE STUDY: EVOLUTION OF IT APPLICATIONS IN BUSINESS

This section briefly sums up the evolution of IT applications in Business.

1930's through 1970's

In this period, IBM achieved spectacular growth with their unique analog computing devices viz., the tabulating/accounting machines, generally called unit record machines (URM), which used 80 columns punch cards for data input and output and also slow speed printers. In the 1960's, many business organizations (including India) used these machines for financial accounting and employees' salary processing and sorting, collating, and tabulating business data. These machines were to be programmed (analog programs) to perform such tasks by wiring the control panels. IBM enjoyed a huge customer base for these machines which later helped IBM in smooth selling their digital computers to them.

Year 1970's—Birth of EDP

Thanks to IBM, second generation (digital or solid state electronics) computers such as IBM 1400 and 7000 series with just single task or single user capability were made available to big business organizations. IBM also established computer centres for the business organization to use them on time share basis. Applications like employee payroll, financial accounting, stores ledger, assets register, dividend payments to share holders, statement of accounts (for suppliers and market channels) etc., were run periodically (batch data processing/electronic data processing) thereby saving great manual efforts otherwise spent by the business organizations in such time consuming and error prone processes.

Either because the business organizations did not have full time job for the computers or they were very costly, business organizations did not venture into buying their own computers except some very large enterprises. These computers did not have the operating system, hard disks or VDU's and only had a few magnetic tape drives to perform business process automation. An IBM assembly language called **autocoder** with its 'assembler' and machine language in BCD codes (binary coded decimals) were used in business applications. IBM was synonymous with computers at that time.

Year 1975's—Birth of OLTPS and MIS

Two distinctive ranges of computers, one named mainframe computers like IBM–S 360, S370, and S390, and the other called super mini or mini computers like IBM S36 and S38 were sold to the business organizations. Other vendors like DEC (Digital equipment corporation) PDP 11 and VAX series, HP 3000 and HP 9000 were also made available to business process automation. All these computers were multi-tasking or multi-user systems.

All of them were proprietary systems (operating systems developed by the computer manufacturers themselves and supplied bundled with the computers which were not compatible with other brands) even though some manufacturers have offered open systems using UNIX operation system. UNIX was a multiuser and multitasking operating system developed by AT&T and supplied as free source codes for all computer manufacturers so as to evolve open standards across the world. This was the first attempt to make the computers from different suppliers to be compatible to one another. However, this did not happen, as individual computer manufacturers started customizing UNIX to suit their computer capabilities and refusing to follow 'open standards' (fearing loosing their market share).

Mainframe computers have very large foot print, proprietary operating system, powerful processors capable of serving 100's of concurrent users, larger data storage devices, efficient database management systems and all of them closely coupled together in order to offer highly reliable and very fast processing capabilities (system response time). Due to their high cost, they are used only by big business organizations.

Mini and super mini computers on the other hand are capable of serving less then 100 users and much less concurrent users. They are far cheaper and offered cost effective computing power to medium and big business organization not requiring higher computing capabilities.

However all these computers enabled connecting number of business functions (say 20 to 100 business users) stationed across entire factory site or number of floors of a big office building, through 'dumb terminals' (monitor and keyboard only, without the local processor, operating system and hard disk). This has led to the implementation of OLTPS and MIS in number of business organizations, medium and big, thereby enhancing the scope of business applications exponentially. This is the stepping stone for the computer revolution to occur in business organizations.

Year 1980's—Birth of personal computers

Personal computers came into existence with Z80 processor from Zilog built on 8 bit micro processor and 64 KB memory which used CP/M (Control Program/for Micro computers) operating systems. However, IBM PCs, built using Intel 8080, an 8 bit microprocessor and PC DOS operation system became more popular, thanks to the brand image IBM enjoyed at that time. In fact they were called IBM PCs. Microsoft which owned a very versatile operating system called **MS DOS** sold the user license to IBM, to use in their computers as PC DOS. Microsoft due to its business acumen yet retained its rights to sell the same operating system as MS DOS to others. That was the great decision which was instrumental for the giant leap forward, for the ever since succes story of Microsoft. Microsoft and Intel joined hands in bringing out more powerful PCs with MS DOS operation systems at cheaper prices. The IBM PC was also successfully cloned by number of leading manufactures like Compaq, HP, Dell and so on, all running on MS DOS.

As the PC population started growing exponentially, general purpose or versatile application software packages like dBASE II (bringing mainframe database functions to the personal computers), VisiCalc (first electronic spread sheet application conceived by an Harvard student Dan Bricklin and programmed by his friend Bob Frankston in 1978) and LOTUS 123 as electronic spreadsheet applications (ancestors to MS-Execl) and WordStar or WordPerfect a full featured word processing software packages became synonymous with personal computers.

Such user-friendly and general purpose application software packages pushed up the demand for personal computers all around the world exponentially. Thousands of Personal computers whose prices were in the range of ₹ 150,000 in India and all the above application software packages put together costing just ₹ 15,000 were sold in great volumes. Such software packages brought great benefits to business organizations around the world. That was the first impetus for astronomical growth of software industry worldwide which developed thousands of application software for varied human interests.

Ever increasing capabilities and usefulness of PCs pushed up worldwide sales of the PCs resulting in favourable scales of economies which in turn led to appreciable cost reduction of PCs and also in the development of thousands of more useful and versatile software packages.

In 1984, Apple introduced Macintosh PCs with graphical user interface (GUI) which later was offered by Microsoft also on its Windows operating system in 1990. Windows became very successful because of its simplicity (graphic or user friendly interface) and the huge installation base enjoyed by Microsoft though MS-DOS. From 1984 onwards, Intel also started releasing faster and more powerful processors like, 80286, 80386, 80486, Pentium I, II, III, IV, and so on, by doubling the processor speeds, every 18 months.

Year 1985's—Unstoppable PC frenzy

The personal computer industry started growing wildly without any planning and no one imagined it is going to impact the business world as we see today. Millions of personal computers were bought by business organizations to automate wide variety of business processes using database management systems, word processing, electronic spread sheets and thousands of other application specific software.

Centuries since, no single device had such profound impact on the business compared to personal computers. Personal computers have placed creative capabilities in the hands of the business users which enabled them automating number of business processes, which hitherto were considered either to be impossible or too time consuming or costly.

Material requirement planning (MRP): Helped by the mainframe and super mini computers, manufacturing organizations started implementing more complex applications such as, material requirement planning (using bill of materials), capacity planning (using process flow charts), manpower planning (using work flow schedules), product costing, cashflow planning and so on which are generally referred as MRP. This was the first attempt in integrating the business processes of different business functions and also the MIS pertaining to entire business. This was the forerunner for enterprise resource planning (ERP) and integrated business applications (IBA).

Year 1990's—Networking of PCs (Local Area Network)

Since large number of PCs started functioning at various departments, data related to all such functions were scattered in different personal computers. It is quite logical for the business managers to expect sharing common information stored in others computers. Also, since the hard disks and high quality printers were costly, people also wanted to share such resources to reduce the costs. So, it naturally created a need for the personal computers to be connected to one another (networked). Thus, the local area networks (LAN) entered the business world.

However, the concept of computer networking was invented way back in 1970 in the name of ARPANET (Advanced Research Projects Agency Network) by US department of defence to connect their project sites and universities involved in research activities. In 1970, about nine interface message processors IMPs, similar to present day routers, connected to the computers were networked together and in 1974 about 46 IMPs were connected to the network. Today millions of computers around the world are networked together through (technical marvel) Internet.

LAN is a computer network that enables managers in sharing the business data or information and other computer resources within a confined geographical area. The computer where common data is stored is called the server and people who access it are called the **clients**. In order to connect them together, network interface cards (NIC) on each computer, communication mediums and network operating system (to interact with native operating system) are used.

Servers need to be high speed computers capable of storing and accessing large volumes of data for the clients. The clients are the personal computers which can function as an independent PC, or executing number of applications on the server, or also accessing the data/information. The controlling software in LAN is a networking operating system like Novel's Netware and Windows NT. A component of this software resides in each client and allows the client application to read and write from the server as if it is in the local PC.

Since the personal computers became cheaper and versatile, they also replaced the dumb terminals used in the mainframe computers. This has clearly led to two distinctive computer architectures as of today.

1. Main frame computers (proprietary systems) connecting hundreds of business users through their PCs to enable perform all business processes on the main computer.
2. Clinets and server computers as LAN (open systems).

Both these architectures are discussed in Chapter 11 and both could be connected to Internet.

Year 1995—birth of Internet (Information Super Highway)

The Internet is a worldwide network connecting thousands of smaller networks and servers and millions of personal computers. Today the Internet is spread worldwide in the form of information super highway that provides information on every subject known to human race, wherever they are stationed on the globe. The Internet has seen phenomenal growth due to two main factors.

First, the Internet enabled millions of people around the world to communicate with one another through e-mail, even if they are connected to different e-mail service providers, using a short and universally unique e-mail address. Secondly, with the advent of GUI based web browsers like Netscape navigator (a killer product in the nineties), Microsoft's Internet Explorer, Mozilla Firefox, Google's Chrome and so on, mighty world wide web (www) became a great platform for the people to learn, share and exchange vast knowledge.

Ironically, the Internet is just a set of standards (protocols) for connecting the computers, communication devices and mediums, application software, operating systems, and electronic devices. It is not controlled by any country or political powers and uses TCP/IP communication protocols. There are millions of host computers connected to Internet today, a host meaning a mainframe or high-end server computers which are always connected to Internet (available online) via high speed mediums. There are billions of clients around the world accessing the Internet using the languages of their choice.

Proliferation of integrated business applications and ERP packages: Thanks to powerful computers capable of executing hundreds of business tasks concurrently, very large capacity data storage devices, efficient database management systems and Internet, the applications like EDP, OLTPS, MIS, OLCPS and so on, pertaining to all business functions of an organizations, even stationed anywhere in the world got integrated through a single suite of application software called Integrated business application software or ERP packages. This has also led to supply chain integration including the customers. This enables any business process to be performed electronically (e-business) very effectively and economically.

Multimedia and entertainment: Universal serial bus (USB) ports which provide hardware interface for low speed devices like scanner, printer, mobile phones, cameras, camcorders, microphones, speakers, LCD projectors and so on enable all such devices to be 'plug and play' devices. USB's hot swap capability allows these devices to be plugged in and unplugged without turning the system off. Operating systems are also capable of handling multimedia like data, images, documents, pictures, voice, audio, video and so on of different standards. The Internet is also capable of sending and receiving multimedia contents at great speeds. This has led the computers and the Internet to be used in entertainment as well in the form of streaming videos, live concerts, live telecasts of games, TV, virtual games and so on.

Year 2000s'—Internet enabled business

The business applications spread across different geographical locations, get consolidated in the form of 'Intranet' and the same way, the supply chain entities in the form of 'Extranet', both using cost effective Internet. This has shrunk the physical business space with regard to its operations and management.

E-business and Internet enabled services: E-business and the Internet enabled services have brought strategic benefits to the business and radically changed the way business is run and managed. They have become strategic tools and the businesses need to reorient the processes in order to realise such strategic advantages or potential benefits. Customers are brought closer leading to profitable interactions.

People around the world are able to complete banking transactions, able to buy the products and services and pay for the services rendered sitting at the comforts of their homes.

Customer relationship management (CRM): Thanks to vast and valuable customer data residing in the computer databases and the Internet which enable mutually beneficial electronic relationship to be established with the customers and the prospects, CRM applications have become highly beneficial among customer focussed businesses. Powerful statistical and mathematical models have also been deployed in creating customer profiles which can be used in profiling more prospective customers.

Year 2010 onwards

Higher bandwidth wireless technologies like 3G and 4G, smart phones, notebook computers, the Internet and so on, enable the business to be managed from anywhere or even while travelling (Pervasive/Mobile/Anywhere computing).

Information processing, communication, knowledge sharing, entertainment, social networking, exchange of ideas, e-business and so on have merged into one vast space called the digital world, with no appreciable demarcation among them.

SUM UP

In this chapter the readers would have easily understood the tactical IT applications that are generally being used in all business organizations today, the benefits they bring to the business and what efforts are needed in making these applications highly effective.

5

BUSINESS TECHNOLOGY
Strategic IT Applications in Business

In this chapter, the readers would understand the following strategic IT applications:

1. Integrated business applications (IBA/ERP)
2. Supply chain IBA/ERP (SC-IBA)
3. Sales force automation (SFA)
4. Customer relationship management (CRM) system
5. E-business—Internet enabled business
6. Logistics and goods in transit tracking systems
7. Product development life cycle (PDLC) management systems
8. Data warehouse and data mining
9. Decision support system (DSS)
10. Expert system (ES)

At the end of this chapter, the readers would find answers for the questions like,

- How strategic IT applications are different from tactical applications?
- What are the strategic benefits such IT applications bring to business?
- What are the additional considerations and efforts that need to be put in to make strategic IT applications successful in business?
- What are the limitations of strategic IT applications?

A few case studies are also given at the end of this chapter to enable readers in understanding some of the interesting applications implemented in reality, in big business organizations.

5.1 INTRODUCTION

Business Technology refers to aligning of IT with business strategies.

The attributes of strategic IT applications have already been discussed in Section 1.10.1. Business organizations could seek specialists' services while choosing strategic IT applications if such skills are not available within the organization. Business Technology Management is discussed in chapter 18.

5.2 INTEGRATED BUSINESS APPLICATIONS (IBA/ERP)

5.2.1 Introduction

In this section, we discuss the functions of integrated business applications (IBA/ERP) covering internal operations and management of the business. In Section 5.3, we discuss supply chain integrated business application (SC-IBA/ERP), which would include external entities, viz. suppliers, sub-contractors, wholesalers, warehouses, distributors, retailers and customers. IBA and ERP software are discussed in Chapter 8.

IBA/ERP is being implemented in many business organizations today in view of the strategic advantages it brings to the business and excellent facilities being offered by IT, in the form of powerful host computers, huge data storage mediums, efficient RDBMS and Internet.

IBA/ERP integrates operations of most of the line and support functions in an organization even if they are distributed across different geographic locations and integrates entire business to function as one single entity in achieving its objectives.

The definition of IBA, the factors that contributed to disintegrated information systems, resources required for IBA and the advantages of IBA have already been discussed in Section 1.13.

5.2.2 Logical Structure of IBA/ERP in Business

The logical structure of IBA/ERP is given in **Figure 5.1**.

5.2.3 What IBA/ERP Does to the Business?

1. Automates most of the business processes in the form of OLTPS, EDP, MIS, OLAPS, OLCPS, programmed decisions, and so on. Many such automated business processes under various business functions are listed in Section 5.2.4.
2. Like a mirror, it reflects the true status of business through data/information stored in its database, thereby enhancing the business perception of all managers engaged in business. The managers are able to get right information at right time.

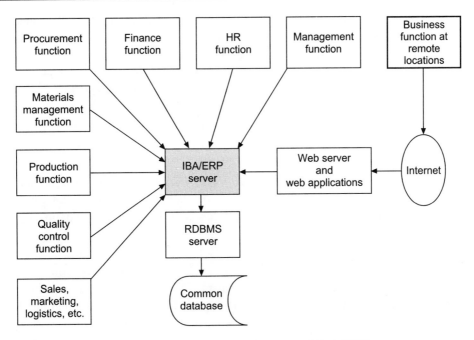

FIGURE 5.1 Logical structure of IBA/ERP.

3. Allows sharing of information related to all business entities and events of all business functions among all managers. It integrates all business and management functions and thus enables close coordination, collaboration and effective communication among all employees and the managers. The advantages of IBA have been discussed in Section 1.13.

4. Makes the business more competitive as discussed in Section 1.16 and leverages the business to a great extent as described in Section 1.18.

5.2.4 Business Processes Automated Through IBA/ERP

Many of the business processes that are automated through IBA/ERP under respective business functions are listed in this section. These applications are not described in detail here, because the readers could logically relate them to any business. However, some applications are described in detail under the case studies given at the end of this chapter.

1. **MIS for all business functions:** In addition to automating the business processes listed below, IBA/ERP would provide hundreds of real time MIS for the managers of all business functions and at all levels of management as explained in Chapter 2.

2. **Sales and marketing**
   - Preparation of sales and marketing budgets/targets
   - Integration of (sales) orders received through various mediums (letters, e-mail, phone, SMS, etc.) and from all market channels and customers

- Creation of sales orders database for all the products and for all channels
- Order acceptance and sending confirmation letters to all channels/customers
- Product allocation from stocks and printing of product delivery notes (to accompany product dispatches) and packing slips at all stock points
- Sales invoicing, collections against sale proceeds and preparation of receipts for the collections
- Preparation of statement of accounts to be sent to all channels of marketing
- Finished stock accounting and stock ledgers for all warehouses/stock points
- Accounting of goods returns
- Recovery of various taxes (e.g., VAT, excise duty, etc.) and preparation of statement of returns for the same (to be submitted to government agencies)
- Sales promotion activities: preparation of schedules and updating completed activities
- Accounting of marketing costs and cost analysis
- Sales promotions, advertisement and publicity expenses accounting
- Market analysis involving market share, TIV, and so on
- Measuring actual sales and marketing performance and comparing the same with the budgets to assess variance (favourable/adverse).

3. **Procurement**

- Preparation of material requisitions (by production and various other business functions)
- Consolidation of material requisitions
- Specifications, drawings and standards database for all raw materials, products and services being procured
- Database of vendors and the materials/products supplied by them
- Request for quotations to be sent to prospective vendors
- Vendor price comparison and selection of vendors
- Printing and the communication of purchase orders to vendors
- Purchase orders delivery schedule follow-up reports
- Preparation of material inwards register
- Closing of purchase orders when all quantities are supplied
- Vendor rating (based on quality, reliability, price, etc.).

4. **Materials management**

- Preparation of goods receipt/material acceptance documents
- Validation of material receipts with purchase schedules
- Accounting of material receipts in stores stocks
- Valuation of accepted materials and creation of accounts payable
- Valuation of stocks and processing of priced stores ledger
- Material issues for production
- Costing of issues and integrating the same with cost of production.

5. **Production**
   - Material requirement planning based on production schedule and bill of materials
   - Accounting of raw materials drawn from stores
   - Capacity planning of plant and machinery to be used up in production
   - Manpower planning for all operations
   - Accounting of product rejections
   - Rejections analysis involving costs and the reasons
   - Accounting of finished stocks in stores
   - Manpower utilization and costing
   - Work in progress accounting for management and control
   - Production history database for tracking product complaints/failures
   - Consumption analysis—specific consumption for all materials and utilities
   - Evaluating installed capacity with utilized capacities (capacity utilization—MIS)
   - Computing cost of production and so on.

6. **Quality control**
   - Database of quality specifications for all input materials and products
   - Database of inspection norms and methods
   - Inspection schedules to perform actual inspections and monitoring time delays
   - Inspection rejections accounting
   - Update purchase orders for the rejections
   - Defective material returns, intimation to vendors and so on.

7. **Plant and machinery: Repairs and maintenance**
   - Breakdown maintenance management and costing
   - Preventive maintenance scheduling and costing
   - Monitoring maintenance work orders
   - Database of plant and machinery indicating cost, depreciation, book values, replacement costs, location etc.
   - Maintaining breakdown history
   - Breakdown analysis in terms of reasons for breakdown (MIS).

8. **Logistics**
   - Database of all transporters/service providers
   - Freight rates and contracts management systems
   - Preparation of distribution schedule in terms of products, quantities, destinations, target dates, etc.
   - Origin to destination route maps indicating shortest distance and lead time
   - Transporter's performance rating
   - Logistics management and product movements tracking systems
   - Payments to carriers/transporters/product handling agencies

- Goods-in-transit management
- Warehouse rentals payment, and so on.

9. **Customer support and services**

- Call centre operations (integration of telecommunication and the customer database)
- Applications related to post-sales customer support services
- Warranty claims processing
- Managing annual maintenance contracts entered with the customers
- Integration of customer touch points (like phone, e-mail, SMS, letters and so on)
- Analysis of customer complaints, and so on.

10. **Finance**

- Books of accounts—daybooks, general ledgers, P&L and balance sheet
- Preparation of finance schedules to accompany the balance sheet
- Maintaining assets registers
- Debtor ledgers and ageing analysis
- Creditor ledgers
- Preparation of payments vouchers and cheques
- Cash flow management—comparing planned and actual
- Product costing
- Responsibility/commitment accounting—target vs. actual analysis
- Expenses accounting and statements
- Capital budgeting: budget vs. actual variance analysis (MIS)
- Revenue budgeting: budget vs. actual variance analysis (MIS)
- Project management in terms of project activities and costs
- Investments management—follow-up on maturing investments, re-investment, computation of return on investments, etc.
- Borrowings management—repayment schedules, closing of loans, computing cost of capital, etc.
- Computing various financial ratios
- Bank accounts management and bank reconciliation
- Systems that help management of financial risks and compliances
- Systems that monitor insurance policies, renewals and claims, and so on.

11. **Human resources management**

- Creation of organization structure with reporting relationships (database)
- Approved vs. vacant positions reports
- Recruitment—systems
- Employee compensation/payroll systems
- Performance appraisal systems
- Increments and promotions—processing system,

- Loan disbursement and recovery monitoring systems
- Attendance and leave management systems
- Retirement/termination processing systems
- Manpower costing system
- Managing statutory compliances with respect to PF, ESI, professional tax, income tax, and so on.

12. **Management functions:** IBA supports most of the management functions. IT applications in management functions are discussed in Chapter 6.

5.2.5   IBA Software Packages (IBASP)

Business organizations can acquire IBASP in different ways, which are discussed in detail in Chapter 8. The relative merits and demerits of each of these alternatives have also been discussed in that chapter.

5.3   SUPPLY CHAIN INTEGRATED BUSINESS APPLICATIONS (SC-IBA)

5.3.1   Introduction

The Internet has brought strategic advantages to business, in the form of electronic connectivity to the supply chain. Supply chain is a complex process involving materials, products, information, time, costs and people both within and outside the organization. It starts from the suppliers, pass through the value addition chain, market channels including the retail outlets and end with customers. The objective of effective supply chain management is to reduce the logistics and inventory carrying costs of the business and positioning of right products at right places at right time.

5.3.2   Supply Chain Entities

The supply chain entities are the suppliers, sub contractors, logistics providers, warehouses, wholesalers, stockists, distributors, retailers and customers. SC-IBASP would integrate all supply chain entities and make the business as a whole to function as one single integrated entity.

5.3.3   Logical Structure of Supply Chain Integrated IBA

The logical structure of SC-IBA is given in **Figure 5.2**.

5.3.4   IT Applications Associated with SC-IBA

SC-IBA effectively convert supply chain entities into extended profit centres, responsible for achieving the business objectives. SC-IBA would automate and integrate all internal business

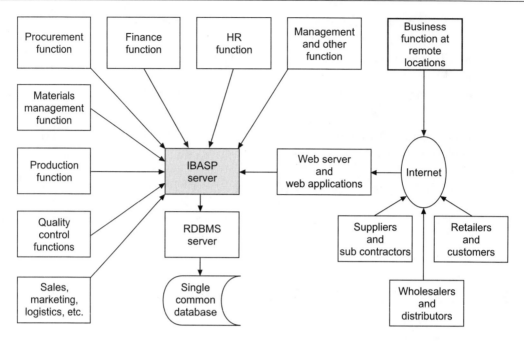

FIGURE 5.2   Logical structure of SC-IBA.

applications discussed in Section 5.2 and in addition enable the following applications/ interactions with the supply chain entities.

Business organizations can share parts of their business database with the supply chain entities if appropriate access controls and secured communication links are established for the purpose.

The applications/automated business processes of SC-IBA discussed below are only indicative and not exhaustive.

1. **Suppliers and sub contractors**

   - Suppliers and sub contractors can easily pick up the requests for quotations and submit their quotations electronically.
   - Similarly, purchase orders of the buyers can be sent electronically to all suppliers and sub contractors.
   - Suppliers and sub contractors can plan and alter their production schedules based on the buying company's (buyers) production plans.
   - Buyer's can instantly know the delivery schedules of all vendors.
   - Product dispatches from the suppliers can easily be tracked by the buyers to assess GIT, cash flow requirements and arrival times of materials.
   - Materials received, inspected, accepted and rejected can be intimated to the suppliers automatically.
   - Electronic payments can be effected for all materials accepted from the suppliers, and so on.

2. **Wholesalers and distributors**

- Manufacturing companies can have instant information of the stocks, product requirements, receivables, etc. of all wholesalers and distributors to plan further product dispatches.
- Wholesalers and distributors can know in advance the products that are being dispatched to them and the goods in transit.
- Manufacturers and market channels can work in synchronization in placing right products at right time and at right places.
- Wholesalers and distributors can pass on important market information as and when new opportunities or threats are sensed in the markets, and so on.

3. **Warehouses and stock points**

- Stocks, receipts and issues of products, stock replenishment, etc. could easily be monitored and synchronized with logistics and distribution.
- Cost of storage of stocks, transportation costs, safety of the stocks, stock to sales performance, etc. can easily be controlled by virtue of readily available information for all warehouses and the stock points.
- Most economical and fastest modes of transport, economic shipment sizes, and so on can be identified with respect to each location and the same can be used in logistics decision support systems.
- The market channels and retailers would also be aware of the availability of stocks at nearest locations.

4. **Retailers**

- Retail management is the most important marketing activity and integration of all retail outlets offer immense benefits to the business. If it is not possible to integrate all retail outlets, key outlets where the sales volumes are high need to be integrated with this system.
- Retailers are very large in numbers and are stationed widespread across the country/countries. SC-IBA enables accurate planning in positioning and movement of stocks with respect to each retail point, based on available stocks, sales plans, competitor stocks, sales pattern, and so on.
- Stocks, sales, goods-in-transit, demand, competitor stocks, etc. can also be consolidated at state/region levels in positioning the products at state/region levels.
- Retailers are the most important link in the supply chain, and real time information on retailer stocks helps in production planning, actual production, marketing and logistics.

5. **Customers**

- Customers are the ultimate link in the supply chain integration. However, it may not be required or possible to connect the customers for all businesses. For business organizations where customer values are high (limited number of customers combined with high business volumes), it is necessary to integrate the customers with SC-IBA.

- Some businesses could be able to sell the products or services directly through Internet (e-commerce discussed in detail in Section 5.6) to the customers.
- In all instances, the SC-IBA systems enable the businesses to have close and beneficial interaction with its customers, be it product preferences, complaints, after-sales support, and so on.

6. **Transporters/logistics providers:** An integrated logistics/transport management system needs to be designed as part of SC-IBA. The model (DSS) should be able to support decisions like,

- Are the finished products to be packed at the factory site or moved in bulk and packed at warehouses or stock points
- Is transportation is to buffer stocks or direct to warehouses or retailers
- Cheapest modes of transport
- Faster and shorter routes
- Type of transport to retail outlets and customers
- Warehouse locations and ideal stocks to be positioned at each location
- Cheaper or better warehouse locations in terms of costs, product safety, rental, retail access, insurance cover, etc.
- Ideal stock to turnover ratio for each warehouse, and so on.

5.3.5 Privacy and Security Concerns

The access rights of the external entities should be restricted to SC-IBA applications (listed in Section 5.3.4) strictly on a need to know basis (for each one of these entities) and other internal business applications should be protected as discussed in Chapter 10. A 'non disclosure agreement' needs to be signed with all supply chain entities.

The data communication between the business and the external entities needs to be fully secured, so that none of the data handled by the supply chain is accessible by unauthorized entities.

5.3.6 Benefits of Supply Chain Integrated Applications

- It reduces the time gap between identification of demand and its fulfilment. This leads to reduction in inventories and working capital in all stages of the supply chain.
- Products by virtue of availability, convenience, prompt delivery, etc. contribute to customer loyalty.
- Unwanted/bottleneck entities in supply chain are identified and eliminated.
- Business is able to respond quickly to changing market/customer requirements.
- The physical infrastructure associated with logistics is optimized in terms of cost and time, e.g. minimum warehouse rentals, cheaper and quicker modes of transports.

- Offers integrated information flow for the entire supply chain which results in better decisions and faster action.

- Supply chain entities function as extended profit centres of the business.

5.3.7 SC-IBASP (SC–IBA Software Package)

All processes listed under Section 5.3.4 need to be automated through well designed application software. Entire SC-IBASP needs to be carefully planned and implemented through SDLC activities discussed in Chapter 8.

ERP packages could be the other alternative, but they may not cover all the applications listed under Section 5.3.4. SC-IBASP is implemented under ERP option, through a number of software products integrated with ERP packages.

5.4 SALES FORCE AUTOMATION (SFA) SYSTEM

Sales forces are the marketing/field officers or sales representatives who are present in the marketplace all the time. They are the key link between the markets and the business.

The notebook computers, 3G enabled mobile phones, IBA and Internet enable the sales forces to be electronically connected to the manufacturing sites, top management, marketing channels and customers all the time. This enables the market information to reach the decision makers at the earliest.

Sales force can feed wide variety of marketing information listed below, to head offices or top management:

- Market potentials, new opportunities and threats
- Customers' shifting preferences
- Product complaints
- Strengths and weaknesses of the products compared to competing products
- Available stocks across all market channels
- Stock replenishment schedules for all channels
- Competitor sales performance
- Total industrial volumes
- Sales promotional exercises—targets and achievements
- Customer/retailer contacts and feedback
- Product positioning data at all retail outlets, and so on

It is also possible to appraise the top management of dynamic market situations and obtain their directions or approvals directly and immediately.

Sales force can also automate sales activities such as

- Booking of retailers/customer orders
- Authorization for release of products from stock points

- Sales invoicing
- Collection of money from retailers/customers
- Controlling Marketing costs
- Follow-up and collection of overdue outstandings, and so on

The biggest advantage of sales force automation is that relevant market data is captured at the point of their origin (markets) at the earliest and sent to the central database immediately. For example, product orders captured through SFA become an important input for production scheduling. SFA has been the forerunner for customer relationship management discussed in the following section.

5.5 CUSTOMER RELATIONSHIP MANAGEMENT (CRM)

5.5.1 Introduction

Most of the businesses today are in buyer markets and the competition is also fierce. Organizations need to deliver products and services tailored to suit individual or group of customers' needs and preferences.

CRM helps business organizations in understanding the customer needs/preferences better and faster, so as to offer right products ahead of competition. It aims segmentation at customers or groups of customers' level (micro level market segmentation). CRM is a suite of integrated business applications which aim at managing the customer interactions more effectively/profitably.

Proprietary and small businesses do establish profitable relationships with their customers by virtue of smaller size and personal interactions with them. But large businesses do not enjoy the luxury of such personal interactions. However, the customer data (captured through various IT applications) residing in the databases can effectively be used in knowing them and learning their behaviour better and use such information in establishing closer customer relations.

5.5.2 CRM Objectives

- To assess customers' needs and preferences accurately and deliver right products that match their requirements
- To improve marketing processes leading to 'efficient customer response', both in pre- and post-sales activities
- To integrate all customer touch points (phone, SMS, letters, e-mail, etc.) and create a single point of reference for each customer across entire business
- To look at each customer as a profit centre and to identify high worth and loyal customers on whom to focus the sales and marketing activities more
- To move from broad market segmentation to high value customers'/group of customers' segmentation
- To identify cost effective sales promotions.

5.5.3 CRM in Knowledge Economy

- Historically, the manufacturers were 'pushing' (push marketing) the information related to their products and prices to the markets and made the consumers buy the products. It was sellers market then. Now the manufacturers need to 'pull' (pull marketing) the information from the customers/markets and need to do customer focussed marketing.

- Retail chains are becoming more knowledgeable of the markets, customer preferences and competing products and are also emerging as most preferred destinations for the customers at large. Such 'power' retailers start dictating prices, thereby reducing the margins for the manufacturers. Producers, hence, need to establish a closer rapport with their customers to tackle power retailers e.g. leading brands establish exclusive retail outlets for their products.

- Today's customers are highly knowledgeable and too demanding. They want the products and services that meet their exact needs. Competition is fierce and product obsolescence is fast. The customer needs are to be understood and serviced fast. It is costlier to gain new customers than keeping them satisfied. And it is easier to sell to the existing customers rather than to new customers.

- Only a part of customers' positive feelings and loyalty are generated by product quality and price and the rest come from things like, prompt customer service, their buying experience, the way they are treated, and so on.

- CRM systems are capable of answering questions like, customers who are most profitable, profitable market promotion exercises, prospective customers for the existing and new products, shifts in their loyalty, and so on.

- The differential value between the sales promotional costs to the profits earned through them are to be reckoned.

5.5.4 Components of CRM System

CRM systems are made up of three categories of IT applications, viz.

1. Marketing transactions processing applications
2. Analytical applications
3. Customer interactive applications.

5.5.5 CRM Applications in Business

Marketing transactions processing applications

These applications could be part of IBA or separate modules added to ERP discussed in Section 5.2.

1. **Point of sales/OLTPS applications:** Point of sales (OLTPS) system enables business organizations to gain good knowledge of their customers both in the past and now, in terms of products, price, who, when, where they buy, and so on.

Though OLTPS are created to meet the operational needs of the business, they contain valuable information about customers, which can be used in CRM effectively.

2. **Customer database:** Business organizations could create and manage exhaustive database of their customers consisting of personal and demographic data. They could collect such data through KYC (know your customer) forms or at the point of sales or through on line registration using Internet. The customers may be given some sort of incentives to get such information (prize schemes, issuing special membership cards, discounts, and so on). This database could be used in establishing closer interaction with the customers like sending greeting cards and to intimate the new products to them first.

3. **Customer feedback/complaints:** There needs to be a system to capture customer feedback, good or bad, and the product complaints. The customers data and the product feedback obtained from them need to be stored in a central database so that they are made known to business functions concerned. The customers need to be told of the action being taken resolving their problems and such instances should be utilized for establishing closer customer relations.

4. **Post-sales services applications:** Post-sales applications include, giving the customers usage tips/guidance, settling warranty claims, annual maintenance contracts, customer/product support services, customer contact programmes customer forums and so on. The business organizations need to ensure that the customers get a fair deal all the time. Customers' loyalty and brand image depend more on these factors than on products and prices.

5. **Sales force automation (SFA):** SFA, which is the forerunner of CRM (already discussed in Section 5.4), also needs to be automated.

6. **Integrated view of each customer:** An important task for the business organizations today is to have an integrated (single window concept) view of each of their customers and all their interactions with the business. All business functions should update this database when they interact with the customers. Integration of customer touch-points to enable this is discussed subsequently. This is yet another important activity that boosts customer loyalty and brand image, but generally not done in India.

Analytical applications

1. **Data warehouse:** The business needs to remember what their customers have done in the past. Data warehouse captures historical customer behaviour information. This is a huge database containing valuable information of all its sales, customers, product complaints, products sold, prices, times of purchase, channels, and so on obtained from the transaction processing applications discussed above, over many years.

Data warehouse is discussed in detail in Section 5.9.

2. **Data mining:** The business needs to learn something new from the data warehouse and such learning is enabled by data mining. Data warehouse contains

valuable customer information. It is up to the management to mine for useful hidden information. Data mining translates historic data into newer marketing plans and profitable customer relationships strategies. The data warehouse provides the enterprise with electronic memory. And this memory needs to be interpreted intelligently. Intelligence allows noticing new patterns, formulating better ideas and making better business predictions.

But finding the patterns is not easy because they are not prominent and sometimes may even be confusing. Recognizing objective/useful patterns from out of the data warehouse is an important role of specialists and it is done through data mining. Data mining is discussed in detail in Section 5.9.

For example, the profiles of existing customers (based on certain/definite attributes) can be obtained from the data mining and such profiles can be applied on to total population (Nearest neighbours) to identify more prospective customers and to target sales promotional efforts on them.

3. **CRM:**   CRM is to act based on what the business has learnt (through data ware-house and data mining) in order to enhance customer loyalty and customer base.

For example, CRM can be applied in planning more effective sales campaigns, acquiring new customers, test marketing, test campaigns, cross selling (selling one product with other), customer retention, customer/(s) segmentation, and so on.

For more information on these types of applications, readers are advised to read the textbooks devoted to CRM, market research and statistics applied to marketing.

4. **Information systems:**   The business organizations need to identify and implement right information systems that would enable taking right customer-oriented decisions, identifying prospective customers, making right offers to them, identifying the right time when such offers are to be made, right channels, and so on. MIS, OLAP and KMS are to be used for this purpose.

5. **Decision support systems/statistical packages:**   Statistical (software) packages come with a number of techniques/models, which help in understanding the customer behaviour based on the data warehouse. Models used in data mining and decision support systems are discussed in Section 5.9.

Interactive applications

Interactive applications have gained popularity thanks to Internet, mobile devices, wireless technologies including 3G, integration of communication devices with the computer databases and responsive customers. This has created great potential for the business organizations in establishing closer customer relations to great levels not witnessed so long.

1. **Integration of customer touch-points:**   Business organizations need to enable their customers to interact, through various mediums such as the websites/portals, telephone, fax, SMS, interactive voice response system (IVRS), call centre, e-mail, letters, etc. and integrate all such interactions into unified customer interaction database. Information/feedback received from all customers, good or bad, needs to

be updated on to this database. All business functions need to interact with the customers through this database and keep updating this database in all their interactions with them.

2. **Call centre:** Call centre is an important link between the customers and the business. It needs to be made known to all customers. They should be able to contact the call centre all the time through toll-free number(s). During the call, the customer interaction database needs to be made available to the call centre operators. Customer interaction needs to be updated on to this database as soon as the call is completed. All business functions need to be made aware of such interactions and initiate necessary action in response to all customer calls.

In order to establish effective CRM, the business needs to become highly responsive to the customer calls and their expectations.

3. **Establishing electronic relations with customers through Internet:** The Internet allows the most efficient and economic collaboration between the business and its customers. Business organizations need to exploit Internet in establishing closer customer relations.

The Internet enables a direct link between the business and its customers anytime and anywhere. Reliable Internet infrastructure needs to be made available for successful implementation of CRM.

Customers are to be attracted to have frequent access to the company's website, to learn about existing and new products, customer/product support services, company contact points for reporting the problems, guide for troubleshooting by the customers themselves, important do's and don'ts, frequently asked questions (FAQs), service outlets, and so on.

Readers may visit websites/portals of DTH service providers is India in understanding how Internet is used in running a service oriented business with minimal human resources.

5.6 E-BUSINESS

Any business process performed electronically (using computers/smart phones and Internet) is called e-business and today most of the business processes (like Intranet, Extranet, e-procurement, e-recruitment, e-commerce, e-mail, e-payments, e-auctions, and so on) are being performed through e-business. E-commerce involving buying and selling is a sub set of e-business.

E-business is another strategic IT application which radically changes the way the business is run. It has brought the supply chain and the customers closer. The business operations distributed across different geographical locations get integrated and are becoming more cohesive, efficient and highly responsive to the customer expectations.

E-business has very broad connotation and include Internet enabled IBA/ERP (Intranet), supply-chain integrated IBA/ERP (Extranet), B2B, B2C, CRM, business portals, websites, and so on. E-business models are discussed in section in 5.6.8.

E-business has virtually shrunk the global business into a local business. Industries having geographically dispersed operations like banking, insurance, travel, hospitality, multinational corporations (MNCs), retail chains, manufacturing businesses having their production facilities and marketing networks spread across the country, and so on, derive great leverage from e-business.

5.6.1 Benefits of E-business

1. **Global exposure and opportunities:** E-business allows exchange of business information in the form of Business-to-Business (B2B), Business-to-Customer (B2C) and Customer-to-Customer (social networks/user groups) around the globe. The business gets global exposure with respect to the products and services offered and required and business association/collaboration.

   It offers global opportunities for business and even a local shop can have the world market at its doorstep. It eliminates the constraints posed by geographic and political boundaries and enables organizations to reach out to the customers and markets all over the globe. Indirectly, it is also making the business organizations to be more efficient and highly competitive.

2. **Effective business communication:** E-business enables efficient and economical communication among all human entities involved in business, both within and outside the organization. This enables relationship-building, negotiations and exchange of ideas among key entities, like the sales force, customers, market channels, business managers, vendors, and so on. People engaged in business are able to collaborate, exchange information and take collective decisions wherever they are positioned.

3. **Business process integration across all geographic locations:** E-business enables the business processes to be integrated among all business functions, value addition chain, supply chain and all external entities in the form of web enabled business applications, irrespective of their geographical location and time zones.

4. **E-commerce (dot com companies):** It means Internet enabled buying and selling of diverse products and services. It may involve products or services that can be delivered electronically or physical products, supported by right logistic infrastructure to complete the deliveries fast. E-payment services offered by the banks and secured payment gateway service providers complete the payment cycle effectively.

5. **Convergence:** Internet enables convergence of multimedia, viz. images, pictures, graphs, animation, audio and video along with conventional text and data. This enables the business to have an integrated approach in storing and accessing business information gathered in all such mediums. The 3G and 4G communication technologies today deliver even audio and video contents instantly (discussed in Section 11.12).

6. **Lower costs:** Since e-business is done in electronic form, there is no need to have physical infrastructures like office, redundant channels of marketing, and so on. This considerably reduces the overheads and such savings are passed on to the customers. Customers get better deal through e-business. Virtual stores selling a variety of products through internet, internet banking, employment portals, tourism portals, etc. are the examples for this.

7. **Search engines and intelligent agents:** Search engines allow business managers in accessing huge volumes of business related information stored in the computers

anywhere in the world. The business managers are able to gain good knowledge of cheaper inputs, improved production techniques, shifting market trends, and so on very easily. Special purpose software called intelligent agents, mimic human intelligence in performing various commercial and personal tasks associated with Internet applications for it's users.

8. **Internet portals:** Internet portals offer single point of contact for the customers for multiple products and services logically related to one another (e.g., the tourists get all services like travel, accommodation, food, local sight seeing, etc. through one single portal). The business can tie up with the suppliers of complementary/ associative products and services in offering integrated services to its customers. This also offers better deals for the customers because of the scales of economy derived by such service providers.

   They are interactive websites that provide a variety of services including web searching (search engines), news, e-mail/e-chat, discussion groups, social network- ing, on line shopping and links to other websites. Internet portals generally offer services related to a particular industry such as banking, insurance, travel, employ- ment, and so on. Business organizations can also have their own corporate portals to offer a wide variety of services to their customers and other business entities.

9. **Internet:** Internet is a set of universal standards/protocols (like OSI and TCP/IP for communication, HTTP for texts, URL for addresses, HTML for programming, POP/SMTP for e-mail, FTP for file transfers, and so on) established and being adopted by all vendors and users around the globe to connect computers to one another and to perform various Internet enabled tasks/applications.

Internet is built on client server architecture, having two types of computers, viz. web servers and the clients. Web servers run on the web server operating system and stores all applications (programs) and data associated with Internet applications. Clients (Users) run on browser software and access web servers. Internet is very cost effective and radically changes the way the business is run today. Internet is also discussed in Sections 5.6.4 and 5.6.14.

10. **Efficient customer response:** E-business makes the business operations faster and enables managing the business resources in real time. It also leads to better coordination, closer collaboration and collective decision-making among all human entities associated with the business. By virtue of real-time information shared among all managers, organisations become more knowledgeable of the customers, markets, competition, suppliers, wholesalers, retailers and so on. This finally makes the business highly responsive to customer/market needs and expectations.

11. **Paperless business:** Everyone is aware that the papers cause destruction of our natural resources viz., forests. Computers convert the paper contents (text, pictures, data etc.) into digital formats that can easily be stored and communicated in electronic mediums. E-business enables the digital contents accessible around the world without using papers. This leads to paperless business and hence the society. For example, airlines and railways in India, allow their customers to carry their tickets in digital form in their mobile phones.

12. **Shrinks physical business space:** Internet and E-business shrink the physical business space in all fronts and enable managing the business from anywhere and on the go. This has also reduced the transaction costs considerably.

Since the benefits of e-business are so many and widely varying, only key advantages are discussed in this book.

5.6.2 Benefits of E-business to the People/Customers

1. **Increased choice:** Customers are able to evaluate many offers made available through Internet and choose the best available products/services at best prices.

2. **Convenience of interaction:** Customers can interact with the business and service organizations and do shopping and other activities sitting in the convenience of their home any time, any day and every day.

3. **Information on demand:** Public can reach the business any time for sales, service or product information.

4. **Where to buy:** Public can easily locate the products or services of their choice either in local markets or in international markets.

5. **Transparency in business transactions:** The prices and product specifications become transparent which leads to fair play among producers and consumers.

5.6.3 E-business Application Software

E-business application software is generally custom built to suit wide and varied requirements of each business. The software provides appropriate and friendly user interface for all the entities interacting with the business. This is developed conforming to Internet standards/protocols and using SDLC activities discussed in Chapter 8. Since e-business brings strategic advantages to business, it is advisable to develop this software in-house. The application software also would undergo frequent modifications to meet the fast-changing requirements of e-business users.

5.6.4 E-business IT Infrastructure

Logical structure of e-business infrastructure is shown in Figure 5.3. Functions of Internet components are listed below.

Internet

The Internet is a set of standards or protocols (discussed in Sections 5.6.14 and 5.6.15) established by various technical committees, stationed across number of countries that enable Internet resources like computers (clients and web servers), communication devices and mediums, operating systems and numerous applications get interfaced with one another, to enable seamless exchange of information among its users. Internet is not owned by any company or country.

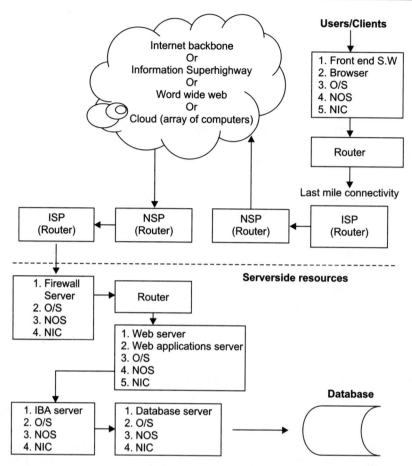

FIGURE 5.3 Logical structure of the Internet or E-business infrastructure.

Client

An e-business user or the Personal computer connected to the Internet is generally termed as a client. Client can only feed and receive information from the server. All processing takes place only at the server side. A client can be connected to the Internet as and when required. When it gets connected, it is given a temporary IP address by the Internet Service Provider (ISP). Such connectivity is also termed as **last mile connectivity** and it does not warrant high bandwidths.

E-business front end (software)

It is the e-business application's front end (screen layouts with menu options, tool bars, icons, check boxes etc. in colours and graphics) loaded on to the client's computer by the application software residing in the web server, as and when the client logs on to the server. The front end is highly user friendly and takes the input from the users as dictated by the application being run in the server. The processed outputs are again sent to the client computer by the server. The front end software makes the users highly comfortable with e-business applications. It hides the technology from the users, e.g. point of sales billing, raising purchase orders, payments to the suppliers and so on.

Browser

It is the utility software that sits on the client computer and takes the inputs or instructions from the application front end and communicates the same to the web server placed on the Internet and vice versa. Browser and web server communicate with one another using standard protocols. Popular Internet browsers are Explorer, Firefox, Chrome and so on.

Web server

Web Server is a high end computer with web server software, where all the Internet processes are performed for the clients. Each web server is given a unique domain name easily remembered by the people. Domain name is also an integral part of an URL (universal resource locator). The domain name is converted into unique IP address by the domain name server (DNS) also connected to the Internet. Web server also interact with the web applications like e-mail, e-commerce, www, IBA and so on. All the Internet exchanges take place between the browser and web server only.

IBA server

In addition to web server, there could also be dedicated business application server for the Intranet and Extranet models discussed in Sections 5.2 and 5.3. Application servers generally do not have the domain names and cannot be accessed by the clients directly.

In addition, there could be firewall server to protect the resources connected to the Internet and database server to manage huge databases efficiently. These servers are required for big e-business applications.

Networking operating system (NOS)

NOS is the system software that digitally communicates to other computers. This component is not used in stand alone computers. NOS comes as a part of the operating system today. Network interface card (NIC) is a hardware that connects the computer to the network through routers.

ISP (Internet service provider)/NSP/NAP

ISPs connect the clients and servers to the Internet backbone (high band width information super highways) and charge the users based on their bandwidth usage. ISPs in turn get connected to network service providers (NSP) and network access points (NAP), which connect the computers around the world together, through high bandwidth coaxial cables laid under deep seas. ISPs and NSPs have also been discussed in Section 3.2.2.

Router

Routers are intelligent communication devices that decide the path for the flow of data from one computer to the other, control the traffic based on given criteria and segment the networks.

5.6.5   E-business Challenges

1. **Security:** Since critical and confidential business data are placed on the communication mediums encircling the globe, there is always a risk of someone eavesdropping into confidential business information. It is therefore necessary to ensure the security of information through data encryption/decryption techniques discussed in Chapter 10.

2. **Threat of hacking:** Since the computers connected to Internet are accessible by anyone, the computer resources need to be protected from unauthorized users/ hackers. Computer resources need to be protected with appropriate firewall to avoid such threats.

3. **Customer privacy:** As more and more data pertaining to customer purchases, personal data, their buying patterns, etc. are captured in the computer database, there is always a possibility that the business organizations can encroach upon the privacy of customers. It is the responsibility of the business to get their customers concurrence in using their personal information.

4. **Lacks human warmth:** Since the business is carried out using inert objects, e-business lacks human touch, warmth and social relations among the buyers and sellers.

5. **Sincerity of sellers and buyers:** Since the products are not seen physically, the sellers need to be sincere and truthful in offering right products to the customers. The buyers also need to discharge their obligation in making payments and should not resort to unethical activities.

6. **Information overload:** Since storing of large volumes of data, text and images is less costly and easy, sellers and buyers should not overload one another with unwanted and redundant data which would confuse and waste others' times.

5.6.6   E-business Strategy

Business organizations need to have definite e-business strategy in place based on its potential to the business.

1. **Business information posted on the websites:** It is highly cost-effective to post business information on to the websites. But the websites need to follow certain guidelines as follows:

    *   The web pages should not freeze up and not lead the visitors to a dead end. From the homepage, forward and backward navigation should be easy (supported by the site map).

- Sufficient and reliable IT infrastructure needs to be in place for the visitors to access the website any time and to get the information fast. E-business site should not frustrate potential users by making them to wait for more than a few seconds or giving unwanted and stale information.

- Information presented should enable the business in tapping the newer markets and getting more customers.

- The site should allow access to popular search engines and intelligent agents. It should also enable the users to communicate to the business through its website.

- Visitors should feel that they learn something new, every time they visit the website. Business organizations need to collect as much information as possible from the business entities and customers accessing the websites.

2. **Establishing better business relationship through web/e-business sites:** Business organizations need to adopt innovative ways in establishing a win-win relationship with the customers and other business entities interacting in the electronic space.

E-business sites need to be interactive and capture the customer responses thereon. Such responses need to be acknowledged and acted upon fast.

The business organizations need to create user groups/forum for opinion-building and sharing their experiences of the products and services offered by the business.

3. **Enabling electronic transactions through web/e-business sites:** The business should allow e-business sites to engage in meaningful dialogues or negotiations. It should have easy to operate e-baskets/e-carts to fill the products ordered and wide choice of payment gateways.

All data communicated through e-business sites need to be highly secured through appropriate and sound data encryption/decryption techniques. The site should establish authentication and non-repudiation of parties engaged in e-business.

4. **Long-term and short-term goals:** E-business strategies are to be finalized by the top management in consultation with the functional heads and with external consultants if so warranted. It is the responsibility of top management to set long- and short-term goals for e-business and realign the business processes so as to tap strategic advantages of e-business. Top management needs to have good understanding of the business, its markets and strategic benefits e-business could bring to the business. This would involve finding answers to the following questions.

- **What business?** E-business strategy depends on the type of the business (product/service being offered, such as FMCG, consumer durables, automobiles, engineering, banking, healthcare, pharmaceutical etc.), the supply chain entities including the customers who could be engaged through it, how the competition is embracing e-business, the technology offerings, emerging trends and so on.

- **What strategic advantages?** The strategic advantages that could be realized through e-business like new markets, new channels, new products, cheaper inputs, integration of business processes, integration of supply chain, adoption of best business practices, highly responsive customer relations, flat and networked organization structures with modified reporting relationships and so on, are to be identified.

- **What contents, what transactions and how much information sharing?** What are the contents to be put in the public domain, responsibilities for content management, the extent of business transactions that would be automated through e-business including payment gateways, how much of business information would be shared among the business entities, access control for sensitive information, type of non-disclosure agreements to be signed to ensure data security etc. are to be finalized. Contents need to be uptodate, crisp, informative, attractive and artistic and meet the psychic and functional needs of the Internet clients. The site needs to be highly flexible to the circumstances and situations and fulfill clients' expectations.

- **What infrastructure (e-business resources)?**

  (i) **Computers and communication hardware:** Web server, web application server, integrated business applications server (IBA), firewall server and database server to support e-business need to be chosen based on their capacity in handling peak business volumes, scalability, maintainability, reliability and availability factors. This should also include hundreds of personal computers required to connect all business users (clients).

  (ii) **Communication mediums and bandwidths:** Communication mediums and bandwidths are to be chosen based on reliability, number of clients, expected data traffic and peak business volumes. Wherever necessary, redundant resources need to be ready as standby.

  (iii) **System software:** The operating system, web server, firewall server, relational database management systems etc. are to be chosen based on the reliability, capacity, scalability, maintainability, and configurability (compatibility).

  (iv) **Application software:** E-business application software like integrated business application software (IBA), supply chain integrated business application software (SC-IBA), e-commerce software, Internet portal software and so on are to be procured or custom built based on the functionality, reliability, user friendliness, upgradability, maintainability, configurability and so on. The application software requirements would vary appreciably depending on the e-business model choosen by the business. The software development activities need to follow SDLC activities discussed in Chapter 8.

  (v) **Skilled managers:** Managers running the business and developing e-business software need to know the scope and potential of e-business applications and should be capable of exploiting the technology, by providing wider functionality, designing friendly and simple user interface and deciding and managing the contents on a day-to-day basis. For all the above resources, initial investments and recurring expenses are to be computed.

- **Responsibility and authority?** A senior level manager needs to be given the responsibility and adequate authority for all e-business initiatives. He needs to be fully aware of the strategic benefits the business would derive through present and emerging technologies.

- **What logistics support?** If the products in physical forms are sold through e-business, highly reliable and supportive logistics need to be in place, even if it is outsourced. For the products and services delivered in electronic mediums there need to be a highly secured communication facilities for such deliveries.

- **User concerns?** E-business initiatives need to take care of users or customers and business's privacy issues. The site needs to have the site map, ease of forward and backward browsing, quick response time with no freezing and lockup of any web page and should not challenge intellectual capabilities of the users.

- **Push strategy?** The business needs to push as much useful information as possible to the users without overloading them with unwanted or unsolicited information. Information presented should enable completion of the intended e-business processes with no ambiguity.

- **Pull strategy?** At the same time it is necessary to ensure that sufficient information is also pulled from the users or clients. The information obtained need to be effectively used by the business in offering more personalised products and services.

- **Mapping newer and emerging technologies?** Business needs to be ready to map newer and emerging technologies like smart or mobile devices, 3G/4G standards, cloud computing, CRM, interactive voice response systems (IVRS) etc., through appropriate e-business applications.

- **What costs and what benefits?** Before the start of the e-business project, initial and recurring costs of all the resources discussed earlier, tangible and intangible benefits of these projects both in long- and short-terms need to be identified and stated clearly. No e-business initiative should be undertaken without taking into consideration the issues discussed so far in this section.

5.6.7 Wrong Notions of E-business

Internet and e-business have become very popular. However, there is still confusion as what E-business can do or cannot do. E-business initiatives need to be based on sound strategy based on the type and spread of the business and its products and services. The technology alone should not be the factor for the business to jump on to this bandwagon.

The false beliefs are:

- Setting up an e-business is easy and can be done fast.
- E-business is economical and profitable always.
- E-business is a sure path for the growth of the business.
- On line retailing is always the best and low cost channel.
- Any product can be sold online.
- E-business companies grow faster and achieve economies of scale.
- Small businesses become par with big businesses, and so on.

This should caution the business organizations and make them formulate right and profitable e-business strategies.

5.6.8   E-business Models

Though numerous other models could emerge, fourteen distinctive e-business models are discussed in this section.

1.   **Website hosting:** Many business organizations just host their business website on the Internet. They publish vast amount of information related to the business such as the products and services being offered or required, installed capacities, business vision, mission and long-term objectives, senior management personnel, contact points, operating results, social welfare schemes, share holding patterns etc. in attractive formats including multimedia, so that people around the world can get to know about the company very easily. All business organizations in India whether big, medium, or small including private business follow this.

In India, it is mandatory for the listed companies to post their quarterly and annual results on their websites in terms of P&L, balance sheet, auditors' reports and so on. This is the easiest and most economical way for the business organizations to publish vast business information compared to all other known media.

Business organizations need to ensure that all the information posted on their website is current and uptodate (i.e. content management). The website (URL) name should be made popular through all business communiqués or documents and media advertisements. People willing to know about the business organization would reach the website either through the domain name already known to them or using the services of search engines. The website needs to be linked to popular search engines.

2.   **Payment gateway:** Many organizations, particularly the utility service providers such as telephones, electricity and water, insurance companies, civic agencies collecting property taxes, statutory agencies collecting turnover or income or service taxes etc., create their websites along with payment gateways, to enable people to make payments using their credit cards or debit cards or Net banking or mobile banking facilities. This saves huge manual efforts for the organizations concerned and enables people at large in making these payments very easily, sitting at home. Through this facility secured money transfers happen instantly. No organization having similar activities can afford to ignore this e-business model. Payment gateway service providers like Verizon, offer highly secured data encryption and communication services between the payee, payer and their respective banks for this purpose.

3.   **E-commerce:** It is a potential model for certain products and services irrespective of the sizes of such business. E-commerce primarily is a sales or purchase transaction processing system over the Internet with a payment gateway embedded in it. E-commerce sites will have the following commercial components:

- Colorful display of products with multidimensional views including animation, if required and their detailed specifications to enable customers to gain good feel and know of the products.
- Products comparisons along with specifications and prices.
- Virtual billing system for the customers to know, the basic prices, discounts, taxes, packing and transportation charges etc., when they select the products online.
- Payment options in the form of debit/credit cards, Internet banking, mobile phones (e-wallets) and so on with fully secured payment gateways.
- Shopping cart, mimicking the shoppers' physical activities in real stores with options to add or delete the products from the cart.
- Secured delivery for digital products and services and prompt delivery of physical items through reliable logistics providers.
- Efficient product delivery tracking systems until the products reach the customers.
- Customer registration and customer feedback systems.
- Post-sales services including the maintenance contracts through e-mail, call center and IVR (interactive voice response systems).
- Highly attractive design with right and intelligent contents so as to tempt casual visitors to the site into buying.

Advantages of e-commerce

- Enable people buy and sell the products and services sitting at the convenience of the home any time and from anywhere.
- Help creating global demand for the products and services.
- Quickens products ordering and payment processes.
- Delivery or product tracking is made possible through GPS.
- Physical infrastructure costs and transaction costs are reduced considerably.
- Enable sale proceeds to be realized immediately.
- Enable customers to do comparison shopping.
- Brings in transparency in product pricing and discount structures.
- Small businesses are positioned on par with big players thereby giving the former a level playing field.
- E-stores are open round the clock around the globe with no geographic and time zone barriers.
- Can be scaled up to include newer products, wider markets and larger customer base.
- Instant service for customers.
- Reduced cost of serving customers and so on.

Factors that drive e-commerce

The factors mentioned below contribute to the success of e-commerce:

- Business reputation, brand image, product quality and demand.

- Crisp, clear, attractive, artistic, innovative website design.
- High quality and informative contents placed online.
- Ease of use by average website visitors.
- Quick downloads.
- Rewarding experience for the website visitors.
- Good content management.
- Intelligent use of colors, images, audio, video, formats and layouts.
- Ease of navigation of the site, back and forth.
- Display of products photos and specifications.
- All possible payment options.
- Secured payment gateways.
- Reliable data communication links.
- Stability of the products and services.
- Post-sales support and consumer confidence.
- Business ethics of buyers and sellers.
- Good and effective e-advertisement.
- Knowledge of customers and their web behaviours.
- Effective web traffic management.
- Links to related websites.
- Quick system response time and so on.

Advertising e-commerce

E-commerce needs to be supported by effective advertisement (both conventional and e-advertisement) and promotional activities like,

- Submitting key references (mega tags) of the products, services and other key attributes to all popular search engines.
- Advertising the products, services and e-commerce sites (URL) in print media along with QR (quick response) codes and other media like TV, movies, telemarketing etc.
- Placing banners or button links in other popular websites (e-advertising) like search engines, social sites, railways, banks, e-news papers, e-publications etc.
- Sending mass e-mails and SMS to prospective customers.
- Knowing your customers (KYC) information systems.
- Obtaining and evaluating site visitors profiles based on the data (hit statistics) obtained from ISPs.
- Profiling customers and effectively using such profiles in enlarging the customerbase.
- Offering personalized products and services based on customer preferences.

E-commerce sites need to pull people to its website, make them interested in the site, create desires and tempt them in making purchase decisions.

E-advertisement profiling and personalization influencing e-commerce are discussed in subsequent sections.

4. **Social portals:** Portals have already been described in Section 5.6.1. Social portals are yahoo, gmail, hotmail, facebook, youtube, twitter, linkedin, skype etc. and the search engines Google, Wikepedia and so on. Though they offer free services to the users, they generate revenue through e-advertisements, placed by various other commercial entities.

5. **Business portals:** In Indian context, the commercial activities such as Internet banking, online trading of listed stocks, railway reservation systems, income tax payments and submission of tax returns, hospitality services including tours, travels and hotels, matrimony and employment services, e-tailing (such as Flipkart, Naptol, Amazon), booking of tickets for movies and plays and many more such commercial activities fall under this model. This model offers much more than what e-commerce offers to the people. All such services are the paid services for the users. Extensive planning and higher investments are required for this model.

6. **Internet enabled CRM/IVR systems:** This has been discussed in Section 5.5.

7. **Intranet:** This has been discussed in Section 5.2.

8. **Extranet:** This has been discussed in Section 5.3.

9. **Cloud computing:** This has been discussed in Section 12.17.5

10. **E-Governance:** This has been discussed in Section 16.4

11. **Internet TV/entertainment:** Many TV channel producers like Sony, Zee TV, Star TV and so on, now offer Internet based TV, which can be viewed through computers or smart phones by paying prescribed subscription charges. This has added mobilty to TV viewership. People even can play virtual games with virtual or real money.

12. **Digital world/online customers:** Internet (Web), smart phones, tablets, computers, various other digital devices and social networking sites joined together are creating digital world of millions of young and resourceful customers, thereby creating worldwide and newer opportunities for the businesses. Business organizations need to take note of this phenomenon and adopt right strategies at the earliest in exploiting the digital world or online customers.

Social media has become a potential platform for the brands to reach out to prospective customers. The brand needs to communicate in the most effective way so as to win the loyalty and trust of new customers. Well designed contents including creative images should grab the attention of online customers. A business's social media strategy needs to include creating of innovative contents, broadcasting strong contents on brands' social channels (e.g., facebook.com/parkerpens, twitter.com/parkerpens), encouraging interactions, responding to user requests, running campaigns and contests on the social media and continuous improvements on all these fronts.

Nearly one-sixth of the world population is on Web based social media. For the business, the data associated with such huge population would carry valuable information. But such vast data need to be analyzed in order to derive business insights from them. Skilled manpower need to be employed for such complex analysis.

13. **Smart phones:** New e-business models need to reach out to smart phones functioning under Windows, Android or Apple iOS mobile operating systems. For example, as of mid-2013, there are about 9 lakh applications (Apps) that are being downloaded by millions of smart phone users around the world. This business has already witnessed a turnover of about INR 60,000 crores worldwide. Business organizations need to look into the avenues of exploiting such newer technologies. Smart phones combined with 3G and 4G technologies would grab all e-business applications now being run on computers. Also, the smart phone users are outnumbering the computer users around the globe.

14. **Virtual economy:** A virtual economy is another emergent model in a virtual world, usually exchanging virtual goods in the context of Internet games. People enter these virtual economies for recreation and entertainment rather than necessity (for instance, players in a virtual economy often do not need to buy food in order to survive, and usually do not have any biological needs at all).

However, some people do interact with virtual economies for "real" economic benefit (for example, betting, lottery, card games etc.). Real money commerce in a virtual market has grown to become a multibillion dollar industry. What avenues they could create for the business organizations need to be watched.

5.6.9 E-Business Life Cycle

E-business life cycle activities discussed below are to be understood by the managers:

1. **Vision, mission and objectives:** A business has its own vision as to what it should achieve in the long run. All e-business initiatives should stand to support such vision. Vision leads to mission so also e-business mission.

Objectives are the targets set to realize business vision and mission in terms of various business performance yardsticks. While setting business objectives, appropriate e-business models are to be identified and implemented.

2. **Requirement planning:** Requirement planning differs for B2B and B2C models.

B2B model

Requirement planning for B2B model need to take into consideration the business process requirements of the business functions stationed all around the globe (Intranet) and also the supply chain (Extranet). All business processes associated with the business need to be automated and included under the purview of e-business initiatives.

The business process requirements could be in the form programmed decisions, data processing, transaction processing, payment gateways, creation of business documents, MIS, knowledge accumulation and dissemination, business integration (digital communication, coordination and collaboration), and relationship management with business entities and the customers.

Simple, user friendly and menu driven interface are to be designed for all business users. The interface and all the functions performed by the application software are to be understood and approved by the business users.

Measures are also to be put in place to ensure accuracy, security, integrity and reliability of business processes and the data associated in all such processes.

B2C

B2C model need to take into consideration the requirements of e-commerce customers based on the type of products or services being offered.

B2C sites need to push as much information as possible to the website visitors and pull as much useful information as possible from them. Such information need to be exploited in offering more customized products or services to the customers and enhancing customer loyalty.

E-commerce site needs to be innovative, artistic, attractive and exhibit creativity so that the visitors find their experience always rewarding. The B2C sites need to be tested with knowledgeable (target) customers to assess ease of navigation, usefulness and crispness of the information presented and overall performance of the site. The feedback obtained from them need to be incorporated into the site.

3. **Infrastructure:** Infrastructure or resources required for establishing e-business have been listed under Section 5.6.4. The infrastructure need to be decided based on the e-business model choosen for the business.

4. **E-business application software—Design:** Since e-business software functions would vary considerably for B2B and B2C models, they are discussed separately.

B2B (Intranet and Extranet)

This would involve hundreds of programs, each program aimed at automating a specific business process. These applications should speed up the business processes though they are more data centric. They would help managing all business entities, events and resources more effectively. Designing software for B2B model is done using software development life cycle (SDLC) discussed in Chapter 8.

B2C (e-commerce)

Software design for B2C model would include the activities like designing interesting and innovative user interface, displaying product specifications and views, transaction fulfilment modules in the form of shopping carts, comparison shopping, virtual billing and payment gateways, product delivery tracking, capturing customer feedback and so on.

Though this activity is less time consuming compared to B2B, creative, innovative and intuitive skills are required on the part of e-commerce application designers. Developing such software in-house or by outsourcing are discussed in Chapter 8.

5. **E-business application software—testing:** E-business application software is tested with a test website, mimicking a live business situation involving all e-business resources, business processes, web contents and e-business users but not in a real business. The testing is done to ensure that the application programs and all other resources perform as per the requirement specifications. Even if something is not performing as expected, concerned software or the resource is modified to

make it work perfect. Since real business is not yet run on new software, there is no inherent threat to the business.

All business processes completed during testing (using the new e-business software), business documents created, computations made, business data collected or updated, programmed decisions made in the software and so on are to be tested thoroughly for accuracy, integrity and consistency. Only when 100% testing is completed the e-business application software is implemented in real-business operations.

B2C software is also tested for the reliability and availability of the IT resources including the network, availability and sufficiency of the bandwidth, user adoptability, content readability, system response time (how much time e-business user needs to wait in completing an intended business task), web traffic assessment and so on.

ACID test

B2C software also needs to pass the ACID test (Atomicity, Consistency, Isolation and Durability.

Atomicity means a business process needs to be treated as completed only when all activities under it are completed, e.g., a sale acknowledgement is to be sent to e-customer, only when the money is received through payment gateway. Consistency means that both buyer and seller agree on common terms and stay committed to them until the completion of the business process. Isolation means each e-business activity is to be independent of other activities. Durability means reversal of a business process in the event of any interruption occuring in Internet environments.

6. **Implementation:** Once all e-business application software are tested thoroughly and corrected fully, the e-business resources are put in place and integrated together. Then actual business data and the contents are loaded onto the websites and the e-business is implemented in real-business environments. At this stage what had been planned meticulously becomes a marvelous reality.

7. **Maintenance and enhancement:** Maintenance of e-business system means, trouble free maintenance of the computer and network resources without disruptions, acquiring sufficient communication bandwidths that would assure good system response time, correcting the software for errors encountered during the run time, incorporating the changes as requested by the business users and the customers while using e-business processes, incorporating the improvements to be made to the business processes (business process re-engineering) and so on.

Enhancement on the other hand, means making major changes to the e-business software to include new and additional business processes, making use of newer solutions offered by the technology, enhancing the scope and spread of e-business processes, installing new computer and network resources and so on.

8. **Attributes of ideal E-business site:** An ideal e-business site has following attributies:

- Needs to be consistent with general e-business practices.
- Users should be able to recognize all processes in the site itself, rather than mental recall.

- Web design needs to be catchy, innovative and interesting.
- HELP menu and search options are mandatory.
- Frequently asked questions and the answers (FAQ) are desirable.
- Easy to remember URL.
- Ease of navigation back and forth with no dead ends and freezing of frames.
- All links (HTML) are to be active and uptodate.
- Contents need to be uptodate, crisp, accurate and informative.
- Good site services like e-mail, contact points, links to related sites and so on.
- Multimedia display wherever needed.
- Quick response to customer queries.
- Websites need to have home page, site map, menu options always displayed in left side of the screen, forward and backward navigation, do and undo options, links or buttons for other pages and so on.

5.6.10   E-business—Management Concerns

The senior management need to pay attention to the factors listed below, while implementing e-business:

- E-business is redefining conventional business models. Business needs to realign itself to accommodate such inevitable changes.
- It is also changing the business structures (e.g., flat organization structure) and decision making cultures, which need to be recognized.
- Business processes need to be highly efficient and effective conforming to global standards.
- Businesses are becoming highly customer focussed and responsive to customer needs.
- Business data, resources, processes and e-business infrastructure are to be secured and protected against fraud, misuse, thefts, forgeries, computer virus, cyber crimes and so on.
- The e-business resources should be capable of scaling up to larger business volumes and shorter processing times, warranted by the changing business environments.
- Not all businesses and processes could be converted to e-business.
- Contents and business data put on the e-business environments are to be correct, crisp and uptodate all the time. Content management responsibilities need to be delegated to right persons in the business.
- At no time e-business users should be overloaded with unwanted information.
- During seasonal surges in e-commerce sales, business should not face product delivery or fulfilment problems. Sufficient logistics support needs to be in place for such situations.

- General shortage of skilled human resources required for designing, developing and implementing good, effective, efficient and reliable e-business models need to be taken cognizance of.

- Since too much product and business information are posted on the public domain, there is always a competitive vulnerability, as critical business information can easily be copied by others and more so the competition.

- Launching of successful e-business means extensive planning, highly skilled and innovative managers and technical personnel, loyal and committed supply chain entities, well-defined business vision, mission and objectives.

- Online customers in the digital world and the scope and potential of e-advertisement techniques discussed in the following sections are to be exploited ahead of competition.

5.6.11 Advertising E-business (Conventional Methods)

In today's business, customers,

- Control the channels.
- Demand innovative products and services.
- Expect one to one personalized relations.

Advertising e-business and e-marketing need to take this scenario into consideration. The following factors contribute to effective e-business advertisement:

- URL needs to be short, catchy and reflect the brand. It needs to be registered. It needs to be made known to the public through advertisements in all media, QR (quick response) codes, letter heads, all business documents and communications, business cards and so on.

- Mega tags (indices and short names/referrals through which the world of users would search for the products and services through search engines), should be submitted to all popular search engines even if they charge for such services.

- If the products or services are in great demand the customers will search and find the websites. Otherwise website needs to be made popular in various media.

- Advertisement can also be placed on TV and Radio mediums and the hoardings erected at vantage points to make the products and websites more popular.

Note: Advertising of e-commerce has been discussed earlier.

5.6.12 E-marketing

E-marketing, also known as online marketing, online advertising, or internet marketing refers to marketing and promotion of products and services over the Internet. Exponetial growth of the Internet users worldwide, attract the attention of business organizations and advertisers to e-marketing. E-marketing offers great opportunities in bringing new customers and existing customers closer.

E-marketing would include contextual advertisements on search engine results pages, banner or display advertisements in other websites, blogs, rich media advertisements, social network advertising, interstitial advertisements, online classified advertising, advertising networks, dynamic banner advertisements, cross-platform advertisements and e-mail marketing, including e-mail spam. Popularity of e-mail, websites, search engines, social sites, such as Facebook, Twitter and so on, has accelerated e-marketing initiatives of the business organizations around the world. Internet advertising has a variety of ways to publicise and reach niche audience and also to focus its attention to specific groups. And so also, conventional advertising is fast loosing its sheen.

History of E-marketing

E-marketing is increasingly becoming significant because millions of digital devices such as mobile or smart phones, tablets, laptops and so on are connected to the Internet and people spend more time on these devices. The online advertising industry burst into magical reality in 2007. Google's sky-rocketing stock price and its forays into industries such as word processing software, online payments and mobile telephones are drawing significant attention.

Businesses began to move their advertising efforts into these areas by making wide use of social media from 2009. The social media includes social networking sites such as Facebook, Twitter, social news sites such as Reddit, Digg Propeller, social photo and video sharing sites such as Photobucket, Flickr, YouTube and so on. One of the advantages of social media advertising is proper targeting of market through the use of the users' demographic information.

Let us discuss some popular e-advertisement techniques being used by business communities and certain other issues the readers need to be aware of, in this context.

E-marketing through Internet

1. **Inbound marketing:** Inbound marketing is advertising a company's products or services through blogs, podcasts, e-books, e-newsletters, social media marketing and other forms of content marketing discussed in the following sections. In contrast, buying attention, cold-calling, direct paper mail, radio TV advertisements, sales flyers, spam, email marketing, telemarketing and traditional advertising are considered outbound marketing. Inbound marketing earns the attention of customers, makes the company easy to be found and draws customers to the website by producing interesting content.

Inbound marketing is more focussed whereas the outbound marketing is like gropin in the dark, as to what it could bring?

It has now become the practice that marketers "earn their way in" (via publishing helpful information) in contrast to outbound marketing where they "buy, beg, or bug their way in" (via paid advertisements, issuing press releases etc.). According to HubSpot, a company associated with inbound marketing, it is especially effective for small businesses and knowledge-based products. In these areas prospects are more likely to get informed. It is associated with five stages viz.,

(i) Attract traffic

(ii) Convert visitors to leads

(iii) Convert leads to sales

(iv) Turn customers into repeat higher margin customers

(v) Analyze for continuous improvement

Complex inbound marketing practices target potential customers at different levels of product and brand awareness. The most scaled tactics attempt to funnel customers from semantically related market segments, who have no product awareness or intention to purchase. This is usually achieved by taking the customer through a structured informational path that builds awareness and increases interest over time.

2. **Search engine listing:** A search engine 'results page' is the listing of results returned by a search engine in response to a keyed in query. The results normally include a list of items with titles, a reference to the full version and a short description showing where the keywords have matched content within the page. Search engines may include different types of listings: contextual, algorithmic or organic search listings, and sponsored listing consisting of images, maps, definitions, videos and so on.

Algorithmic listings are the natural listings generated by search engines based on a series of metrics that determines their relevance to the searched term. Webpages that score well on a search engine's algorithmic test show in this list. These algorithms are generally, based upon factors such as the content of a webpage, the trustworthiness of the website, and other factors like news, sponsorship advertising and so on.

3. **Banner advertisement:** A web banner or banner advertisement is another form of advertising on the World Wide Web. This form of online advertising entails embedding an advertisement into other websites. It is intended to attract traffic from more popular websites (e.g., railways portal) by linking to the website of the advertiser. Web banners function the same way as traditional advertisements are intended to function—notifying consumers of the product or service and presenting reasons why the consumer should choose the product in question. It is mostly a paid service.

However, web surfers regard these advertisements as highly annoying because they distract them from the actual content of a web page or waste bandwidth. Newer web browsers often include options to disable pop-ups or block images from selected websites.

Banner advertisements can be targeted on the Internet users in different ways in order to reach the advertiser's most relevant audience. Behavioral targeting, demographic targeting, geographic targeting, and site based targeting (discussed in subsequent sections) are all common ways in which advertisers choose to target their banner advertisements.

4. **Display advertising:** Display advertising appears on web pages in many forms, including web banners. Such displays can consist of static or animated images, as well as interactive media that may include audio and video elements. Display advertising on the Internet is widely used for branding. This may change in the future as display advertising is becoming much more targeted on users, much like how search engine advertisements can be extremely relevant to users based on what they are searching for.

Display advertisers use cookies and browser history to determine demographics and interests of users and target appropriate advertisements through browsers (discussed subsequently). Banner advertisements standards have changed over the years (different sizes) due to increased resolution and sizes (tablet PC) of present day monitors. It offers advertisers better impact for their investment.

5. **Web log (blog):** A blog is a discussion or informational site consisting of discrete entries ("posts") typically displayed in chronological order. Until 2009 blogs were usually the work of a single individual, or a small group, and often covered a single subject. Now "multi-author blogs" have come into existence, with posts written by large numbers of authors. Blogs from newspapers, universities, interest groups and other institutions account for an increasing quantity of blog traffic now.

A majority of blogs are interactive allowing visitors to leave comments and even message and it is this interaction that distinguishes them from other static websites. In that sense, blogging can be seen as a form of social networking too.

Many blogs function more as online brand advertising of a particular individual or company. A typical blog combines text, images and links to other blogs, Web pages, and other media related to the subject matter. The ability of readers to leave comments in an interactive format is an important contribution to the popularity of many blogs. Most blogs are primarily textual, although some focus on art, photographs, videos, music and audio (podcasts).

6. **Corporate blogs:** A blog can also be for advertisement purposes. Blogs used internally to enhance the communication and culture in a business organization or externally for marketing, branding or public relations purposes are called corporate blogs.

The Blogosphere is the collective community of all blogs. Since all blogs are on the Internet by definition, they may be seen as interconnected and socially networked. Discussions "in the blogosphere" are occasionally used by the media as a gauge of public opinion on various issues. It is common for blogs to feature advertisements either to financially benefit the blogger or to promote the bloggers' favorite causes. The popularity of blogs has also given rise to "fake blogs" in which a company will create a fictional blog as a marketing tool to promote a product.

7. **Interactive media:** Interactive media refers to products and services on digital or computer systems which respond to the users actions by presenting content such as text, graphics, animation, video, audio, games, etc. Interactive media is related to the concepts like interaction design, human computer interaction, digital culture, and includes specific cases such as interactive television, interactive narrative, interactive advertising, algorithmic art, video games, social media, ambient intelligence, virtual reality and so on. An essential feature of interactivity is that both user and machine take active roles.

8. **Social network advertising:** Social networking advertisement is a term that is used to describe a form of online advertisement that focuses on social networking sites. One of the major benefits of advertising on a social networking site (e.g., Facebook, Orkut etc.) is that advertisers can take advantage of the users' demographic information and target their advertisements appropriately.

9. **Interstitials/hyperstitials:** Interstitials are web pages displayed before or after an expected content page, often to display advertisements or confirm the user's age (prior to showing age-restricted material) or passing on important information in its context (warning users of 'phishing' before they enter their passwords). Full-screen interstitial advertisements are referred to as hyperstitials. Impact of hyperstitials on the users is more profound.

Some business organizations use such pages to present online advertising before allowing users to see the content they were trying to access. Less controversial uses of interstitial pages include introducing another page or site before directing the user to proceed or alerting the user that the next page requires a login, or has some other requirement which the user should know about before proceeding. In this context, interstitial is used in the sense of "in between". The interstitial web page exists between a referenced page and the page which references it, hence it is in between two pages.

10. **Classified advertisement:** Classified advertising is a form of advertising which is particularly common in newspapers, online and other periodicals which may be sold or distributed free of charge. Advertisements in a newspaper are typically short, as they are charged for by the line, of a newspaper column width. Today, "classified ads" has expanded from merely the sense of print advertisements in periodicals to include similar types of advertising on e-marketing, radio and television.

11. **Online advertising network:** An online advertising network is a company that connects advertisers to websites that host advertisements. The key function of an advertisement network is aggregation of advertisement space supply from publishers and matching it with advertiser's demand. It is increasingly used to mean "online advertisement network" as the effect of aggregation of publisher advertisement space and sale to advertisers is most commonly seen in the online space. The fundamental difference between traditional media advertisement networks and online advertisement networks is that online advertisement networks use a central 'Ad server' to deliver advertisements to consumers.

12. **Lean advertisement:** Instead of buying costly TV advertisement slots, some enterpreneurs shoot very catchy, interesting and short duration advertisement videos and upload them on to You Tube. Some such videos do capture millions of eyeballs in the digital world. Since it costs a fraction of the TV advertisement cost, it is termed as lean advertisement. As millions of people use smartphones, tablet phones and laptop computers, less number of people watch TV advertisements. Moreover, since the customers in the digital world have distinctive profiles, highly differentiated products and services can be offered to them. This can be done by the business istself without going to advertisement agencies or entrust this work to freelancing professionals who could create excellent and creative contents at fraction of costs.

However, creation of good contents and effective distribution of the same alone could spell success of lean marketing. The contents could be posted on the websites or on to YouTube and to attaract more viewers the services of 'inbound marketing' agencies could also be sought. This gives better opportunities for small companies on par with big companies.

13. **E-mail marketing:** E-mail marketing means directly mailing a commercial message to a group of people using e-mail. It usually involves using e-mail to send advertisements, request for business or solicit sales, and is meant to build loyalty, trust, or brand awareness. Email marketing can be done to either cold lists or current customer database. Broadly, the term is usually used to refer to:

    - Sending e-mail messages with the purpose of enhancing the relationship of a merchant with its current or previous customers to encourage customer loyalty and repeat business.
    - Sending e-mail messages with the purpose of acquiring new customers or convincing current customers to purchase something immediately.
    - Adding advertisements to e-mail messages sent by companies to their customers.

E-mail marketing can be carried out through different types of emails:

- **Transactional E-mails:** Transactional emails are usually triggered based on a customer's action with a company. Triggered transactional messages include dropped basket messages, purchase order confirmation emails and email receipts.

The primary purpose of a transactional email is to convey information regarding the action that triggered it. But, due to its high open rates, transactional emails are a golden opportunity to engage customers; to introduce or extend the e-mail relationship with customers, to anticipate and answer questions or to cross-sell or up-sell products or services.

Many email newsletter software vendors offer transactional email support, which gives companies the ability to include promotional messages within the body of transactional e-mails. There are also software vendors that offer specialized transactional e-mail marketing services, which include providing targeted and personalized transactional e-mail messages and running specific marketing campaigns.

- **Direct E-mails:** Direct email involves sending an email solely to communicate a promotional message (for example, an announcement of a special offer or a catalogue of products). Companies usually collect a list of customers and their email addresses to send direct promotional messages, or they can also buy a list of email addresses from service companies.

- **Permitted E-mail advertising:** Permitted E-mail marketing is a method of advertising via email whereby the recipient of the advertisement has consented to receive it. This method is one of the several methods developed by marketers to eliminate the disadvantages of email marketing.

Permitted e-mail marketing may evolve into a technology that uses a handshake protocol between the sender and receiver. This system is intended to eventually result in a high degree of satisfaction between consumers and marketers. If this type of advertising is used, the material that is emailed to consumers will be "anticipated." It is assumed that the consumer wants to receive it, which makes it different from unsolicited advertisements sent to the consumer.

A common example of permission marketing is sending a newsletter or product catalogues to customers. Such newsletters inform customers about upcoming events or promotions, or new products. In this type of advertising, a company that wants to send a newsletter to its customers may ask them at the point of purchase if they would like to receive such e-mails.

With such customers' database, marketers can send out promotional materials automatically, known as **Drip Marketing**. They can also segment their promotions to specific market segments.

- **E-Mail spam:** E-mail spam, also known as **junk e-mail** or **unsolicited bulk e-mail** is a subset of electronic spam involving nearly identical messages sent to numerous recipients by email. Clicking on links in spam email may send users to phishing websites or sites that are hosting malware. Spammers collect email addresses from chatrooms, websites, customer lists and newsgroups and viruses which harvest users' address books, and are sold to other spammers.

14. **Other avenues for e-marketing:** The other avenues are listed below:
    - **Content marketing:** It refers to the process of creating specialized content such as infographics, blog articles and e-books to attract more customers.
    - **Video marketing:** This type of marketing specializes in creating videos that engage the viewer into a buying state by presenting information in video form and guiding them to a product or service. Online video is increasingly becoming more popular among the Internet users and companies are seeing it as a viable method of attracting customers. This kind of advertising is the most prominent in television, and many advertisers use the same clips for both television and online advertising.
    - **Floating advertisement:** An advertisement which moves across the user's screen or floats above the content.
    - **Expanding advertisement:** An advertisement which changes size and which may alter the contents of the webpage.
    - **Polite advertisement:** A method by which a large advertisement is downloaded in smaller pieces to minimize the disruption of the content being viewed.
    - **Wallpaper advertisement:** An advertisement which changes the background of the page being viewed.
    - **Trick banner:** A banner advertisement that looks like a dialog box with buttons. It simulates an error message or an alert.
    - **Pop-up:** A new window which opens in front of the current one, displaying an advertisement or entire webpage.
    - **Pop-under:** Similar to a Pop-up except that the window is loaded or sent behind the current window so that the user does not see it until they close one or more active windows.
    - **Map advertisement:** It is text or graphics linked from, and appearing in or over, a location on an electronic map such as on Google Maps.
    - **Mobile advertisement:** It is an SMS text or multimedia message sent to a mobile phones.
    - **Frame advertisement:** It is an advertisement that appears within an HTML frame, usually at the top with the site logo. As the user browse the site, the frame would not change.

- **Behavioural targeting:** In addition to contextual targeting, online advertising can be targeted based on a user's online behaviour. This practice is known as behavioural targeting

  For example, if a user is known to have recently visited a number of automotive shopping and comparison sites based on clickstream analysis enabled by cookies stored on the user's computer, the user can then be served auto-related advertisements when they visit other sites.

- **Predictive behavioural targeting:** A further refinement to behavioural targeting is predictive behavioural targeting, where machine learning algorithms overlay behavioural patterns with sampled data, to create data-rich predicted profiles for every user.

- **Semantic advertising:** Semantic advertising applies to semantic analysis techniques to web pages. The process is meant to accurately interpret and classify the meaning and/or main subject of the page and then populate it with targeted advertising spots. By closely linking content to advertising, it is assumed that the viewer will be more likely to show an interest (i.e., through engagement) in the advertised product or service.

- **Streaming video or audio:** In addition, advertisements containing streaming video or streaming audio are becoming very popular with advertisers.

- **Cross selling:** It is the process of telling the customers that one particular product is generally bought with one or more other products.

15. **E-marketing through television:** E-marketing can also be classified as digital promotions. Digital promotion with respect to television industry is the one in which TV networks use digital resources to promote their new programmes or shows. An example of digital promotion on television is the network CBS in which new digital technologies of Bluetooth-enabled mobile devices are incorporated that are able to download a thirty-second clip of a new show on their devices. It is also possible to see one minute video clipping of any TV content by the mobile phone users. Television viewers are also able to get the programme schedules of various channels on their mobile phones via SMS.

16. **Film and television marketing:** Industries such **as** film and television are also loading the contents on the Internet (e.g., YouTube) Film trailers, television show schedules and so on came on the scene quite quickly as the content that promoted such products. This major media platform was developed with investments of millions by the film studios and television networks because it was a valuable marketing tool.

17. **E-marketing approaches:** Different approaches of e-marketing are discussed below:

One-to-one approach: In a one-to-one approach, marketers target a user browsing the Internet alone so that the marketers' messages reach the user personally. This approach is used in search marketing, for which the advertisements are based on search engine keywords entered by the users.

Appeal to specific interest groups: When appealing to specific interests, marketers place an emphasis on appealing to a specific behavior or interest, rather than reaching out to a broadly defined demographic. These marketers typically segment their markets according to age group, gender, geography and other general factors.

Appealing to specific users can be achieved through behavioural targeting, which refers to the use of behavioral patterns and putting up the relevant content suitable to the viewer's interest obtained from the users, through cookies and other tools.

Contextual advertising refers to the publishing of advertisements based on the context the user is into a site. For example, if the user is searching for coffee, the search engine publishes advertisements related to coffee.

- **Niche marketing:** In conventional niche marketing, clusters of consumers (the niche) are identified in order to more economically and efficiently target them. Similarly, niche internet marketing attempts to create a more direct advertising message for those who are seen as most likely to buy the product being advertised.

Niche internet marketing focuses on marketing products and services which are, tailor-made for a specific subset of consumers who are expected to buy the product or service with a specific motivation. The online advertising message can then be tailor-made to target that assumed motivation.

- **Geotargeting:** In the Internet marketing, geotargeting is the method of determining the geolocation of a website visitor with geolocation software, and delivering different content to that visitor based on his or her location, such as latitude and longitude, country, region or state, city, metro code or zip code, organization, Internet Protocol (IP) address, ISP and other criteria.

- **Cookies:** A cookie, also known as an HTTP cookie, web cookie, or browser cookie, is a small piece of data sent from a website and stored in a user's computer while a user is browsing a website. When the user browses the same website in the future, the data stored in the cookie can be retrieved by the website to notify the website of the user's previous activity. Cookies were designed to be a reliable mechanism for websites to remember the activity the user had undertaken in the past, e.g. pages that were visited by the user even months or years ago.

Cookies are used as ways to compile long-term records of individuals' browsing histories (could amount to privacy intrusion). Cookies can also store passwords and forms the users filled in, such as credit card numbers or addresses. When a user accesses a website with a cookie function for the first time, a cookie is sent from server to the browser and stored with the browser in the local computer. Later, when that user goes back to the same website, the website will recognize the user because of the cookie stored with the user's information (e.g., the user gets information as when he visited the site last).

Information stored in cookies could be used in establishing more profitable interaction with web customers.

- **Profiling:** This process is also called 'Knowledge Discovery in Databases' which provides the business with sets of correlated data that are used as "profiles". What characterizes profiling technologies is the use of algorithms or other mathematical techniques that allow one, to discover patterns or correlations in large quantities of data, e.g., of the customers, residing in databases. When these patterns or correlations are used to identify they are called profiles.

Profiling is used in,

- Identifying loyal customers.
- Segmenting the markets based on the customer groups.
- Retaining existing customers.
- Offering new and premium products to prospective customers.
- Moving profitable customers up the value chain.
- Applying the profiles to identify target customers in the newer markets.

- **Personalization:** Business organizations need to collect relevant data from the customers based on which personalised products or services can be offered to them. Personlisation can be based on the check box selection by the site visitors or rule based personalisation based on the parameters captured in the database.

5.6.13   E-business/E-marketing—View Points

Additional view points related to E-business and E-marketing are discussed in this section.

1. *E-mail marketing—Advantages and disadvantages*

E-mail marketing is popular for the following reasons:

- An exact return on investment can be tracked since the targets are known. E-mail marketing is considered as second only to customer contact programmes.
- E-mail Marketing is significantly cheaper and faster than traditional mail, mainly because of high cost and time required in a traditional mail campaign, which involves producing the artwork, printing, addressing, mailing and so on.
- Advertisers can reach substantial numbers of e-mail subscribers who have opted (i.e., consented) to receive e-mail communications on the subjects of interest to them.
- More and more people check or send e-mail nowadays.
- Percentage of population who are exposed to conventional advertisements is fast shrinking.

Whereas the disadvantages of e-mail marketing are:

- According to reports, legitimate e-mail delivery rate is only 56% (who access mails), 30% of the messages are either rejected or are filtered.
- Companies using e-mail marketing program have to ensure that they do not violate spam laws, privacy policies and so on.

2. *E-marketing: Competitive advantages*

- E-marketing is inexpensive when examining the ratio of cost to the reach of the target audience.

- Companies can reach a wide audience for a small fraction of traditional advertising budgets. The nature of the medium allows consumers to research and to purchase products and services conveniently. Therefore, businesses have the advantage of appealing to consumers in a medium that can bring results quickly.

- Internet marketers also have the advantage of measuring statistics easily and inexpensively. Almost all aspects of the Internet marketing campaign can be traced, measured and tested. The advertisers can use a variety of methods, such as pay per impression, pay per click, pay per play and pay per action.

- Marketers can also determine which messages or offerings are more appealing to the audience. The results of campaigns can be measured and tracked immediately because online marketing initiatives usually require users to click on an advertisement, to visit a website and to perform a targeted action.

- Benefit of online advertising is the ease of publishing of information and content that is not limited by geography or time. The emerging area of interactive advertising presents more opportunities for advertisers.

- Another benefit is the efficiency of the advertiser's investment. Online advertising allows for the customisation of advertisements, including content and the websites. For example, Yahoo! Search Marketing and Google AdSense enable advertisements to be shown on relevant web pages or alongside search results.

3. *Problems associated with E-marketing*

1. **Privacy:** E-marketing impringes on the privacy and anonymity of users. Hosting the banner images on its servers and using third-party cookies, the advertising company is able to track the browsing of users across these two sites.

   Third-party cookies can be blocked by most browsers to increase privacy and reduce tracking by advertising and tracking companies without negatively affecting the user's Web experience. Customers' data also get sold to other companies thereby exposing it to the rest of the world.

2. **Malware:** There are also some advertising methods which are unethical and illegal. These include external applications which alter system settings (such as a browser's home page), spawn pop-ups, and insert advertisements into non-affiliated webpages. Such applications are usually labelled as spyware or adware. They may mask their questionable activities by performing a simple service, such as displaying the weather or providing a search bar. These programs are designed to dupe the user, acting effectively as Trojan horses. These applications are commonly designed so as to be difficult to remove or uninstall. Millions of online users, many of whom are not computer savvy, frequently lack the knowledge and technical ability to protect themselves from these programs.

4. *E-business limitations*

- One of the challenges that the Internet customers face is that many products are promoted with deception, making it difficult to know which one is worth buying. And so also ethics that is still missing in online marketing.

- The consumer is unable to physically feel or try on the product which can be a limitation for certain goods. However, a survey of consumers of cosmetics products shows that email marketing can be used to interest a consumer in visiting a store to try a product or to speak with sales representatives from where a purchase decision can be made.
- The marketer is not able to use personal interaction to influence the audience as the marketing is completely based on the advertisement.

5. *Security concerns in E-business*

- Information security is important for the consumers. Consumers are hesitant to purchase items over the Internet because they do not believe that their personal information will remain private. Some companies offer the option for individuals to have their information removed from their promotional redistribution, also known as opting out. However, many customers are unaware that their information otherwise is being shared.
- Additionally, companies holding private information are vulnerable to data attacks and leaks. Web sites routinely capture browsing and search history which can be used to provide targeted advertising. Privacy policies can provide transparency to these practices. Spyware prevention software can also be used to shield the consumer.
- Another consumer e-commerce concern is whether or not they will receive exactly what they purchase. Online merchants have attempted to address this concern by investing in and building strong consumer brands (e.g., Amazon.com).

6. *Ethics*

- Online advertising encompasses a range of types of advertising, some of which are deployed ethically and some are not. Some websites use large numbers of advertisements, including flashing banners that distract the users, and some have misleading images.
- Websites that unethically use online advertising for revenue frequently do not monitor what advertisements on their website link to, allowing advertisements to lead to sites with malicious software or audience-inappropriate material.
- Some argue that website operators who ethically use online advertising typically use a small number of advertisements that are not intended to distract or irritate the user, and do not detract from the design and layout of their websites.
- The use of technologies like Adobe Flash in online advertising has led to some users disabling it in their browsers, or using browser plug-ins like Adblock or NoScript.
- Some companies perform customer engagement studies in online marketing to insure consumer satisfaction.
- Based on the customers' profiles, the advertiser may offer different type of products or different prices for select groups.

7. *E-marketing trends*

- Technological advancements in telecommunications have dramatically improved online advertising techniques. Many firms are shifting the focus of advertising methodology from traditional text and image advertisements to those containing more recent technologies such as JavaScript and Adobe Flash.
- Advertisers more effectively engage and connect their audience with their campaigns that seek to shape consumer attitudes and feelings towards specific products and services.
- Some new trends for the internet marketing are inbound marketing, mobile marketing and improved usage of analytics. Inbound marketing refers to information and display of content and design which is relevant and attractive enough to entice the audience.
- Mobile marketing is huge, with over 75% of the world having access to a mobile devices, it is imperative that companies also focus their marketing on to mobiles.
- Analytic improvement can now discover sentiment to forecast emerging trends in the industry, giving companies the knowledge they need to determine best strategies for increasing sales.

8. *Effects of E-business on various industries*

- The number of banks offering the ability to perform banking tasks over the Internet has increased. Online banking appeals to customers because it is often faster and considered more convenient than visiting bank branches.
- The effect on the advertising industry itself has been profound. In just a few years, online advertising has grown to be worth ten billions dollars annually.
- Several industries have heavily invested in and benefited from the Internet marketing and online advertising. Some of them were originally brick and mortar businesses such as publishing, music, or automotive while others have sprung up as purely online businesses, such as digital design and media, blogging and Internet service hosting.

5.6.14 Internet Applications Standards

Internet applications standards and their basic functions are discussed very briefly in this section.

1. **TLS (Transport layer security)/SSL (Secured socket layer):** TLS and its predecessor SSL are cryptographic (discussed in Chapter 9) protocols that provide communication security over the Internet. They use asymmetric cryptography for authentication of key exchanges and symmetric encryption for confidentiality, authentication and integrity of messages and documents. Several versions of these protocols are in use in applications such as web browsing, electronic mail, instant messaging and so on.

In the TCP/IP communication model (discussed in next section), TLS and SSL encrypt the data of network connections at a lower sublayer of its application layer. TLS and SSL work on behalf of the underlying transport layer, whose segments carry encrypted data.

2. **HTTP (Hyper text transfer protocol): HTTP** is an application protocol for distributed, collaborative, and multimedia (hyper) information systems. HTTP is the foundation of data communication for the World Wide Web. Hypertext is a multilinear set of objects, building a network by using logical links (the so called hyperlinks) between the nodes (e.g., text or words). HTTP is the protocol to exchange or transfer hypertext.

3. **HTML (Hyper text markup language): HTML** is the main markup language for creating web pages and other information that can be displayed through a web browser. HTML is written in the form of HTML elements consisting of *tags* enclosed in angle brackets (<html>), within the web page content. HTML tags most commonly come in pairs like <h1> </h1> <h2> </h2>.... The first tag in a pair is the *start tag*, the second tag is the *end tag* (they are also called *opening tags* and *closing tags*). In between these tags web designers can add text, tags, comments and other types of text-based content.

The purpose of a web browser is to read HTML documents and compose them into visible or audible web pages. The browser does not display the HTML tags, but uses the tags to interpret the content of the page.

HTML elements form the building blocks of all websites. HTML allows images and objects to be embedded and can be used to create interactive forms. It provides a means to create structured documents by denoting structural semantics for text such as headings, paragraphs, lists, links, quotes and other items. It can embed scripts (programmes) written in languages such as JavaScript which affect the behaviour of HTML web pages.

4. **FTP (File transfer protocol):** FTP is a standard network protocol used to transfer files from the server to a client, over a TCP-based network, such as the Internet. FTP is built on client-server architecture and uses separate control and data connections between the client and the server. FTP users may authenticate themselves in the form of a username and password, but can connect anonymously if the server is configured to allow it. FTP is often secured with SSL/TLS.

The first FTP client applications were command-line applications developed before the operating systems had graphical user interfaces and are still shipped with most Windows, Unix and Linux Operating Systems. Dozens of FTP clients and automation utilities have since been developed for desktops, servers, mobile devices, and hardware, and FTP has been incorporated into hundreds of productivity applications, such as Web page editors.

5. **SFTP (Secured file transfer protocol):** SFTP protocol supports the following:
   1. User id based login (User-id/Password combination)
   2. Hierarchical folders
   3. File Management (Rename, Delete, Upload, Download, Download with overwrite, Download with append)

6. **DNS (Domain name system/server): DNS** is a hierarchical distributed naming system for computers, services, or any resource connected to the Internet. It

associates lot of information with domain names assigned to each of the participating entities. Most prominently, it translates easily memorised domain names to the numerical IP addresses needed for the purpose of locating computer services and devices worldwide. By providing a worldwide, distributed keyword-based redirection service, the Domain Name System is an essential component of the functionality of the Internet.

An often used analogy to explain the Domain Name System is that it serves as the phone book for the Internet by translating human-friendly computer hostnames into IP addresses. For example, the domain name www.example.com translates to the addresses 192.0.43.10. Unlike a phone book, the DNS can be quickly updated, allowing a service's location on the network to change without affecting the end users, who continue to use the same host name. Users take advantage of this when they use meaningful Uniform Resource Locators (URLs) and e-mail addresses without having to know how the computer actually locates the services.

The Domain Name System distributes the responsibility of assigning domain names and mapping those names to IP addresses by designating authoritative name servers for each domain (like a country). Authoritative name servers are assigned to be responsible for their particular domains, and in turn can assign other authoritative name servers for their sub-domains. This mechanism has made the DNS distributed and fault tolerant and has helped avoid the need for a single central register to be continually consulted and updated. Additionally, the responsibility for maintaining and updating the master record for the domains is spread among many domain name registrars, who compete for the end-user's (the domain-owner's) business. Domains can be moved from registrar to registrar at any time.

7. **NFS (Network file system):** NFS is a distributed file system protocol originally developed by Sun Microsystems in 1984, allowing a user on a client computer to access files over a network in a manner similar to how local storage is accessed. The Network File System is an open standard, allowing anyone to implement the protocol.

8. **POP (Post office protocol):** POP is an application-layer Internet standard protocol used by local e-mail clients to retrieve e-mail from a remote server over a TCP/IP connection. POP and IMAP (Internet Message Access Protocol) are the two most prevalent Internet standard protocols for e-mail retrieval. Virtually all modern e-mail clients and servers support both. POP has been developed through several versions, with version 3 (POP3) being the current standard. Most webmail service providers such as Gmail and Yahoo! Mail provide both an IMAP and POP3 services.

9. **SMTP (Simple message transfer protocol):** SMTP is the Internet standard for electronic mail (e-mail) transmission across Internet Protocol (IP) networks. SMTP and Extended SMTP are the protocols in widespread use today. While electronic mail servers and other mail transfer agents use SMTP to send and receive mail messages, user-level client mail applications typically use SMTP only for sending messages to a mail server for relaying. For receiving messages, client applications usually use either POP or IMAP or a proprietary system (such as Microsoft Exchange or Lotus Notes/Domino) to access their mail box accounts on a mail server.

10. **SNMP (Simple network management protocol):** SNMP is the "Internet-standard protocol for managing devices on IP networks". Devices that typically support SNMP include routers, switches, servers, workstations, printers, modem racks, and more. It is used mostly in network management systems to monitor network-attached devices for conditions that warrant administrative attention. It consists of a set of standards for network management, including an application layer protocol, database structures, and a set of data objects.

11. **Telnet:** Telnet is a network protocol used on the Internet or local area networks to provide a bidirectional interactive text-oriented communication facility using a virtual terminal connection. Historically, Telnet provided access to a command-line interface (usually, of an operating system) on a remote host. Most network equipment and operating systems with a TCP/IP stack support a Telnet service for remote configuration (including systems based on Windows NT). However, because of serious security issues when using Telnet over an open network such as the Internet, its use for this purpose has waned significantly in favor of SSH. SSH File Transfer Protocol (also called Secure File Transfer Protocol-SFTP) is a network protocol that provides file access, file transfer, and file management functionalities over any reliable data stream.

5.6.15 Internet Communication Standards (TCP/IP)

Internet communication standards viz., Transmission Control Protocol/Internet Protocol (TCP/IP), which is functionally comparable to OSI model (Open System Interconnection), is where two or more layers of OSI are combined in to one as illustrated in Table 5.4.

OSI is an ISO (International Standards Organization) standard for worldwide communication that defines the framework for implementing communication protocols in seven layers. Control is passed from one layer to the next, starting at the application (top) layer in one station (client) and proceeding to the bottom layer and then over the communication cables (mediums) to the next station (server). On the server side the same process is reversed back up the hierarchy in the same way. Since OSI was loosely defined, it was not followed in the Internet, but most of its functionality are incorporated in TCP/IP mdoel.

5.6.16 E-business in India

India paints quite different e-business/Internet picture by virtue of its unique characteristics. Though India is a thickly populated country and stand to gain by virtue of Internet's extensive reach through wired and wireless links, there are number of hurdles not conducive to e-business.

Factors affecting e-business in India are:
- For Internet/E-business to penetrate in India, the contents need to be made available in about 30 different regional languages. Only a small percentage of Indian popupation comfortable with English only are using the Internet mostly in urban areas. Facebook as an exception is available in select regional languages.

Layer No.	OSI Model	TCP/IP Steps 7 to 1 at origin and 1 to 7 at destination
7	**Application Layer** Defines type of communication like, e-mail, file transfer, and client/server processes.	7, 6 and 5 are combined into following standards: TLS (Transport Layer Security)/ SSL(Secured Socket layer)
6	**Presentation Layer** Data encryption for securing data communication through the mediums, and conversion of ASCII (or EBCDIC) form data in to binary codes.	HTTP (Hyper Text Transfer Protocol) FTP (File Transfer Protocol) DNS (Domain Name System) NFS (Network File System) POP (Post Office Procol) and IMAP (Internet Message Access Protocol)
5	**Session Layer** Starts and stops the session and maintains the order of communicating the data packets.	SMTP (Simple Message Transfer Protocol) SNMP (Simple Network Management Protocol) (Please see section 5.6.14 to learn more of these standards)
4	**Transport Layer** Ensures delivery of entire file or message.	TCP
3	**Network Layer** Routes data to different computers, Lan, WAN etc., based on network Addresses.	IP (Address)
2	**Datalink Layer** Transmits data packets one address to the other	Same as in OSI
1	**Physical Layer** Electric, electromagnetic signals and the mediums (cables/wireless)	Same as in OSI

Table 5.4 is showing seven layers of TCP/IP protocol.

- Governments' (both central and state) initiatives in the form of e-governance, which deliver contents in local languages, have good reach because it meets the day today needs and expectations of the people (discussed in Section 16.4).
- The Internet finds favour to some extent because the schools and the colleges publish the results through Internet, enable people to get their mark sheets printed

online and the books, the syllabus and academic information related all educational institutions in India are posted on to hundreds of academic websites.

- Computer population in India is far less compared to developed countries. However, more than 70% of Indians use mobile phones (wireless technology). Due to this Indian banks are offering various banking services through mobile phones. If e-business has to grow in India, the mobile phones (need to become smart phones) are to be part of e-business.

- Internet bandwidths are very low and even small percentage of e-business users find this very frustrating. Some service providers who have laid fibre optic cables in big cities to offer higher bandwidths, have left them unused for many years now.

- There is no transparency in business operations and pricing and buyers, sellers, supply chain entities and logistics service providers do not trust one another. There are no Government policies, regulations and enforcement agencies to oversee e-business related issues/problems.

- However, in spite of this, millions of urban youth well-versed with web, smart phones, social networks and with good buying power are still placing India on e-business map.

- Many big business organizations are still investing in IT to integrate their business processes across different geographic locations though not much is happening in supply chain integration.

5.7 LOGISTICS AND GOODS IN TRANSIT TRACKING SYSTEMS

Logistics has already been discussed in Section 5.3. Logistics means product handling, transportation, positioning, distributing up to the retail outlets. The objectives of logistics are the least cost of transportation, quickest reach to the markets and safety of the products handled. Logistics is integrated with market planning.

Logistics is a dynamic activity and computer applications like decision support systems supported by a good logistics model, knowledge management systems, OLTPS and GPS help providing timely information to the managers in making right logistic decisions. Good and reliable logistics models are to be built by the experts to suit individual business environments.

5.7.1 Global Positioning System (GPS)

It is a system supported by Internet and mobile/wireless devices for identifying earth locations of the products being moved across the country or the globe. For example, a moving truck can be located anywhere from its origin to destination. This is utilized by logistics operators to identify the consignment movements throughout the physical space. Fedex, a logistics company based in USA and also a few companies in India are able to inform the consignors the exact location of their consignment until it reaches the consignees. These are dedicated applications used in product movement tracking systems. They help speeding up product delivery and safety.

5.8 PRODUCT DEVELOPMENT LIFE CYCLE (PDLC) MANAGEMENT SYSTEM

In PDLC management, first and foremost, the emphasis is on products. It starts from the stage when the customer preferences are identified and ends when matching products are sold to them. PDLCMS again is a set of integrated IT applications put in place to enable the manufacturers to develop new products faster, in order to capture the market opportunities first.

PDLC management system automates the product life cycle activities starting from identification of new products/services that have good market potential or changing existing products to meet customer expectations and include technical design, product specifications, process design, process specifications, specifications for input materials, bill of materials, workflow design, prototype development, production, test marketing, and so on.

PDLC management system also involves establishing the procedures for production planning and control, capacity planning, quality assurance, inspection/quality control, marketing, sales promotions/campaigns, after-sales service and support until the life time of the products.

PDLC management system offers the following advantages to manufacturing organizations:

- People involved in the product life cycle activities are the engineers engaged in R&D, product design, production, quality assurance, etc. the managers engaged in purchase, materials management, quality control and marketing, suppliers, the market channels and the customers. All of them can easily collaborate and share their knowledge in capturing, evaluating and controlling the product information/specifications/project activities until right products are identified by all these entities.

- Results in better utilization of intellectual assets of the organization and collective decision making.

- Leads to better product innovations, cheaper products, shorter time to market and better product quality through real time collaboration at workplace.

PDLC management system is developed as a separate software package and is totally different from other business applications. However, it could be integrated with IBASP/ERP or the software vendors can also offer integrated solutions for specific industries if so required by business houses.

Knowledge management systems, CADD, proto type design, production engineering, controlled production of sample products, sales campaigns, test marketing, etc. are the components of the PDLC management system.

5.9 DATA WAREHOUSE AND DATA MINING

Business organizations have now realized the strategic importance of historic business data that have been accumulated over the years (say, last 5 years) in their computer databases. By analysing such historic data, it is possible to gain new information/knowledge of the business, its customers, vendors, raw materials, finished products, markets, and so on hitherto hidden in them.

This can be achieved through efficient and systematic historic data management systems in the form of 'data warehouse' and model based analytical systems, in the form of 'data mining' and 'decision support systems'.

5.9.1 Data Warehouse

A data warehouse is the accumulation of historic business data associated with all its entities and events pertaining to previous years in electronic mediums to support future business decisions. Data warehouse builds up the organizational capability in creating huge database and accessing accurate, complete and reliable data pertaining to past business performances.

This is a well planned and elaborate activity. Relevant data elements from various files are extracted, converted into data warehouse formats and loaded into data warehouse. This involves reformatting, filtering inconsistent and incomplete data, creation of summary records, defining the key data elements, establishing logical relationships among various files/tables, collection and adding of additional data, and so on. These activities are performed using dedicated software or RDBMS. The selection of right and appropriate data elements decides the scope and benefits of the data warehouse.

Data warehouse also maintains the data dictionary (also discussed in Section 13.3), which is information about warehouse data elements themselves. It is used for building, maintaining, managing and using the data warehouse.

Data dictionary contains details like,

- Data elements that are to be picked up from transactions/MIS files
- Name and description of all such data elements
- Destination tables of data warehouse, rules for conversion, validation, etc. for each data element
- Data warehouse and table structures, access keys and relations
- Access rights, backup and restoration procedures, and so on.

5.9.2 Business Usage-based Classification of Data (Files/Database)

Business data can be classified into three categories, viz. transactions/operations files, MIS files and data warehouse files.

1. Transaction/operations files consist of data elements associated with all business events that are captured in the course of business process automation/transaction processing. Such files grow in volumes fast, since large numbers of transactions are processed every day. The transactions in such files have a definite life span and get closed as soon as the activities associated with an event is completed (e.g., when a material is received, a payable transaction is created and this transaction is closed when the payment is made).

These transaction files contain two types of data, viz. operation oriented data, like addresses, product description, taxation details, etc. and MIS oriented data which are useful in extracting MIS, like product, quantity, price, discounts, dates, etc.

2. MIS files contain only information oriented data related to business entities (like quantities or money values related to stocks, suppliers, employees, customers, plant and machinery, banks, and so on). Pertinent data contained in the transactions files are posted on to MIS files regularly for easier and quicker access of management information. MIS files generally pertain to current year.

3. Data warehouse (files) contains MIS oriented data, related to all business events and entities pertaining to previous years which are used in the applications like DSS, OLAPS and data-mining. This database is updated once in a quarter or a year.

5.9.3 Advantages of Data Warehouse

The advantages of data warehouse are as follows:

1. Automate the process of building one single and integrated enterprise-wide data warehouse (and also called data store or data mart for individual departments) consisting of both internal and external data, to enable the business organization to refer back.

2. Exploit the capabilities of cost-effective technologies in the form of large volume data storage devices, efficient RDBMS, complex statistical techniques made possible through special purpose software (like, PAS-preventive analytic software, LP-linear programming, finance and mathematical models) with which even complex data could be converted into convenient graphs or charts, leading to a better perception of the business.

3. It incorporates the procedures for aggregating, processing and extracting the management information to make them more relevant and useful for the managers. It facilitates understanding the overall performance of the business and its customers, which hitherto is unknown to the business.

4. It ensures accuracy of historic data. While creating massive data bases, data warehouse techniques filter unwanted data, correct erroneous data, fill up incomplete data, check and eliminate inconsistencies and improve the quality of entire business data warehouse.

5.9.4 Components of Data Warehouse System

Data warehouse processes with reference to **Figure 5.4** are explained as follows:

1. **Data warehouse database:** Data warehouse database is created by the transformation of MIS files related to business entities and MIS data extracted from business events/transactions. Pertinent external data is also added to this. Data warehouse systems automatically create data dictionary to help data warehouse administrators and users.

2. **Data warehouse management:**   Data warehouse administration and management are carried out by data warehouse management system (like RDBMS) to optimize data warehouse functions and performance.

3. **Data warehouse tools:**   Many tools/software are available to extract information from the data warehouse in the form of reports, tables, graphs, answers to the queries, etc. for business users. There are a number of statistical and other analytical tools which bring out valuable/hidden information from the data warehouse. The data warehouse is also used in the applications like data mining and DSS discussed subsequently. The data warehouse is also used to feed BI applications.

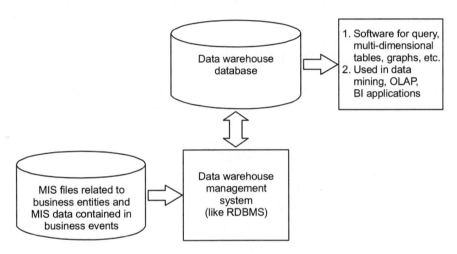

FIGURE 5.4   Logical structure of data warehouse.

Though computers are capable of storing large volumes of data and extracting multidimensional information fast and accurate, the human mind has limited capability in perceiving/understanding multidimensional information (e.g., sale of about 20 different products and their profit margins over last 5 years, across 20 states in India). Such information needs to be presented in the form of tables, formats, charts, graphs, animation, and so on with different views and colours so as to enable the managers in understanding the business situations better.

The report writers (user-friendly software) and SQL (structured query languages) can be used by the managers to extract MIS or any other exceptions from the data warehouse.

There could also special software modules written and stored in the computers to save the managers from the complexities of SQL, report writers, and so on. Such software stores pre-programmed queries in the form of simple menu options so that the managers can select an appropriate query based on the business situation.

5.9.5   Data Mining

Data mining software has great potential in yielding new information hitherto unknown to the business. It is the process of discovering meaningful new correlations (among the data variables), patterns (e.g., in customer behaviour) and trends (e.g., inflation eating into profits) by digging into (like mining) past data stored in data warehouse using, statistical, mathematical and financial models and other techniques. Business organizations that resort to data mining techniques could gain newer insights into their customers, markets, suppliers, employees, and so on.

Data mining is a specialist job done by the business analysts or statisticians or model experts. It is capable of revealing surprisingly new relationships, definite patterns, and so on. But the specialists need to tell data mining systems, *what to look for?*

Data mining involves extracting "hidden" patterns in business. Data mining applications automate the process of searching the mountains of data to find patterns that are good predictors of the future.

5.9.6   Models Used in Data Mining

Model is a simplification of a real-world event or the behaviour of an entity (which is too complex to comprehend) constructed for the purpose of studying and understanding them (better).

A model is intended to resemble the actual event/entity as closely as possible, but does not have the same depth of detail as the original one.

A model discussed here could be either the program logic/algorithm, or a set of rules/formula, or complex computations, or statistical techniques or the combinations of them, which could enable ascertaining many characteristics of the actual event or the entity. It connects a number of data variables to a particular business outcome. A model can give an insight into how the given data element/elements, influence the business outcome.

Some of the statistical techniques used in data mining are classification, affinity grouping, clustering, nearest neighbour, decision trees, histograms, correlation, clustering, and so on. These techniques are not discussed as they are outside the scope of this book. However, readers interested in them can refer to books dedicated to models and statistics.

It is also possible to build complex models interlinking all associated data elements in the form of long formula or expressions or program algorithm or combining different models. But this is the specialist job of statistical experts or economists.

For example, agricultural departments in India use rain forecasting models, based only on statistics which would tell the probability of rain in a given city/town for a given week. These models make use of the data warehouse consisting of weekly rainfall statistics of all cities and towns in India for previous 20 to 50 years. A complex statistical model has been developed for this purpose.

US Government is using a complex model which would indicate probable cost of pork, beef and poultry products for the next 10 years. This model has been working at 90% accuracy in the previous years.

5.9.7   Advantages of Data Mining to Business

Following are the advantages of data mining:

   1. **Discovering knowledge hitherto unknown to business:** Explicit/unknown relationships/correlations among business data variables, patterns in customer and

vendor behaviours, etc. are discovered using the organizations' data warehouse. Data mining is used in newer segmentation and classification of business entities based on such findings. However, as indicated earlier, we need to tell the system what to look for.

2. Predictive models are also capable of supporting managers' decisions. And adjusting such models based on the feedback obtained from the past decisions could lead to better models.

3. Successful data mining applications could also offer the following advantages:
   - Planning and implementing cost-effective sales campaigns/promotions
   - Identification of cheaper/economic marketing channels
   - Identification of customers who can be moved from current contribution levels to higher levels, and so on.

5.10 DECISION SUPPORT SYSTEMS

There are situations in business where decisions are complicated and beyond managers' skills and abilities. Some decisions would require application of statistical techniques or other decision models. Decision support systems assist the business managers in such situations. It provides a set of software programs that could provide the managers with potential decision alternatives (to support their decisions). Here we need not tell the systems what to look for?

5.10.1 Components of DSS

DSS processes with reference to **Figure 5.5** are explained as follows:

1. **DSS database (RDBMS):** The DSS database organizes, stores, updates and retrieves relevant business data used by the DSS. The DSS database is like any other RDBMS whose functions are discussed in detail in Chapter 13.

The MIS data is drawn from operational database and data warehouse (DSS does not take direct inputs) at periodic intervals. The DSS is not allowed to access operational database since it would delay other routine business applications.

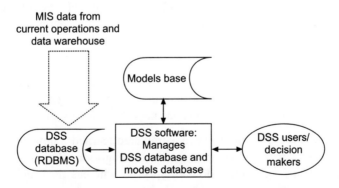

FIGURE 5.5 Logical structure of DSS.

Internal data from IBA applications like sales, material management, purchases, finance, etc. are taken to DSS database. External data are also collected and added to DSS database, as required by the DSS models. External data would include the data from the industry, competitors, and so on. However, identification of right data for DSS would require lots of foresight, efforts and skills.

2. **Models base (MBMS):** We have already discussed what a model is in the previous section. The model database consists of carefully selected statistical, financial, mathematical and other quantitative and rule based models as required for the DSS applications in the business. Model database of the DSS systems makes them unique compared to other computer applications discussed in this book.

The ability to run individual models or combined models or to construct new models makes the model base management system (MBMS) a powerful component in DSS. Some of the models have already been listed in Sections 4.9 and 5.9.6. The DSS also uses a number of analytical tools and such tools are managed through (MBMS). The main components of MBMS are modelling software and models library.

Modelling software allows creation of new decision models (software) or extracting from existing models, provides a mechanism for the linking or chaining of multiple models and allows users to modify the models dynamically.

Most commonly used statistical modelling software is predictive analytic software (PAS, formerly known as SPSS), which can run on any operating system and is capable of performing a number of statistical modelling like regression analysis, correlation, analysis of variance, normal distribution, scatter plots, trend analysis, and so on. These models are extensively used in market research and sales forecasts.

Models library stores a collection of mathematical, qualitative, statistical, financial and analytical models that can easily be accessed by the DSS user.

When the factors contributing to the final outcome are known, quantifiable and such factors can be combined in the form of formulae or other type of relations, such models are deterministic, e.g. the impact of increase in input costs on profits. There are a number of mathematical and finance models belonging to this category being used in many organizations today.

When the conditions stated above are not met, it is not possible to build deterministic models. However, certain statistical or mathematical models could be established to predict probabilistic occurrence of an event. For example, based on the sales for previous years, it could be possible to make a sales forecast for the coming year using statistical models.

3. **DSS software:** The DSS software allows easy interface with users, the models base and the database. It allows adding and modifying the models to the model database and adding the data from business applications to the DSS database.

DSS knowledge base is where the accumulated/learned knowledge is stored. DSS knowledge means rules or trial and error processes leading to a solution. The knowledge base contains information that is generally domain specific whereas data and models are useful across several business verticals or decision contexts.

People who actually build up knowledge base are called knowledge engineers (statisticians, economists, etc.). Knowledge engineers interact with business managers (domain experts) to acquire domain knowledge.

The entities interacting with DSS are the decision makers/managers (responsible for running the business), model experts (having good knowledge of the models and business domain knowledge), DSS software engineers who develop specific software and DSS data entry operators.

5.10.2   Benefits of DSS to Business

1. DSS offers managers a powerful tool in decision making, e.g. sales forecast. Managers can handle large scale, time-consuming and complex business problems through DSS.

2. Even some structured decisions in business are highly complex and time-consuming. DSS can solve such problems and save managers' time and efforts.

3. DSS improves the reliability of business decisions or reduces the risks of bad decisions. DSS provides the decision maker with more alternatives.

4. DSS supported by KMS enable the groups in taking collaborative decision (GDSS).

However, it cannot replace human cognitive skills in decision-making like creativity, imagination, intuition, intelligence, inference, and so on (wisdom). The power of DSS is limited to the knowledge of knowledge engineers and the models used in developing the DSS. DSS may not also be able to offer precise information to its users which are readily actionable.

5.11   EXPERT SYSTEM

Expert systems are used in selective business applications and special software has to be procured for the purpose. Expert systems work based on the statement of facts fed into the system by business experts, e.g. if the machine failure affects the production more than 20%, replace the machine.

Expert systems have two components, viz.

1. Expertise data base
2. The inference software (engine)

Expertise data base would consist of thousands of facts or statements or the rules stated by the experts which are captured in the system in the form of facts, statements, rules, do's and don'ts, and so on. New findings of the experts are added to the expertise database regularly.

The present conditions or the problems for which the solution or a decision is required are fed into the expert system as a series of structured statements. For the statements presented to it, the inference software draws its conclusion using the expertise database and presents possible solutions to the users in the form of statements.

Expert system uses a knowledge base of human expertise for problem solving. Its success is based on the quality of the statement of facts and the extent of rules added to the expertise database. It derives possible solutions by running the knowledge base through the inference software/engine.

Examples of uses of expert systems are, preventive maintenance schedules for plant and machinery, investment decisions, logistics, and so on. Another typical application is processing of insurance and medical claims for settlement.

5.12   CASE STUDIES (Part 1)

The following case studies are presented to enable readers in understanding how various applications discussed in Chapters 4 and 5 are applied in reality in business organizations. The case studies discussed in Part 1 pertain to a big automobile manufacturing company (hereafter referred as the company), where the author had implemented a number of IT applications.

5.12.1   Materials Purchases and Suppliers' Bills Payable System

Process

Purchase orders are released to the suppliers for the purchase of materials. The suppliers' bills are processed through the computers and get paid automatically through bank cheques and payment vouchers both printed by the computers. The suppliers' bills payable system processes hundreds of supplier bills and makes payments of millions of rupees daily. Exhaustive controls are built into the system (discussed in Section 9.7.1) such that payment vouchers and cheques printed by the computer are always accurate. This system is in operation for more than two decades now.

Steps involved in the process (IT applications)

1. Purchase orders are placed with the suppliers for the purchase of materials.
2. Materials supplied by the suppliers are acknowledged through good receipt notes (GRNs) prepared by the company (for receipts).
3. Materials are inspected for quality, and defective materials are rejected and sent back to the suppliers.
4. Accepted materials (= Supplied-rejected) in GRNs' (after inspection) are accounted in stocks.
5. The suppliers' bills are processed through the computers and they get paid automatically (based on the GRNs' accepted quantities) through bank cheques and payment vouchers both printed by the computers.
6. The bills paid are accounted in the books of accounts.

These activities are explained further to enable the readers in understanding the automated processes better.

STEP 1: The company buys thousands of inputs in the form of raw materials, small components, finished and semi finished automobile parts, from hundreds of suppliers. The purchase orders are placed with the suppliers for the supply of these materials indicating the price, taxes, and other costs and delivery schedules for the quantities to be supplied. The purchase orders are captured in the computer database.

STEP 2: The suppliers supply the materials through various means of transports always accompanied by supplier delivery notes (SDNs) prepared by them. They contain the details of the materials supplied, purchase order number, quantities, mode of transport, and so on. Based on the SDNs, the computer system prepares a document called goods receipts notes (GRN) after validating the SDNs with the purchase orders and the delivery schedules contained in it. The copies of GRNs are sent to the suppliers acknowledging the receipt of the materials. The GRNs are added to computer database.

STEP 3: The materials accompanied by SDNs and GRNs are inspected by quality control functions and if the materials are found to be defective, they are rejected. The accepted quantities (supplied-rejected) are updated in the GRNs database. The rejection intimations are sent to the suppliers accompanying the materials returned back to them. After this activity, GRNs are priced with the purchase order rates and the GRNs data contain the accepted quantities and corresponding payable values.

STEP 4: The accepted materials along with SDN's and GRNs are sent to the stores for accounting the materials in stocks. Once the materials are accounted in stock, payable transactions are created by the computer for the accepted quantities contained in the GRNs'.

STEP 5: When the suppliers submit the bills, the bills contain the reference to SDN numbers. The suppliers' bills data are entered into the computers along with respective SDN details. The computer systems match the suppliers' bill amount with the values contained in the priced GRN's (payable to the suppliers) data by linking the two through SDN numbers and make the payments to the suppliers depending on the payment due dates. Bank cheques and payment vouchers are printed in the process and sent to the suppliers.

STEP 6: The payment vouchers indicating GRN, SDN and supplier bill numbers are processed in the books of accounts and subsequently used in preparing the statement of accounts for the suppliers.

This application has eliminated the manual efforts and made the processes highly efficient.

5.12.2 Retrospective Price Increases

This application is an example of OLCPS and also involves a data warehouse. It is a logical extension of the previous case study. The purchase orders released to the suppliers are valid for a year and contain the delivery schedules and the quantities to be supplied over 52 weeks.

Some suppliers, for valid reasons, request the company to increase the prices for the materials supplied by them. The company negotiates such requests and agrees for higher prices with retrospective effect, if their requests are justified. This means all bills paid earlier need to be reprocessed to pay for enhanced prices.

The purchase orders are also updated with the revised prices. All bills paid so far and respective GRN data are stored in the data warehouse.

All earlier bills from the date from which the new prices are to be paid, are reprocessed to find out the incremental value to be paid with respect to each bill. This statement will have details of all the bills and the amounts paid earlier in old rates and corresponding new amounts to be paid for all such suppliers. Hundred of bills are involved for each supplier in such re-processing.

Since these processes are fully automated, additional amounts to be paid to the suppliers are computed very accurately. There is no need for the suppliers to counter check such statements.

5.12.3   Retrospective Revision of Taxes

This case study is also an example of OLCPS and similar to the previous one (involving data warehouse), but involved the bills to be reprocessed for previous three years.

The company had a dispute with the commercial taxes department of Government of Tamil Nadu, over the rate of tax to be paid by the company while buying the inputs from various suppliers.

This dispute went to the court and court gave the verdict favouring the company after a lapse of three years. The company actually was paying 8% tax on many number of input materials for which it had to pay only 4%.

The company reprocessed all the bills pertaining to the previous three years from the data warehouse wherein higher tax had been paid. This statement contained hundreds of pages accurately indicating revised and old tax amounts against individual bills.

The total value to be paid by the commercial taxes department back to the company was printed in the last page. This process was completed in a few minutes. The department honoured the payment very promptly because of the assured accuracy of the computer statement.

5.12.4   Extension of Vehicles Warranty Period

This case study relates to data warehouse and data mining. The company was offering the warranty period of one year for its vehicles sold to its customers.

The company was building the history of all the warranty claims preferred by its customers, in terms of the problems reported, causes for such breakdowns and the costs of replacement parts on all such warranty claims. The company also was maintaining data on all vehicle failures reported by the customers even after the warranty period.

Such data warehouse contained valuable information about the reasons for breakdowns, components involved in frequent breakdowns and the costs of settling warranty claims. A number of statistical analysis was made on such data to get lot of new information which hitherto were not known to the management. The management was able to perceive what was happening with regard to warranty claims better.

The management was also able to estimate the likely cost of warranty claims if the warranty is extended to 3 years. They also identified the components whose quality are to be improved for this purpose. With all such information available with them, the management decided to enhance the warranty period to three years, which gave a competitive advantage to the business.

5.12.5 Vehicles to Reach the Markets Quicker

The company is producing hundreds of vehicles daily through its assembly line, which starts with just four wheels and all other components and the sub systems are added one by one until a vehicle comes out of the assembly line. The vehicles coming out of the assembly line undergo about 10 more processes before they could be sold to the customers.

Such processes involve fitment of shortages, test driving, rectification of defects, retesting, payment of excise duty, drive up to dealer points, and so on. All these processes involve delays and locking up of working capital.

A system has been developed to record time and date of all activities completed with respect to all vehicles produced. The managers who are responsible for all such 10 activities are also given time targets for the completion of each activity. Actual time taken is compared with the targets to monitor time delays very objectively.

This has also enabled improving all these ten processes further so that the time targets could still be reduced. What is measured is managed better in business.

5.13 CASE STUDIES (Part 2)

The following case studies are associated with chemicals and fertilizers manufacturing company (referred as company in the case studies) where the author had about 14 years of experience implementing very successful IT applications, including IBA.

5.13.1 Integration of Business Functions

This company had implemented a number of IT applications related to finance, marketing, materials management, HR, and maintenance management functions across different locations on different application and computer architectures as indicated in sections 11.11 & 12.17. These applications were disintegrated and the business information was not easily shared among different business functions.

Management wanted to integrate all business functions so that the business information could be shared by all functions. The responsibility was given to the head of the IT services division (the author of this book holding the position at the time) to decide on such transition.

The requirement specifications were prepared covering all the above functions as per the procedures discussed in Chapter 8. Two alternatives were considered, one involving an ERP package and the other developing IBASP (integrated business application software package) in-house.

In the process of mapping the requirement specifications on to the capabilities of ERP, it was found that the ERP option required extensive custom programming since many of the requirement specifications were not readily handled by ERP. At the same time, the company had sufficient software engineering skills in-house.

A presentation was made to the management appraising the merits and demerits of both options including the costs, and the management decided to go for in-house development of IBASP.

IBASP associating the business functions mentioned above was developed in-house and was implemented in eight months involving 10 software engineers. IBASP developed for the company involved about 400 programs, 120 files related to various business entities and events (contained in the database), about 150 formats for feeding input data to the computers and about 400 outputs involving business documents, reports, statements, MIS and many more electronic files.

5.13.2   Executive Information Systems (EIS)

The chairman of the company was also managing another 11 companies belonging to the group. He wanted an EIS (executive information systems) to be designed for him through which he will come to know the status of all operations of these 12 companies on a day-to-day basis on the computer screen. He did not want to see any report in paper. Accordingly, effective EIS was implemented covering all 12 companies, for the chairman and also the senior management of those 12 companies. The EIS system was implemented using LAN. The user interface was menu driven and was made operational just using the mouse (no key board operations)

The first menu consisted of the names of all 12 companies for which EIS was implemented. In addition to this, it enabled flash news to be given to the management about anything important happening within the group any day and time.

The second level of the menu consisted of all business functions within a company. And the third level menu consisted of about 10 to 15 EIS pertaining to each business function. EIS also contained the information about the markets and the competitors. Thus, about 200 EIS formats were made available to the Chairman which could be selected very easily depending on the situation in which he wanted to access particular EIS. Colour monitors made the reading a pleasant experience for them. The adverse conditions were also indicated in red. Some EIS were also in the form of graphs and charts.

A group of business analysts also used to analyse the performance of all 12 companies very critically and submitted confidential reports to the chairman both in quantitative and qualitative terms. EIS were updated every day, some EIS in real time (like the companies share prices). The whole system operated without any paper being sent to the chairman.

Such vast information was made available to the management instantly.

SUM UP

Readers would have understood the scope and usefulness of all strategic applications that could be used in business and how they are different compared to tactical applications discussed in Chapter 4. Now they will also be in a position to identify the types of business that could derive these benefits.

It needs to be understood that not all business organizations would benefit through these applications and lot more efforts are needed in making these applications successful. Top management needs to formulate right strategies and support all organizational initiatives directed towards these applications.

Many case studies have also been discussed to enable readers in understanding practical aspects of some of these business applications.

CHAPTER

6

INFORMATION TECHNOLOGY APPLICATIONS IN MANAGEMENT FUNCTIONS

Chapter Quest

In this chapter, the readers would easily understand and appreciate the immense benefits IT offers to the management functions, viz.

- Planning (strategic and tactical)
- Organizing
- Staffing
- Coordination and collaboration (integration)
- Communication
- Control
- Compliance management
- Risk management
- Decision making
- Innovation
- IT strategy
- Business relationship management
- Knowledge management

A case study has been presented at the end of this chapter to enable readers in understanding how performance appraisal for the managers is linked to their responsibilities.

After reading this chapter, the readers would have a clear understanding of how IT supports these management functions.

6.1 INTRODUCTION

The readers would have understood all tactical and strategic applications discussed in earlier two chapters and understood how these applications support the business operations. Extensive MIS generated through such applications also help the management at all levels and in all management functions.

This chapter discusses IT applications aimed at management functions. The management functions have also been discussed in Section 1.7.3.

The management hierarchy consisting of three levels, viz. top, middle and operational, each level having distinctively different roles and responsibilities, has already been discussed in Section 1.7.

There are two phases in the life span of any business, viz. establishing a business and running it. The management functions discussed below are applicable to both phases and all levels of management.

6.2 SELECTION OF BUSINESS, SETTING OBJECTIVES AND FRAMING POLICIES

Type of products and services to be offered, value addition processes, acquisition of right technologies, identification of the markets, capital required, sales volumes, ROI, market share, time period in setting up business, organization structure, etc. are decided by the top management or the promoters of the company.

Most of the data associated with such activities and decisions are unstructured, stay external to the business and are not available readily. Such decisions are also not based on any rules or formulae.

6.2.1 IT Support in Selection and Setting Business Objectives and Policies

Management needs to rely on market research reports, industry specific surveys, process/technology owners' specifications, existing markets' analysis, other formal/informal sources and the Internet. Internet offers global information on various products and services, the technology, know-how suppliers, markets, and so on.

KMS (knowledge management systems) could help accumulation of widely varied information (data, graphs, tables, charts, audio, video, animation, and so on), from all possible sources and share the same among all managers involved in such decision making. KMS enables sharing of such vast knowledge across the entire organization, collaboration among all managers in setting organizational objectives and policies, brainstorming and collective decision making leading to firm business plans.

Decision support systems (DSS) making use of statistical techniques and appropriate decision models could also help in the business/sales forecasts. Office automation systems also help synchronizing the efforts of the management functions in this regard.

6.3 ESTABLISHING SYSTEMS AND PROCEDURES (Business Process Manuals)

Top management or the specialist consultants appointed by them and the functional heads need to establish systems and procedures (business process manuals, by incorporating best business practices) and organization and methods (O&M) for all business functions. It is also necessary to create organization rules, regulations and policies for all business functions and their operations.

6.3.1 IT Support in Establishing Systems, Procedures

Business process manuals covering all business functions including support functions need to be part of KMS discussed in Section 4.7. KMS enables adding, accessing and updating these manuals, kept in a central database, by all employees. As the business learns new and better procedures/processes, the same could be updated into the KMS. The organizational rules, regulations and policies can also be made part of KMS. This ensures prompt compliance with the stated business rules and procedures all the time by all functions. Employees can never plead ignorance of their responsibilities.

6.4 PLANNING

Planning is the most important function for all managers. Any business management activity starts with planning.

6.4.1 Strategic Planning

This activity is mainly to look for new business opportunities, expansion of existing business, mergers, acquisitions, introducing innovative products, and so on. Enormous information, both structured and unstructured, needs to be collected stored and analysed.

Establishing a new business would involve lot of planning and the planning period could be a few months or years. The starting of a business (project) would involve hundreds of activities, each activity involving huge costs and time.

IT support for strategic planning

Most of the data associated with these activities are unstructured and available external to the organization. However, IT applications like Project management systems, Internet, DSS involving statistical, financial and other models, KMS and office automation systems (OA) are of great use in strategic planning.

6.4.2 Tactical Planning

Project planning

All activities involved in establishing new business (project) are to be exhaustively identified and accurately estimated both in terms of cost and time. Database consisting of all these activities need to be created for this purpose. This database would become the input to project management software package (PMS).

Daily MIS can be obtained from PMS, indicating the activities completed, activities delayed, costs of completed activities, cost over runs, earliest date of completing the project, and so on accurately.

Project planning is necessary to monitor all activities and to arrange the required resources in time. An appropriate KMS (section 4.7) can also be used by the people to accumulate, update and share right information related to the project activities (delays, bottlenecks, fix for the problems, and so on), which eventually would lead to completion of the project in time.

Business (operations) planning

Business planning (operational budgets) for each financial year needs to be prepared in advance. It would include sales forecast (of both sales volumes and turnover), marketing planning (including all income and expenditure), material requirement planning, procurement planning, capital/cash flow planning, capacity utilization plans, manpower planning, logistics planning, production planning and plans for all support functions. These operational plans set targets of performance for all business functions.

Business planning associated with key business functions are discussed below. Business planning is done by respective business functions using IT applications like MIS, IBA/ERP, OLCPS, electronic spread sheets, DSS and KMS. Most of the data associated with such planning are structured and available within the organization (except the sales forecast). These plans get converted into budgets, which set the performance targets for respective business functions.

The actual performances of these functions are measured by OLTPS and are compared with the budgets to assess actual performance.

Sales forecast

Sales forecast is made ahead of the commencement of the financial year. DSS, data warehouse, MIS related to sales volumes of previous years, management objectives, industry publications, economic indices, competitor plans, etc. are used in sales forecasting. Management may alter this by superimposing their strategies. Sales forecast will identify the product mix, sales volumes, prices, markets, channels, and so on for all products and all days/weeks/months in a year.

Marketing planning

It states monthly/weekly/daily marketing plans in terms of all products, sales volumes, prices, channels, warehouse stocks, dealers, retail-outlets, and so on. It also specifies the costs of marketing like transportation, promotional expenses, advertisements, trade margins, discounts, delays in sales realization, marketing HR, inventory carrying costs, marketing overheads and so on such that all income and expenses could be monitored against the budgets. Marketing plans (budgets) direct the marketing functions in planning and controlling the market operations.

IT applications like data warehouse (to know earlier years market plans and actual performance) and MIS would help marketing functions in finalizing the marketing budgets and controlling their operations.

Material requirement planning

For all end products, the inputs/raw material requirements are maintained in a database called bill of materials (BOM). Based on the production plan and product mix, the (input) raw material requirements are assessed using the bill of materials and the software developed for this purpose (OLCPS-online complex processing systems). Material requirements eventually become the procurement plans/purchase schedules.

Capacity planning

All production operations to be performed and various plant and machinery required in the conversion of raw materials into finished products, plant and machinery required for each operation, conversion time, setup time and manpower required for each operation are stored in the capacity planning database. Based on the sales forecast and available capacities, the production schedules are prepared using the computer. Capacity planning software (OLCPS) performs these tasks during business planning and actual production.

Manpower planning

Manpower required for all production processes (direct labour involved in the conversion of raw materials into finished products) are also maintained in the computer database. Based on the production plans, it is also possible to assess the manpower requirements. If sufficient manpower is not available, additional manpower is either recruited or covered by 'overtime'. Manpower planning software (OLCPS) performs such tasks during business planning and actual production.

Manpower planning for indirect labour is done based on volumes of business operations to be performed by functions concerned and based on MIS reports of previous years.

Production scheduling

With available resources like machines, men and materials, it is possible to draw a production schedule using the computer model (DSS based on mathematical model). Issue of raw materials to production, manpower deployment, controlling production, packing and logistics, etc. are also managed through production planning, scheduling and control systems. Production plans can be prepared for a year, a month, or a week in advance so that all required resources are mobilized at right time.

Because all planning is done through computers, it is possible to alter production schedules dynamically, at a short notice, based on the market requirements/situations.

Financial (working capital/cash flow) planning

Marketing plans are associated with sales incomes and marketing costs, and business plans related to all other business functions have all other costs. Daily/weekly/monthly income and expenses data related to all business functions are fed into the financial planning model (electronic spreadsheets or OLCPS or IBA). Such systems help finance managers in cash flow budgeting/planning and enable acquiring necessary funds (working capital) for the business operations at right time.

Sales planning

This involves the planning of points of sales, stocks at each point of sales, logistics, order booking, invoicing, product delivery, sales realization, selling expenses, sales promotional expenses, sales accounting, and so on. Sales forecast is mandatory for sales planning. Finance models and multidimensional MIS from the data warehouses (containing previous years' sales information) are used in sales planning.

IT applications in tactical planning

Planning is done for all business and support functions and at all the three levels of management. IBA/ERP, MIS from the data warehouse, financial models, OLCPS and office automation systems are used in tactical planning.

6.5   ORGANIZING

Organizing has two connotations, viz.

1.   Organizing the tasks in order to establish the business and running it to achieve the business objectives
2.   Establishing right organization structure for the purpose.

Organizing needs to start as soon as the business objectives/targets are set. A number of activities are to be organized to mobilize the resources required for establishing and running the business, like technology, capital, production infrastructure, land, plant and machinery, government/statutory approvals, sourcing the raw materials, establishing marketing channels, business partners and other support infrastructures. Organizing transfers the business from planning to fulfilment stage.

IT applications in organizing: IT applications like KMS, project management systems, IBA, and office automation systems are used in organizing.

6.5.1   Organization Structure

Organization structure is associated with human resources. There are two types of organization structure—one at the project stage and the second at operations stage. These two stages require different skill sets, the first one being one time activity. Appropriate and right organization structures need to be in place for both stages.

Human resources necessary for running and managing the business, managers at all levels and the employees under them are to be identified in terms of the tasks to be performed (job specification), job responsibilities, reporting relationships, and so on for each position in the organization structure. The skill set, experience, qualifications, etc. required for each position are to be stated exhaustively.

Organization structure involving all positions and their reporting relationships can be incorporated in a computer database. Type of organization structure like hierarchical functional, matrix or networked, with established line of control and command can also be obtained as organization chart using the graphics software package. Organization structure and reporting relationships need to be made known to all employees through KMS.

The head of HR function, in consultation with the functional heads and top management, needs to finalize the organization structure and also compute HR costs of the organization. Employee costs need to be justified by the departmental heads and need to have commensurate returns/benefits for individual departments.

The available manpower can always be compared with approved organization structure to assess either vacant positions or excess manpower.

IT applications associated with organization structure: IBA/ERP, MIS, graphics software and KMS are used in managing the organization structure.

6.6 STAFFING (HR Positions and Recruitment)

Once the organization structure gets approved by management, the organization needs to be staffed with right people at right cost. This is very crucial for the success of any business. Unlike other resources, the human resources bring in their emotions, feelings, sentiments, own beliefs and social values in addition to the skills and knowledge of the business.

Requisite knowledge, qualifications, experience, skill sets required to handle the positions effectively and efficiently, age limits, compensation levels (minimum and maximum), etc. are to be clearly defined and stated for each position.

Staffing is to identify the right person for a right job at right cost. Computers enable creating the database of all approved positions in the organization in terms of position names, description, responsibilities, skill levels, qualification, experience, reporting relationships (like to whom the position is reporting to and positions below who will be reporting to him), compensation (cost to the company), and so on. It is possible to identify all approved positions, positions occupied by people and position lying vacant from the computer system.

Human resources management: It is possible to have the integrated application software that can perform all functions of HR management. HR functions like recruitment, payment of salaries, performance appraisal, job rotation, job enrichment, employee leave and attendance, promotions, transfers, separation from service, and so on can be efficiently managed through such software.

IT applications in staffing: IBA/ERP, EDP (Batch processing systems), OLTPS, MIS, office automation systems and Internet are used in staffing functions.

6.7 COORDINATION/COLLABORATION (Integration)

There are thousands of independent and interlinked business activities that need to be performed by the employees (and the managers) in perfect coordination in order to achieve organizational synergy. This has been discussed in Section 1.13. This would lead to faster decisions and actions and make the organization as a whole highly responsive.

All activities need to be coordinated towards optimal utilization of organizational resources and in achieving business objectives in a systematic and structured way. In order to achieve good coordination, all employees, managers, suppliers, marketing channels and other external entities need to have close collaboration.

IT offers excellent support for business coordination and collaboration in the form of the applications mentioned below.

6.7.1 Work Groups Applications/KMS

KMS enables all business functions to interact with one another and work in close coordination in successfully completing the business tasks. It leads to organizational synergy (the organization to be more capable than the sum total of individuals' capabilities).

KMS (discussed in Section 4.7) provides a mechanism that helps groups to collaborate and keep track of ongoing business activities. The responsibilities like who is to do what, the activities completed, the activities where the bottlenecks are encountered, etc. are made known to the entire group. KMS is a messaging system, which notifies the group of all the things happening in business, sending alerts on pending tasks and responses to others' requests.

Other applications under KMS include group 'Decision Support Systems' (GDSS) document sharing, document management, group appointments, meeting schedules, minutes of the meetings indicating the responsibilities and target dates, group contacts points, project management, discussions, brainstorming, collective decision making, text chat, file transfers and audio and video conferencing.

KMS is a central repository of organizational knowledge in all forms (multimedia) which allow the employees and managers to accumulate, share, access and update organizational knowledge on a continual basis. KMS makes employees knowledge workers and the organization itself knowledge based and learning organization. This helps in achieving close coordination and collaboration among employees since the project/process status is constantly updated in the system.

6.7.2 Workflow Management and E-Approvals

Workflow management systems allow messages and documents to be routed to different business functions and the managers. Since the business data pertaining to the operations are converted into electronic mediums, everyone is able to access them and come to know of what are the tasks pending and what needs to be done to finish the tasks in time.

Approvals can also be given by managers and top management over electronic documents/computer files and this eliminates physical flow of documents and speeds up the business processes. The approvals can also be given using digital signatures which are authenticated and which cannot be repudiated. Such issues are discussed in Chapter 10.

6.7.3 Networked Organization Structure

Computer networks enable creation of networked organization structures within the business. It enables employees and managers within the organization to get networked into a number of groups, each group responsible for performing a specific task or solving business problems or resolving business bottlenecks. All the members in the network are able to interact with one another very effectively. Well coordinated efforts result in completing the tasks in time and achieving organizational efficiency. KMS support creation of networked organization structure.

6.7.4 Integrated Business Applications

Integrated business applications have been discussed in Sections 1.13, 5.2 and 5.3. IBA maintains a common database pertaining to all business functions in a central place such that everyone is able to update and access business information in real time. Integrated business applications enable close coordination and collaboration (integration) among all human entities associated with business and creates unity of purpose among them. SC-IBA enables close coordination and collaboration even among all supply chain entities.

6.8 COMMUNICATION

Information technology has revolutionized business communications within and outside the organization around the globe. Communications involving conventional voice, short messages (SMS), documents, data, electronic/digital files, images, graphs, pictures, drawings, audio and video are being effortlessly communicated by the business organizations today.

Internet enables people around the globe to communicate effortlessly, 24 hours a day and all 365 days with no barrier whatsoever, across varied time zones, cultures and political/geographical boundaries. Internet has shrunk the world into a close neighbourhood with respect to communication.

E-mail, voice mail, video conference, voice over internet, call centres, IVRS (interactive voice response systems) and e-chat are the facilities being used extensively by business organizations today.

People need not travel to meet the business entities stationed at distant locations and instead transact/manage the business using modern communication systems sitting in one place. People on the move can still manage the business as if they are stationed at the workplace.

Internet enables the organizations to communicate their business objectives, company profile, product brochures, operating results, business offers, career opportunities/recruitments, contact addresses and so on through their websites very economically but effectively.

IT support in communication: Internet, e-mail, IBA/ERP, KMS, call centres, IVRS, etc. offer excellent support in business communications.

6.9 CONTROL

Management control is yet another great benefit of IT to business which was realized as soon as MIS reached the managers. IT enables scores of management controls, at micro and macro levels, to be exercised on business which otherwise is too difficult to manage. Organizational rules, best business practices, management directives, standing orders, policies, statutory rules, etc. can easily be embedded in the application software. It ensures automatic compliance of all the above.

By virtue of IBA, real time data pertaining to all business entities and events are readily available for the managers. This enables extraction of any type of information for management control and initiating timely action (like management by exception and management by objectives discussed in Section 1.18).

Though there are endless possibilities by which the management can control the business using IT, a select few are discussed below.

6.9.1 Budget Control (Targets vs. Actual)

Budgeting has already been discussed. What cannot be measured in business cannot be managed. Effective management means setting business objectives in measurable terms (budgets) and measuring the actual business performance objectively.

Information technology applications enable measuring the business performance in quantifiable parameters like, production and sales quantities, sales turnover, cost of sales, inventory carrying cost, direct and indirect expenses, cost of capital, ROI, cost of production, capacity utilization, cost of warranty claims, specific consumption, sales realization delays, financial ratios, and so on.

The time taken for all business processes and delays, if any, can also be measured and compared with the norms/targets, to locate the reasons for delays.

Employees/managers' performances, customer satisfaction, etc. though cannot be quantified accurately, the subjective assessment could still be obtained on a number of decision parameters and be converted into quantifiable values based on rightly chosen rating scales for each parameter.

Responsibility/commitment accounting

Management control can also be exercised over the performance of each employee/manager by setting the performance parameters in quantifiable terms for each of them as discussed above. Once the performance parameters are set, the IT applications can easily measure the actual performance and compare the same with the targets. Such systems lead to very effective performance appraisal (also discussed in a case study in Section 6.17).

Another important management control is to measure time delays in critical business activities and take steps to reduce such time delays (also discussed in a case study in Section 5.12.5).

6.9.2 Functional Controls

Numerous controls at functional levels like, expenses control, cost control, inventory control, quality control, production control, debtor control, finance control, etc. are easily implemented in business through various IT applications.

IT support for management control: OLTPS, IBA/ERP, MIS, etc. help management in controlling the business very effectively.

6.10 COMPLIANCE MANAGEMENT

Business organizations need to comply with statutory rules and regulations either by way of paying or collecting and paying of various taxes in time, complying with statutory rules and regulations, submission of information/returns to authorities concerned, abiding by national/international laws, and so on, on a continual basis. The failure to do so would lead to fine, legal action, punishment or stoppage of the business itself. It is the management responsibility to ensure that the business comply with stated rules, regulations and other statutes without exception.

Management needs to ensure that all rules, regulations and statutory requirements related to all business functions and operations are fully identified and documented by respective functional heads along with time targets. The compliance needs to be monitored by the top management.

IT applications enable the business organizations in the creation of compliances database consisting of what needs to be complied with, when is to do it, who is to do it, to whom it is to be submitted, and so on. And in the event of actual compliance, the data like who did it, when it was done, etc. can also be posted into this database. This enables identification of non compliances, if any, immediately.

Management thus can exercise good control on all types of compliances. This would make the business a compliant organization all the time.

IT support for statutory compliance: Batch processing systems, IBA/ERP and OLTPS perform all processes in accordance with the stated rules and regulations (programmed decisions) and also prepare the supporting documents like statement of returns, registers, etc. to be submitted to the regulating agencies as part of the compliance procedures. Rest of compliance management can be done through KMS and MIS.

6.11 RISK MANAGEMENT

Any business is exposed to different types of risks. Risks can arise through its own operations and risks external to it. Risks vary in their characteristics like, their predictability, levels to which they can be mitigated, risk management, impact on the business like disruption, losses, compensation to the affected entities, etc. insurable risks, and so on.

Management needs to assign responsibilities to all the functional heads and the managers in identifying and documenting

- All possible risks under respective business functions
- Risks that can be insured
- Risk mitigation procedures
- Risk management procedures in the event of its occurrence
- Damages/disruptions they can cause to business
- Costs of overcoming/reducing the risks
- People who are responsible for risk mitigation and management
- Elaborate documentation on all risk associated business operations.

All such information needs to be put into a central computer database so that all employees in the organization are aware of all the risks and their roles in risk management. Responsibilities need to be fixed on employees/managers as to who has to do what for each type of risk. This can be part of knowledge management system discussed in Section 4.7.

IT support in risk management. KMS and MIS help ensuring effective risk management in business organizations.

6.12 DECISION MAKING

Decision making is the unique function of the managers. However, as the programmable decisions get embedded in the application software, it considerably reduces the human efforts involved in taking structured decisions in daily operations.

By virtue of real time MIS, Business intelligence systems, EIS and KMS, the managers are able to perceive the business in right context and take right decisions at right time.

In situations where decision making is not based on structured data and the decision variables are too many and too complex to be correlated, DSS and Data Mining Systems can guide the managers in strategic decisions (discussed in Sections 5.9 and 5.10). However, IT has a limited role in decision making processes involving unstructured data and strategic management.

6.13 INNOVATION

Innovation is associated with all business functions and activities. It could be like, introducing newer and cheaper products to the markets, enhancing their utility value, attractive pricing, value added packing, logistics leading to minimum inventories, high return sales promotions, intelligent inventory management, saving organizational resources, efficient business processes, and so on. Innovation still is the domain of the human resources in business. However, IT applications indirectly contribute to innovation such as:

- All IT applications discussed in this book greatly relieve the human resources from non-intellectual activities. They, in turn, can focus their cognitive skills to innovate and identify better and newer ways of doing business.
- Knowledge management systems allow all employees and the managers to brainstorm and offer suggestions that would finally lead to innovative products and processes.

- The customer relationship management systems and data mining applications can help the business in identifying innovative ways of enhancing customer loyalty and customer base.

- Internet is the source of valuable information and knowledge for any business today. Efforts need to be made to look for all possible avenues of innovation from such vast knowledge.

6.14 IT STRATEGY

IT itself can be used in formulating right IT strategies for the business. The business needs to create a database consisting of (file drawer system):

- Various IT applications that are being used around the world and by similar industries and possible benefits that would bring to the business.
- Emerging technologies that are likely to offer newer applications that would bring competitive advantages to the business.
- Vendors who are offering state-of-the-art hardware, software and other solutions which are likely to make the business more competitive, and so on.

The head of the IT division needs to use such database in formulating right IT strategy for the business.

This book is aimed at enabling top management in identifying right IT strategy for their business. The technology, its applications, five key constituents of IT applications and the issues to be taken care with respect to each of them are discussed in simple terms to enable top management in identifying right IT strategy for their respective business.

Evolving trends like 'Business Technology' and its management are discussed in Chapter 18.

6.15 RELATIONSHIP MANAGEMENT

Business organizations today need to establish profitable/beneficial win-win relationships with the business entities like,

- Customers
- Retailers
- Market channels
- Logistics operators
- Employees and the managers
- Vendors and various service providers
- Investors and banks
- Governments and regulating agencies
- General public.

Management needs to set right strategies and establish supporting organization structure in maintaining beneficial and profitable relationship with all these entities. Necessary systems and procedures are to be in place, with responsibilities earmarked among various business functions/managers in establishing winning relationship with these entities.

Customer relationship management (CRM) and IT support for CRM are discussed in detail in Section 5.5.

Supply chain integrated business applications, discussed in Section 5.3, would also help in gaining profitable relationships with the retailers, market channels, logistics-operators, vendor and service providers.

Internet and websites and other IT applications designed for such purposes would help establishing better relationships with the investors, banks, governments, regulating agencies and the general public.

6.16   KNOWLEDGE MANAGEMENT

Business knowledge in various types, forms and mediums is being held by all employees and managers in the business. They use such knowledge in business operations and decision making. Such knowledge is an organizational asset and the management needs to exploit it for the benefit of the organization (to get better mileage).

The modern management needs to ensure that knowledge possessed by individuals are ploughed back into the organization's knowledge base, so that it is made available to the entire organization. When the employees and managers leave the organization, the knowledge possessed by them needs to be left behind for the benefit of others and new employees joining the organization. Knowledge management systems are discussed in Section 4.7.

6.17   CASE STUDY: Performance Appraisal through Responsibility Accounting System

A fertilizer and chemicals manufacturing company consists of a number of strategic business units (SBUs), each being run as an independent profit centre. Each SBU is headed by Vice President (VP) and the Managing Director (MD) is responsible for entire company. There are hundreds of managers of different business functions and levels working in these SBUs.

In big business organizations, rewarding a bad performer is worse than not rewarding a good performer.

MD wanted to have an effective performance appraisal system for all managers covering both objective and subjective performance parameters. The objective performance is given a weight of 50 points and the subjective performance 50 points and the system works as explained below.

1.   **Objective performance/responsibility accounting system:**   The business performance yardsticks for the managers of all business functions which can be measured (as applicable to individual managers) have been identified very exhaustively in terms of:

- Employee costs of all people working under each manager including his costs
- Office administration expenses like electricity, maintenance, consumables, rent, etc.
- Costs and expenses related to all business equipment used including computers
- Costs of borrowings
- Return on investments
- Realization delay for the cheques deposited in the banks
- Sales quantities
- Discounts offered
- Sales promotional expenses and other marketing costs
- Delay in sales realization
- Stock to sales turnover ratio for each stock point
- Inventory carrying costs of raw materials and finished products
- Cost of production
- Product rejections
- Plant and machinery breakdowns and capacity utilization
- Number of other such parameters carefully selected for the purpose.

For each manager, performance targets in terms of the above factors (for all months in a year) have been set depending on their function and in consultation with them. These yardsticks have become the individual manager's business objectives. Actual performances of the managers in terms of these parameters are measured through IT applications (IBASP) implemented in the business. The objectives set earlier and actual performance by them are reckoned in performance appraisal.

2. **Performance appraisal based on subjective parameters:** For this assessment, **six** different subjective performance parameters (like quality of work, leadership, quantity of work, dedication, delegation, and so on) have been identified for each manager, depending on the responsibilities and job description. A weight is given to each of these **six** parameters (say 1 to 12) such that the total weight equals 50. And the manager's actual performance against each such parameter is given a rating of 1 to 5. Based on such rating, the points are given against each parameter (e.g., if the weight is 12 and rating is 5, the point earned is 12 for such parameter). Thus, the total points earned by each manager (against a total of 50) are computed through the application software.

Performance appraisal systems for the managers take into consideration the outcome from both systems discussed above and is also made known to the respective managers.

SUM UP

By now, the readers could have understood modern management functions and the IT support for management functions. If the readers are not clear about any of the IT applications mentioned in this chapter, they can go to respective sections in Chapters 4 and 5 and get to know such applications better.

7

PRACTICAL APPROACH FOR MANAGERS IN IDENTIFYING RIGHT IT APPLICATIONS

The following questions would guide the readers in navigating through this chapter:

1. What is the step-by-step approach recommended for the business managers in identifying right IT applications for their respective business functions?

2. What are the critical success factors (CSFs)? What decisions are to be made in reaching them, the information needs and the sources of information for such decisions for business functions like procurement/materials management, production, marketing, finance and HR?

After finishing this chapter, the readers would have clear answers for these questions.

7.1   INTRODUCTION

This chapter discusses practical approach in mapping right IT applications/solutions to business problems. The technology needs to be looked at from the business perspective and not vice versa.

There are two ways by which the business needs to be looked at in understanding the business, its internal operations and interaction with external entities very clearly.

1. **Top down approach:** The business needs to be looked at from the wider perspective in terms of its interaction with external environments like the customers, market channels, suppliers, competitors, investors, regulators and the general public. The flow of organizational resources, data/information, decisions, control, feedback, etc. between the business entities themselves and the external entities are to be studied and understood. The IT applications need to address all requirements of internal and external interactions of the business. (Please refer **Figure 1.5**)

2. **Bottom up approach:** A business is made up of a number of business functions and sub functions. They in turn consist of a number of departments. The functions of each of these departments, their interaction with other departments and other business functions, the flow of organizational resources, data/information, decisions, commands, controls, approvals, feedback, etc. among them are to be studied and understood.

In addition, the data that is being created and used, business documents/transactions being generated, the organizational resources committed, roles and responsibilities of the employees, type and extent of value addition made, management controls being exercised, the registers/books that are being maintained, and so on are to be studied with respect to each department.

7.2 POTENTIAL BENEFITS OF IT AND ASSOCIATIVE APPLICATIONS

Potential benefits offered by IT (discussed in Section 1.1.3) to business and associated applications are summed up in **Table 7.1**, to enable managers to have a clear understanding of IT applications in business.

7.3 STEPS INVOLVED IN IDENTIFYING RIGHT IT APPLICATIONS FOR EACH DEPARTMENT/BUSINESS FUNCTION

A step-by-step approach as outlined below needs to be followed by each manager (with respect to each department or business function).

1. Identify the critical success factors (CSF)/key result areas (KRA) and the factors contributing to the same.
2. List the decisions to be made by the managers in reaching the CSF/KRA.
3. Assess information needs for all such decisions both for business operations and effective management (planning, organizing, controlling, and so on).
4. Identify the sources of data and information, internal or external, available or to be obtained, structured or unstructured, and so on.

TABLE 7.1 Potential contributions and associative applications of IT

Potential contributions of IT to business	*Associative applications*
1. Business process automation. (Involving programmed decisions, creation of business documents, complex computations, bookkeeping, large scale printing, and so on)	• Batch processing (EDP) • On line transaction processing systems (OLTPS) • Integrated business applications (IBA/ERP) • On line complex processing systems (OLCPS) • Supply chain integrated systems (SC IBA/ERP)
2. Storing large volumes of data and accessing the same fast	• All IT applications in business
3. Enhancement of business knowledge and knowledge sharing among managers	• MIS • DSS • EIS/Business intelligence (information dash board) • Multidimensional MIS offered by data warehouse • On line analytical processing systems (OLAPS) • Data mining applications • Knowledge management systems
4. Integration of business functions including the supply chain	• Integrated business applications (IBA/ERP) • Supply chain integrated IBA/ERP
5. Establishing electronic relationships	• E-business • Internet enabled Intranet and Extranet applications • Knowledge management systems • Web sites and portals • Sales force automation • Customer relationship management (CRM)
6. Shrinking the physical business space.	• E-business • Internet enabled Intranet and Extranet applications supported by mobile devices
7. Global reach for the business	• Internet and E-business

All these applications have been discussed in great detail in Chapters 4 and 5.

5. Identify all the business processes that could be automated (choose from various applications discussed under Chapters 4, 5 and 6).
6. Consolidate all the above requirements into business requirement specifications (discussed in Chapter 8) for each department/function.

The next step is to consolidate the requirements of all departments and business functions into the organizational requirements. This should lead to the logical database and application software development activities discussed under Chapter 8.

The roles and responsibilities of the top management, the functional heads and the business users in implementing ideal IT applications in business have already been discussed under Chapter 3.

7.4 INDICATIVE LIST OF CSFs AND KRA

CSFs/KRA pertaining to marketing, procurement/materials management, production, finance and HR functions are listed below, so as to guide the managers in identifying CSFs and KRA related to their respective business functions.

The types of decisions to be made, information needs for such decisions and the sources of data for obtaining such information are also indicated for these functions.

The details shown are only indicative and not exhaustive.

7.4.1 Marketing

Critical success factors/Key result areas:

- Offer right products at right prices
- Right positioning so as to liquidate stocks at the earliest
- Right market promotion (best return on promotional expenses)
- Understanding customer needs
- Minimum inventory carrying costs
- Quick realization of sale proceeds
- Pull market strategies
- Good control on marketing costs
- Order to product delivery to realization to be quick, and so on.

Decisions to be made:

- Product characteristics and specifications
- Product mix-volumes and prices
- Quality specifications and control procedures
- Market promotion activities and costs
- Marketing budgets covering all marketing operations
- Positioning—where, when, how much, and so on
- Sales forecast, and so on.

Information needs and the sources for such information (given within brackets):

- Total industrial volumes—TIV (competitor sales, annual reports, media, etc.)
- Company sales—previous years (MIS)
- Market share—previous years (OLAPS)
- Sales forecast (decision support system)
- Products' strengths and weakness (market survey, customer feedback, competing products' brochures, etc.)
- Customer preferences (market survey, customer feedback, 'pull market' strategy, etc.)
- Customers buying power (economic indices, per capita incomes, cost of living, inflation, etc.)
- Market trends (customer/channel feedback, 'pull market' strategy)

7.4.2 Production

Critical success factors/key result areas:

- Produce quality products
- Optimal utilization of production resources like men, materials and plant and machinery
- Do right value addition for which the customers are willing to pay
- Production cycle time to be the least (minimum work in progress)
- Implement right quality assurance techniques
- Maintain production history so as to track product complaints to its origin

Decisions:

- Production schedule (for all days in a year)
- Plant and machinery capacity utilization schedules
- Material requirements
- Manpower requirements
- Logistics and movement of products at right time
- Quality control techniques/methods to be followed

Information needs and the sources for information (given in brackets):

- Production targets (sales—budget)
- Production cost (finance—costing)
- Product characteristics/requirements (market survey/competitors product specifications)
- Production techniques (competitors, vendors and current technologies)
- Source of supply for all input materials (industry, vendors and Internet).

7.4.3 Procurement/Materials Management

Critical success factors:

- Buy materials at rates that sustain end product prices
- Buy quality materials
- Maintain database of current and prospective vendors
- Keep identifying cheaper and better sources for all inputs
- Maintain minimum inventory of raw materials
- Strict and close control on surplus/obsolete stocks
- Conduct value engineering on all inputs

Decisions:

- Right vendor/right material selection
- Cost of materials to be procured and EOQ

- Purchase schedules
- Inventory carrying costs
- Ideal stock levels for all raw materials

Information needs and the sources of information (given within brackets):

- Material specifications (product specifications brochures/standards)
- Sources for all inputs (enquiries, brochures and Internet)
- Delivery schedules (production plans)
- Quality inspection norms for inputs (engineering specifications, industry norms)
- Value engineering for all materials (vendors/industry norms)

7.4.4 Finance

Critical success factors/key result areas:

- Funds to be made available at right time
- Least cost of funds
- Ideal debt/equity ratio
- Accurate/transparent accounting and profit reporting
- Statutory compliance related to finance
- Effective management of all assets and assets safeguard
- Good investment management
- Effective cost control
- Cordial investor relations
- Preempting financial risks
- Prompt debt servicing and payments to suppliers, and so on

Decisions:

- Funds/cash flow requirements
- Where and when to borrow and the interest rates
- Investment decisions
- Cost control methods
- Selling price, and so on

Information needs and the sources for information (given in brackets):

- Business funds requirement (sales budget, procurement budget, etc.)
- Statutory compliances (government and statutory regulations)
- Levels of financial controls (management directives)
- Source of funds and costs (banks and financial institutions)
- Cost of products (financial accounting systems)

7.4.5   Personnel (HR)

Critical success factors:

- Flat and thin organization structure
- Clearly defined job specifications
- Objective recruitment
- Right compensation to attract best talents
- HR career planning
- Performance appraisal and compensation
- Establish accountability for all employees

Decisions:

- Organization structure
- Employee costs to turnover ratio
- Recruitment policy and recruitment decisions
- Employee compensation
- Performance appraisal criteria

Information needs and the sources for information (given in brackets):

- Employee costs (industry survey, recruitment agencies)
- HR sources (Internet/recruitment agency/media/educational institutions)
- Employee performance (performance appraisal, responsibility accounting)
- Employee morale (exit interview, open house)
- Type of personnel to be recruited (functional heads/job specifications)
- Appraisal system (industry norms, management policies).

All business processes/operations that are automated in business, through integrated business application software package (IBASP) have been listed in Sections 5.2.4 and 5.3.4.

SUM UP

The logical steps involved in identifying right IT solutions for each department or business function can easily be understood by the business managers having specific domain knowledge.

Knowledge of IT applications discussed in Chapters 4, 5 and 6 and specific applications listed in Sections 5.2.4 and 5.3.4 would help managers in identifying right solutions for their respective functions.

8

DESIGN AND IMPLEMENTATION OF INTEGRATED BUSINESS APPLICATION SOFTWARE PACKAGE (IBASP) FOR BUSINESS
Software Development Life Cycle Activities—SDLC (Waterfall Method)

Chapter Quest

The following questions would guide the readers in navigating through this chapter:

1. What are the ways by which integrated business application software package (IBASP) could be developed/acquired and implemented in business and the merits of each such alternative?

2. What is SDLC and what are the activities involved in it (steps leading to the design and implementation of IBASP)?

3. What are high level design (HLD) activities and what is accomplished through them in terms of 'As is' business study, the requirement analysis, requirement specifications, systems analysis, feasibility analysis, system design and systems specifications?

4. What are the roles to be played by the business managers in developing highly useful, reliable, effective and efficient IBASP?

5. What are the quality assurance techniques that need to be followed while implementing reliable IBASP?
6. How the software development skills/efforts are estimated and how IBASP project costs are computed?
7. How to design and choose right IT Infrastructure and how their costs are estimated?
8. What are the processes involved in getting the software projects approved by the top management?
9. What are the low level design (LLD) activities performed through programming, testing, documentation, implementation and maintenance of IBASP?
10. What are other activities that are to be completed prior to the implementation of IBASP (in terms of installation of computer resources, creation of database, training the business users and so on)?
11. What are the alternative ways by which the IBASP could be implemented and made operational and what are relative merits of each alternative?
12. What are the activities involved in system maintenance, data backup, ensuring of data integrity and systems audit (post implementation) of IBASP?
13. What is end-user computing and what are the merits and demerits of this alternative?
14. What is outsourcing of software development (SDLC) and when such alternative should not be attempted by the business?
15. What are the situations conducive for the business to go for ERP solutions?
16. What is configuration management and what are the steps involved in effective configuration management?
17. What are SDLC project metrics and measures and why they are used in software projects?
18. What are the objects that are delivered to the business at the end of the IBASP project?
19. What is rapid application development (RAD) methodology?
20. What are joint application development and waterfall methods?
21. How small businesses need to acquire application software?

After finishing this chapter, the readers would have clear answers for these questions.

8.1   INTRODUCTION

Integrated business applications (IBA) software is an important and intellectual entity in business and its usefulness, reliability and quality depends on how it is developed. This chapter dwells in great detail on the steps involved in getting the best IBA software for business.

Integrated business application software package (IBASP) automates most of the business processes and integrates all business functions. It enables close coordination and collaboration among all employees and provides real-time information for the managers. It is also referred to as enterprise integrated applications (EIA) or simply integrated information systems (IIS).

IBASP can be implemented in business by any of the four ways mentioned below:

1. A fully customized IBASP can be developed from scratch in-house if necessary skills are available within the organization.

2. A fully customized IBASP can be developed from scratch through third party SW development service providers.

3. An ERP (enterprise resource planning package like SAP, etc.) can be acquired, customized and implemented.

4. An IBASP which is in use in similar industries and which meets the company's requirements can be procured and used straightaway (generally done by the banks and insurance companies).

Eight steps of SDLC activities discussed in this chapter are necessary for the first two options. For options 3 and 4, all eight activities are not warranted. Some other methodologies that can be used in business are also discussed at the end of this chapter.

Software engineering is a technical, intellectual and creative process involving eight SDLC activities that need to be performed one after the other (waterfall method) in a systematic way to produce the end product, viz. IBASP. Waterfall method is discussed in section 8.16.

IBASP in its fold will have:

- Hundreds of application programs (thousands of automated processes)
- Common user interface (GUI) menu driven
- Database consisting of hundreds of files related to business entities and events
- Relational database management system (RDBMS)
- Hundreds of input formats in different mediums
- Hundreds of output formats including business documents in different mediums.

A fully operational IBASP would be automating most of the processes listed in Sections 1.1.3, 5.2.4 and 5.3.4, by way of EDP, OLTPS, MIS, OLCPS and EIS, discussed in Chapter 4.

Software engineering demands good knowledge, expertise and skills involving

- The business domain, its objectives, processes and interaction with internal and external entities
- Software engineering skills
- Current and emerging IT trends and their usefulness to business
- Quality assurance techniques leading to reliable and efficient IBASP (hundreds of programs)
- Methods of ensuring reliability, accuracy and integrity of business data
- Effective and efficient software project management
- Scope and functions of systems audit
- Documentation standards for all SDLC activities
- User-friendly GUI, user manuals and online HELP for all users.

IBASP projects may vary in size, depending on the extent of automation and the complexity of the business processes.

Software development life cycle (SDLC) consists of eight milestone activities, viz. High level design (HLD) activities:

1. Requirement/Systems analysis and requirement specifications
2. Infrastructure design, project costing and implementation time estimates
3. System design and specifications

Low level design (LLD) activities:

4. Programming and testing
5. Implementation of IBASP
6. Documentation and system maintenance

Support activities:

7. Life cycle support activities

Post implementation:

8. Systems audit

Other methodologies associated with IBA discussed in this chapter include

- End user computing
- Ready to use application software packages and ERP
- Application development (IBASP) outsourcing
- Customized IBASP—merits and demerits
- Rapid application development (RAD) methodology.
- Joint application development
- Application software for small business.

The activities to be performed under SDLC are discussed exhaustively in the following sections.

8.2 REQUIREMENT ANALYSIS, SYSTEMS ANALYSIS AND REQUIREMENT SPECIFICATIONS

At the end of this activity, the scope of new IBASP and the extent of business process automation are clearly identified, documented and agreed among the business managers and software engineers.

This milestone activity involves the following sub activities:

1. 'As is' study of existing business/Requirement analysis
2. Systems analysis/Business process re-engineering
3. Feasibility analysis
4. Data dictionary/Logical database
5. Requirement specifications ('To Be' processes).

8.2.1 'As is' Study of Existing Business and Requirement Analysis

This activity enables the IBASP project managers and software engineers in understanding the existing ('As is' processes) business processes thoroughly so as to enable them mapping the most appropriate IT solutions/applications on to all such processes. Readers can review Section 1.11 where enormity of the business processes is illustrated.

'As is' business process study requirement analysis needs to cover the following:

1. **Exploitation of IT:** Emphasis at this stage is to exploit the existing and emerging technologies so that the business gets the maximum leverage out of them. Business process automation needs to automate the business processes to a great extent and provide right information to the managers. Extensive discussions including brain-storming sessions need to be held with all business functions and the managers (end users of IBASP). The business managers and employees are to be educated of the technology, its applications in business and their advantages beforehand. Readers can revisit Section 1.1.3 where potential contributions of IT to business are highlighted.

2. **All outputs from IBASP:** IBASP as a system consists of three components viz., input, process and output as shown in the diagram below. A computer output is a collection of data elements assembled together and presented in a specific format and medium to meet the requirements of the business. All outputs like business documents, statements, MIS reports, ledgers, books of accounts, and so on are to be identified and finalized in consultation with all business functions. This is the most important and a threshold activity in a software project because the outputs decide all computer processes and the inputs.

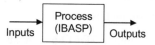

All outputs need to be identified in terms of:

- Unique identification (serial) number, name and description
- The format (identifying all data elements that are to be assembled together indicating their relative positions) leading to better readability and comprehension
- The mediums like paper prints (plain or pre-printed stationery), VDU and electronic/computer files
- The category of output, viz. MIS, query, business report, statement, document, ledger, register, and so on
- Frequency of processing (daily, weekly, monthly, annually, on demand, etc.)
- Business use/users for all outputs.

Note: Please refer MIS formats 1 and 2 discussed in Section 2.3 for better understanding of the formats. This and all other activities discussed in this chapter are highly laborious and computer-aided software engineering (CASE) tools discussed in Section 12.13 are made use of to automate these activities as well.

3. **MIS contents and formats for each business process:** Information needs of managers at all levels and functions, which would enable them in taking right decisions, are to be evaluated and designed. Identification of the information needs of the managers have been discussed in Chapters 2 and 7. The effectiveness of managerial decisions depends on the contents, quality, reliability and availability of right MIS to the managers. This involves great efforts to be put in by business managers.

It is to be noted by the readers that **activities 2 and 3 are the most important** activities while developing an IBASP.

4. **All input data:** The availability and sources of all input data that are required to produce the desired outputs are to be identified and recorded. This would also involve identifying, the data structures, complexity involved in the collection of the data, the computer process to be performed on such data, and so on. Efforts involved in data collection, entering them into computers and ensuring data integrity are also to be assessed.

All inputs need to be identified in terms of

- Unique identification (serial) number, name and description
- The format (identifying all data elements that are to be fed together and indicating their relative/specific positions)
- The medium like document, computer files and other input devices, and so on

5. **Business process automation:** The objective at this stage is to automate the business processes at optimal levels. The processes that can be automated are discussed in Section 1.1.3. In addition to this, tactical applications discussed in Chapter 4, strategic applications discussed in Sections 5.2.4 and 5.3.4 and IT applications related to management functions discussed in Chapter 6 are to be included in the scope of IBASP.

6. **Reliability and availability of computer resources:** All business functions/ employees/managers who are likely to use IBASP (users), their locations, time periods for which the computer resources are to be made available to them (like 24×7 or 9 to 5 basis), degree of reliability for the computer resources, etc. are to assessed. If IT resources are highly critical for running the business (like manufacturing, banking, railway reservation systems), fault tolerant systems are to be designed.

7. **Data storage volumes:** Volumes of operational data related to all business entities/events and historic data in the form of data warehouse are to be assessed to decide disk storage and data back-up resources.

8. **User interview:** Employees and managers of all functions are to be interviewed so as to include their BPA requirements within the scope of IBASP. They need to be told and convinced of all benefits the business would derive by virtue of new IBASP. This needs to be documented extensively using CASE tools.

9. **Continuation of existing applications:** Existing IT applications which need to be replaced by new IBASP and those that can still be continued are to be identified. Possibilities of upgrading the existing application software (software re-engineering) to take care of the new requirements of the business also need to be assessed. This would reduce the cost and time required for developing new IBASP.

10. **Industry-peer comparison:** The extent of usage of information technology by the peer industries and competitors and the benefits derived by them also need to be assessed. Business organizations can be forerunners in adopting IT, but cannot afford to lag behind the competition.

11. **Supply chain integration:** All interactions the business has with the supply chain entities such as the suppliers, customers, market channels, retail outlets, banks, etc. are to be studied. Possibilities of integrating the entire supply chain through SC-IBA are also to be assessed.

12. **Interfaces:** Of other strategic IT applications discussed in Chapter 5, the applications that could be interfaced with the new IBASP are to be identified and necessary interface needs to be included in IBASP.

13. **Management participation:** The management policies and strategies need to support information technology initiatives. The management needs to stay committed to IT initiatives and allocate sufficient funds to IT projects. They need to entrust the authority and responsibility to a senior position in the organization to spearhead all IT initiatives. This has also been stressed in Section 6.14.

14. **Documentation of requirement analysis:** Exhaustive documentation needs to be done by the software engineers and the project leader covering all the above issues and get the same approved by the respective functional heads. This document needs to be exhaustive and easy to understand as this is the basis for subsequent life cycle activities. CASE tools discussed in Section 12.11 are used in this process.

8.2.2 Systems Analysis/Business Process Engineering

Systems analysis is a process of examining the business processes with the intent of improving the business's

- Effectiveness (optimal utilization of business resources)
- Ease of management
- Efficiency (speed of operations)
- Competitiveness
- Responsiveness (speed of getting adjusted to markets and customer expectations)
- Profitability/Return on investments (ROI)
- Cost of operations and cost reduction
- Innovative products and processes
- Customer satisfaction, brand image, and so on.

Systems analysis is also referred to as business process (re)engineering, wherein the existing business processes are critically examined by asking questions like, why this way and why not some other way? who does it and why not some other person? where it is done why not some other place? when it is done and why not earlier? and so on.

Though systems analysis and business process (re)engineering are to be done on a continual basis, it is better done at this stage since all such requirements could easily be incorporated in the scope of new IBASP. Modifications to IBASP later will be more costly and time-consuming. IBASP needs to incorporate the best business practices at first instance.

This activity requires good assessment of existing business processes and the problems faced, excellent business domain knowledge, managerial expertise, innovative ideas, creative thinking, change management, and so on.

Systems analysis is to be done both with respect to business and technology.

Systems analysis—business perspective

The following activities need to be done at this stage:

1. Business process automation needs to be extensive as it speeds up the business processes, saves manual efforts, ensures automatic compliance to business rules, incorporates best business practices and leverages the business as indicated in Section 1.18.

2. Employees and managers need to be told of the changes to be made to the business processes, arising out of new IBASP. They need to understand the ultimate benefits IBASP would bring to the business and willingly participate in all SDLC activities.

3. Identifying right MIS (attributes of ideal management information has been discussed in Chapter 2) for each manager is a challenging task as it needs to be designed for each decision making situation in business. MIS should reflect the true status of the business in real time. MIS needs to be accurate, reliable and complete. There should not be information overload on the managers.

4. Incorporation of effective cost and other management controls and establishing accountability among all employees and the managers are also to be taken into consideration.

5. All programmable decisions are to be identified and automated as this would enable employees and managers with lesser skills to perform the business operations.

6. It is necessary to incorporate all business/statutory rules, procedures and policies in IBASP, so that they are complied with automatically with no exception.

7. Simple user interface (GUI) to make average business users comfortable in interacting with IBASP, sufficient training, user manuals and on line 'Help' are to be provided.

8. Exhaustive system and integrity controls are to be incorporated in IBASP (abled to be managed by the business users with ease) in ensuring the accuracy, integrity and reliability of the application programs and the data, as discussed in Chapter 9.

9. Business needs of IT are to be looked at as total system (top down approach) and all business functions as sub systems to understand the interaction between the sub systems and the flow of decision/information/resources/control among them. The business processes also need to be understood at the department/micro levels (bottom up approach). New IBASP should be aimed at bringing better synergy by integrating all business functions and IT applications.

Systems analysis—technology perspective

The following technology related issues need careful evaluation at the system analysis stage:

1. **Application architecture:** Right application architecture for the business needs to be identified, from the alternatives discussed in Section 12.17. The application environments in terms of the operating systems, RDBMS, CASE and front end tools and the programming languages need to be identified rightly.

2. **Computer architecture:** Appropriate computer architecture needs to be identified for the business from the alternatives discussed in Section 11.11.

3. **Network architecture:** Network architecture required for IBASP needs to be chosen from the alternatives discussed under Section 11.12 and associated networking hardware are also to be identified.

4. **Communication mediums and bandwidths:** Among the wired mediums like coaxial cables, ISDN, PSTN and the fibre optic cables and wireless mediums like VSAT, microwave links, 3G (discussed in Chapter 11), etc. right medium needs to be chosen based on the volumes of data flow, reliability and costs. Backup/standby mediums also need to be in place for business critical applications. For each remote location, the bandwidth requirement needs to be estimated based on the transaction volumes and sufficient speeds need to be provided.

5. **Integrated application software:** The mode of acquiring the IBASP needs to be finalized out of four options discussed in the beginning of this chapter.

6. **Data security:** Security of the business data, based on their confidentiality and sensitiveness, needs to be ensured. Various alternatives like data or record or file level locking and access control through user id and password, biometrics, RFID cards, data encryption, etc. need careful evaluation. These issues are discussed in detail in Chapter 10.

7. **Data quality, accuracy and integrity controls:** Extensive integrity controls need to be built into the application software to ensure quality, accuracy and integrity of business data at all stages of data processing, viz. data capture, data manipulation, computations, programmed decisions, information reporting, printing of business documents/statements, data backups/restoration and so on. (Various types of controls and systems audit issues have been discussed in Chapter 9.)

8. **Data creation efforts:** Data feeding efforts (manual process) in capturing the data related to all business operations and time required for the same are to be assessed. Sufficient computer and manpower resources need to be provided for database creation. If the data is to be taken from the electronic mediums/data migration, additional programming efforts need also to be identified. Various methods of capturing data are discussed in Section 13.18.

9. **Number of users:** Number of business (operational) users and the managers, their locations and duration for which they will be entering the data or accessing the information or taking print outputs or performing various other processes are also to be estimated. Computers need to be provided for all such users and also make provisions for additional users who are to be added later.

10. **Supporting infrastructure:** The supporting infrastructure like power generators, UPS, structured cabling, air conditioners, fire alarm systems, physical security, etc. are also to be finalized.

11. **Interface to other systems:** Types of interfaces to be provided to the other existing and new systems and other manual processes are also to be decided.

12. **User competence:** Levels of training to be given to the users and capabilities of users in learning the computer operations are also to be assessed correctly. Training programmes, on line help and user manuals are to be so designed such that people with low IQ levels are able to manage all automated processes.

13. **Infrastructure for the creation of new database:** Computer and software resources are also required for creating the new database consisting of master (business entities) data and open transactions (business events) data while implementing new IBASP.

14. **Infrastructure for software development and testing:** Computer resources, RDBMS, case tools, etc. are to be in place for software development and testing throughout the life cycle activities.

15. **Resources for training the users:** Users need to have hands on training on the fullfledged working of IBASP. Computer resources with test database need to be in place for the users to gain good experience and confidence in using new IBASP.

16. **Preliminary flowcharts:** It is necessary to develop data flow diagrams (DFD) indicating the flow and direction of business data between all business entities both within and outside the business, system flowchart as discussed in Section 4.3, decision tables, etc. at this stage to have a good understanding of the business and computer processes. Dataflow diagram has been discussed in Section 4.14.

8.2.3 Feasibility Analysis

The feasibility analysis needs to be made in terms of technical, financial, administrative, organizational, functional and other statutory/regulatory aspects before the project is initiated. However, feasibility is not a deterrent while implementing IT applications in business today.

1. **Financial feasibility:** The project needs to be financially and economically feasible and necessary funds need to be made available for the project. For example, small business cannot invest on IT infrastructure required of IBASP/ERP or E-business applications.

2. **Administrative feasibility:** Top management needs to support all activities associated with IBASP and also needs to fix responsibilities and assign authority among all business functions for timely implementation of the project. Management needs to spearhead IT projects. If the management support is lacking, the organizations would resist changes brought out by IT applications. Employees' cooperation and participation in all SDLC activities also need to be ensured by the top management.

3. **Technical feasibility:** The computers, computer networks, operating systems, RDBMS, communication infrastructure, etc. required by IBASP are to be available within the country including the maintenance support. Installation of computer infrastructure at all remote locations and reliable communication bandwidths to connect them also need to be feasible. The computers and the database need to be protected from sabotage, hacking, 'phishing', computer virus, and so on. Data encryption/decryption should ensure security and confidentiality of business information communicated across the networks.

4. **Organizational feasibility:** It should be possible for the people to be trained in the usage of the new IT applications. All employees need to operate the IBA on

their own. IBA may change the working styles of the employees and they should be willing to accept the changes arising out of it (e.g., trade unions may have to be taken into confidence).

5. **Statutory and regulatory feasibility:** New information technology initiatives like e-business, supply chain integration, CRM, etc. need to conform to statutory and regulatory laws, rules and regulations of the respective countries. Rights of all external entities interacting with IT applications need to be protected and safeguarded.

6. **Functional feasibility:** New IBA needs to be made operational for all business functions and the external entities associated with business. The customers, suppliers, market channels, employees, managers and all other external entities need to work with the new system with ease and without exception.

8.2.4 Logical Database

1. **Logical database:** All data elements (thousands of them) associated with various business entities and events that are to be captured by IBA (as required/identified by the business managers in the process of requirement analysis) are called the logical database. Logical database has been discussed in detail in Sections 2.14 and 13.6.

2. **Data structure/attributes:** Data structure/attributes of individual data elements need to be fixed as explained in Section 13.3.

3. **Responsibilities:** Logical database is to be conceptualized and constructed by respective functional managers purely based on the business requirements (like MIS or operational or statutory requirements). They are the custodians of the logical database. They need to fix responsibilities for the creation and update of individual data elements and their access rights.

4. **New data elements:** When existing business processes undergo changes or better processes are introduced, it would become necessary to introduce new data elements or alter the attributes of existing data elements. The logical database is also to be modified accordingly. Logical database is maintained in the computer so that the business managers and the software engineers are able to share and update it.

5. **Data dictionary:** The process of converting the logical database into data dictionary and physical database are discussed in Section 13.6.

8.2.5 Requirement Specifications/'To Be' Processes Documentation

This is the most important document in the project because it is the main and only interface between business managers and the technical team.

This is a detailed and exhaustive document prepared on completion of steps discussed in Sections 8.2.1 to 8.2.4. All the alternatives discussed under these sections are to be evaluated and finalized with respect to a given business and its operations. The factors contributing to final decisions are also to be stated.

Requirement specifications are prepared in two parts, one in business perspective and the other technical perspective. Step by step approach for the business managers in consolidating the business requirements of IT are discussed in Section 7.3.

Requirement specifications/'To be' processes are final statements of what the new IBASP would perform. It will include the 'As is' processes (as discussed earlier) fully and state all processes and the functions that will be automated through IBASP.

Requirement specifications—business perspective

This would clearly state the processes associated with all business functions that would be automated through new IBASP. This would also state the efforts to be put in using the IBASP and the responsibilities of all the business users in a (non technical) language clearly understandable and agreeable by them.

This document needs to be approved by the heads of all business functions (they should not be allowed to plead ignorance later).

1. **Automation:** The business processes/activities that would be automated through IBASP need to be stated clearly along with their merits. The processes that are **not** automated also need to be stated with reasons.

2. **Inputs:** All inputs and their formats as discussed under Section 8.2.1 need to be annexed to the requirement specifications. The responsibilities to enter input data, data validation rules, error correction procedures and reconciling the integrity controls (discussed in Chapter 9) as built into the system are to be stated and concurred with the respective users.

3. **Programmed decisions:** All decisions that would be automated through IBASP, decision rules/formulae, the data associated with such decisions, responsibilities for feeding the decision rules, etc. are to be clearly stated.

4. **Outputs:** All outputs that would be obtained from IBASP as discussed in Section 8.2.1 are to be annexed. The responsibilities for reconciling the integrity controls (discussed in Chapter 9) of all outputs are also to be stated and concurred with respective users.

5. The time frame for implantation of IBASP, the schedule for user training and other responsibilities of the users during SDLC are to be clearly stated in order to get their cooperation. Their efforts involved in the course of the project and in working with IBASP are to be clearly stressed.

6. Changes to the existing business processes or procedures and any other changes envisaged in the IBA need to be brought to the users' notice.

7. **Exceptions:** The processes that are expected to be automated by respective business functions but cannot be automated need to be stated with reasons.

8. **Errors in data:** All possible errors in input data need to be filtered by the software and erroneous data should never be allowed to enter the system. Users need to be informed of all such filters and the procedures for rectifying the errors and feeding the corrected data again without fail.

9. **Agreement between business functions and project leader:** At this stage, the project manager and the functional heads have to agree on the scope and limitations of the new application package. Their respective roles and responsibilities are also to be clearly stated and agreed.

10. The 'To be' processes/requirement specifications need to be fully documented and given to user functions for feedback, enhancement of its scope and approval.

11. Subsequent activities under life cycle methodology need to be initiated only when the users agree on the 'To be' processes/the requirement specifications and sign these documents as proof of their acceptance.

Requirement specifications—technical perspective

1. All technical issues discussed under Section 8.2.2 are to be carefully analysed and the best alternatives are to be chosen to suit respective business. Final decisions made on all these issues and the factors that contributed to such decisions are to be stated.

2. The preliminary system flowchart prepared and attached to the requirement specification should lead to costing of subsequent SDLC activities like system design, programming, and so on.

3. The architectures chosen for computers, computer networks, application software and communication mediums are to be clearly stated. The type of main computer, data storage devices, the operating system, the RDBMS, number of user computers, etc. are to be listed exhaustively so as to compute the infrastructure cost fairly accurately. The reasons for choosing each of these entities also need to be stated.

8.3 IT INFRASTRUCTURE DESIGN, PROJECT COSTING AND IMPLEMENTATION SCHEDULE

This is a crucial step, wherein the IT infrastructure required for implementing IBA including their costs, cost of developing IBASP, and time frame for implementing IBA are known. Based on the costs and the benefits the management gives their approval to proceed further with the project. The following activities need to be performed at this stage:

1. Infrastructure design
2. Software engineering—efforts and costs estimation
3. Project—cost estimation
4. Project measures and matrices
5. Management approval for the project

8.3.1 Infrastructure Design

Infrastructure design is a technical process requiring good knowledge of all the components of the IT infrastructure and relative merits and demerits of all the alternatives/architectures discussed under Section 8.2.2.

New IBASP would require investments in IT infrastructures in terms of:

- Computers (servers and clients)
- Operating system (software)
- Application software (IBASP)
- RDBMS
- Communication infrastructure (hardware)
- Communication mediums and bandwidth costs
- Web server, firewall server, etc.
- Support infrastructures like power generators, UPS, air conditioning, secured site for the server, and so on.

Infrastructure costs need to include both one time investments and recurring expenses for their operations and maintenance.

All the alternatives discussed under Section 8.2.2 are to be evaluated and the best suited infrastructure (after cost benefit analysis) is to be finalized in this phase.

Factors to be taken into considerations in the infrastructure design are:

- Processors, types and speeds
- Data storage capacities (volumes) and access speeds
- Business processes' response time
- One time and recurring costs
- Reliability of hardware and software
- Compatibility/connectivity of all hardware and software components
- Vendors' reputation/support
- Communication bandwidths
- Number of users
- Availability/reliability of IT resources to the users and so on

Selection criteria for the computer hardware and software are discussed in Chapters 11 and 12, respectively.

Computer infrastructure cost: Costs of computer infrastructure (one time and recurring) required for IBASP implementation need to be estimated based on the infrastructure design.

8.3.2 Software (IBASP) Development Efforts Estimation

There are different methods by which software engineering efforts and the costs of software projects are estimated.

But before that, we need to understand why IBASP is split into a number of independent programs (IBASP would consist of hundreds of programs), each one performing distinctively different business process/task.

We also need to understand that each program would consist of a number of program functions which in turn would consist of sequence of instructions arranged as per the program logic/algorithm to accomplish the task.

This hierarchy is illustrated through the following figure.

IBASP (huge software package)

100s' of programs, each performing a distinctive business activity

Each program having a number of program functions

↓

Each program function having a series of instructions written as per the program logic

1. **Programs under IBASP:** We have seen that IBASP consists of hundreds of individual programs. The reasons for splitting the IBASP into a number of programs are as follows:

   - The business processes taking place at different time periods,

     e.g. the materials received today are inspected the next day, accounted in stock the third day and the payment is made based in the due dates.

   - Activities are performed in a logical order (one after the other),

     e.g. materials received could be posted to the stock only after inspection.

   - Activities are performed by different departments or persons or places,

     e.g. for the materials received by the stores department the payment is made by finance.

   - Complex programs are split into a number of smaller programs to reduce the complexities of programming.

   Thus, IBASP is logically split into hundreds of individual programs.

   Programming takes the longest time in IBASP projects. The IBASP cost and time estimation is done based on the programming efforts. Costs of other SDLC activities are taken as certain percentage of cost of programming.

2. **Programming efforts estimation:** Programming efforts estimation could be done through any one of the following methods:

   (i) *Based on experience:* Estimation is done based on past experience/thumb rule. For each program, based on its complexity, the programming efforts are estimated in terms of hours by virtue of experience. This is not a scientific method and is not followed in big projects.

   (ii) *Estimation based on program variables methodology:* The efforts in hours are estimated for each program depending on the number of files accessed/updated/created, number of screen inputs accepted, number of outputs created, and so on. This is also not an accurate method and also not used today.

   (iii) *Function-point methodology:* This is the most popular method used in software projects in estimating the programming efforts and its costs.

   Programming efforts of each program are estimated based on the type and the number of functions performed in each program (functional decomposition of a program). Functional decomposition means breaking down of a program into logically different and non-redundant function like

- Input files/tables accessed/updated
- Data elements handled/manipulated
- Output files created
- Computations made
- Types of GUI provided to the users
- Formats for screen inputs and outputs
- Formats for print outputs
- Programmed decisions and so on

To understand this better a case study for functional decomposition of a program is explained below.

The process: A computer program validates suppliers' delivery note SDN (supplier delivery note accompanying the materials being supplied), is validated against the vendor and purchase order files before accepting the materials. Once the materials are accepted, this program prints the good receipt note-GRN (document acknowledging receipt of materials) and creates an electronic file for the same.

The system flowchart for the program is shown in **Figure 8.1** indicating various functions performed by this program.

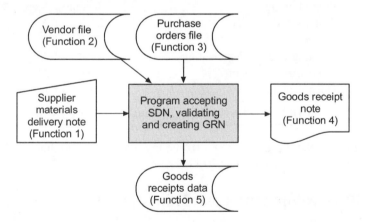

FIGURE 8.1 System flowchart depicting GRN processing.

The above program performs five logical functions as mentioned below.

Function 1: Accepting SDN data into the system

Function 2: Validating supplies against vendor data file

Function 3: Validating supplies against purchase orders/delivery schedules data file

Function 4: Printing of GRN document

Function 5: Creation of GRN data file

Function points: Certain standard weight, called **function points** (say x = integer value from 1 to 10), is assigned for each of the above five functions (performed by the program), depending on their complexity.

The sum total of all function points (of five functions performed by this program) is added up (x1 + x2 + x3 + x4 + x5) = X. 'X' points is converted into programming efforts in hours based on certain standards being followed in the industry, which gives, say, 'Y' hours of programming efforts for this program.

To Y, further weight is added depending on the programming environments like COBOL or Oracle or MS SQL or other programming languages, the programmer's experience and their skill. Let us take, say, 'Z' hours (= Y ∗ weight factor) is computed for each program. Z is the programming efforts in hours required for the program.

If this is done for all programs, we get man hours like Z1, Z2, Z3, Z4 ... for all programs covered under IBASP, whose total is, say, 'A' hours.

The estimation of time and efforts for other life cycle activities (like system analysis, system design, program testing, etc.) is worked out as percentage of 'A' as illustrated below.

(iv) *Total IBASP project time estimation:* The programming efforts for the entire project are worked out as A hours. The efforts required for other life cycle activities are taken as a percentage of the programming efforts A.

SDLC efforts	SDLC Man Hours
Programming	A hours
System design	25% of A
Testing	20% of A
Training and implementation	15% of A
Project management	10% of A
Documentation	10% of A
Total IBASP project efforts in hours	**1.80% of A**

For example, if the programming efforts involved are 100 hours, the total project software engineering efforts would be 180 hours.

8.3.3   IBASP Development Cost Estimation

The software development cost is computed based on the cost of programming and certain weight added for other life cycle activities which are relatively costlier compared to programming.

If the cost of programming is, say, ₹ C/hour,

Cost of programming for the entire project would be computed as	INR. 1.00 A∗1C
Cost of system design efforts taken as ₹ 3C/hour is computed as	INR. 0.25 A∗3C
Cost of testing IBASP is taken as	INR. 0.20 A∗2C
Cost project management effort is taken as	INR. 0.10 A∗5C
Cost of training and implementation effort is taken as	INR. 0.15 A∗1C
Cost of documentation effort is taken as	INR. 0.10 A∗1C

The total project efforts in hours are 1.8*A hours. Based on the programming costs per hour C, total IBASP development cost is computed as above.

Thus, software development cost for the entire project is computed. This is taken as the budget and the actual cost incurred in IBASP development is compared with the budgets through the process known as 'Metrics and measures', discussed next.

8.3.4 Metrics and Measures

Metrics is a process of setting the performance yardsticks for

1. All SDLC (software engineering) activities
2. Computer resources
3. Automated business processes

The expected performance targets are set for these entities and events before the commencement of the project. The actual performance is then measured when the project is completed, implemented and running. The actual performance is compared with the target values for all these entities. This is an important project control activity.

Project managers always insist their team members to establish metrics (and measures) for all life cycle activities, computer infrastructure and the automated business processes.

Examples of metrics and measures are given below:

1. **SDLC/software engineering activities**

    (i) For each program, the estimated programming effort (in hours) is set through the function point method discussed earlier. The actual time taken to complete individual programs is also measured.

    Similarly, the actual time taken for all other life cycle activities are measured and compared with original estimates.

    SDLC performance variance = Actual hours – Estimated hours

    If the actual hours taken are more than the estimated hours, the project performance is not considered good. Such metrics and measures could also help improving the accuracy of efforts estimation for subsequent projects.

    (ii) *Programs quality metrics:* Quality of the programs is measured in terms of 'defect code density', which expresses the number of defects per thousand lines of program source code. Generally allowed defect density is 2 to 5. Programs that have more defects density reflect bad programming.

2. **Computer resources:** Metrics are also set for the computer resources like, CPU utilization, data storage volumes, number of users, data communication bandwidths, and so on.

3. **Automated business processes—Computer process metrics:** These metrics are set to control the speed of the processes/system response time, which means the time required for the computer to complete a task. The designed response time is set for all business processes.

For example, the time to be taken for completing the employee payroll is set, say, x minutes during the design stage. Then, the actual time taken by the system in completing the payroll process is measured as y and compared with the process matrices already set.

It could also be for the number of transactions that can be processed per second through the system.

Metrics and measures are management control for software engineering activities.

8.3.5 Project Approval

The IT project costs of computer infrastructure and the IBASP needs to be approved by the management before the commencement of the project.

The proposal to the management needs to include the following:

1. **Existing business problems:** The business problems being faced (in the absence of right IT applications) like inefficiency/ineffectiveness of the business processes, losses to organizational resources, missed business opportunities, high costs of operations, time delays in product delivery/business cycles, and so on need to be stated.

2. **IBASP advantages:** The tangible benefits of the new IBASP, like the reduction in costs of operations, business cycle time, manpower, inventories, etc. are to be stated. The intangible benefits like quicker response to customer needs, employee morale, the brand image, etc. are also to be elucidated.

3. **Investments:** The investments required for implementing the new IBASP, both for IT resources and IBASP, both one time (capital investments) and recurring (operating expenses), are to be stated.

4. **Implementation schedule:** Time frame for training the users, conversion of existing systems into the new IBASP and the final schedule for implementation are to be stated.

5. **Responsibilities:** The responsibilities of employees/managers in the organization, who are responsible for all project activities, are to be stated clearly.

6. **Change management:** Organizational/procedural changes required to make the new IBASP operational also need to be approved by all business functions and the top management.

Top management may also seek the opinion of external consultants while approving the project. Once approved, the activities required for implementing IBASP would commence under the leadership of a project manager nominated by the top management.

8.4 SYSTEM DESIGN AND SYSTEM SPECIFICATIONS

System design is a technical activity leading to detailed system specifications based on which the programming activities could commence.

System specifications are also important documents as they serve as an interface between the system designers and the programmers.

The sub activities under this are

1. Data flow diagram (DFD)
2. System design
3. System flowchart
4. System specifications
5. Systems audit issues and data integrity controls
6. Quality assurance in design, programming, testing and implementation

8.4.1   Data Flow Diagram

The data flow diagram depicts the movement of data/information/decisions in a business organization, between various business entities, functions, locations and computer systems. It is a pictorial representation of the flow of data encompassing all business entities. It also indicates the source, intermediate storage and destination for all business data, the process carried out using them and the type of action being initiated (refer case study 4.14).

Data flow diagrams can be drawn at macro and micro levels. It helps visualizing the physical information systems in its entirety in business.

8.4.2   System Design

System design is a technical, intuitive, intellectual and creative activity requiring both business domain knowledge and software engineering skills. System design involves decisions/finalization of the following activities.

1. **Output design:**   Directory of all the outputs from IBASP, their formats, contents and the mediums with unique identification for each output as discussed in Section 8.2.1 is to be prepared. Individual formats need to be approved by the business functions/managers.

2. **Input design:**   Directory of all the inputs to the IBASP, their formats, contents and the mediums with unique identification for each input as discussed in Section 8.2.1 is to be prepared. Individual formats as approved by the users are to be appended to the system specifications.

3. **Database design:**   It involves design of physical database through data dictionary and the logical database, consisting of master files (for the business entities), transaction files (for business events), decision tables, and so on.

    (i)   All data elements of the logical database need to be logically grouped into

        (a) Master data (of entities), like suppliers, customers, etc.

        (b) Transaction data (of the business events like sales, purchase, etc.)

    (ii) Other data elements to be added to special tables are,

        (a) Parameter data (like M for Male, F for Female)

        (b) Decision table (like sales tax based on the products)

The process of converting the logical database into data dictionary, physical database and RDBMS are discussed in Section 13.6.

(iii) The file/table organization and access methods need to be designed in order to have quick access and easy update for all data elements in the database (discussed in Section 13.4).

4. **Design of programs/system flowcharts**

(i) The business processes to be carried out by the entire application package need to be split into a number of individual programs as discussed under Section 8.3.2, i.e. IBASP is converted into hundreds of programs.

(ii) Individual programs need to be indicated in the system flowchart. The tasks to be performed by each program also need to be described.

(iii) All decision tables and business rules used in the IBASP need to be finalized. The data elements associated with each of these decisions need to be clearly stated.

(iv) Programmed decisions incorporated in the software and subsequent action initiated (automatically) in the system are to be clearly stated.

5. **Design of data integrity controls:** Integrity controls need to be designed for all critical processes and data elements as discussed in Chapter 9.

6. **Design of data security features:** A comprehensive system for ensuring data security needs to be designed. The access rights for all types of users, data/record/file locking systems, data encryption, user identification and password management systems, etc. need to be adequately incorporated as discussed in Chapter 10.

8.4.3   System Flowchart

Systems flowchart is the pictorial representation of all business processes automated through IBASP shown in a logical order in terms of individual programs along with all inputs and outputs for each program. System flowcharts for purchase and sales functions are shown in Sections 4.3.1 and 4.3.2.

System flowchart depicts:

- All the programs identified under IBASP, their names and numbers
- Tasks being performed by each program
- The logical flow of the business processes (showing the tasks performed by the preceding and the following programs) through all programs
- The files/tables (of the database) which are accessed/updated/created by each program

8.4.4   System Specifications

System specifications are the detailed technical documentation covering all issues discussed in this chapter so far. Since this is the document that enables the software engineers to proceed further with the programming and implementation, this document needs to be exhaustive and made very clear to all.

In addition to documenting all issues discussed/decisions made so far, system specifications should necessarily include the following:

1. **The business functions being automated:** The business functions/processes that are being automated including programmed decisions and MIS are to be described in detail. This section needs to describe the functions being carried out by individual programs. Critical programs are to be explained in greater detail.

2. **Exceptions:** The business processes that are not covered by the new application package need to be stated indicating the reasons for the same.

3. **Efforts in feeding input data:** Formats in which the inputs need to be entered into the system and the efforts involved are to be stated to enable the users to organize themselves for feeding the inputs.

4. **Decision tables:** The programmed decisions made through IBASP, the data elements associated in the decisions, decision rules/tables, action taken in the system for each decision outcome, responsibilities of maintaining right decision tables, procedures to be followed in ensuring their authenticity and integrity, etc. are to be stated.

5. All files/tables in the database need to be specified along with record layouts/ formats, file organization, access methods and key data elements. Relationships between the files are to be stated.

6. **Inquiry:** The types of information that can be obtained from the system through queries, the types of queries, scope of information obtained, etc. are also to be indicated.

7. **Computations:** The formulae used, the computational logic, action taken by the system based on the computed values, etc. are to be stated.

8. **Database creation:** The process by which the initial database consisting of the master data, decision tables, the opening balances, open ended transactions, etc. are created are to be stated. If manual efforts are involved in feeding such data, efforts and time estimates for the same are to be indicated.

9. **Integrity controls:** Integrity controls need to be put in place for the critical data elements like quantities and money values. To ensure accuracy and integrity of all such data elements, the type of integrity controls built in the system and the procedures to be followed by the users in ensuring this also need to be stated. Please refer the case study in Section 9.7.1.

10. **Implementation schedule:** The project manager needs to prepare the project schedule for implementing IBASP. The business functions and the external entities like the suppliers and the market channels are also to be told of the schedules.

11. **Demarcation of responsibilities:** The responsibilities of the business users and the IS professionals in terms of who is to do what and when are to be stated clearly.

12. **Data validation rules:** Data validation rules like range check, check against the list of variables, existence check, check digit, hash totals etc, for critical data

elements are to be stated. This enables the accuracy and integrity of the data as discussed in Chapter 9.

13. **Error data:** Errors, if any, in the input data need to be detected at the first instance. Users need to be told of all of data validation rules so that they feed the data, free from errors. Procedures for handling error data, its rectification and re-entry into the system are to be stated clearly.

14. **Retention of business data for on-line processing:** The master data would be retained in the system on a permanent/ongoing basis. The transactions/operations data related to the business events grow over a period of time. Based on the require-ments of the business, the transaction/operations data are maintained for a specific duration (say for 12 months). The transaction data pertaining to the previous periods need to be removed and taken to data warehouse. Such periods and the procedures are to be stated in the system specifications.

15. **Data backup procedure:** Backup procedures for the master and transactions data, periodicity for such backups, retention periods, the mediums, etc. are to be stated. People who are responsible for backup and restoration are to be identified and told of their responsibilities.

16. **Software backup:** Backup procedures for the application software, operating systems and RDBMS also need to be stated clearly. These activities need to be performed by system administrators or the computer operators.

17. **Standby systems/infrastructure:** Business processes being performed through the computers, though generally are reliable, they could fail due to any one or more reasons:

   ● Disruption in power supply

   ● Breakdown of computer hardware

   ● Malfunction of the application software

   ● Malfunction of the operating system, RDBMS, etc.

   ● Computer virus, sabotage, hacking, and so on.

   Various means by which the computer systems could be made fully reliable are discussed in Chapter 11. The working of the 'backup' systems and the procedures to be followed in such eventualities also need to be explained in detail.

18. **Manual system:** The business processes could also be continued using the manual system during such interruptions. Procedures for manual operations and subsequent updates in the system are to be stated.

19. **Security:** Various ways and means by which business processes, data, computer infrastructure, etc. are secured need to be stated (discussed in Chapter 10).

20. **IBASP project deliverables (summary):** The deliverables at the end of the IBASP project and what the project team would deliver to the business are to be stated. The deliverables would be like (not exhaustive):

(i) *System documentation.* Documentation associated with all SDLC activities under IBASP including requirement and system specifications.

(ii) *Application software.* Application programs both in source and executable forms.

(iii) User/operations manuals both in physical and digital form including on line help.

(iv) *Control procedures.* The procedures to be followed in ensuring the quality of all business applications including data integrity, the data backup/restoration, software maintenance, periodic fine tuning of the system, and so on are to be stated.

(v) *User training.* The levels of training to be given to the users at different levels, and the duration of training need to be stated.

(vi) *Assumptions.* All assumptions made by the system designers also need to be stated.

(vii) *Constraints.* Constraints if any, in terms of technology, investments, people, statutory regulations, external agencies need to be stated. Action plan needs to be in place when such constraints are removed subsequently.

(viii) *Responsibilities.* Responsibilities of the systems engineers and the users are to be stated clearly.

8.4.5 Systems Audit Requirements

Business organizations make investments in IT in order to gain good leverage and gain competitive edge from it. Hence, the management needs to be assured that the investments made in IT, bring commensurate benefits.

Management also needs to be assured that the IT applications implemented enhance organizational effectiveness, improve operational efficiency, support all management functions including decision making and management control, ensure data integrity and reliability, IT resources are made available to the business all the time, and so on. These are the concerns of system audit functions.

The needs and functions of the systems audit are discussed in Chapter 9. Necessary provisions are to be made in the application package at the design stage to enable the systems auditors to test periodically whether the IT applications have brought the above benefits to the business.

Integrity controls

Valuable and critical data related to business (like stock quantities, prices, payables, receivables, fixed assets, cash and bank balances, and so on) are stored in the computer database. Strict controls need to be exercised by all IT applications, to ensure that the data are right, reliable, accurate, and what it is, is exactly what it needs to be, not altered by anyway, anytime (data integrity). The integrity controls discussed in Chapter 9 are to be incorporated in IBASP at the design stage.

8.4.6 Software Engineering—Quality Assurance

1. SDLC activities are to be performed very carefully and defects, if any, encountered in any life cycle activities are to be identified and remedied immediately. All quality assurance techniques and CASE tools are to be used in the life cycle activities.
2. The extent of coverage of the 'To be' processes and quality of requirement specifications, system analysis and design, system specifications, etc. need to be evaluated by the quality assurance managers/engineers.
3. All SDLC activities are to be performed as per the established standards.
4. Norms for testing individual programs (unit testing) and entire application package (integration testing) need to be stipulated. Exhaustive test database incorporating all extreme conditions in the business data needs to be created. All programs need to be tested thoroughly before IBASP is implemented.
5. The tested programs are to be taken to the production directory (base line), having tight access controls.

8.5   PROGRAMMING AND TESTING

Programming is a critical activity engaged in creating an intellectual asset for the business in the form of IBASP. IBASP would become integral part of the business operations and management for many years. If not done properly it would lead to chaos in business. The following activities are to be performed at this stage:

1. Program specifications
2. Program flowchart
3. Programming
4. Program walk-thru
5. Program (unit) testing
6. Application package (integration) testing

8.5.1   Program Specifications

Program specifications are also the most important documents in SDLC because the quality of IBASP depends on program specifications.

A program performs a specific business task/process through computations, comparisons (logical decisions), programmed decisions, accepting input data, accessing and updating the database, data manipulation, creating new outputs, developing integrity controls, securing business data against unauthorized access, and so on.

Program specifications need to state all the tasks/processes to be performed by individual programs exhaustively and clearly with no ambiguity. The programming personnel need to understand the processes/tasks to be performed by each program very thoroughly. The objective for creating the program specification is to make the programmers produce good and quality programs (coding) right, at first instance. Subsequent modifications would delay the project and escalate the project costs more than proportionately.

The programs need to run without errors (bugs), i.e. it needs to perform exactly as stated in the program specifications and as expected by the business (program integrity). It also needs to run efficiently, i.e. it has to make use of the computer resources optimally and take minimum time in completing a task.

Hundreds of programs covered under IBASP would be in operation for many years. During this period, the business processes would undergo changes for valid reasons and accordingly the programs also need to be modified.

The program specifications are very important resource while making such modifications. The program specifications are also to be modified when the programs are modified. The program specifications are configurable items and need to be managed through configuration management, discussed later.

Program specifications need to include:

- Program number, name and brief description of it
- The inputs accepted (electronic mediums or keyboard) and the formats
- All the outputs generated, their formats and mediums
- All updates made to the database
- The computations made
- The rules and the formulae used
- The decisions made, the decision parameters and the decision tables
- Systems audit and integrity controls incorporated
- The operating system and RDBMS environments in which the program needs to run
- Database structures, file formats and relationships, file organization and access methods used
- Response time expected while the program is executed by business users
- Running of the program in batch or on line mode
- Usage of the program to be in stand-alone or network or Internet mode
- Types of security to be incorporated for users and the data
- Criteria for testing and creation of the test database
- Planned interrupts to be incorporated in the program, and so on

8.5.2   Program Flowcharts

Program flowchart is a pictorial representation of the program logic/algorithm and all the operations carried out by it. Program flowcharts are necessary to enable the programmers in clearly understanding the program logic and to improve its performance/efficiency. Program flowchart makes subsequent program modifications easy, even if some one else does it.

8.5.3   Programming

Programming is the actual coding of the computer instructions in a logical order/established algorithm using a programming language. The programs are to be written conforming to the syntax rules of the programming language being used (Program 'syntax' errors are detected by the language processors).

Logical errors committed in the programs cannot be detected by computers, unless the programs are tested with carefully created test data. Hence, it is necessary to produce error-free programs at the first instance. Programming, testing and fixing program errors (bugs) are intellectual activities demanding good IQ and programming skills. The program complexity depends on the number of lines of the program and the number of functions performed by it.

Programs should always be supported by good program specifications and the program flowchart. Thorough understanding of the programming language and formulating right program algorithm are necessary to produce efficient programs. Right database organization, the file structures and the access methods also contribute to the efficiency of the programs.

There is no automated mechanism to check whether the program is written efficiently or the logic used is correct. Hence, special care needs to be taken by the programmers in delivering efficient and correct programs.

8.5.4 Program 'Walk-thru'

This is the activity in which a programmer, after writing the program, reads the program source code line by line and goes through the program logic mentally, to ensure that

- Right instructions and right program syntax are used.
- The program will perform the intended task precisely and not otherwise.
- The program logic used is efficient.
- File organization is appropriate.
- Files are accessed and updated efficiently.
- There are no loose ends (dead ends) in the programs.
- Necessary explanatory notes are embedded in the program.
- The computations and the programmed decisions are correct, and so on.

This is the exercise to ensure that the programs run in conformation with the program specifications. Most of the defects could be rectified at this stage if this activity is performed with care. This could also be carried out by other programmers or the software quality engineers.

8.5.5 Program Compilation and Unit Testing

Programs written using the programming languages (source programs) need to be compiled and converted into an executable form (object programs) before they could be run on the computers. Compilation is the process of converting a source program into an object program (discussed in Section 12.7).

Unit testing

Each program is independently tested on the computer, using a carefully created test database presenting all business situations/conditions for which they are written. All inputs as expected by the program are to be entered into the computer. New outputs would be created by the program. The test database would also be updated in the process. The outputs and the updates need to be tested thoroughly to ensure that the program performs exactly as per the program specifications.

The computations, programmed decisions, logical decisions, etc. made by individual programs also need to be tested thoroughly. In addition to the programmer himself testing the program, an independent testing is also to be carried out by the software quality assurance team.

All the defects encountered while testing a program need to be recorded. The programmer needs to modify the program to rectify these defects. Individual programs need to be tested repeatedly until it is error free. The results of the program testing and subsequent rectification are also to be documented.

The defects density (errors per thousand lines of a program) targeted originally and actual defects density encountered while testing are to be compared as part of 'programming quality metrics'.

Please refer section 8.18 for other types of program testing.

8.5.6 Application Package (IBASP) Integration Testing and Moving to 'Base Line'

IBASP would consist of hundreds of programs having logical relationship to one another. Outputs of one program would be inputs to some other programs. Though individual programs are tested, there could still be defects when the programs are tested in relation to the rest. This could arise out of the defects, either in the system design or in system specifications or in program specifications or any other life cycle activity which had not been done correctly.

Hence, all programs under IBASP are tested together. In case of inconsistencies, concerned programs are to be modified to rectify such inconsistencies. The application package IBASP needs to be tested repeatedly until all such inconsistencies are resolved.

Once unit and integration testing is completed successfully, both source and executable programs need to be moved to a 'control area'/production directory (base line) on the hard disk. The programs should be protected from other programmers and unauthorized modifications. The control area/production directory needs to have tight access controls.

The results of the integration tests and subsequent rectification are also to be documented. Now IBASP is ready for implementation subject to the following activities which are also to be completed.

8.6 USER TRAINING, INSTALLATION OF COMPUTER RESOURCES AND IBASP IMPLEMENTATION

Once IBASP is tested fully, the other three entities associated with IBA viz., computer resources, business data and business users are to be made ready.

The activities to be performed under this are:

1. Business users training
2. Acquisition and installation of computer resources
3. Data conversion/migration
4. Business process conversion/parallel run

    5.   User manuals/operations manual

    6.   Intimation to business managers and the business associates

    7.   Implementation

8.6.1 Business Users Training

Once the IBASP is ready for implementation, the business users (operational users and the managers) are to be trained in the use of the new IBASP in their respective business functions/operations/processes. There are four types of users for IBASP.

Operational users

Operational users are responsible for feeding data, transactions processing and performing various other automated business tasks. They are also responsible for preparing the business documents (invoices, purchase orders, payment vouchers, etc.), statutory reports and statements, MIS reports, reconciling data integrity controls, and so on. Some computer operations like data backup, system start up and shut down, etc. are also entrusted to the users. They need to be trained on all such activities. They will have access/update rights only to the data (and not the programs).

They also need to be trained in identifying errors/problems encountered with application programs and the data. They need to know 'to whom' the problems are to be reported. In the case of complete system breakdowns, they should know how to use the standby systems.

It is a good management policy to entrust the responsibility of overseeing the activities performed by the operational users to the respective business managers.

Success of IT applications in business rests in their hands.

Business managers

Business managers would access information from IBASP. They need to have only access rights for extracting the information. Managers need to have good knowledge of all MIS available in the system and should be able to access it with least efforts. They also need to be trained in querying the database using simple SQL commands.

Top management

Top management would access EIS/BI (information dashboard), to guide them in taking strategic and tactical decisions. They need to have only access rights. Top management needs to have good knowledge of the extent of information made available through EIS/BI and should be able to access it in the form of charts, graphs and diagrams (tools for better perception). They need to have very friendly user interface with IBASP.

Computer operators

Computer operators are the people who will be performing the tasks common for all business functions from the main computer (server room) room. The tasks carried out by them could be like starting the server, taking periodic backups for the programs and data, performing batch oriented processes like pay roll, financial accounting, and so on.

8.6.2   Acquisition and Installation of Computer Resources

Implementation of new IBASP would require acquisition and installation of the following infrastructure (generally from different vendors):

- Computer servers/mainframe computer
- Client computers (network of PCs)
- Operating system
- RDBMS and front end and GUI tools
- Various input/output devices
- Networking hardware and software
- Communication mediums linking to network/Internet
- Support infrastructures like power, UPS, fire alarm and security systems

Since these infrastructures would require different time frames for delivery and install-ation, these activities need to be planned in advance so that all infrastructures are available as soon as the IBASP is tested and ready for implementation. It is necessary to ensure that all these entities are compatible to one another (as discussed under configuration management).

8.6.3   Data Conversion/Data Migration

Once IBASP in its entirety is tested and the computer infrastructures are in place, the business data need to be loaded into the new database designed for IBASP.

The business data would include the master data (data related to all business entities), business transactions (events) like receivables, payables, and so on and the decision tables.

Data could be loaded into the new system by:

- Converting the old database into new database (data migration)
- Posting the transactions in electronic mediums to new database
- Manual data entry from available records into the new database, and so on

Additional software has to be developed for this purpose and such efforts also should be included in the programming efforts estimation and costing.

When the new database is created, care needs to be taken to:

- Validate and correct existing data as per the requirements of the new IBASP.
- Collect and feed the missing data to ensure completeness/integrity of new database.
- Remove redundant data to ensure consistency of the new database, and so on.

The creation of a new database is an important task and sufficient care needs to be taken to ensure its accuracy, completeness, consistency and currency.

8.6.4   Implementation of New IBASP

The implementation of new IBASP would mean switching over from the existing system to new IBASP. There are four ways by which new IBASP could be made operational. Each method has its own merits and demerits. Most appropriate method suitable for each business needs to be selected.

1. **Parallel run:** The new IBASP is run on real business environments parallel to the existing systems (which could be either manual or automated). It is run either for a few days or weeks depending on the complexity of the business operations. The new processes, outputs, results, MIS, etc. obtained through new IBASP are compared with the existing systems. The accuracy, completeness and consistency of the all the outputs from the new system are to be checked and certified by all business functions.

This is the safest conversion process since inconsistencies, if any, in the new system are eliminated before its final adaptation. Even if major problems are encountered in the new system, the business still functions using the existing system without interruption.

But the parallel runs involve additional efforts to be put in by the users, since both systems need to be managed by them simultaneously. It would also involve additional costs.

Sometimes the people who are reluctant to accept changes incorporated in the new package, may develop a tendency to continue with the existing systems. This method cannot be used when the customers and the external entities are also interacting with IBASP, e.g. SC-IBASP, e-business, and so on.

2. **Direct cutover (conversion):** The implementation date for the new IBASP is fixed with the consent of all user functions and the management. On the conversion day, the new system is implemented and all business processes are carried out only with the new system.

This is the quickest method of implementing the new system and people are forced to change on the day one.

If all SDLC activities are performed perfectly and all the programs are tested thoroughly, this method of conversion can be adopted. The problems encountered in parallel run methodology are eliminated in this method. This method needs to be used when the new system interacts with the customers and the markets directly.

3. **Pilot approach:** When a business has their manufacturing or marketing operations spread across different locations, it is quite reasonable to implement the new system in one of the locations first and extend to other locations subsequently. This eliminates the drawbacks discussed in earlier methods.

This method is considered good since process improvements as suggested by the users at pilot locations can be incorporated in IBASP before it is extended to other locations. This is the best alternative for the business applications where the customers and the external entities are interacting with the new system.

For example, IBASP in banking sectors can be implemented at select branches first and extended to others when the systems are doing fine at pilot locations.

4. **Phase in method:** IBASP can logically be split into a number of modules for the purpose of phased implementation, e.g. OLTPS can be implemented first and the MIS in the second phase. This allows the users to adopt the changes slowly. However, the benefits envisaged in the new application package also will be delayed to the extent of phased implementation.

When the conversion is successfully completed, the system is ready for real time implementation. User manuals/operations manuals are to be made available to the users at this stage.

8.6.5   User Manuals/On line Help

IBASP should guide all users through a simple 'menu driven' interface. The menu at the first level should list major business functions like purchase, production, logistics, marketing, finance, HR, and so on.

All sub functions (departmental operations) within each business function will be listed at the second level of menu options and the actual business processes to be carried out/the tasks to be performed at the third level. The menu options should not go beyond 4 or 5 levels. Any business activity needs to be performed by the users, just by selecting an appropriate menu option.

And fully documented user manuals need to be made available to all business users before IBASP is implemented. User manuals need to be both in printed and electronic mediums (On line help). The user manual in electronic medium needs to be properly indexed and the users should be able to access the electronic manual based on the key words or based on the business operations being carried out by them.

The user manuals need to be exhaustive and need to include the following for each process:

- The name of the program/menu option to be used for each business process
- Input files that are accessed by the program
- New files created or updated by the program
- Data and other parameters to be entered during run time
- Naming standards for the transaction files/tables
- Various validity checks performed on the data
- The files that are to be backed up/restored before initiating the process
- The procedures for integrity controls to be checked and tallied
- Actions to be taken when exceptions are encountered, and so on

The user manuals could be of two categories:

1. User manuals for business users (separately for each business function),
2. Operations manuals for computer operators (discussed earlier).

8.6.6   Intimation to Managers and Business Associates

Employees need to be told of the changes in their work styles, new methods and procedures.

A business is always interfaced with its suppliers, channel partners, customers, banks, regulatory agencies and various external entities. When new IBASP is implemented, it will have an impact on all such entities. All business entities need to be informed beforehand of the changes the new IBASP would bring to respective business processes.

The changes could be like:

- New formats for the business documents like sales invoices, purchase orders, payment vouchers, etc.
- New formats for the data in electronic mediums (file transfers) which are interfaced with the applications used by the business associates
- Revised time schedules/targets for the completion of the business activities
- Approvals to be obtained from the statutory agencies for the new outputs/formats, and so on.

8.6.7 IBASP Implementation–Feedback

All business processes and operations carried out using new IBASP are to be closely monitored to check whether:

- All business processes have been automated as planned.
- MIS obtained is right and useful.
- The business users find IBASP very user-friendly.
- The system response time is quick.
- Application package runs without errors/bugs.
- User manuals are clear and easy to use.
- Business processes have been speeded up.
- Business associates are comfortable and agreeable to the new system.
- IBASP is reliable.
- Human efforts in running the business are saved considerably.
- All other business expectations are fairly accomplished.

Business managers need to advice the software engineers to modify IBASP suitably if any of the above objectives are not fulfilled.

8.7 IBASP—DOCUMENTATION AND MAINTENANCE

Once IBASP is implemented in business, the following activities are to be carried out regularly without let up.

1. Documentation of SDLC activities
2. System reliability
3. Backup systems
4. Projects measures and metrics
5. Post-implementation audit
6. Data backup
7. IBASP maintenance
8. Configuration management
9. Network/computer infrastructure maintenance and support

8.7.1 System Documentation

We have seen that IBASP is developed through SDLC activities involving different technical skills. The IBASP is an intellectual asset of the business. IBASP would be in operation for many years and the functioning of it should not rely on specific individuals. IBASP needs to function independent of individuals.

Hence, it is necessary that all life cycle activities are adequately/exhaustively documented as per the established standards. Software quality assurance teams need to develop the documentation standards and ensure that the project team is creating good documentation, as per the standards.

Documentation standards need to specify the numbering system to be adopted for all documents, formats, contents, version number and effective date of implementing the procedures mentioned therein. The documents also need to be managed through the configuration management (discussed in Section 8.7.7).

System documentation needs to:

- Cover all SDLC activities.
- Be exhaustive enough and easily understandable for others to make subsequent modifications easily.
- Ensure all subsequent modifications are updated in the documentation (configuration management).
- Be protected against unauthorized use/modifications.
- Be identified by unique SDLC activity, document number, version, section and page numbers.
- Have effective date of commissioning of changes in all sheets.

8.7.2 IBASP System Reliability

The reliability of IT application depends on the following entities:

1. **Computer hardware:** Computer hardware consisting of the processor, memory, data storage devices, monitors, PC's, printers, data back up devices input/output devices, etc. could fail due to electrical, mechanical, ageing, fatigue, bad maintenance and for other reasons and disrupt the business processes. If IBASP is to run with no disruption, certain redundancy needs to be built into computer resources, e.g. fault tolerant systems.

2. **System software:** Operating system, RDBMS, networking software (server and browser), etc. could fail due to software errors (software bugs) or when software gets corrupted due to the malfunction of hardware or computer virus. When any bugs are noticed (generally they are bug free), the vendors concerned need to be told of this to rectify such problems. If the system software gets corrupted, they need to be loaded afresh from the original/back up mediums.

3. **Application software:** Often we find that the failures of business applications are due to the errors in application software. To avoid this, application software needs

to be fully tested before implementation. Problems encountered in application software need to be reported to the software maintenance engineers, who can rectify the program errors by correcting respective source programs and testing them again. If they get corrupted due to hardware problems/virus, the right programs need to be restored from the baseline directory.

4. **Power supply problems:** Power failures, voltage fluctuations, power surges/ frequency variations, etc. would either stop the system as a whole or damage the hardware or corrupt the software. They could create havoc on data storage devices and the data stored in them. Installation of uninterrupted power supply (UPS), voltage stabiliser and standby power generators, etc. would solve such problems.

5. **Communication hardware:** Breakdowns in communication hardware like modems, routers and switches would affect the activities at the remote locations. It is necessary to maintain redundant hardware to take care of these situations. Physical communication mediums like cables, wireless mediums, VSAT, etc. could also fail. It will also affect business operations at the remote locations. It is necessary to maintain redundant communication links such that when one medium fails, the other can be used. Normally, the dedicated leased lines will have a standby ISDN link for this purpose.

6. **Computer virus:** Computer virus is the devil the technology has created for its own peril. There are hundreds of virus (villainous software) which could play havoc on the software and data stored in the computers. Care needs to be taken across the organization to protect computer systems and the applications from the onslaught of computer virus. If the system is inflicted with the virus, data storage mediums need to be cleared of all the data and programs (by formatting). Clean data and application programs are to be loaded afresh. Appropriate anti-virus software can also be used to rectify/filter/detect computer virus.

7. **Fault tolerant systems (FTS):** FTS consists of two independent computers systems each having their own CPU, memory, hard disks, database and the application software which are logically connected in parallel and all business processes are carried out independently and simultaneously on both computers. It is possible to house these computers at two different geographic locations so that the natural calamities, like fire, floods, earthquake, etc. at one location do not affect the other. This is also discussed in Section 11.11.

8.7.3 IBASP Project—Metrics and Measures

This has already been discussed in Section 8.3.4.

8.7.4 Post-implementation Audit

After implementing IBASP, the business processes need to be evaluated to ascertain whether the benefits as anticipated earlier (as stated in the requirement specifications) are realized by the business. The post implementation audit need to check:

- Extent of business process automation accomplished and the activities yet being carried out by manual process and the reasons for the same
- Accuracy of the computations and programmed decisions
- Usefulness and timeliness of the MIS being made available to the managers
- Response time for all automated processes
- Degree to which the stated objectives are realized in the business
- Safety of the organizational resources committed through new IBASP
- Reliability/availability of the computer resources
- Extent of usage of the computer resources during peak business volumes (like CPU time, data storage volumes, number of users, etc.), and so on.

Systems audit is also discussed in Chapter 9.

8.7.5 Data Backup

The procedures need to be clearly stated for backing up the data on to reliable mediums so that the data and the software stored in the hard disks, even if get corrupted or damaged, could be restored with least interruption to the business. Data back up procedure needs to cover:

- Schedules for periodic backups
- Incremental/full backups
- Data restoration procedures
- Responsibilities for performing data backup and restoration, and so on.

These issues are also discussed in Section 13.14.

8.7.6 Software Updates and Upgrades

The IBASP though has been designed to take care of business processes as stated in the requirement specifications, it would undergo changes to take care of the defects found in them (updates) and improvements (upgrades) for the following reasons:

- Business processes undergo changes as dictated by the external environments or to incorporate business process improvements.
- Program bugs get fixed.
- To improve throughput/response time of existing processes.
- To include additional MIS/other reports as requested by the business functions.
- To adopt to the new/better technologies.

Procedure for software modification

The IBASP consisting of hundreds of programs, which are in operation are in two forms, viz.

1. Source programs as written by the programmers
2. Executable/object programs that are used in the business processes.

Both are kept separate in well protected directories in the hard disk. When the programs are to be modified, the systems manager needs to assess the impact of such program modification on entire IBASP, the business and the users. Necessary approvals need to be obtained from the business functions for the incorporation of such changes. Systems manager also needs to work out the time schedule for such program modifications, testing and implementation.

The affected programs will then be requisitioned from the baseline system (library of current operational programs in source form). These programs will be copied to the development directory away from actual production directories. The development directory is under the control of the programmers/system developers.

The affected programs will then be modified to incorporate the changes as documented in the software upgrade/modification specifications. Activities like program modifications, testing, documentation, user training, etc. will again be carried out, before the modified program is made operational. The modifications carried out to the software also need to be updated in the respective IBASP documentation.

8.7.7 Configuration Management

A fully operational IBASP will have the following configurable items (items whose configuration or the structure or the attributes or the interfaces change independent of one another with respect to time). However, they need to be compatible to one another and function in unison all the time.

Configuration management ensures compatibility among the following configurable items:

- Computer processor, memory, hand disks etc.
- Operating system
- RDBMS
- Hundreds of programs under IBASP
- Communication hardware and the mediums
- User manuals
- System documentation
- The business processes

In the course of using IBASP, the above configurable items would undergo changes independent of others due to technological changes, innovations, product improvements, changing business environments, and so on.

For example, computer processors are identified by their model, name, release number and other technical standards like the clock speed, MIP's rating, etc.

Disk storage and other input/output devices are identified by their storage capacity, model number, interface standards, access time, data transfer speed, and so on.

The system software like the operating system, RDMBS, web server and browser are referred by their version and release numbers. The new releases need to be tested for its compatibility with other configurable items before they are put into operation.

The IBASP consists of hundreds of programs. Any program would undergo changes for the reasons discussed earlier. Programs are identified by program name, program number and the version number, e.g. MA104/001. The modified program will have to be given new version number, e.g. MA104/002 to distinguish it with its earlier version.

A new program being introduced will be given a new number, e.g. MA456/001.

When an existing program is modified or a new program is introduced, it needs to be compatible to the rest of the configurable items.

The user manuals and other system documents are identified by their respective document number, release number and the release date (effective date). If an existing document is modified, a new release number and release date is given to it.

All configurable items need to be compatible to one another all the time and produce the same results always. Old versions need to be taken out of operations.

Care of configuration management:

- Configurable items are to be managed such that the changes to any one do not affect the working of the rest.
- All active configurable software are to be stored in a controlled area of the hard disk with strict access control.

8.7.8 Managing Computer Resources (Network Support)

The computers, input/output devices, computer networks consisting of communication hardware and communication mediums, the Operating Systems, RDBMS, IBASP and the support infrastructures like A/C, UPS, security systems and so on need to be maintained properly for trouble free and uninterrupted business operations. This is necessary to ensure the reliability/availability of the computer system to the business all the time (24/7 basis).

The hardware failures need to be reported to respective vendors for speedy rectification. Appropriate maintenance contracts need to be in place for this purpose.

The problems encountered with the software need to be reported to the respective software vendors and these problems need to be rectified promptly.

The data storage mediums need to be properly administered (by database/system administrators) so as to get optimal utilization of available data storage space and faster data access.

8.8 LIFE CYCLE SUPPORT ACTIVITIES

8.8.1 Procurement of Computers

The factors that need to be taken into consideration while computer resources are acquired are discussed in Section 11.10.

8.8.2 Procurement of Software

The factors that need to be taken in to consideration while software resources are acquired are discussed in Section 12.16.

8.9 SYSTEMS AUDIT

Systems audit requirements related to all business processes need to be taken into consideration in SDLC activities. Systems auditors also need to be part of the software development projects.

System audit issues which are discussed in detail in Chapter 9 need to be given top priority while designing, implementing and running the new IBASP.

8.10 END USER METHODOLOGY

The business users in medium and small businesses, who are responsible for running the business, develop their own application software without depending on professional programmers. This is called end user application development methodology (end user computing).

Small and medium businesses which cannot afford in-house software professionals and big business where the efforts of central ITSD team are directed mostly towards corporate application requirements (not towards departmental requirements), lead to end user computing.

Availability of personal computers at affordable costs, highly user friendly application development tools like 4GL languages, electronic spread sheets, simpler DBMS packages and rich domain expertise possessed by end users have ushered in end-user computing. These tools are easy to learn and use, since they come with interactive and self-learning tutorials.

The business users, thus, are able to design, develop and implement applications by themselves. They can create their own database, access required information (MIS), print reports and develop fully functional departmental applications.

Since the software is developed by the domain experts themselves, such software gives best fit to the business processes. Because of the widespread popularity of the technology, the users also show keen interest in learning these tools and applying them in their work.

However IBASP or e-business type of applications cannot be developed through end-user computing.

8.10.1 Benefits

- Improved requirement determination for the software.
- User involvement in application development gives raise to job satisfaction.
- End user computing gives best fit to departmental processes.
- Ease of maintenance of application software.
- Cheaper application development skills since software engineers are costly.

8.10.2 Drawbacks

- Applications may not run efficiently since they are not developed by professionally qualified software engineers.
- Such applications are not integrated with other business applications.
- Lacks standards.

8.11   READY TO USE APPLICATION PACKAGES AND/ERP

It is possible to procure ready to use IBASP if it is being effectively used in a similar industry elsewhere and use the same package immediately if it meets the business requirements fully (out of box solutions). It saves lots of time and efforts involved with SDLC activities.

As an alternative, a good ERP package can be procured, customized and used in business. However ERP packages can not be used straightaway.

8.11.1   Circumstances When ERP Software is Chosen

- When the business wants to implement IT applications in its operations earlier and cannot wait for developing an IBASP.
- Availability of ERP which meets the requirement specifications of the business fully.

8.11.2   Merits of ERP Packages

- Efforts and time to be spent in programming and testing are greatly reduced.
- The ERP products which are in existence for long and being used by the business organizations around the world come with the best business practices incorporated in them.
- Software vendors supply periodic upgrades and updates to keep the business applications abreast of emerging technologies, like Internet and mobile devices.
- These application packages come with extensive documentation, user manuals and self learning tutorials.
- These packages make use of the computer resources efficiently. They also meet the requirements related to systems audit, data security and integrity.
- Users can observe these package in operation elsewhere (reference sites) and fully understand and appreciate its features and benefits before acquiring them.

8.11.3   Demerits of ERP Packages

1. **Customization:** Though ERP packages are massive in terms of business functionality (come with the solutions for many thousands of business processes) and the best business practices incorporated in them, they do not offer 100% out-of-the-box solution to any business.

Since ERP packages come with the solutions for thousands of business processes and any business needs to choose a few hundreds from them that suit their business requirements, these packages need to be **customized** by feeding right parameters (choosing from number of options for each business process) as applicable to the business in context.

This requires very rich business domain expertise and also thorough knowledge of all the capabilities incorporated in the ERP packages. In other words, it demands special skills of customization (selecting right parameters) before the ERP package could be implemented.

Bad customization would lead to confusion and chaos in business. While programming efforts are saved, it is replaced by costlier customization skills.

2. **Proprietary programming:** ERP packages expect the business processes to be carried out as per the procedures incorporated in these packages. If the business processes are to be carried out differently (like VAT, Income tax, etc. in India), other than what is possible through 'customization', it would involve additional programming using proprietary programming languages. Such programming skills are scarce and also costlier.

So, successful ERP implementation requires good 'customization' and programming using 'proprietary programming languages'. ERP packages also need to match the requirement specifications of the business.

8.12 IBASP DEVELOPMENT—OUTSOURCING

To avail of the benefits of the customized IBASP which gives best fit to the business processes, the management could decide to go for IBASP. If the software engineering skills are not available in-house, the organizations can go for outsourcing of all or some of the SDLC activities (using software development vendors).

8.12.1 Benefits

- The software development vendors have right technical skills in the current and emerging technologies. They also use quality processes in all SDLC activities.
- Since the vendors have to keep the clients satisfied all the time, they offer their best services.
- The quantum of application development services required by the business varies over a period of time and such services can be availed from these vendors as and when needed. In-house skills cannot be planned for such fluctuating demands.
- In addition to application development, the computer maintenance, computer operations, database and system administration, etc. can also be outsourced.
- The business can concentrate on its core activities instead of getting involved in information technology related issues.

8.12.2 Disadvantages

- The business would lose control on IT expertise/know-how and become dependent on the vendors.
- The vendor can have access to trade secrets of the business and could misuse the same.

- The vendor personnel may not be loyal to the business organization and may not be aware of the critical success factors of the business.
- The interpersonal relationships between vendor and the business organization could turn out to be fault finding and finger pointing for anything going wrong.

8.12.3   When Not to Outsource

- When the organizations need to focus on information technology applications that are strategically important and bring competitive edge to the business, such applications should not be outsourced.
- Applications where the rewards for excellence are high and penalties for failures are serious, such applications should not be outsourced.
- Applications which are very critical for the business should not be outsourced.
- When the organizations need to possess right IT expertise/know-how so as to gain competitive edge and for its future business growth, it cannot be outsourced.

8.13   CUSTOMIZED IBASP (Developed In-house or Outsourced)

8.13.1   Merits

- Since IBASP is developed using SDLC activities (software engineering), starting from the business requirements analysis, this would automate most of the business processes and give best fit to the business including the supply chain.
- IBASP upgrades and maintenance is easier and quicker since the source programs are owned by the business.
- It could be more user-friendly for the business users within and outside the organization.
- This is the desired route for the service industries like banking, insurance, retailing, airline/rail reservation systems and so on, as innovative business strategies could be rolled into IBASP.
- It is possible to build exhaustive controls in making the applications more reliable and accurate.
- Since the process overheads are less, these applications could give better system response time for all types of applications.

8.13.2   Demerits

- Business organizations need to meticulously perform all SDLC activities discussed in Chapter 8 and this may take 6 to 12 months depending on the requirements of the business.
- Business organizations and the management need to possess sufficient technical skills required for SDLC activities.

8.14 RAPID APPLICATION DEVELOPMENT (RAD)

Business organizations could also implement IT applications in specific business functions like sales, financial accounting, employee payroll, inventory management, etc. which are very critical to business and are to be implemented in a very short time. To do this, business organizations develop application software required for specific functions immediately. Enterprise wide automation is done at later stages.

This method enables business organizations to reap the benefits of IT immediately. This was generally done by the business organizations during the 1980s when affordable computers in the form of mini and super mini computers were entering the markets (as against costly main frame computers). Additional processes were automated later or in stages. Such applications could not bring in all benefits of IT discussed in this book, to business.

8.15 JOINT APPLICATION DEVELOPMENT (JAD)

Though JAD is a part of SDLC activities discussed earlier in this chapter, emphasis is made here again, to stress the need for the business users to be associated with all life cycle activities along with software development professionals. The responsibilities of the business users are to be clearly stated and agreed with them.

The business users are the human entities who are incharge for running day-to-day business operations, the managers and would also include the suppliers, dealers, wholesalers, logistic service providers, retailers and the customers when the scope of the application software is widened to cover such business processes. Customers are to be consulted necessarily while developing e-commerce applications.

The business users need to understand and agree the scope of the software, what processes that would be automated or not automated, input and output layouts, contents and formats, data entry efforts to be undertaken by them, data validation rules, procedures for rectifying the errors in data, ease of using the software and so on. The business users are to be associated with all life cycle activities and the feedback received from them need to be incorporated in the software without fail.

8.16 WATERFALL METHOD

Under waterfall method, SDLC activities are performed one after the other, the same way as the waterfall, which gets materialized only when one level gets filled up before water could cascade down the lower levels. Waterfall method is a proven, structured and systematic way of getting reliable and functional application software in place. But this method could not be useful when business requirements could not be established in advance with certainty like e-commerce applications which would see more and frequent changes as dictated by the customers and market environments and CRM applications which could evolve as good systems only over a period of time.

In such business situations software prototypes could be developed and tested much faster.

Advantages

- Delivers high quality and reliable software at the end of designated activities.
- Milestone activities get clearly defined with extensive documentation.
- Easy to fix responsibilities in terms of well-defined deliverables and project metrics.
- Best suited when the requirements can be stated fairly clearly in advance like manufacturing industries.
- Easy for the business users to perceive and understand how the new software would function meeting their expectations.
- Easy to manage and complete the software project in time.

Disadvantages

- Success or failure could be assessed only when all designated activities are completed.
- Business requirements need to be established fairly accurately in advance.
- Needs to be done by experienced people who have good business domain knowledge and technical skills. Else going back and forth of the completed activities would lead to higher costs and longer time.
- Unless one activity is completed the subsequent activities can not be started.

Note: Other methods used in software development such as spiral method, iterative and incremental development method, and Agile development are used in very specific instances. Since they are the combination of one or more methods already discussed in the book, they are not discussed separately here.

8.17   SOFTWARE FOR SMALL/MEDIUM BUSINESS

For small and medium business organizations planning to automate their business processes, it is not recommended to go through SDLC activities since they would be costly and more time consuming. Instead these organizations can adopt one or more of the following strategies:

- Buy ready to use application software which meets the business requirements fairly well or buy the software which is in use in similar business environments.
- Implement business applications through cloud computing architecture as explained in Section 12.17.
- Outsource software development and acquisition and maintenance of IT resources through third parties (vendors) as discussed in Section 3.2.2.
- End users can be encouraged to develop their own software in line with end user methodology discussed in Section 8.10.
- However while procuring computer hardware and application software, factors discussed in Sections 11.10 and 12.16 are to be taken into consideration.

8.18 PROGRAM TESTING-OTHER METHODS

Since program testing is a crucial activity ensuring trouble free functioning of application software, various other types of testing, as stated below, are also performed at this stage.

- Acceptance testing is done by the business users and customers to ensure that the software meets their requirements fully.
- Alpha testing is done to ensure the functionality of individual programs and also the overall software package.
- Beta testing is done by select business functions for whom the software plays crucial role.
- Black box testing is done by software quality assurance team and systems auditors based only on the requirement specifications.
- Regression testing is done to ensure that all errors encountered in the programs earlier are rectified promptly without exception.
- Security testing is done to ensure that business data, database, programs and other resources are well protected against unauthorized or unintentional misuse.
- Functional testing is done to ensure that software performs all business functions as intended by the business functions.

SUM UP

The readers would have got a good understanding of various methods by which IBASP could be acquired and used in any business.

The SDLC activities have been discussed so thoroughly the sincere readers would become as knowledgeable as professional systems analysts.

Readers would also have understood the circumstances when the business can opt for ERP packages and relative merits and demerits of such option.

It is also suggested that the best way of implementing IBASP is to acquire similar packages working in similar industries elsewhere which would not require SDLC activities to be performed (some banks do this).

Readers are exposed to another alternative, viz. outsourcing of SDLC activities, in order to gain the benefits of a fully customized IBASP. The relative merits, and the circumstances when this should not be done are explained.

Finally, the advantages of developing IBASP from scratch (either in-house or out-sourced) and merits and demerits of IBASP packages have also been explained in detail. These issues would guide top management in identifying right strategies in acquiring IBASP/ERP packages.

9

IT APPLICATIONS' INTEGRITY, AUDIT AND CONTROL AND ATTRIBUTES OF IDEAL IT APPLICATIONS IN BUSINESS

Chapter Quest

The following questions would guide the readers in navigating through this chapter:

1. What are the business expectations of IT and attributes of ideal IT applications in business?
2. What is systems audit and its' role in business?
3. What are the controls to be exercised by the top management and the head of IT services division?
4. Discuss various controls to be incorporated in the IT applications in ensuring integrity, accuracy, reliability and security of business applications and data.
5. What are the quality assurance techniques to be followed while implementing IT applications in business?
6. A few case studies illustrating the need for integrity controls in IT applications are also discussed at the end of this chapter.

After finishing this chapter, the readers would have clear answers for these questions.

The readers should be aware that the actions to be taken and the care to be exercised in implementing ideal IT applications in business have been stressed throughout this book.

9.1 BUSINESS EXPECTATIONS OF IT

Business organizations make huge investments in IT and implement a variety of applications in order to achieve broad goals viz:

- Speeding up the business processes/operations (efficiency) and to make the business highly responsive to the customer needs and market expectations.
- Ensuring optimal utilization of organizational resources and managing the business with least efforts (effectiveness) so as to offer products/services at affordable prices to the customers.
- Integration of all business functions including the supply chain such that the whole organization functions as one single monolith focussed on organizational goals, customer satisfaction and market growth.
- Making all employees and the managers knowledge workers enabling them to take well informed decisions.
- Exploiting the business opportunities offered by IT, Internet, wireless communication and mobile devices.
- Establishing profitable/win-win relationship with the investors, supply chain, market channels and the customers.
- The management needs to be assured of the quality, reliability and availability of all IT applications implemented in business.

In the process of gaining these advantages, sufficient system integrity and security controls are to be incorporated in all IT applications. Such controls are discussed in this chapter.

9.2 CHARACTERISTICS AND ATTRIBUTES OF IDEAL IT APPLICATIONS IN BUSINESS (20 Points Approach)

Let us discuss 20 important characteristics and attributes of ideal IT applications in business. The management, business functions, systems auditors and software engineers need to take these into consideration while planning, designing and implementing IT applications in business.

Though these issues have been highlighted throughout this book, these factors are summed up here to present a consolidated and single point of reference for the readers.

1. **Business process automation at optimum levels:** Business processes need to be automated to optimal levels including programmable decisions and management information. Since the manual process leads to delay, monotony and human errors (to err is human), it is necessary to delegate the same to the computers. The manpower instead needs to be deployed in more productive and innovative business pursuits. Automated processes also ensure strict compliance with the stated business rules and procedures and other statutory regulations.

2. **Right and real time information:**   Right information needs to be made available to all managers in real time so that they know precisely what is happening in business and take appropriate decisions that could keep the business on right track.

Information contents and the formats need to be carefully designed based on the type of the decisions to be made and the levels of the managers.

MIS should be sufficient, relevant, easily perceivable, conclusive and explicit. At the same time, it should not result in information overload on the managers. It should save managers' time and efforts in taking decisions.

3. **Quality/reliability of the data and application software:**   If a customized application software is developed, the software engineering activities (discussed in Chapter 8) need to be thorough and conform to quality standards and good documentation. Any shortfall of this could lead to serious defects in the IT applications.

If ready to use applications/ERP packages are bought, such packages need to meet the requirements of the business fully.

The reliability related to IT applications mean:

- The management information needs to be reliable and accurate since the business decisions are dependent on them. Wrong information should lead to wrong decisions and consequent losses to business.

- The business transactions/documents also need to be accurate and conform to business rules, since the transactions once completed cannot be re-enacted.

- Quality assurance and quality control techniques extensively discussed in the subsequent pages are implemented without exception.

4. **System availability/reliability:**   The IT infrastructure, including the computer networks and bandwidths, needs to have sufficient capacities to support all IT applications at peak business volumes and with good response time. The infrastructure needs to be reliable and available for the business all the time. Non-availability of IT infrastructure would lead to stoppage of business, loss of opportunities, and so on. For critical business applications, 'fault tolerant systems' need to be in place.

5. **Information security/confidentiality:**   Business information needs to be highly confidential and the access rights need to be given only to the authorized persons (on need to know basis). Access rights need to be controlled through strict user-id and passwords for all users.

6. **Data accuracy and integrity:**   Data accuracy and integrity are to be ensured at the data entry, processing and output stages. Necessary control systems need to be built in the application software to ensure this. User functions need to be fully trained in ensuring data accuracy and integrity through effective integrity control systems implemented for the purpose (discussed in subsequent pages).

7. **Conformation to organizational objectives:**   Information technology applications need to conform to organizational objectives and integrate all business functions and the supply chain in achieving this.

8. **Integration of business functions and collaboration among employees:** All business functions and the supply chain are to be integrated so that all of them are aware of what is happening in business all the time. The business operations to be performed, when and who to perform are to be made known to functions concerned all the time.

The business managers should be able to take collective decisions in dealing with dynamic business/market situations. The activities of individual business functions and the supply chain including logistics need to be synchronized.

IT applications should enable close collaboration among all the employees, managers and the external entities. IT should enable the networked groups to freely exchange and communicate the business progress and the bottlenecks with one another. IT applications should make the working of the groups highly effective and efficient.

9. **Business effectiveness:** IT applications should enable businesses to be managed with least resources and efforts. Best business practices need to be programmed into all automated processes. IT and the business opportunities created by it need to be exploited fully.

10. **Efficiency of business operations:** IT applications should speed up the business processes and reduce the time delays in all value addition activities. The elapsed time between the procurement of raw materials and the realization of sale proceeds needs to be kept to the minimum. Business needs to have efficient customer response management systems in place.

11. **System response time:** The infrastructure installed needs to have sufficient capacity and speed in order to complete the business tasks in the shortest time. The communication infrastructure and bandwidths also need to have sufficient speed and capacities.

12. **User interface, training and operations manuals:** IT applications need to have a very simple and friendly interface for all types of business users. All business users and managers need to be fully trained in using IT applications. The user manuals need to be clear enough to make them comfortable in using all IT applications. 'Self learning' tutorials need to be made available to them. There needs to be exhaustive 'Help' menu as part of the applications with 'search' facility for the users to get contextual help. Frequently asked questions (FAQ) and answers to them also need to be included under help menu.

13. **Responsibilities of business users:** The employee(s) who can perform each business process needs to be stated clearly and the same be captured in respective transactions. The business users need to be made accountable for their activities such that they cannot repudiate their actions subsequently. Passwords assigned to the users need to be kept confidential by each user.

14. **State-of-the-art technology:** Information technology is evolving fast and is bringing new benefits and applications to business. The technology needs to be exploited continually in order to get optimum leverage out of it.

15. **Selection of appropriate IT applications:** The management needs to lay down a clear strategy with regard to IT. A senior executive needs to be made responsible and accountable for all IT initiatives of the business. Right applications need to be chosen among all tactical and strategic applications discussed in Chapters 4, 5 and 6.

16. **Responsive organization:** By virtue of right IT applications, the business organizations need to be highly responsive to external business environments and their customers' needs, preferences and expectations (high performance organizations HPO).

17. **Compliance:**
    - The IT applications and the processes need to comply with organizational rules, policies and procedures.
    - The IT applications and processes should also conform to the national and international rules, laws and regulations.

18. **Assets safeguard:** By virtue of business process automation, the organizational resources are either committed or controlled through IT applications. All such organizational resources need to be safeguarded through appropriate and right control mechanism built into IT applications. Physical verification, managerial authorization and approvals are to be integrated with the IT applications.

19. **Systems audit:** All IT applications implemented need to be audited regularly and the scope and benefits of existing applications need to be enhanced all the time. Periodic feedback surveys need to be conducted among the business users and the external entities to achieve this.

Systems audit also needs to evaluate the usefulness and effectiveness of all IT applications. It should ensure that adequate controls are built into the applications to ensure accuracy and reliability. All assets and other resources managed and operated through IT applications are also to be safeguarded.

20. **Establishing and managing business relationship:** Internet and wireless technologies need to be exploited fully in establishing enduring business relationships with the investors, supply chain, employees, managers, market channels, customers, statutory bodies and the regulating agencies.

9.3 INTEGRITY OF IT APPLICATIONS

IT applications are constituted by five entities, viz. people, business processes, computer infrastructure, software and the data. Necessary controls need to be incorporated in the IT applications to ensure the integrity of all five entities. (These five entities are discussed in detail in Chapters 3, 11, 12 and 13.)

Integrity of people

- Only authorized people should be allowed to interact with the IT applications. All such employees and managers need to be given unique and confidential 'user id' and password and should be allowed to perform only the activities assigned for them. All such transactions should capture respective 'user ids' as audit trails.

- Responsibilities need to be clearly stated for all personnel associated with IT applications, viz. IT managers, software engineers, users involved in transaction processing, managers involved in accessing MIS, system auditors, system administrators, computer operators, and so on and all of them need to be made accountable for their activities.
- IT resources should not be allowed to succumb to employees' misdeeds either intentional or unintentional, fraud and external hacking. Sufficient and ingenious controls need to be incorporated in the application software suitably supported by manual/independent controls.

Integrity of business processes

- Management needs to ensure that well documented business procedure manuals exist for all business functions and are being followed without exception. The automated processes need to include the same in the application software.
- Management should establish transparency in all its operations and report true financial performance to the stakeholders, investors and regulating agencies.
- IT applications need to incorporate sufficient integrity and system audit controls in individual programs/business processes.

Integrity of computer infrastructure

- Integrity with respect to hardware refers to compatibility/perfect interface between the computers, operating systems, RDBMS, application software, GUI, networking hardware and software, communication mediums and the Internet.
- All the resources need to be protected from unauthorized use or access both within and outside the organization.
- Proper maintenance support (annual maintenance contracts) and configuration management systems are to be in operation to ensure integrity of computer infrastructure.

Integrity of application software

- Application programs need to be thoroughly tested and made error-free before implementation.
- All tested programs need to be moved to 'controlled directory' and only authorized personnel be allowed to access this directory.
- When the programs are to be modified, only the affected programs need to be released to the programmers. Once these programs are modified, they need to be thoroughly tested and only the tested programs be moved back into 'controlled directory'.

- The modified programs need to be identified by right version numbers and the earlier versions should be removed from controlled directory (configuration management).

Integrity of data (data need to be what it should be and nothing else and truly reflect what the physical business entity or event is)

- *Input stage.*   The data entering into the system need to be correct and complete in the first instance.

- *Processing stage.*   Only the authorized modifications (updates and manipulations) are to be allowed on the data. Data need to be protected from unauthorized modifications either intentional or non intentional either by the software or by the employees.

- *While held in storage or accessed.*   Data need to be secured while they are held in storage or are being accessed. Breakdown of the data storage mediums and the drives, data corruption due to computer virus or faulty software, etc. need to be taken care of. Damages caused by extraneous factors like humidity, fungus, physical storage environments also need careful consideration.

- *Output stage.*   Data contained in the outputs need to be checked and the integrity controls be tallied before the outputs are put into actual use.

- In the event of anything going wrong in the data in any of the stages mentioned above, there need to be ingenious system and manual controls in trapping such errors and rectifying the same at the earliest.

- Software engineers should be denied access to the business data and business users should be denied access to application programs.

Various system and manual controls that are to be exercised in order to make the applications and the data highly reliable are discussed in Sections 9.5 and 9.6 of this chapter.

9.4   INFORMATION SYSTEMS AUDIT AND CONTROL

Information systems audit and control is the process of collecting relevant details/evidence and evaluating them to determine whether the IT applications comprising business processes, application software, data, computers and people's performance meet achieving the business/ stated objectives.

It is a systematic method to enable incorporating all attributes of ideal IT applications (20 points discussed earlier) in all IT applications before they are implemented in business and also to testify the degree to which they are achieved subsequently. Systems audit needs to be a continuous activity.

IT infrastructure and the applications are to be periodically audited to ensure that:

- Stated business objectives of IT are met.

- IT applications are reliable.
- Data processed and the MIS provided to the managers are accurate.
- The business users are comfortable with the technology enabled applications.
- The technology is exploited to the maximum.
- Investments made in IT infrastructure bring in commensurate returns.
- Organizational resources are well protected and accounted.
- All attributes of ideal IT applications are realized.

Need for systems audit?

If the IT applications are not implemented with care and perfection, they may lead to one or more of the problem situations mentioned below:

- Errors in record keeping and wrong reporting
- Business interruption/delays and hence loss of revenue
- Wrong decisions leading to loss of business resources
- Fraud and embezzlement
- Excessive cost of products and business operations
- Lost revenue or opportunities
- Loss or destruction of assets
- Loss of organizational focus/disintegration of business functions
- Bad employee morale
- Violation of statutory rules and regulations
- Customer dissatisfaction and bad brand image
- Bad business relations with external entities
- Competitive disadvantage and so on

9.5   IT MANAGEMENT CONTROLS

Necessary and sufficient controls need to be incorporated in all IT applications to ensure that the business is safeguarded against all problem situations listed above. In addition, sufficient management controls are also to be in place.

9.5.1   Top Management Control

- Management needs to clearly state its policy with regard to IT, the extent up to which it will support the business now and in the near future.
- Organizational policies are to be clearly stated with regard to in-house development/ outsourcing of application software, the size of the IT division who will spearhead IT initiatives, IT applications that bring strategic advantages to business, and so on. Sufficient funds are to be made available accordingly.

- Management needs to support the information technology initiatives and create a senior executive position to be in charge of the IT services division and delegate necessary powers to them.

- The functional heads need to be made responsible for the successful deployment of IT applications in their respective business functions.

9.5.2 Information Technology Services Division (ITSD): Management Control

- ITSD needs to set its long-term and short-term objectives with regard to IT in line with organizational objectives. It needs to rightly map IT solutions on to the business processes such that the business gets best leverage from IT.

- ITSD needs to possess best software engineering (SDLC) skills and adopt right quality assurance techniques and documentation standards.

- ITSD needs to ensure that all IT applications implemented bring in the attributes discussed under Section 9.2.

- Need to possess in-depth knowledge of the technology and also the business domain.

9.5.3 General Controls to be Followed by ITSD

- All data and programs need to be backed up regularly onto reliable mediums and stored at different locations.

- Computer centre operations need to be carried out by experienced personnel and they need to maintain the log of all the operations. In case of breakdowns, the maintenance agencies need to be notified. People need to be trained in disaster recovery.

- Appropriate security systems for the computer resources, data and programs need to be implemented.

- Computers and communication networks need to be reliable and necessary redundancies need to be provided for critical business applications (e.g., disk mirroring, fault tolerant systems, etc.).

- Power supply needs to be backed by UPS or generators.

- The operating systems and RDBMS need to be reliable and should be capable of taking up additional loads (scalability) of new/peak business transactions.

- The application software needs to utilize the IT resources fully and system response time should be quick for all business applications/users.

- As the technology brings in new and innovative concepts, the same need to be made available to the business.

9.6 IT APPLICATIONS/SYSTEMS INTEGRITY CONTROLS

Various controls that are to be incorporated in the IT applications to ensure that all five constituents involved in it are performing well in delivering quality applications are discussed below.

However, the controls discussed below are not exhaustive or conclusive as more and additional controls may have to be incorporated depending on the type of the applications being implemented.

9.6.1 Authenticity Control

- It is to be ensured that the business users, software engineers, computer operators, systems auditors, database administrators, network/maintenance engineers and so on, interact with IT applications only to the extent of the rights and responsibilities assigned to them. Wherever possible such rights need to be incorporated both in the application software and RDBMS.
- All users need to have 'read only' rights to the data, except the business users who need to perform data entry and database updates. Highly secured password controls are to be in place for such users.
- Modifications to the existing application software need to be performed only after necessary approvals from the user/IS managers are obtained.

9.6.2 Accuracy Control

- For critical numeric data elements like sales quantity, selling price, money values, etc. 'hash total' controls need to be implemented. The hash totals at each stage need to be tallied with manual totals or totals obtained through alternate software independently for this purpose.

Hash total: It is a simple arithmetic total of a given data element (which is in numeric form) contained in all records of a given file, e.g. the hash total of basic salary of all employees in employees' file.

All programs accessing or modifying the computer files need to print the hash totals for such data element before and after the process. Variations in hash totals need to be supported by the audit trails, e.g. the hash total for the basic salary for the employees in the employee file will show an increase equal to the basic salary of new employees who have joined the organization during the database update.

- All computed values like employee salary, invoice value, sales discounts, etc. and programmed decisions need to be checked thoroughly at program testing and parallel run stages. These values also need to be validated through other independent computations, either through alternate computer programs or manual calculations.
- It is to be ensured that all programmed decisions conform to the stated business rules/approved formulae.

- The responsibilities of creating and modifying the decision tables/formula need to be entrusted to the managers. The modifications made to them should have supporting audit trails printed on paper and the same be approved by concerned functional heads.

9.6.3 Integrity Control

Integrity of IT applications and business data mean their completeness, soundness, purity, accuracy and true reflection of physical business. Integrity related to five key constituents of IT applications have already been discussed in Section 9.3. Integrity controls with respect to the business data are discussed further below.

Data integrity, in other words, means that the data or information needs to be what it ought to be, no more and no less.

- **Range check:** Certain data elements can be validated against a range of values, which alone are valid, while they are entered into the computer. Data falling outside the range need to be shown as error (e.g., employee salary can only be in the range of ₹ 8,000 to 9,000 for a particular designation with increments of ₹ 100).

- **List of variables:** The data elements like percentage of tax, discount, etc. need to be picked by people from the list of variables displayed by the system. The users should not be able to feed any other values into the system.

- **Existence check:** The entities held in computer database are always identified by unique number or mnemonic code to avoid ambiguity. Data elements like employee number, product number, vendor number, etc. can be checked for its validity by ensuring such data is present in the database, e.g. when materials are received from the suppliers, existence of corresponding purchase order number needs to be checked in the purchase orders file.

- **Audit trails:** This is the technique in which the data elements that are modified in the database are printed with present and previous values. The modified values are to be manually checked in relation to the previous values. The audit trails are to be printed, approved by managers and filed permanently as proof of such change.

- **Manual validation:** This is generally done for the critical business documents like sales invoices, material purchase orders and payslips printed by the computers. These documents are manually verified and signed by competent persons as a proof of validation. Though it is a highly reliable control, it involves more efforts and time. To reduce the manual efforts, it is customary to perform manual validation for representative samples of such documents or high value documents.

- **'Checklist':** The data as entered into the computer is printed as a 'checklist' before they are processed. People need to go through the 'checklist' and validate the data entered into computer for its correctness. The 'checklist' needs to be signed by the person who validates it, as a proof of validation. The checklists are to be stored as permanent proof of validation and as audit trails.

- **Confirmation:** This is the method by which the data pertaining to the external entities, which are stored in the computer database, are printed periodically and sent to them for their concurrence, e.g. debtors and creditors statement of accounts.

- **Integrity controls:** Critical data related to business entities and events like stock quantities and values, amounts payable, assets value, receivables amount and so on are stored in the computer database. Extensive integrity controls need to be ingeniously designed and implemented to ensure that the data is correct and accurate always (please refer a case study in Section 9.7.1).

The possibilities for such data/information to go wrong could be due to any of the following reasons:

- Errors in application software

- The error committed by users while feeding input data or decision tables

- Unauthorized changes made to the application software/data (fraud)

The objectives of system/data integrity controls are to trap these anomalies instantly.

9.6.4 Completeness Control

Data elements entered into the computer, pertaining to an entity or an event, need to fully describe them, without missing the mandatory data elements. Examples of mandatory data for the employees are, employee name, date of birth, father's/spouse's name, designation, basic salary, and so on.

9.6.5 Redundancy Control

It is necessary to ensure that the transactions through which organizational resources are committed are performed only once and is not duplicated. For example, the goods' receipts note (GRN) for the receipt of the materials (from the vendors) needs to be prepared only once through the computer. System should not allow duplicate GRN to be printed in the system. When a payment is made for the materials supplied by the vendor, the suppliers' bill number needs to be tagged in the system so that the same bill is not processed twice in the system.

9.6.6 Data Security Control

- Confidential and sensitive data need to be made available only to the authorized persons in the organization. 'User id' and passwords are to be assigned for such users.

- Wherever necessary, data level/record/file level access are also to be controlled through user id and password.

- For data passing through computer networks, appropriate encryption/decryption needs to be done to protect such data against unauthorized access and modifications.

9.6.7   Existence Control

Management needs to assign responsibilities to the managers/auditors to monitor whether sufficient/necessary control systems and procedures are in existence and being followed without exception.

Examples of existence checks to be done are:

- System documentation is done as per the established standards for all SDLC activities.
- Data and software backups are done as per the documented procedures.
- Integrity controls are tallied by all user functions.
- The audit trails are duly verified, certified and filed.
- Exhaustive testing is done on all application programs and their results are certified by the system auditors.
- Physical security measures do exist at all computer sites and so on.

9.6.8   IT Assets Safeguarding Control

The computers and supporting infrastructures are to be safeguarded and protected all the time. The following needs to be checked towards this.

- Existence of annual maintenance contracts executed with vendors for the maintenance of computer hardware, software, computer networks and all other IT resources.
- The fire alarm systems are in effective use.
- The computer resources are appropriately insured against insurable risks.
- Inventory of all hardware and software are checked and verified physically often.
- Data and programs are backed up regularly.
- Support facilities like UPS, generators, A/C's, etc. are in working condition.
- Effective configuration management systems are in place.

9.6.9   Effectiveness Control

The effectiveness of IT applications needs to be audited regularly. For example,

- Cost/benefit analysis needs to be carried out once in a year to assess both tangible and intangible benefits of all IT applications versus their costs.
- All automated processes need to incorporate the best business practices and all processes are to be performed with least manual resources.
- User feedback to be obtained from all business functions so as to assert the effectiveness of the IT applications including MIS.
- Right information is to be made available to the managers at right time such that they need not chase the information.
- Managers are able to rightly perceive what is happening in business through appropriate MIS and become knowledgeable.

- For key business functions like purchase, production, sales, etc. noticeable reduction in business cycle time are realized (business efficiency).
- Information technology applications need to eliminate manual efforts and free the human resources to perform more productive/innovative tasks.
- Periodic feedback needs to be given to the senior management indicating the extent to which the stated objectives are met through IT applications.

9.6.10 Efficiency Control

- Business users need to complete the business transactions and the queries in a few seconds. RDBMS need to be fine-tuned periodically and unwanted data need to be backed up and removed from on line storage devices.
- IT resources need to be scalable to take care of higher business volumes.
- Suitable system performance evaluation software need to be used to keep track of levels of utilization of CPU, memory, disk storage, on line connect time of all users and so on. Periodic reports need to be taken from this software to identify system bottlenecks.

9.6.11 Testing Control

- All outputs obtained during program testing phase need to be documented and adequacy and sufficiency of testing needs to be evaluated by the systems audit/ quality assurance functions.
- Results of parallel runs and acceptance from the users need to be documented and approved by the systems auditors.
- Program bugs reported during the operations need to be recorded and corrected. Subsequent test results are also to be certified and documented as part of configuration management.

9.6.12 Documentation Control

- Adequacy and sufficiency of system documentation including the user manuals need to be verified and certified by competent persons.
- Documentation standards followed within the organization also need to be approved for its adequacy and sufficiency.

9.6.13 Preventive Control

- Wherever the data is coded, it needs to be short and mnemonic so that people do not make mistakes while using the codes. The codes need to be displayed along with their description.
- Data entry efforts need to be minimum and simple, so that people do not make mistakes while entering the data into the systems.

- Business users need to be made accountable for errors or mistake committed by them.
- All the data entered need to be validated by the software without exception.

9.6.14   Detective Control

- Input data, database updates, all processes performed by the application programs and the outputs are to be checked manually or through alternative programs regularly to detect possible errors.

9.6.15   Corrective Control

- When the errors are detected after an automated process is completed, immediate steps need to be taken to reprocess the same after restoring the input files from the backup and rectifying the causes of error.
- If some of the transactions are found to be in error after they had been posted on to the master files, suitable adjustment/correction entries need to be passed to rectify such errors.

9.6.16   System Controls

1. **Input control:** All inputs to the system need to have associative controls (for example, hash totals for numeric data, checklist for descriptive data and so on) and need to be ensured that the database is altered only to the extent of legitimate inputs fed into the system.

2. **Process control:** Computer process would involve updates to the database or creation of new records and such updates should conform to the input data fed into the system. Necessary controls (like audit trail) need to be printed for all such processes carried out based on the input data.

The process also would involve computations and programmed decisions. Appropriate and ingenious controls need to be printed by respective application software to ensure that all processes carried out by the application programs are always correct.

3. **Output control:** All outputs obtained through the application programs in the form of electronic mediums, business documents, statements, reports, etc. need to accompany printed integrity controls and the user functions need to tally these controls before the outputs are put into business use.

4. **Backup control:** Daily back up of the database, transactions and the application programs also need to have appropriate controls built into such activities to ensure that the back ups and restoration are accurate and reliable.

5. **Design of right and appropriate controls:** System auditors, software quality assurance engineers and user-functions need to design ingenious controls for all the four stages mentioned above.

The business users should be trained in tallying all system/integrity controls and ascertaining that all application programs run correctly and accurately.

9.6.17 System Audit Controls

Necessary provisions are to be made in the application software such that the systems auditors can test the system without affecting live business operations/data.

9.6.18 Quality Assurance

- Defects in the programs need to be identified and rectified at the programming and testing stages.
- The extent of coverage of the requirement analysis, requirement specifications, system specifications, etc. need to be assessed by the systems manager and the heads of the respective business functions.
- All activities associated with SDLC and their documentation are to be performed as per the standards.
- Norms for testing individual programs (unit testing) and all programs together (application package-integration testing) need to be stipulated before the system gets implemented. The programs need to be tested thoroughly before they are implemented.

Even though many control aspects have been discussed so far, it is once again brought to the notice of the readers that they are not all conclusive. A number of other ingenious and innovative controls need to be incorporated based on the type and complexity of the business applications and data.

9.7 CASE STUDIES

9.7.1 Data Integrity Controls Established in Materials Purchase and Supplier Bills Payable System

This case study is an extension of the case study discussed in Section 5.12.1 and the readers would be able to understand how the organizational resources are protected through data integrity controls incorporated in IT applications.

Logical activities involved in the process (repeated from Section 5.12.1):

1. Purchase orders are placed with the suppliers for the purchase of materials.
2. Materials receipts are acknowledged through goods receipt notes (GRNs) by the company.
3. Materials are inspected for quality and defective materials are rejected and sent back to suppliers.

4. Accepted materials (supplied-rejected) in GRNs (after inspection) are accounted in stocks.

5. The suppliers' bills are processed through the computers and they get paid (based on the GRNs' accepted quantities) through bank cheques and payment vouchers both printed by the computers.

6. The bills paid are accounted in the books of accounts.

The bills payable system processes hundreds of supplier bills and makes payments of millions of rupees daily. Exhaustive controls are built into the system such that the payment vouchers and the cheques printed by the computer are always accurate.

The table below shows the format in which the integrity controls are maintained in the computer processes of this case study.

Step	Activities involved in the purchase of materials and bills payable system	Hash totals for material quantities	Hash totals for material values
1	Purchase orders released for the materials	Q555	V555
2	Goods received as captured in GRNs' file	Q444	V444
3	Materials inspected and defective materials rejected	R111	RV1
4	Accepted materials taken to stocks—GRN's payable	Q333	V333
5	Materials for which suppliers are paid—GRNs' paid	Q222	V222
6	GRNs paid and taken to accounts	Q111	V111

This table is explained with respect to logical business activities performed in the purchase/bills payable system. The hash totals of quantities and the values shown in the table above will undergo changes only to the extent of the business activities performed in each of the stages listed above. The procedures related to data integrity controls are elaborated as below:

STEP 1: All purchase orders for the purchase of raw materials/inputs are captured in the computer file. Each order contains the materials ordered, quantity and order value. Any program accessing this file will print the hash totals (as explained in Section 9.6.3) for order quantity and order value summed up from all purchase orders (records) contained in purchase orders' file (Q555 and V555 shown in the table).

When a new order is added to this file, hash total for quantities and values of this file should show corresponding increase (only) to the extent of the new orders released. Purchase managers always tally these controls to ensure the integrity of purchase orders file.

STEP 2: The suppliers deliver the materials based on the orders placed with them. The system values the GRNs with the purchase orders and prepares goods receipts note (GRN) through the computer for each material received from the suppliers and the same is added to the GRNs file. The computer prints hash totals for the received quantities and values for all the GRNs contained in this file. When a new GRN is added to this file, the hash totals should show an increase (only) to the extent of the new GRNs added (Q444 and V444 as shown in the table). Thus materials management functions ensure the integrity of the GRNs file.

STEP 3: Inspection functions inspect the materials and rejects defective materials. These values are posted as R111 and RV1 in the table above. The quantities of materials sent back to the supplies are reconciled with this. The accepted quantities and payable values are updated in the GRN's file.

STEP 4: Stores department counts the materials received through each GRN, confirms the quantity and takes them into stock accounting and updates the GRNs' as payable. Such GRNs' quantities and the values become the payable (Q333, V333 shown in the table). Hash totals for the payable value is printed by the computer for all such GRNs and stores functions reconcile these totals.

STEP 5: When the supplier submits the bill for the material supplied by him, corresponding GRN records are identified in the GRN file and converted as paid values. The suppliers are paid exactly to this value. Hence, the computer prints the values of the bills paid from the GRNs file (Q222 and V222 shown in the table). These values are reconciled by finance functions.

STEP 6: When the bills are paid, the suppliers bills and associated GRNs' are accounted in the books of accounts, the GRNs file will show (Q111 and V111) as the totals of paid and accounted in finance. These totals are reconciled by finance functions.

Thus, the materials ordered, delivered, rejected, accounted in stocks, paid, and accounted in the books of accounts get reconciled by the materials and finance managers at each such process. This is how the business resources in the form of materials and money are safeguarded through IT applications.

If any other unauthorized processes take place in these files, these totals would show variances that can be detected by managers concerned.

9.7.2 Employee Fraud

This has happened in a company some time back. But it shows how people could beat control systems. But to understand this case study, readers need to understand some aspects of financial accounting systems.

Companies release payments to suppliers in the form of bank cheques. The cheque books are held in safe custody by finance managers and when the cheques are released, it is signed by two authorized signatories of the company. Cheques released by the company are cashed by the payees through their banks. Cheques released by the company are accounted in the books of accounts and also taken for reconciling with the company's bank passbook (bank statement). This process could lead to three possibilities as shown below.

Cheque issued by the company	Realized by the payees as shown in bank pass book	Values will be reconciled
Cheque issued by the company	Not realized by the payee	Waiting time for realization
Cheque **not** issued by the company	Realized by the payees as shown in bank pass book	Possibility of fraud. Payment needs to be investigated (AAAA)

(AAAA): This is one situation described in this case study.

Journal vouchers: Journal vouchers are critical accounting documents and are used for accounting of transfer of funds from one account to the other. This is an important document and needs to be signed by the finance managers entrusted with such responsibilities. Journal vouchers (JV) are created through computers and in some instances they are written manually. Such manual JVs are entered into the computer off-line and computer checklists are printed to ensure the accuracy of data entered into the computer as discussed in Section 9.6.3. When the checklists are corrected for data entry errors, such checklists are also to be signed (as audit trail) by the same finance manager. (BBBB)

BBBB: This is another situation of the fraud discussed in this case study.

A senior employee in finance function used to steal bank cheque leaves when the manager concerned went away from his seat for discussions or meetings. He used to forge the signatures of two authorized signatories and issued the cheques favouring a person who was his relative but living in a far away city. Such payments will appear in bank reconciliation as (AAAA) mentioned above, because these payments are not made by the company and hence not accounted in the books of accounts.

But the same person used to counter such situations by making unauthorized entries in the JV checklists after it is signed by managers concerned at (BBBB) stage mentioned above. When such entries are taken to accounts, situations arising out of (AAAA) are taken as reconciled. What a clever move by an individual and it was not detected for some time.

It so happened, that this person went on leave due to some unavoidable reason and could not make unauthorized entries in the JV checklists. Situation (AAAA) was detected by finance managers and the person was caught.

There are some frauds which cannot be detected even by strict control mechanisms, e.g. credit card and ATM frauds.

9.7.3 Manager's Unethical Practice

This was done by a regional manager not to gain any personal favours but to get best performance award from the company.

The company was selling its products to the dealers on credit terms, credit period ranging from a month or two. Each regional manager was managing the sales through hundreds of dealers in their region. Management directive to the regional managers is to collect money promptly at the end of the credit periods. Some dealers were prompt in payments and some others chronic defaulters. This created the problem for the regional manager concerned.

What he did was to collect the payments (cheques) from the regular dealers and credit them against those dealers whose outstanding are far beyond the due dates. For some reason or other, he never used to send the statement of accounts or the receipts to them and the dealers also did not care about it, as they are supplied the stocks as and when they required them.

This was revealed by the company' auditors when they audited these accounts.

SUM UP

Managers are generally aware that IT leverages the business to a great extent and also brings many competitive advantages. However, the readers now would have become aware of the attributes of ideal IT applications in business and the efforts to be put in by the employees, managers, top management and IT professionals in achieving such ideals.

IT is a double edged sword and if proper care is not taken in the design and implementation, it would bring more problems than benefits.

Readers would also have understood the need and functions of the systems audit and what the top management expects from the systems auditors.

Many facets of system controls and the need/importance of such controls are also discussed exhaustively in order to enable the readers to understand how such controls need to be incorporated in the application software (IBASP) during SDLC activities. This would also guide the readers in incorporating more ingenious, innovative and tighter system controls in their respective businesses/associative IT applications.

The case studies discussed at the end of the chapter would enable readers in appreciating the relevance of various controls and other security issues discussed in this book.

10

SECURITY OF IT RESOURCES INCLUDING BUSINESS DATA AND INFORMATION

The following questions would guide the readers in navigating through this chapter:

1. What is the need for securing the IT resources including business data and information?
2. What are the various security issues to be addressed by the business and what possible solutions are offered by the technology to this effect?
3. What is cryptography and how data encryption and decryption ensure confidentiality and authenticity of business data/information?
4. What are digital signatures and digital certificates? How they enable non-repudiation of business documents/agreements by the respective owners?
5. What are good data encryption and authentication procedures to be followed in the business?
6. What are various other issues such as firewalls, software piracy, cyber crimes, hacking, etc. that need to be taken care by the business?

10.1 INTRODUCTION—NEED FOR DATA SECURITY?

1. Business critical/sensitive information in digital form flows within and out of the business in electronic mediums all the time and they carry the risks of being accessed by unauthorized/unscrupulous entities (e.g., industrial espionage).

2. Many operating systems including network OS, and communication infrastructure like Internet, follow universal standards/open protocols to enable the computers to communicate to one another. Such protocols also enable unscrupulous entities to gain unauthorized access to others' computers, software and data.

Business organizations need to be cautious and pre-empt such threats since business processes and data transfers get completed so fast by the time such intrusions are detected, the damage is already done.

In this chapter, we discuss security and other related issues, possible solutions, and care the businesses need to take, to safeguard the computer resources and the data.

However, the subject discussed is this chapter has limited purpose.

10.2 SECURITY ISSUES CONCERNING IT APPLICATIONS IN BUSINESS

1. **Confidentiality:** When a message is sent electronically from the sender to the receiver, it needs to be confidential between them.

2. **Information or message integrity:** When a person receives the message/information from the sender, it needs to remain the same as sent by the sender and not altered on the way.

3. **Authentication:** For the receiver of the electronic message, the identity of the sender needs to be authenticated in terms of his personal id, password, private key (discussed later), fingerprints, digital signature, and so on.

4. **Non-repudiation:** Non-repudiation means undeniable proof of ownership for the document/message on its sender. The sender and the receiver cannot deny having sent or received the message.

5. **Access controls:** It means limiting the access to data and information resources, only to the authorized users.

10.3 SECURITY TECHNIQUES

10.3.1 Data Encryption

Data encryption is the process of encoding data for security reasons such that no one eavesdrops on them. The 'original text' is converted into an 'encoded text' via an encryption program using an encryption key (a string of bits). The 'encoded text' is decoded (decrypted) at the receiving end using the same key and the program and turned back into 'original text'.

10.3.2 Cryptography

Cryptography is the science of converting the 'original text' into 'encoded text' (encryption) using innovative algorithm/program logic and a secret string of binary digits (key bits). In other words, it is the process of sending the message in disguise over computer networks/ Internet. Encrypted message/text, depending on the program logic and the length of the key bits used, is either extremely difficult or totally not possible to decode or de-cipher.

The encryption program produces key bits, which is a binary number that can typically be from 8 to 256 bits in length. The more the number of bits in the key, the more are the possible key combinations and the more difficult to break the 'encoded text' (cipher strength). Complex program logic (mathematical algorithms) creates higher cipher strengths but takes more processing time to encode and decode the original text.

The original text is encrypted, by combining the bits in the key, mathematically with the bits of the original text. At the receiving end, the same key bits are used to "unlock" the code and restore the original text. If the 'encoded text' is intercepted, it cannot be read by any person not possessing the secret key. In order to understand the encrypted message, it needs to be decrypted using the same secret key.

There are various methods, standards and software used in encrypting the original text enabling different levels of security for the message/information transferred over the communications mediums/Internet. Three such methods are discussed in simple terms (cryptography is a big subject) to illustrate the process of encryption and decryption and their relative merits and demerits.

1. Symmetric cryptography (fast but not very safe)
2. Asymmetric cryptography/public-private key cryptography (safer but slow)
3. Combination of the two (to derive the benefits of 1 and 2 referred above)

The strength of the data encryption is dependent on:

*   Length of the key (number of bits) and number of keys used
*   Strength of the cryptographic program logic/software
*   The security involved in storing and forwarding of the keys
*   Number of scrambling cycles used

10.3.3   Encryption Program Logic

Encryption involves either an algorithm or mathematical formula used in turning the original text into secret text. The program uses a string of bits known as "key bits or key" to perform the calculations/conversions. It is obvious that the longer the key bits, the greater the number of potential patterns that can be created, thus making it harder to break the secret text.

Most encryption programs code fixed blocks of "original text", which are typically from 64 to 256 bits in length.

10.4   SYMMETRIC CRYPTOGRAPHY

It uses a common key at both sender and receiver ends. This key needs to be maintained as a secret by both parties.

It breaks the original text into 64–256 bit blocks before encrypting them. It uses the 64–256 bit key and converts them into 64–256 bit block of coded text. There are a number of symmetric encryption software in the market. Symmetric cryptography is very fast and widely used. The key which is to be kept a secret can also be used to repeatedly encode the original text any number of times (scramblings) and decoding also needs to be repeated same number of times. Or, a key can be randomly generated for each session, in which case the new key is to be transmitted to the recipient using a more secured system discussed under Section 10.5.

It is also possible to use more than one distinctive keys and the message be encrypted repeatedly with different keys. The receiver also needs to have all the keys and decrypt the message in the same order as it was encrypted. It should be noted that encryption and decryption involve additional processing time.

10.4.1 Symmetric Encryption Method (Ensuring Message Security)

The process of transmitting a message using symmetric encryption is shown in **Figure 10.1**. Though it is the fastest method, transmitting the secret key to the recipient needs to be highly secured. The strength of the encryption can be enhanced by increasing the block size of texts and the key and performing more number of scrambling rounds. The safety of this type of encryption depends on the users, on how secured they transmit and use the keys.

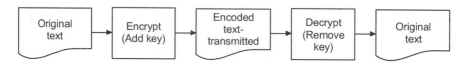

FIGURE 10.1 **Transmission of symmetric encrypted message.**

10.5 ASYMMETRIC CRYPTOGRAPHY (ENSURING CONFIDENTIALITY AND AUTHENTICATION)

Asymmetric cryptography involves a complementary pair of keys (key bits), a public key and a private key pair, known simply as key pairs.

The public-private key pair is obtained from a 'mathematical function' with an intentional 'provision for entry'. The mathematical function can be performed in one direction only and not possible in reverse direction. The 'provision for entry' makes the reverse computation possible if some precise information is known. Such precise information which uses the 'provision for entry' is the owner's secret (private key) password. Thus, one can freely publish his public key (which is a sure complement of private key) without the fear of the private key being derived out of it. One such method is discussed below.

The private key is kept only by the owner and the public key is published. Data is encrypted by the sender, using the recipient's public key (since it is known to public), which can only be decrypted by the recipient's private key. Only the receiver can do this, as he alone holds his private key.

Such programs are also implemented in hardware chips (firmware). As the chips get faster, the encoding and decoding also becomes faster.

●

10.5.1 Key Pairs Used to Provide Confidentiality

Each recipient has a private key that is kept secret and a public key that is published for others. The sender looks up the recipient's public key and uses it to encrypt the message. The sender is assured that the message can be read only by the receiver, because it is encoded with the receiver's public key which can only be decrypted by the receiver's private key. Thus, the confidentiality of the text is ensured.

The recipient uses his private key to decrypt the message. Users never have to transmit their private keys and hence are not vulnerable.

But the receiver is not sure that the message has come only from an intended sender. Anyone can encrypt the message using the receiver's public key. So, still the authenticity needs to be established. The process of transmitting a confidential message using asymmetric encryption is shown in **Figure 10.2**.

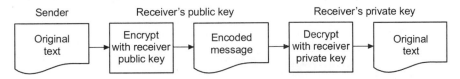

FIGURE 10.2 Transmission of asymmetric encrypted message (confidential).

10.5.2 Key Pairs Used to Provide Authenticity

The sender wants to ensure that only his message reaches the receiver. The sender encodes the message with his private key as he alone knows it. He sends it to the receiver who has the sender's public key and decodes the message with the sender's public key. However, published message does not have confidentiality as anyone having the sender's public key can access it. Transmission of asymmetric encrypted message which ensures authenticity is shown in **Figure 10.3**.

FIGURE 10.3 Transmission of asymmetric encrypted message (authentic).

10.5.3 Key Pairs Used to Provide Authenticity and Confidentiality

To combine authenticity and confidentiality, the encryption and decryption performed in Sections 10.5.1 and 10.5.2 are combined.

The sender can encrypt the message with his private key first and with the receiver's public key second. The double encrypted message reaches the receiver.

The receiver first decrypts with his private key and again decrypts with the sender's public key second time.

This is theoretically a sound mechanism to ensure authenticity and confidentiality. However, such conversions and re-conversions would take longer processing time. The larger the message, much more time for such conversions. Asymmetric encryption is not fast as the symmetric encryption, discussed earlier.

10.5.4 Combining of Symmetric and Asymmetric Cryptography

To reduce the processing time and at the same to maintain authenticity and confidentiality, a combination of symmetric and asymmetric key methodologies which provide more efficient and secured communications is used.

In this method, the message is encrypted (symmetric cryptography) with a key (1), by the sender and the encrypted message is sent to the receiver. The key (1) is still a secret and not known to the receiver. The key (1) is encrypted through asymmetric cryptography (digital envelope) by the sender and again decrypted by the receiver using the method described in Section 10.5.3. Since only the key (and not the text) is encrypted and later decrypted using asymmetric cryptography, this method is much faster.

10.6 DIGITAL ENVELOPE

Symmetric encryption provides the fastest decryption and asymmetric encryption provides a safe method for transmitting the secret key. So what is done is both the symmetric encrypted text message and the secret key needed to decrypt it using the asymmetric method are sent to the receiver. This is called a "digital envelope".

Asymmetric encryption is very computation intensive. Thus, it is often used to create a digital envelope, which holds an asymmetric encryption of symmetric key and symmetric encrypted message/information.

Cryptography techniques undergo rapid changes as the computers are getting faster. Any encryption code can be broken given enough computer time. However, it may take months to break a strong key. As computers get faster, the keys get longer and the program logic become more complex to make the message more secured.

10.7 HASHING

Hashing is yet another program logic (mathematical function) that turns a variable length text into a numeric value (hash value). In cryptography, it is a mathematical function that converts a text message into string of numbers. However, it is not possible to convert the numbers back into text. This number is called the original message's digest or 'check value'. If it is a single digit, it is called check digit. If the message is altered in any way, a different 'check value' will be obtained. Hash functions are used in creating digital signatures.

10.8 DIGITAL SIGNATURE

Digital signatures bind the message to the private key owner. Digital signatures are more authentic than physically signed signatures. Public and private keys are used in digital signatures. Since the private key is a secret code known only to the user, it binds him to his digital signature.

In order to compute the digital signature, hashing program is used to first compute a 'message digest' for the message. The message digest is a unique number that can only be calculated from the contents of the message. The message digest will vary when the message is altered.

The sender's private key is used now to encrypt the message digest. The encrypted message digest is called the (sender's) digital signature. The message concerned is considered to be digitally signed by the sender and binds the sender. The message's contents cannot be denied by the sender any time subsequently.

The message and the digital signature both are sent to the receiver. The receiver uses the sender's public key to decrypt the message digest received from the sender (say it is X). The receiver also uses the hashing algorithm to recalculate the message digest from the message received (say it is Y).

The receiver ensures that X and Y are same. If so, the message binds the sender (authenticated) and the message integrity is also validated. This provides for both non repudiation of origin and security of the message.

10.8.1 Digital Certificate/Digital ID

Digital certificates are issued by trusted third parties known as certification authorities after verifying that a public key belongs to a certain owner.

The digital certificate is actually the owner's public key that has been digitally signed by the certifying authority's private key. The digital certificate is sent along with the digital signature to verify that the sender is truly the entity claiming so. The recipient uses the widely known public key of the certification authority to decrypt the certificate and extract the sender's public key. Then the sender's public key is used to decrypt the digital signature. The certificate authorities keep their private keys very secure all the time.

10.9 CERTIFICATION AUTHORITY

To ensure authenticity of public and private key pairs, they are generally registered with a trusted third party agency called 'certification authority'. Key management and certification agencies are important players in authentication, message integrity and non-repudiation security processes. Such authorities are appointed and controlled by the Government agencies with statutory powers.

10.10 GOOD ENCRYPTION/AUTHENTICATION PRACTICES

Password management: Passwords are very useful in authentication and access controls. Password needs to be of longer lengths, beyond anyone's guess, needs to be kept secured and is to be changed often. If the passwords or private keys are not secured, the respective owner is accountable.

Key length: Key lengths need to be at least 64-bit long. For financial transactions, it needs to be at least 128 bits. Highly secured encryption algorithms use up to 256/512 bits.

Compressed files: In order to reduce the message transmission time, data is compressed based on certain program logic. If the files are to be encrypted, the files need to be compressed before such encryption to make the process faster.

Steganography: To improve the effectiveness of encryption, extra meaningless characters are inserted into the clear text message before it is encrypted. Extra meaningless characters are made known only to the recipients.

Smart cards: Smart cards have in-built microprocessor and memory. These cards are also used for authentication. The password and other user information are stored in the memory cards.

Two factor identification: This method which is generally used by the users of ATMs, combines two factors like ATM card and the PIN number to draw money from the ATM booths.

Challenge-response technique: This is an interactive procedure in which the user must prove something by answering a question to the other. The questions and the answers are known only to the user and the other person/system.

Biometrics: This is another form of authentication that requires some physical and unique characteristics of the users for identification. Finger prints, voice recognition, retina scans, DNA mapping, etc. would fall into this type of authentication.

Time stamps: Electronic documents can also be sent through e-mail service providers offering time stamping services. Digital time stamping is used to know the time in which a message was created/sent/received.

Confirmation services: Mail messaging services and the certification authorities provide additional services that provide the proof of delivery/origin of the message binding the individuals to the message. It is also possible for the confirmation service provider to attest to the integrity of the message through message digest.

10.11   FIREWALLS

Firewalls (servers) consisting of hardware and software provide protection/access control to the computer resources that are connected to the Internet.

It offers protection to the computer infrastructures and Internet users from the intruders. Firewalls are also used to protect IT resources from within the organization itself.

The following are the attributes of effective firewalls:

- The data, files and access to the websites as approved by the management alone are allowed to pass through it.
- Firewall itself needs to be protected from hacking.
- Firewall needs to be treated as one of the security systems and not the sole one.
- Continuous monitoring is needed on both what comes in and what goes out.

Various technical issues concerned with the firewalls are not discussed as they are vast and outside the scope of this book.

10.12   SOFTWARE PIRACY/SECURITY

Software is an intellectual property and is protected by the copy rights, operational worldwide. Software is valuable assets and hence is exposed to theft, unauthorized copying and unauthorized (pirated) use. The purchase of a software package means buying the rights/ license to use it. Software consists of source programs and executable/object programs. The owners only sell the rights to use the object programs.

Unauthorized use of software is a crime. The software owners, in order to protect their software, adopt many techniques so that their software is not pirated. Some of these techniques are discussed below.

Password: The authorized users are provided with the passwords by the software owners so that others cannot use it. The software can be accessed only by giving the right password. But it is not a safe method since the users may give the passwords to others, thereby making the software vulnerable for piracy.

Key strings: Some software is protected by a special algorithm which generates a key string that allows the software to be loaded only once on any computer. The software itself prevents loading it on any other computer. If the authorized users need to copy the software on other computers, they need to contact the software owner to alter the software.

Hardware locks: Hardware locks are electronic adopters with hardware coded password embedded in it. The software while running checks the presence of the adopter (in any of the computer ports). The software will not function in the absence of hardware lock concerned. Of course, the hardware lock cannot be copied by anyone. However, it adds to processor overheads.

10.13   INTERNET (INFORMATION) ROBBERY

The data/information carried over the Internet can be tapped by unauthorized people to gain access to organizational/sensitive information. They can also cause damage to the computers connected to networks by deleting the software or the data.

10.14   CYBER-CRIMES

The acts listed below are construed as cyber-crimes:

- Unauthorized access to computers, or destruction to computer software, data or network resources
- Unauthorized release of information to others
- Unauthorized copying of software or data

- Denying users to access their own computer resources
- Obtaining information like user id and passwords of others illegally (phishing)

Note: Cyber crimes are also discussed in Section 17.7.

10.15 HACKING

Some common hacking tactics used by hackers are as follows:

1. **Denial of service:** It means initiating/submitting too many requests to the web server with the intention of clogging/choking the server. The server could slow down appreciably or they can even crash the system. The hackers would use computers for this purpose. This is the reason many web service providers ask the users to identify the alphabets/integers displayed in graphics, manually.

2. **Scans:** It means hackers probing the Internet to identify the ports which are open, the type of computers, O/S, web servers, routers, etc. and to look for possible weakness in any of these components so as to get unauthorized entry into them. This is the reason the banks ask their Internet customers to close the sessions as soon as the transactions are completed.

3. **Sniffer:** The hackers use technical skills in searching the individual packets of data illegally as they pass through Internet/information super highway so as to capture confidential information, secrets or the passwords. Strong data encryption methods are to be used to avoid this.

4. **Spoofing:** It is the faking of a web site of important service providers like the banks, to trick users into passing their critical information like passwords, credit card numbers, account numbers, and so on. This is the reason the banks are telling their customers to use correct URLs and that the banks never would ask their customers user id, password, and so on.

5. **Trojan horse:** This refers to the bad programs hidden in real application software that delete the programs, data, etc. from the user computers or corrupt the operating systems/RDBMS.

Other techniques used by the hackers are back doors, malicious applets, war dialing, logic bombs, buffer overflow, password crackers, social engineering and dumpster diving. Readers are requested to refer to the books on Internet security if they are keen to know about them.

10.16 CYBER THEFT

Many computer crimes involve money. The credit cards stolen from others are used to make big purchases. It may also involve electronically breaking into banks' computer systems and transferring money from various accounts to the accounts operated by cyber-thieves. Users of these services need to be very careful while using such services.

10.17   CONSUMER PRIVACY ISSUES

Information technology makes it technically easier and economically feasible to collect, store, integrate, interchange and retrieve vast amount of data and information related to their customers. However, the power of information technology could also encroach into the privacy of the customers. The employers, banks, the Government agencies and various other service providers maintain huge database of people (personal and sensitive information), which should always be protected against any misuse. Else it may lead to invasion of privacy, fraud and injustice to the people.

Some more topics like ethical issues, social concerns, cyber terrorism and privacy concerns related to IT are discussed in Chapter 17.

SUM UP

Security is the main concern for the businesses' reluctance to switch over to e-business environments. The readers would have understood the need for security of IT infrastructures including business data and information.

The readers should be able to appreciate how today's technology offers facilities like confidentiality, message integrity, authentication, non-repudiation and access controls in electronic form which are as good as found in the physical world.

The process of data encryption and decryption and various issues that need to be taken into consideration are explained in simple words.

Cyber security associated with IT applications and Internet is too complex and the business organizations need to entrust such responsibilities to the specialists in such/emerging technologies.

CHAPTER

11

COMPUTERS
Structure, Networks and Architectures

Chapter Quest

The following questions would guide the readers in navigating through this chapter:

1. Explain the logical structure of a computer.
2. What are the types, functions, capabilities and capacities of processors, memory, cache memory and system bus and how they interact with one another and with input/output devices?
3. How the data is represented inside computers? What are BITS, BYTES, and ASCII standards?
4. What are the capabilities, capacities and limitations of various data storage and data backup devices?
5. What are the input devices (multi media) that can be connected to the computers and what are their functions and capacities?
6. What are the output devices (multi media) that can be connected to the computers and what are their functions and the capacities?
7. What are computer networks and hardware components used in networking? What is structured cabling?
8. What are the criteria for the selection of right and reliable hardware?
9. Discuss various computer and networking architectures used in business with their merits and demerits.
10. How the computers are classified into different generations?

11.1 LOGICAL STRUCTURE OF COMPUTER (John Von Neumann Architecture)

Most of the computers used today are 'stored instruction computers', where the instructions stored in the memory are brought into the CPU in the sequence in which they are stored, interpreted and executed by the CPU. The software and data are stored in the main memory.

Logical structure of the computer and its key components are shown in **Figure 11.1**.

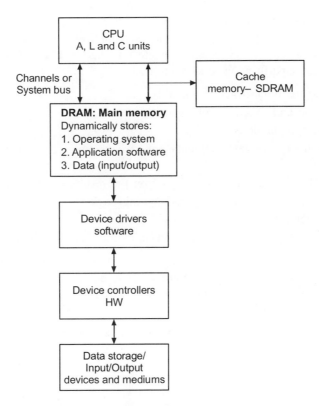

FIGURE 11.1 Logical structure of computer.

The components constituting the computers are discussed in the following sections. The input, output and data storage devices are also discussed in the later part of this chapter. Each device needs to have its own device driver (SW) and device controller (HW).

11.2 CENTRAL PROCESSING UNIT (CPU)

Central processing unit, called the processor, is considered to be the brain and nerve centre of the computer. It consists of three sub units, viz. arithmetic, logical and control units (ALC units), each unit performing distinctively different tasks.

Arithmetic unit (A), as the name implies, performs arithmetic computations, logical unit (L) compares two given entities and decides whether they are equal or which is lesser and the control unit controls A, L and memory units. Based on the decision outcome (of the logical unit), the control unit alters sequential execution of instructions.

The processor performs each operation through definite number of discrete steps, each step taking one millionth to one billionth of a second. Such discrete steps are synchronized with an internal electronic clock which oscillates at a specified number of cycles per second (cycle time) and each oscillation means a completed step of its operation. The cycle time is measured in terms of MHz (megahertz-million cycles per second)/GHz (gigahertz-billion cycles per second). Hence, the CPU speed is referred to in terms of MHz/GHz. However, this is the absolute speed of the processors and the user applications may not be utilizing such speeds fully. For example, a simple addition could take hundreds of CPU cycles (steps).

CPU is capable of performing tasks such as:

- Fetching instructions from the memory
- Interpretation and execution of instructions
- Arithmetic computations
- Comparison of two data elements and decide equal or higher or lower (logical capability)
- Follow different execution paths based on the results of the above comparison
- Fetching data from the memory and writing back
- Data manipulation
- Detecting errors (like parity errors) in its own circuits (registers), and so on.

CPU capability is also referred by the number of distinct instructions it can execute, called the 'instructions set' of a given computer. There are two families of CPUs, viz., CISC or RISC, classified according to the type of their construction.

11.2.1 Complex Instruction Set Computers (CISC Processor)

Complex Instruction Set Computers (CISC) are capable of executing about 100–150 different instructions, which are of variable lengths (e.g., 1 to 16 bytes). However, the electronic circuits (electronic estate) in them are designed for the longest instruction. Hence, the electronic estates are wasted for the shorter instructions which are also part of its instruction set. It also takes more time to execute the instructions as the circuits are designed for the longest instruction. Still majority of computers today use CISC processors since they have become faster due to design improvements.

11.2.2 Reduced Instruction Set Computers (RISC Processor)

Reduced Instruction Set Computers (RISC) have only about 50–60 instructions which are of fixed length (e.g., 1 to 8 bytes). These instructions are executed faster and the electronic estates are utilized better. The missing instructions (compared to CISC processor) get executed through software. RISC processors have not gained sufficient market share, as the CISC processors have become faster ever since.

11.3 SYSTEM BUS/CHANNEL

System bus (also called channel) connects the CPU with the Memory (Dynamic Random Access Memory—DRAM). The instructions and the data are transported between the two through this electronic pathway. A 16-bit bus carries 16 bits of information in parallel using 16 wires and 64-bit bus using 64 wires. The bus comprises two paths, viz. the address bus and the instruction bus to carry addresses of the data and the instructions separately. There are other pathways or channels to connect various input/output devices (through respective device controllers) to the memory and the processor.

Bandwidth: Computers are also referred by their internal bandwidths, viz. 16, 32, 64, 128 bits of the internal pathways/circuits/registers in the processors and the system bus. The higher the bandwidths, the faster are the processes and the larger are the electronic circuits (estate).

11.3.1 Other Ratings Used for the Processors

Other ratings used to measure processor capabilities are MIPS (million instructions per second) rating, TPS (transactions per second) rating and FLOPS (floating point operations per second) for science and engineering related applications.

11.3.2 Computer Instructions

CPU instructions (machine codes) are in binary digits (bits) consisting of two parts, viz. instructions (operation codes) and the operands (one or more operands). The operands are the memory addresses of the data on which the CPU operation (instruction) is performed.

Processor speed needs to match the expectations of the business applications, in terms of:

- System response time (waiting time) for the completion of each transaction/event
- Transaction volumes that can be performed in a second (TPS)
- Number of concurrent users it can support and so on.

11.4 COMPUTER MAIN MEMORY (DRAM)

Memory capability is referred by its size in bytes and access time required to access and transfer a piece of data from the memory. Processor needs to wait until the instructions and the data are brought into the CPU by its control unit. Memory access time could be a few micro/nanoseconds. Memory access is through its internal addresses (like the ward, street and house numbers).

Before we discuss the memory, it is necessary for us to understand how data (alphabets, numbers and the special characters (@ # $ % & * ( ) + " : ; '. , = and so on) are represented inside the computers.

BIT: Computers are capable of recognizing only the **B**inary Dig**it**s viz., 0 or 1 corresponding to two states of internal electronics, as conductive or non conductive modes (semi conductors).

BYTE: A string of 8 bits, which can have 256 combinations of 0 and 1 bits, is used to represent alphabets A to Z, a to z, numerals 0 to 9 and other special characters.

Two standards, ASCII and EBCDIC, are being used in such representation. Each standard recognizes the characters through different combinations of 0's and 1's in the string of 8 bits (one byte).

ASCII (American Standards Code for Information Interchange) is the standard which specifies the exact combination of 0's and 1's in a byte for each character.

EBCDIC (Extended Binary Coded Decimal Interchange Code) is another standard using different combinations.

DRAM (Dynamic Random Access Memory): All programs (software) and the data are to be stored in the computer memory (DRAM). The programs and the data are copied into memory from the hard disk.

Memory is analogous to the post office (letter) sorting box, where each pigeon hole holds letters of one particular destination. Each pigeon hole has an address and associated contents.

Computer memory consists of millions (MB)/billions (GB) of such (pigeon holes) memory cells, each having an address (memory location) and one byte of information stored in it. Each memory location can be accessed by the CPU independently and hence the name DRAM. As new data enters into memory cells, their previous contents are lost.

Once the data is stored in memory, it can be manipulated (calculated, compared, modified, copied, and so on) by the CPU as commanded by the software.

Memory is identified in terms of the storage capacity in bytes. It is normally indicated in terms of Mega Bytes (MB-million bytes or precisely 1,048,576 bytes) or Giga Bytes (GB-billion bytes or precisely 1,073,741,824 bytes).

DRAM, simply referred as Memory, is used to store the instructions, data and results of computations. The instructions need to be loaded into the memory before the CPU can start executing the instructions. The memory requires electric power (replenishing cycles) to keep its contents intact. Else its contents are lost and hence the memory is said to be volatile.

To overcome this problem of volatility, the instructions and the data are stored on the hard disks through magnetic coding and brought to the memory only when they need to be processed. The data or instructions stored on the hard disks are not dependent on power and hence they are not volatile.

11.5   CACHE MEMORY

It takes a few milli/nano seconds for the instructions and the data to be brought into CPU from DRAM since CPU needs to search the DRAM through its vast addresses and the data transfer rate is relatively slower.

To reduce this time delay, an intermediate memory called CACHE memory, made up of Static Dynamic RAM (SDRAM) is used. CPU could access instructions and data much faster from SDRAM. But SDRAM, though is faster, is also costlier compared to DRAM. However, a smaller capacity SDRAM (to save cost) is used in between the CPU and the DRAM, as cache memory (buffer memory).

The instructions and the data which are accessed by the CPU from DRAM, are brought into cache memory in bigger parcels such that immediately following instructions and data are made available from SDRAM itself instead of getting them from DRAM. This increases the processing speeds of the computers considerably. CACHE memories are allocated separately for data and the instructions.

11.5.1 Special Memory Units

The Read Only Memory (ROM) is a special type of memory for which the electric power is not required to retain its contents (micro codes). Programmable Read Only Memory (PROM) and Erasable Programmable Read Only Memory (EPROM) are two types of ROM used in the computers. They are programmable and reusable chips that hold certain instructions (firmware) permanently until erased under ultraviolet light. These chips are used in device controllers and BIOS (Basic Input Output System) chips which are the interface for various input/output devices.

11.6 DATA STORAGE (Multimedia) DEVICES

Data storage devices act as input, output and update (of existing data) devices. These devices consist of a drive mechanism and storage mediums. Data logically is stored in these mediums in the form of electronic directories and files (tables) under such directories. The operating systems and the RDBMS can have access to the mediums and the data stored on them only when the mediums are mounted on to the respective devices. Such data become 'online data'. The data recorded on to the mediums but not mounted on the devices are called 'offline data'.

Device drivers: Device drivers are the software needed to access the respective data storage devices and the mediums. The operating systems interact with the device drivers which in turn interact with the device controllers, respective devices and the mediums. All devices come with the device driver software for this purpose.

Device controllers: Device controllers are the hardware needed to interface respective input/output/data storage devices with computer hardware. The operating system accesses the devices through their respective device drivers and device controllers.

Hard disk: Hard disk is the mass storage device, which is highly reliable and considered as an integral part of the computer. Transfer of data from the hard disk to the memory is also faster compared to other data storage mediums and input/output devices. Hard disk capacity is referred as Giga Bytes (billions)/terabytes (trillions).

Hard disk consists of a number of magnetically coated recording discs stacked one above the other on a common spindle. Data is recorded on virtual tracks (circles of the same radius) and sectors (segments in a track) on the surfaces of these discs. Set of tracks of the same radius on all recording surfaces together is called virtual cylinder. Thus, hard disk consists of millions of virtual cylinders. The computer is capable of identifying data storage location in terms of the cylinder, track and sector. With this capability, the computer can fetch data stored anywhere in the hard disk (hence called direct access device).

Hard disks are high precision devices. Their recording surfaces are coated with highly sensitive magnetic materials and the read/write arms fly over the recording surfaces at a very minute gap. The polarity is set on the magnetic mediums depending on the bit patterns of the data being recorded.

Due to electrical or mechanical problems, the read/write arms flying over the recording surfaces can crash on to these surfaces and the data could get lost permanently. Even external electrical or magnetic fields could damage the data. Hence, it is always necessary to back up the data on to other mediums like CD, DVD or DATS.

Hard disks capabilities are measured in terms of its data storage capacity, the speed of accessing data from the hard disk (by way of rotational delay before a sector could pass through read/write heads and seek time for the heads to reach the required track) and also the speed with which the data is transported to the memory.

Hard disks are also referred as on-line data storage devices or auxiliary memory because it is the logical extension of computers main memory. The operating system (software), RDBMS, application programs and the business data are stored on the hard disks. Hard disks are an essential part of computers, as without it, no processing could be performed effectively.

The ability of the hard disks in storing large volumes of data, accessing the data fast (direct access) and selectively (at random) are also the factors that lead to widespread use of computers in business. They could be internal or external devices.

Floppy disks: Floppy disks which are obsolete now, also operate on the same principles of hard disks. But the recording medium is a single circular sheet of flexible plastic material, coated with magnetic compounds. This can store only 1.44 MB of data. This medium is encased on a thick plastic enclosure with a slot through which the medium is exposed to the read/write heads of the floppy drive. There were of 8", 5.25" and 3.5" sizes.

Since floppy disk is small and light, the data stored in these mediums could be transported across easily. This is a cheaper device but is not as reliable as the hard disks. This was used for data backups for small volumes of data. This medium had been phased out by the CDs/DVDs.

Compact disks (CD): Compact disk, as the name suggests, is compact in size like floppies but can store larger volumes of data (up to 800 MB). The medium consists of thick plastic sheet coated with photosensitive compounds which cannot be damaged easily. The recording is done through optical technology (using bright/dark spots) which makes it optically readable. The data stored is not easily destroyed or damaged. They come with two options, viz. write once and read many times (WORM/R) and read and write many times (RW)

Digital Video Disk (DVD): It is also like a CD, but uses superior optical technologies in recording and reading the data. They can store data of 8 GB and more.

Pen drive: This is a solid state (no moving parts) data storage device, which is growing in popularity due to its reliability, affordability and miniature size. It is possible to read and write data on to this medium. This is highly reliable since no electro-mechanical device is involved in it. The data is retained without the need for electric power. This is much more rugged and reliable compared to CD/DVDs. They come with data storage volumes of 64 GB and more. It is considered a technical marvel as it stores huge volumes of data, its compactness and portability.

Solid state hard disks: Today's computers also come with 320/720 GB and more solid state hard disks having no mechanical movements. They are highly reliable and can be placed as internal or external devices.

Magnetic tapes: In the 1970s, magnetic tapes were used in data processing (to store and access) and subsequently were used for only data back up. Magnetic tapes have become obsolete long back. Big business organizations used to have thousands of magnetic tapes to store backup data. Its usage is replaced by CDs, DVDs, digital audio tapes (DAT) and external/offline hard disks now. The magnetic tapes consisted of 2400 feet long and 0.75 inch width plastic tape coated with magnetic compounds, wound on a plastic spool. The tape drives were huge devices. Though large volumes of data could be backed up, it was a slow process to record and restore the data. These mediums were not reliable as they are susceptible for physical damage and fungal attacks.

Compact/Cassette tapes: Compact cassette tapes were used as an alternative to magnetic tapes. Though much smaller in size compared to tape drives, their reliability was poor. It also lacked standards. With the emergence of better backup devices, these tapes stayed in use only for a short period.

Digital audio tapes (DAT):   This is another data backup device used by some organizations in the 1990s. These back up mediums are very compact in size and capable of storing large volumes of data. The DAT devices are fairly reliable. DAT uses 4 mm magnetic tapes, is very compact in size and large volumes of data stored (up to 128 GB) on it could easily be transported across.

ZIP disk: A 3.5" disk (looking like a floppy disk but thicker and more sturdy) that can store data up to 100 MB data compressed in the Zip file format came into use for a few years which had also become obsolete.

External hard disk (for data backup):   Today, since very large size external hard disks having capacities like 500 GB, 800 GB have become cheap, the external hard disks themselves are used for data backup. They are highly reliable and easily portable. They can be connected to the computers through USB (universal serial bus) ports.

11.7   INPUT (Multimedia) DEVICES

As the name implies, the input devices could feed data or other multi media inputs to the computer.

Keyboard: Keyboard is the most predominantly used device to enter business data into computers. There are two ways by which the data is taken to the computers using the keyboards, off-line and on-line, which are discussed in Section 13.18.

As of today, data entry through the keyboard is a slow, error-prone and time-consuming activity and hence a bottleneck in business process automation. Many ergonomically designed and wireless keyboards (infrared access) are available today to make data entry less tiresome. However, the business functions necessarily need to enter data related to the business activities mostly through these devices.

Mouse: Mouse is the most fancied and user-friendly pointing (input) device. It is called a mouse because it resembles one, with the connecting cord looking like its tail. Interactive user interfaces (GUIs) make use of the pointing devices extensively. This device is used as a pointing device, to pick the tasks to be performed or selecting a data element from out of listed variables displayed on the computer screen. Mouse movement is relative. The right and left click buttons located over it allow the people to perform two different categories of tasks. Many interesting varieties of mouse are available today including the cordless ones.

Touch screen: The video display unit, or simply called the monitor, is the most user-friendly part of the computer. Video display allows data to be viewed before they are fed into the computer.

Touch screens are much easier to feed inputs to the computer but with limited scope (only a few pre-assigned data elements could be fed) into business applications. These devices are costly but highly suitable for the applications where the general public is expected to interact with the computers in harsh environments. Options/data displayed on the VDU screen is picked up when a particular location is touched by a finger. However, only limited input could be fed into the computers using the touch screens.

Electronic pen/stylus: This is another interesting pointing cum input device which enables capturing signatures, hand drawn sketches and diagrams. This device consists of a stylus which is used to write on a magnetic pad or a film. It is also possible to write the alphabets and numerals which can then be converted into text in ASCII format. The sketches drawn using electronic pens are stored as bit map files.

Scanners: Scanners are available in varying sizes from A0 to A4 standards. The images, drawings and documents can be scanned using these devices and stored in the computer as bit map files. Such images can be shrunk, enlarged, cut and pasted using special software. Some desk top printers have scanning and copying facilities built into them. The scanned texts can be converted into ASCII formats using OCR software (discussed in Section 4.5).

Digitizer: Digitizers are used in engineering applications. A digitizer can capture complex drawings and enable storing them in the computers. A digitizer consists of an electronic drawing board which allows creating new drawings or tracing the existing ones. The pen or puck is connected to the board by cross wires to establish contact with the electronic board. The puck is preferred for tracing highly detailed engineering drawings because cross hairs visible through a glass lens let the users to clearly and precisely pinpoint the ends and corners. As the user moves the puck over the board, the screen cursor makes the drawing on the screen. The drawing is stored in the hard disk in a digital form in a series of x–y coordinates (vector graphics). The digitized drawings can easily be modified using CADD software. Digitizers help even complex drawings to be converted into electronic formats with ease and fast.

Bar code readers: Bar codes are short bars of varying thickness placed either horizontally or vertically with varying spacing between one another. Bar codes are read by the bar code readers which return a particular value for each bar code configuration. This value can be picked by the application program and associate the same with a business entity (product or material). Bar codes are generally used to identify the products which are sold over the counter or the materials that are moved in and out of the warehouses.

Labels or stickers containing the bar codes are pasted on to the products. At the points of sales (POS), the products are scanned by the bar code readers (hand held or fixed to the sales counter). Application software picks up corresponding description and price details of the products from the computer database. Bar codes help in automatic identification of the products and eliminate the need for manual data entry which is time-consuming and error-prone. Though it is faster and accurate (compared to manual data entry using the keyboard), it has limited scope.

QR code readers: QR (quick response) codes, which are more powerful and versatile compared to bar codes, are becoming popular now. This consists of two-dimensional black codes in a matrix form placed inside a white square box. QR codes can contain descriptive, numeric and binary codes and can be made to denote names, addresses, website addresses, etc. that can be read by mobile phones (having such capability). QR codes printed on products, documents, product brochures can convey more information for the users (compared to the bar codes).

Microphone: Microphones are used to feed voice inputs to the computer. The voice can be stored as an audio (sound) file in digital form and played back through the speakers connected to the computer. If right voice synthesizer software is used, the spoken words can be converted into a text file (ASCII format), which can then be edited using the word processor software (this has been discussed in Section 4.5.3). Microphones are also useful in creating multimedia presentations. Audio files in digital form could easily be sent to others through e-mail.

Digital still camera: Digital cameras take the pictures like conventional cameras, but store the images in digital formats as electronic files on its memory cards. Digital cameras also come as part of the computers today and enable the pictures to be taken and transferred to the computer hard disk. The photo is stored as picture files. The picture can be displayed on the VDU of the computer or can be printed using photo quality papers. There are software packages which allow modifications to be done to the pictures (editing, enlargement, altering colours and so on). These pictures can be copied on to other computers and also be sent through e-mails. Digital cameras are useful in making multimedia presentations where pictures or images are mixed with business data to make presentations more effective and pleasant.

Digital video camera: This allows capture of objects in motion (movie) by capturing the pictures as a stream of frames. All other advantages discussed above are applicable for this device also. The video captured as a stream of frames can be edited, titled and communicated through computer networks.

11.8 OUTPUT (Multimedia) DEVICES

Output devices are capable of converting data/multi media stored in the computers in digital/ electronic formats, into a form which can be viewed by people.

VDU: Video display units (VDUs) are used as output device in all computers. The VDU has become a preferred alternative to print medium. As the business information is changing continuously, the managers prefer to access the same through VDUs instead of the reports. VDUs are capable of displaying the business information along with graphs, images and pictures. The monotony of printed reports is eliminated thanks to colourful/ animated displays made on the screens. VDUs have made the computers, multimedia machines. VDUs are available in a number of variants, in terms of screen sizes, varying display resolutions, number of colours and different technologies (like CRT, LCD, Plasma, LED, HD and 3D).

Since hundreds of colours could be displayed, this device is used extensively in visual communications. This has also become a close competitor to TVs.

VDU resolution (clarity) is measured in terms of discreet picture elements (pixels of 600×400, 1080×600 and more) that can be displayed in its screen.

Line printer: Line printers are capable of printing an entire line of information in one strike and at the speeds ranging from 300 to 2400 lines per minute (LPM). These printers are used where large volume printings are done. The stationery used is continuous, their widths ranging from 9" to 15". The dotted holes punched on both edges of the stationery enable the matching sockets in the printer to roll the stationery continuously. Using carbon interleaved stationery, multiple copies could also be obtained. A sturdy metal band or a chain embossed with alphabets and numerals revolving at high speeds are used in (impact) printing. These printers use pre-inked ribbons.

Line matrix printers are also used as an alternative to line printers. The line matrix printers have a number of print heads, each consisting of matrix of pins (as in dot matrix printers). Line matrix printers generally have 3 print heads spaced equally across the paper front, which print a line at a time but character by character.

Pre-printed stationery with multiple colours used in such printing improves the clarity and aesthetics of the business documents, statements and reports.

Dot matrix printer: Dot matrix printers are compact and cheaper printing devices generally used with the personal computers. Dot matrix printers are slower compared to the line printers as printing is done character by character. The print head consists of a number of pins arranged in a matrix form which, in various combinations, prints all alphabets and numerals. The print resolution varies depending on the size of the matrix. Generally, the print heads with 24 pins (3×8 matrix) are used.

This is used for small volume printing. The print head and the printer ribbons need to be changed often to maintain good quality of printing. Dot matrix printers can also print graphics and images (consisting of dots). Dot matrix printers are used for taking multiple copies of the business documents and for printing the labels.

Instead of the print head, a daisy wheel embossed with alphabets and numerals is also used (they are called daisy wheel printers). These types of printers are capable of printing high resolution text but at very slow speeds.

Impact printers: The above two types of printers are called impact printers as the printing is done through the impact of the pins or the precast dies. It is possible to make carbon copies only through the impact printers.

The other two types of printers discussed below are non-impact printers and carbon copies cannot be made through non impact printers.

Laser printer: It uses a laser beam and electro photographic methods to print a full page at a time. The laser is used to paint a charged drum with light to which a black toner is applied and then transferred to paper. Cut sheets are used in these printers. The resolutions of the laser printers vary from 300 to 1200 dpi (dots per inch) and can do textbook quality printing. These printers can print 4 to 32 ppm (pages per minute) depending on their capacity.

Colour laser printers are also being used to get a high quality colour print outputs. In addition to text, high resolution graphs, images, photographs and pictures can also be printed using both black and colours. Laser printers are very useful in DTP (desk top publishing) applications where product brochures, company profiles, etc. are printed. Colour laser printers eliminate time-consuming and elaborate type setting processes.

Ink-jet printer: It propels droplets of ink directly on to paper. Both colour and plain black printing are possible. A colour ink cartridge uses 3 basic colours (cyan, magenta and yellow) to produce other colours by combining these basic colours. A black ink cartridge is used to get plain black/grey prints. These printers are quiet, affordable and popular. However, they do not provide the colour quality or text resolution of laser printers. Special thermal papers are also used to improve the quality of printing.

Plotter: It is a graphics printer that plots drawings and images with ink pens. It can draw lines and curves from the drawing files. It can print graphics and full size engineering and architectural drawings. It can print the drawings in multiple colours. The drawing sheet of A0 size goes up and down many times over the print bed before the drawing is finished. The plotting head consisting of multiple colour pens also moves horizontally across the sheet. Such bi-directional movements enable any type of curves and diagrams to be drawn by this device.

Speaker: It is used for audio outputs and is an integral part of the computers today. The speakers are very useful in multimedia presentations. Higher capacity speakers can also be connected, external to the computers.

LCD projector: It displays video contents stored in the computers, on to big screens and is useful for making presentations to a group of people. High resolution display and brighter light source are the desired factors in selecting the LCD projectors. Its compact size and light weight make it portable. Some LCD projectors function even without the computers and just take the inputs from the CDs/pen drives.

LCD projectors are replacing conventional cine projectors (arc light) so far being used in cinema theatres. And the conventional film roles are being replaced by electronic movie contents stored in DVDs/hard disks.

11.9 NETWORKING HARDWARE

In addition to input, output and data storage devices discussed so far, there are other hardware components that are required to network the computers. Since computer networks and Internet have become so popular, the functions of such hardware are also to be understood by the readers.

11.9.1 Network Interface Cards (NIC)

Network interface cards are necessary for connecting individual (stand alone) computers to the computer network. NIC cards are integral part of the computers today. They are identified by the bandwidths of data that can be passed through them (like 10 mbps to 100 mbps). The NIC connects the computers to the network using special type of cables. Today's computers even come with wireless NIC.

The software required for communicating with other computers is part of the operating system today and this software interacts with NIC while establishing the networks.

11.9.2 Modems

Modems (enabling modulation and demodulation) are required to connect the computers (which are digital devices) to analog communication mediums (like conventional telephone lines-PSTN). They are either built-in or external to the computers. If the communication mediums use digital technology, routers are required to connect the computers to the network. Connectivity for the computers in networking (on one side) is shown below.

Computers → NIC → Modems or Routers → cables/mediums (of the networks)

11.9.3 Structured Cabling

Hundreds of computers installed at various departments spread across a vast manufacturing site or different floors in a high rise building get connected in the form of local area networks (LANs). All such computers (clients) are connected either to the server or mainframe computer installed in a common location/computer centre.

Structured cabling, as the name implies, enables all client/user computers to be connected to the server/mainframe computer in a structured way. Structured cabling enables shifting of user/client computers from one location to other without disturbing the connecting cables. Structured cabling has become an integral part of local area computer networks today. It makes the network management easy and practical. It enables balancing of network traffics across all segments of the network. Any client can be placed in any segment of the network irrespective of his physical location.

The user computers/clients can be stationed across different locations. At each of these locations, standard network sockets are provided (like cat 5 sockets). These sockets are provided at vantage locations similar to the provision of electric power sockets. A connecting cable (like cat 5 jacks) connects the computers to the sockets. Sockets in turn are connected to the structured communication cables wired across the office buildings/premises, which are terminated at the patch panels (A) kept near the computer room. Patch panels have hundreds of sockets serially numbered.

There are complimentary patch panels (B) connected to the server/mainframe computer, through switches/hubs/routers. These patch panels are also serially numbered. This enables the connectivity between the two sets of patch panels (A and B) to be established in various combinations. These two patch panels connect all client computers to the server or main frame computer. This offers flexibility in connecting the user computers to any of the switches/hubs/dynamically based on the network traffic (data traffic). The hardware components used in structured cabling are depicted below.

Server computer + NIC → Switches/Routers → Patch → Patch → Sockets → Client computers
Panel B   Panel A

Note: → symbol represents communication cables.

11.9.4   Hubs/Switches/Routers/Gateways/Bridges

All these hardware are passive or active or intelligent communication devices being used in computer networks/data communications including Internet. They connect computers and communication cables encircling the globe. They operate based on established communication standards/protocols (like OSI, TCP/IP) and ensure that the data from one computer is sent to the other, anywhere in the world intact and fast.

These devices help data communication as stated below.

- Establish physical connectivity.
- Segment the network so as to manage the flow of data across each segment of the network.
- Pack the data into packets before they are sent across the communication mediums.
- Unpack the packets that are received and convert them back into original data.
- Selection of paths and routing/rerouting of the packets based on the destination address.
- Securing of the data passing through the networks against unauthorized users and so on.

11.9.5   Computer Network—Mediums

Network communication mediums allow the data to be carried around the world and connect all communication hardware and computers across all geographic locations. The mediums are classified based on the technology used like, PSTN (public switched telephone network), ISDN (integrated services digital network), broad band co-axial cables, fibre-optic cables, very small aperture satellites (VSAT), micro-wave (wireless) links and so on. Each medium is capable of handling certain range of communication bandwidths. Business organizations need to choose the right mediums based on the volumes of data traffic flowing across the business, reliability, availability and costs.

11.9.6 Mobile Devices

Mobile devices like the smart phones, note book computers, i-pad, tablet PCs, (wireless connectivity to Internet), etc. have enhanced the scope of IT applications in business, to the extent that the business could be managed from anywhere (mobile computing). This enables even multinational corporations to be managed like a local business.

11.9.7 Wireless LANs

Many computers come with wireless interface cards to establish connectivity to wireless computer networks within the office premises. However, it has limited range (distances) of operations. They are also discussed in Section 11.12.

11.9.8 Power Supply—Generators and UPS

Computers require uninterrupted power supply with specified voltage, current and frequencies. Any variation to such specifications and power interruptions would cause extensive damage to the computer hardware, software and the data. Hence, all computers need to be supplied with uninterrupted power with specified voltage, current and the frequencies as warranted by their design.

If public electric power distribution systems do not provide such facilities, it should be supplemented by appropriate electric power generators, voltage stabilizers and uninterrupted power systems (with sufficient battery backup) for all computers and associated resources.

11.10 CRITERIA FOR THE SELECTION OF COMPUTER HARDWARE

The following issues need to be taken into consideration in selecting the computer, data storage, and input/output devices and networking hardware:

1. **Proprietary vs open systems:** For highly secured, reliable, high volume and business critical applications like e-business, IBASP/ERP, Internet banking, web search engines, etc. the proprietary systems supplied by vendors like IBM, SUN, HP are considered as better choice.

   The open systems like windows/Unix/Linux, etc. could be cost effective for other application environments. The open systems allow wide variety of applications to be made available to the business. However, the open systems are vulnerable to computer virus and external hacking. These issues are discussed further in Section 11.11.2.

2. **TPS rating:** Computer systems are generally benchmarked against TPS (Transactions per second) ratings. The TPS rating is dependent on the processor speed, bandwidth of inner circuits of the computer and the system bus, access time of disk drives, database organization and access methods, size of the database,

complexity of the business applications/processes, efficiency of the application software, the operating systems and RDBMS.

The business processes and the tasks need to be completed within a few seconds or minutes depending on the tasks. The computer systems should be capable of handling the business transactions at peak loads. TPS rating needs to match the business requirements comfortably.

3. **Processor and memory:** CPU speed measured in terms of MHz, processor speeds in MIPS (million instructions per second) or flops (floating point operations per second) are to be higher. Facility to connect more than one processor (multi-processor) is preferred. Possibility for concurrent processing (the instructions to be executed in parallel or multithreading) is also preferred.

If the memory capacities (GB) are larger, it enables more concurrent users to be serviced simultaneously by the server and also enhances system response time.

Cache memories with sufficient capacities are to be present as they enhance the system response time.

4. **Data storage devices:** Volumes of data to be stored on line (on-line data storage capacity), disk access time, disk rotational delay, seek time and the reliability of disk drives expressed as mean time between failures (MTBF) are to be taken into consideration.

5. **Data backup devices:** The data backup devices need to be reliable (DAT, CD, DVD, pen drive, external hard disk, etc.) and need to have sufficient capacities.

6. **System response time:** The time in seconds up to which the users need to wait for completing a transaction is called system response time. The system response should not exceed a few seconds even when all users are interacting with the system (peak loads).

7. **Cost:** One time cost in acquiring and installing the computer resources and re-curring costs of maintaining and upgrading them are to be taken into consideration.

8. **Reliability:** Uninterrupted and trouble-free performance of computer hardware, availability of prompt and efficient maintenance support at all business locations, etc. are the prime factors to be considered to ensure reliability of the systems. The installation base of similar systems in operation elsewhere is an important indicator in this respect.

9. **Scalability:** Possibility of adding additional computer resources later (like higher capacity processors and hard disks) to handle growing volumes of business transactions need to be ensured.

10. **Compatibility:** All configurable components of the computer systems discussed in Section 8.7.7 need to be compatible with one another. The interfaces need to function well.

11. **State-of-the-art technology:** Proven and upcoming/emerging technologies being incorporated in the hardware and software are the desirable factors to be taken into consideration.

12. **Ease of use:** The hardware, operating systems and RDBMS are to be user friendly. All types of users should be able to interact with the operating system, RDBMS and the application software with confidence and ease.

13. **Skill availability:** Technical skills required for maintaining the computer resources need to be available at all locations.

14. **Vendor reputation:** Vendors of all computer resources need to have good reputation in the market, good market share, wide installation base and expertise in respective business verticals. They need to be in a position to offer maintenance services until the life span of the computer hardware.

15. **Statutory compliance:** The computer systems and the applications need to be in compliance with statutory and regulatory laws of local governments and other regulating agencies.

11.11   COMPUTER ARCHITECTURE

The computer architecture, required capacities/speeds of the processor, memory, on-line storage devices, various input/output devices and the communication hardware to be used in business are to be decided based on the:

- Type of the business, competitors, IT strategies and the market environments
- Number of users at peak business periods
- Volume of business transactions at peak hours
- The applications to be implemented (as discussed in Chapters 4, 5 and 6)
- Geographic spread of the business
- Criticality of the IT applications to business
- Volumes of data to be made available to the business
- Size of the data warehouse
- Levels of reliability of the computer resources required
- The duration, the IT resources are to be made available to business, and so on.

Speeds and capacities of all components of the computers have been discussed in detail in earlier sections of this chapter and they need to be chosen based on the parameters listed above.

The computer architecture needs to be selected among the alternatives discussed below.

11.11.1   Proprietary Systems/Main Frame Computers

Proprietary systems are those wherein the computer, operating system and DBMS are closely coupled together and associated technologies are owned by the same vendor. The business applications need to be ported on to the proprietary system. The vendors like IBM, Sun and HP offer such systems. The computer, operating system, DBMS and the application software get closely coupled to one another thereby making them look like a single entity. Mainframe computers are proprietary systems.

The following are the merits of proprietary systems:

- Capable of handling high volumes of business transactions with good system response time because of the high end processors used and matching efficiency of both operating systems and DBMS.
- Highly reliable and less susceptible for virus attacks, external hacking, etc. since the interface between the operating systems, the computers and the application software are not made public (not open).

The demerits of proprietary systems are as follows:

- The business gets committed to single vendor.
- Relatively costlier.
- All application software/packages available in the market cannot be used (unless the vendor ports them on to the proprietary systems).

11.11.2 Open Systems/Client Server Architecture

As the name implies, the open systems have the computers and the operating systems whose functions, standards, interfaces, etc. are made known/open to the public so that anyone can develop RDBMS and other application software that can be run on these systems. This has given rise to hundreds of ready to use application softwares that can be used on such open systems. The Intel processors and Microsoft Windows fall under this category.

The merits of the open systems are:

- Involves lesser investments and the business need not be tied up with single vendor.
- There is a good scope for using variety of application software for the users.
- The open systems are cheaper because of large scale production and ever growing customer base.

The demerits of the open systems are:

- Relatively less reliable
- Cannot take very high volumes of business transactions or larger number of users (say more than 100)
- Susceptible for virus attacks and external hacking
- In case of problems encountered by the users, one vendor points finger on other

1. **Two tier system:** The client server architecture is said to be two tier systems when both the application software and the RDBMS reside in one single server (one tier). The clients constitute second tier. For small and medium size business, the two tier systems would be sufficient.

2. **Three tier system:** The three tier systems have two exclusive servers for the application software and the RDBMS (two tiers) and the clients, third tier. For big business organizations, three tier is recommended.

Internet based applications will have additional tiers like web server, firewall server, e-business applications servers, and so on.

3. **Disk mirroring:** Disk mirroring is the architecture wherein redundancy is introduced in data storage devices. Generally, this is done through the RDBMS. Two identical databases are maintained in two different hard disks, such that even if for some reason one hard disk fails, the applications would run with no interruption making use of the second hard disk.

4. **Fault tolerant systems:** Fault tolerant systems offer redundant computer resources to business critical applications like banking, airline/railway reservation systems, IBASP/ERP, e-business, etc. such that even if one computer system fails, the other one continues the business processes with no interruption.

Two different computer systems, preferably located at distant locations each having their own/independent servers, operating systems, RDBMS, network infrastructure and IBASP/ERP, are made to run all business applications concurrently. Though costlier, they make the computer resources to be available to the business all the time.

11.12 NETWORK ARCHITECTURE

The network architecture could be any one or more of the alternatives discussed below. The computer networks can also either be proprietary systems (WAN) or open systems (Internet, VPN, etc.) or a combination of both.

1. **Local area network (LAN):** As the name implies, the computers stationed in a local area, like a multistorey office building, manufacturing site, etc. get networked as LAN. The communication is restricted to the local area and it is possible to have the network speed up to of 100 MBPS. Since people located in the local area alone could use the LAN, it very much limits the scope of the business applications (to a local area). It still brings all the benefits of computer networks to the business within the local area.

2. **Metropolitan area network (MAN):** It is a wider computer network compared to LAN. MAN spans across a city or large factory premises or university campuses. MAN interconnects number of LANs through higher capacity backbone connectivity like fibre optic/co-axial/microwave links. MAN also enables connectivity to WAN/Internet.

3. **Wide area network (WAN):** It connects the computers stationed across different/distant geographic locations generally within a country through dedicated networks which can be accessed only by those entities authorized by the business organization, e.g. Indian railways is using dedicated wireless network for their operations. WANs are generally private and costly as they use dedicated lines/microwave links.

4. **Internet:** It is just a set of open standards and protocols established for connecting the computers, communication hardware/devices, all types of mediums, variety of business and personal applications and the users/clients in establishing worldwide connectivity among all above entities (Internet has also been discussed in Section 5.6.1.9).

Internet has emerged as the universal standard for connecting the computers around the globe. It has very largely enhanced the scope of all business applications discussed in Chapters 4, 5 and 6.

Internet standards are set by a number of technical bodies stationed in different countries but not controlled by any governments.

Because of low cost of Internet based communications, many business organizations are able to implement their own VPN (virtual private networks) to interconnect their LANs through Internet. There are number of vendors who offer necessary products and services to establish such VPN networks using INTERNET. VPN for business organizations is cost effective compared to WAN.

5. **Wireless/3G technologies:** In 1876, Alexander Graham Bell invented the telephones (still there is a dispute that it was actually invented by Elisha Gray a month earlier). Ever since it was invented, telephone communications mostly have been happening through wired networks only. The so-called land lines even today use wired connections established between the caller and the called person. Such networks are called PSTN (public switched telephone network) or ISDN (integrated services digital network). It is also called circuit switching, since the circuit needs to get established between the caller and called persons, before the voice communication starts.

Because physical wires are to be laid and it involves huge costs, many of our villages till date do not have wired telephone communications. Thanks to the wireless technology, our villagers are able to communicate with the rest of the world through their mobile phones, which uses wireless technology. Today 75% of Indian population have access to mobile phones and no other technology so far had penetrated so fast to this extent.

In 1900, Marconi invented the radio systems, where he proved that signals could be sent through atmosphere without using the wires.

It is another sad story for India. Jagadish Chandra Bose from Calcutta, studying and researching in UK, invented the radio systems way back in 1894. He demonstrated in public and ignited the gun power placed a distant away using microwaves generated through magnets. He was not aware of the patents and the advantages of patenting. As a true scientist, he showed his invention to the public, so that others can improve on his invention.

Cell/mobile phones being extensively used today are wireless communication devices. Cell phones today make use of 2G/3G technologies.

Wireless communication over the years have evolved through various stages, numbered, Zero G, 1G, 2G, 2.5G, 2.75G, 3G and 4G technologies. If we have to learn about 3G, we need to start from Zero G.

Zero G: Zero G is mobile radio telephone system which came into existence in the 1960s. We can see these systems being used by police, installed in their vans, jeeps and motor cycles. It has transmitter with a long antenna rod, receiver and a handset. All these devices work only in a close range of a few kilometers of radius. Since original voice signals are distorted by intervening electromagnetic and electric field disturbances, this communication generally is not clear and is too noisy.

Similar systems are also being used by call taxi owners and their drivers to communicate to each other about their customer locations and which driver needs to pick up the nearest customer. Zero G sends and receives analogue signals over a limited geographic area.

1G: This is similar to Zero G, but can cover wider geographic areas. Indian Railways, for example, are using this technology since the 1970s. They have installed microwave towers at intervals of 30 to 50 km (with clear line of sight) across the length and breadth of the country (WAN) so that the analogue signals could be picked up from the nearest tower and sent to destination point, jumping across number of towers (signal repeaters), however far the receiver is within India.

Transmission of TV programs using the TV towers in Indian cities also belong to this generation.

2G: 2G technology is what we use in our mobile phones today. The voice is very clear because it uses digital technology to transmit voice signals. 2G came into existence in the 1990s.

In digital technology, the voice is converted into mere zeros and ones when they are transmitted over the mediums. At the receiving end, the magnetic and electric disturbances to zeros and ones are detected and eliminated so that zeros and ones as originated from the caller is again converted back to voice and given to the receiver. Hence clear voice and good quality conversations.

In digital technology, the speed of communication is measured in terms of how many digits (0 and 1 bits) the network can transmit in a second. 2G speed range is about 100 kilo bits/sec, depending on the technology and infrastructure put in use. An alphabet needs 8 bits to be transmitted using digital technology. Voice, text, pictures, songs, movies and all other media are converted into 0 and 1 before they are transmitted through the digital networks.

2G adopts two technology variants:

(i) GSM (Global system for mobile communication) uses TDMA (Time division multiple access) technology. It is digital cellular circuit switched network. It provides individual time slots for each mobile user. When the users get saturated, the networks gets busy. Majority of cell phones around the world and in India are using this technology.

(ii) CDMA (Code division multiple access) uses channel access method wherein several users share a band of frequencies (bandwidth). Some countries including India use this technology.

Both technologies use subscriber identity module (SIM card) to store service information and the phone book. Both technologies have their own advantages and disadvantages and hence they co-exist.

2.5G: Some cell phone service vendors also offer GPRS (General packet radio service) over GSM and it is called 2.5G technology. This is also available in India but at additional cost. This gives data transfer speeds up to 114 kilo bits/sec. People who access their e-mails through cell phones are using this technology.

2.75G: If the cell phone service providers offer EGPRS (Extended general packet radio service), it is called 2.75G technology. This is capable of increasing the data transfer speeds further.

3G Breakthrough in wireless communication: 3G (3rd generation) wireless technology allows large volumes of digital data to be (upto 1 MBPS) transmitted in a second through wireless (microwave) links.

Mobile phone users will be able to do lot more activities using 3G.

(a) Make video calls (people can see one another while they converse).

(b) Surf internet and send and receive e-mails with file attachments (text, data, audio, video and images).

(c) Download movies and see them on mobile phone screens.

(d) Watch live TV, movies, cricket, news and so on (live streaming) on their mobile phone screens.

(e) Perform mobile computing and can access organization's MIS from anywhere.

(f) Can download music and mobile phones can be used as mobile juke box.

(g) Play online games.

(h) Video conferencing, and so on.

Today, there are already about 400, 3G networks around the world and one-fourth of the world population have access to this technology.

3G will become more affordable and fully exploited by people probably in next 2 years. Further advanced technologies like 3.5G and 4G would also become operational in 1 or 2 years. Thanks to higher bandwidth wireless technologies, human race will witness yet another revolution by way of newer mobile applications that would enhance the quality of human race around the globe.

6. **Wi-fi (wireless fidelity):**   This technology enables personal computers, note book computers, smart phones, etc. get connected to internet through wireless network access points. An access point is also called 'hot spot' and has a range of 20 to 30 meters. Multiple overlapping access points could increase this range further. To connect to this network, the computers need to have wireless network interface controller card (WNIC). Such facilities are being offered at the hotels, airports, big railway stations, etc. as free service to their customers.

7. **Bluetooth:**   Bluetooth is a proprietary open wireless technology standard for exchanging data over short distances using radio transmission wavelengths ranging from 2400 to 2800 MHZ between fixed and mobile devices. This enables people talking through the mobile phones with their hands free (through hear phones/microphones).

8. **WiMax:**   Wireless interoperability for microwave access (WiMax) is the fourth generation technology for wireless broadband which is used for providing Internet access to locations where it is difficult to provide conventional cables. Communication towers used in this technology can provide wireless broadband services within a radius of 15 km. Unlike the limited access area, that a WiFi hotspot serves, WiMax can link up larger areas.

It is worldwide interoperability for microwave access and is a trademark for a set of telecommunication protocols which offer both fixed and mobile internet access.

Users stationed within 1 km radius of a WiMax towers can access Internet using a USB dongle, users within 2–5 km radius would require indoor equipment while other far away users would need to hook up with outdoor equipment.

11.13 GENERATIONS OF COMPUTERS

Computers are classified into different generations based on the technology on which they are built.

I Generation (1950s): They were built using diodes and triodes. The memory capacity was up to 4 KB. These computers generated lot of heat and its use was very much limited to specific applications like tabulation of census results, decoding secret messages sent by different countries during world-war II and other analogue processing.

II Generation (1956–1970): These computers were built using the transistors which are very tiny compared to diodes and triodes. These were the first computers to be used in business applications. These machines had memory capacity up to 16 KB. Still there were no operating systems. Machine language and assembler languages were used for programming. EDP/batch processing applications (only) were implemented using such machines. They were single task/single user machines.

III Generation 1980: These computers were built using integrated circuits (ICs) where thousands of circuits were embedded on tiny silicon chips. This is the first revolution in computer technology. Very powerful computers were built by the companies like IBM, HP, SUN micro system, DEC, and so on. Operating systems allowing multi tasks to be performed on the computers came into existence. OLTPS and MIS applications came into operations in business.

IV Generation 1990: These computers were built using very large scale integrated circuits (VLSIC's) where hundreds of thousands of circuits are embedded on very tiny silicon chips. Micro processors, more powerful computers and so also personal computers came into existence. This has led to table top, lap top, notebook computers, and so on.

V Generation (yet to come): These computers may be built based on neural networks mimicking the functioning of human brain to some extent. They are expected to have some sort of artificial intelligence like natural language processing, voice recognition, etc.

SUM UP

The readers would have clearly understood the logical structure and functioning of the computers.

The functions, capabilities and capacities of the components like processors, memory, cache memory and system bus are explained in simple terms.

Need for internal representation of data in binary codes (semiconductor technology) has been explained.

On-line storage and back up devices which are integral part of computers, their functions and capabilities are explained.

All input and output devices including multi media devices that could be connected to the computers and their functions and capabilities have been covered very exhaustively.

The computer networks, components of computer networks and the benefits of networking have been discussed in a logical order.

The criteria for the selection of computer hardware and the issues that need to be taken care while buying the computer resources are explained in detail so as to enable the readers in selecting right hardware for their business.

The computer and network architectures are discussed with their relative merits and demerits to enable readers in identifying right networking architecture to suit their respective business environments.

12

COMPUTER SOFTWARE, CASE TOOLS AND GOOD PROGRAMMING PRACTICES

Chapter Quest

The following questions would guide the readers in navigating through this chapter:

1. What is computer software and what are various types of software?
2. Explain the layers of interface between the users and the computer hardware.
3. What is an operating system and what are its functions?
4. What are other types of system software and their functions?
5. Explain various categories of programming languages and their relative merits and demerits.
6. What are the types and uses of application software in business?
7. What is integrated business application software (IBASP)/ERP, which are being used by most of the business organizations today?
8. What is graphical user interface (GUI)?
9. What are the principles of good programming and good programming practices?
10. What are CASE (computer aided software engineering) tools, their functions and advantages?
11. What is computer virus? What damage they could make to the business and what are the ways by which the IT resources could be protected from virus?

12. What are various types of interfaces between the software, the hardware and business applications?

13. What are the criteria for the evaluation and selection of right software (O/S, RDBMS, ERP/IBASP)?

14. What are various software architectures?

15. What is cloud computing? What are their relative merits to business?

A case study is also presented at the end of this chapter, to enable the readers to understand the application architecture in relation to a business situation.

12.1 INTRODUCTION

Computer software is an intellectual, versatile and potent entity, which enables computers perform wonderful and unbelievable tasks. However, all such tasks get executed using only the 'instructions set' of the computers, discussed in Section 11.2, and as per the algorithm designed by software engineers.

In other words, computer software is made up of thousands of computer executable instructions written in a sequence as per an algorithm or program logic which alone can perform/complete any designated task.

The computer software made up of computer instructions and program logic, as the name implies, is 'soft' as it can easily be written and modified to suit varying business requirements.

12.2 CLASSIFICATION OF SOFTWARE

Computer software is broadly classified as system software and application software (**Figure 12.1**). Most of the discussions in this book relate to applications software only.

1. **System software:** It is a set of generalized programs that interface with the computers and manage the computer resources. They also act as an intermediary between the users, application software and the computer hardware. They are

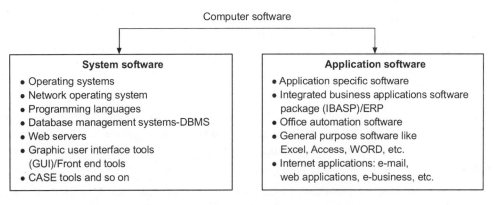

FIGURE 12.1 Classification of software.

supplied by the computer manufacturers or other vendors. They are not developed by the business organizations.

2. **Application software:** It refers to the programs written to perform specific tasks of individual users or the business organizations. The users generally interact with the computers through application software and the operating system (system software).

12.3 INTERFACE LAYERS BETWEEN USERS AND THE HARDWARE

The users need to go through the layers shown in **Figure 12.2** to exploit computer capabilities. The processor/operating systems also interact with various data storage, input and output devices through their controllers.

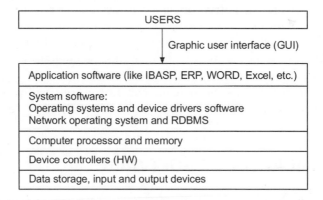

FIGURE 12.2

12.4 OPERATING SYSTEMS (O/S)

Operating system (O/S) is system software which is considered to be an integral part of the computer. The O/S interacts with the users (GUI), the application software, RDBMS and the computer hardware. Operating systems perform variety of operations commonly required for all types of users and applications.

The operating system is a master program that runs the computer and is mandatory. O/S is the first software loaded when the computer is turned on. Its main part, the "kernel," resides in the memory always (firmware). The other segments of operating system are brought to memory from hard disk as and when required. The operating system sets the standards for all application programs that can be run on the computer and all devices that can be connected to it. The operating systems perform the following functions.

1. **User interface:** Most users today are conversant with user-friendly GUI (graphic user interface), while interacting with the computers. GUI includes windows, menu

options, symbolic commands (icons), tool bars, etc. displayed on the computer screen, by clicking which the computer performs requested tasks. Thanks to GUI, the users need not remember or memorize the functions of the computers as all such interfaces are self explanatory.

Prior to the 'Windows' or Macintosh (Apple) operating systems, all interactions with the computers were based on plain English like commands entered through the keyboard. Users were to be trained specially for this purpose. Operating systems today have overly simplified the user interface thanks to GUI. And similarly, all applications software also provide very highly user-friendly and simple interface to their users, e.g. MS Word, Excel, E-mail, IBASP, ERP, Internet banking, Internet explorer, and so on,

2. **Job management:** It controls the order and time in which various programs are to be run. It is possible to create and feed the list (batch) of programs to be run in a sequence (like IBM's JCL) and can also be scheduled to start at a given time. The operating systems also pick up the jobs based on organizational priorities. Applications can also be prioritized to run faster or slower depending on their priority.

3. **Task management:** Multitasking is the ability of the computers in executing multiple programs/user requests simultaneously. The processors are generally capable of executing only one program/task at a time. However, the operating systems slices the processor time into number of micro seconds segments and enable different programs to be run in each time segment. However, since such shifting takes place so fast, all users feel that their tasks are being executed continuously.

In personal computers, multitasking keeps several applications (windows) open at the same time so that users can go back and forth among them.

4. **Memory management:** The operating system allocates necessary and sufficient memory space for all the users, their programs and associative data in main memory. If in the process, the memory size is not sufficient, the users are not handicapped for that reason. To do this, the O/S makes use of the hard disk space (virtual memory) by swapping the memory contents back and forth from the memory and the hard disk space.

To utilize the memory space better, big programs are converted into number of virtual pages and are stored permanently in the hard disk. Relevant virtual pages are loaded into the memory only when particular page segments are to be executed. This makes the memory space to be available for all concurrent users. This also enables the programs of any size to be written without being constrained by the memory capacity.

5. **Data management:** It keeps track of the data physically stored on the hard disk. The application programs identify the data through directory name, file name, keys of records contained in a file and the record structures. The operating system's file system knows where that data is physically stored (in terms of sectors, tracks or cylinders on the disk).

Whenever an application needs to read or write data, it makes a call to the operating system (through API—Application Program Interface) and the O/S actually performs read or write operation through the device drivers and the device controllers. API is a language and message formats used by an application program to communicate with the operating system or RDBMS or communication protocols.

6. **Device management:** It controls all devices (data storage, input and output devices) by sending them commands in their own proprietary language. The software that knows how to deal with each device is called a "device driver." The operating system needs to have the device drivers for all the devices attached to the computer. When a new device is added, that device's driver is generally installed into the operating system automatically. Device driver is software and the device controller is the hardware that physically connects the device to the computer (through I/O channels). Today most of the devices are 'plug and play devices' (with universal serial bus-USB interface) if respective device drivers already exist in the operating system.

7. **Security:** The operating systems enable the users to access the computers through user id and passwords. Certain operating systems also maintain activity logs and their usage time. They also provide backup and recovery routines for starting over in the event of a system failure.

8. **Directory/File management:**
   - Organizes data into files and places the files into different folders and directories with logical names easily understandable by the users.
   - Allows creation and deletion of files, folders and the directories in the hard disks and all other data storage devices.

9. **Data backup and restoration:** Performs backup and restoration of all software including the operating systems and data even in the absence of RDBMS. RDBMS has better capability in backing up and restoration of high volume data/database.

10. **Self diagnostics:** Runs self diagnostics on all computer resources like memory, internal electronics, hard disk, power supply, various input output devices and so on. Problems encountered in them are promptly reported to enable the users to take appropriate action.

In addition, there are a number of other tasks performed by the operating systems which the author feels are not needed for the target readers of this book.

Examples of operating systems:

Microsoft: DOS, Windows Professional, Windows 7, and so on.

IBM: PC DOS, Aix, OS/VS, O/S2

Others: Linux, Solaris 9, Unix, HP-Ux, Apple Macintosh, and so on.

12.5 OTHER SYSTEM SOFTWARES

1. **Device driver:** It is software that links an input/output/data storage device to the operating system and is supplied with the device. This software is written by

respective vendors who have the detailed knowledge of the device's command language and O/S characteristics. The software contains the precise machine language necessary to perform the functions requested by the application program on a given device. The operating system first calls the device driver and the device driver drives the device through respective device controller.

2. **Micro-codes/Firmware:** Firmware is a tiny hardware that holds the instructions for certain computer operations where such instructions are retained even without the power supply. Examples are, ROM, PROM, and EEPROM (Erasable Programmable Read Only Memory). Firmware is also called "hard software" or micro-codes since they hold program codes. This has already been discussed in Section 11.5.

3. **Database management systems (DBMS):** The database management systems which are also system software are discussed in detail Chapter 13.

12.6 NETWORKING OPERATING SYSTEM (NOS)

'NOS' is system software designed for the computers to be networked with one another. This mostly comes bundled with the operating system now.

'NOS' resides in each client (user) and in the server (central computer). It allows disk drives on the server to be accessed as if they are local disk drives on the client machine. It allows the server to handle requests from the clients to share files, applications and many other devices such as printers and hard disks.

12.7 PROGRAMMING LANGUAGES

We have seen that computers are capable of executing a set of instructions (program) upon given data. The instructions consist of two components, viz. operation codes (instructions) and operands (memory addresses of the data) all in binary digits. And instructions are also to be resident in the computer memory to enable the processor to pick them.

Since computer electronics could identify only two states (conduct/non conduct of semiconductors), the instructions also need to be written in binary form (binary codes-bits) called the 'machine language'. But it is too difficult to write and understand even simple programs in machine language. Hence, various easier methods of programming have evolved over a period of time.

Before we discuss various methods of programming, let us understand some terms associated with computer programming.

Source programs (source code) and object programs (object codes): Source programs are the computer instructions written in a form which is easy for the programmers to write, understand and modify (using mnemonic codes/abbreviations resembling natural language) them. The source programs need to be translated into machine language, called object code/object program before it can be executed by the computer. The object code cannot be read or modified by the programmers.

Programming: Programming is the process of writing series of instructions in logical order (algorithm) (either in machine language or using any other programming languages), so as to solve a problem or to perform a specific task.

High and low level languages: Programming languages which are less structured and whose commands resemble natural language are called high level languages. They are easily understandable by people. However, they need to be written as per simple programming rules (syntax rules), e.g. SQL, which is also called 4th generation programming language..

Low level languages are highly structured and need to follow highly disciplined syntax rules and commands of respective programming languages. Such programs could only be written by the programmers who are specially trained in respective programming languages, e.g. Assembler.

12.7.1 Types of Programming Languages

1. **Machine language:** Machine language is the native (binary) language of the processor. It is generally used in the device drivers and the firmware. Programmers used to write programs in machine language in the 1970s when computers had limited memory (8 to 16 kB) and small instruction sets (about 20 instructions). Today, it is not possible to write application programs using the machine language. Machine languages are also referred as first generation languages.

2. **Assembler language:** Assemblers allow programs to be written using easily discernible mnemonic codes (but far away from natural language) for both instructions and data. Assembler language is more nearer to the machine language. The assembler software converts the assembly language into corresponding machine language line by line.

Assembly languages though are easier to write and understand compared to the machine language, they are more cumbersome and difficult to write, compared to the compilers and IV GL (fourth generation language) languages discussed subsequently.

Since assembly languages are nearer to the machine language of the computer, assemblers allow fuller exploitation of the processor capabilities. Assemblers are referred as second generation language.

3. **Compilers:** The compilers allow the source programs to be written in a near natural language form (source codes) and convert them into executable form/object code through the process called compilation. Examples are, COBOL (common business oriented language), PL/1 (programming language), FORTRAN (Formula translation), and so on. Since the programming languages look like a natural language, it is easy to write, understand and modify these programs. However, certain rules called 'Syntax rules' as required by the compilers are to be used in writing these programs. The program written using natural language like commands is called the source program.

The compiled program is called object program/executable program. If the application programs are to be modified, the source programs need to be modified first and compiled again to get the new executable programs.

One statement written using the compiler language is converted into a number of instructions in the object program. The compilers allow writing of even complex programs in easier and clearly understandable form. Compiler languages are referred as third generation programming language.

4. **Interpreters:** Interpreters are also similar to compiler languages. But they do not create the executable/object programs. Interpreters retain the programs in its native/source form and convert them into executable form only when the instructions are taken for execution. Since every time the source instruction is converted to executable form, this took more time for execution. But this does not require compilation. The source programs can be modified any time. It is generally used for developing prototypes of applications so that the programs could be modified more frequently and used without the overheads of program compilation. Interpreters are also referred as third generation languages. Interpreters generally are not used now.

5. **Fourth generation languages (IV GL):** Fourth generation languages allow the programs to be written more or less in a natural language and in less structured way. It enables the end users, managers and other business functions to write programs for themselves. This is used mainly for extracting the information from the existing database. Since it takes more time to process, this method of programming is not used in regular data processing/OLTPS applications. IV GL languages also do not exploit the processor capabilities fully. SQL (Structured query language) of the popular RDBMS packages falls into this category.

12.8   APPLICATION SOFTWARE

As the name implies, application software enables the computers to be used/applied to varied business and other user applications. The business applications could widely vary depending on the business verticals like manufacturing, trading, engineering, banking, insurance, logistics, communication, healthcare, travel, hotel management, and so on.

12.8.1   Integrated Business Application Software Package (IBASP)

The scope of the IBASP has been discussed in Chapter 5. Big business organizations would require thousands of application programs to automate their business processes. Development of application programs in such environments would require high levels of software engineering skills. Developing IBASP has been discussed in Chapter 8.

12.8.2   General Purpose/Utility Software Packages

General purpose software, as the name implies, is useful for all categories of users and versatile applications. If they perform user applications, they are called 'General purpose application packages'. If they perform system related activities, they are called 'Utility programs'.

12.8.3 Utility Programs

Utility programs help all users in every day operations of the computers. Utility programs include file management functions (creating, copying and deleting the directories, folders and files), searching for files, performing diagnostics to check performance and current health of the hardware, and so on. Many of the utility programs are contained in the operating systems. Using utility programs, the files can be (sort programs) sorted or two or more files can be merged (merge program) or reports could be printed (report generators).

12.8.4 General Purpose Application Packages

General purpose application packages have certain generic capabilities built into them and the users can make use of such capabilities in performing designated tasks without writing programs. They come with user manuals, help menus and excellent user-interface (GUI) so that the users can learn and use such packages without difficulty. These packages could also take care of business process automation (BPA) requirements of small and medium business organizations.

Examples of such packages are:

1. **Word processor:** For creating letters, documents, labels, and so on.

2. **Database management systems:** For creation of simple database and performing general data processing jobs including MIS, e.g. MS-Access, Foxpro.

3. **Electronic spread sheet:** In performing computations and manipulation of data (cells) held in the form of rows and columns (tables).

4. **E-mail:** For communication through Internet.

5. **Internet browser:** To access/browse web sites.

General purpose software packages have largely contributed to the growth of end user computing which has been discussed in Section 8.10.

12.8.5 Application Specific Software Packages (ASP)

Application specific software packages are used in specific business functions like, financial accounting (e.g., tally), payroll, materials management, project management, sales management, and so on. The users of these packages need not be computer experts. These packages are aimed at the functional users and come with self learning tutorials to understand and use them. When such packages are run on the computer, the users can easily interact with the application software by virtue of the business domain knowledge possessed by them. No programming skills are required in using these packages.

However, these application packages cannot be modified by the users. These applications do not integrate the business functions as they are developed for individual business functions. Such packages also tend to create islands of information within the organization, normally not shareable by other business functions.

12.8.6 ERP Packages

The ERP packages like SAP, People Soft, Oracle, JD Edwards, Baan are popular among big and MNC organizations. IBASP is a customized software package developed by business organizations concerned from scratch through SDLC activities. IBASP and ERP packages have been discussed in Sections 5.1, 5.2 and 8.11.

12.9 OFFICE AUTOMATION SOFTWARE

Office automation software automates a number of office administrative functions. OA software is available as ready to use software packages. OA software packages have already been discussed in Section 4.5.

12.10 FRONT END TOOLS

Front end tools refer to software aids, used in developing highly user-friendly interface for the business applications/users, adopting graphics, icons, animation, pull down menus, buttons and other user-friendly interactive facilities. For graphical interface, it provides the tools and libraries for creating menus, dialog boxes, fonts and icons.

Examples of front end software tools are Visual Basic, C++, PowerBuilder, SQL-Windows, Visual dBASE, and so on. These packages interact with all popular RDBMS and programming environments.

12.11 BATCHING OF PROGRAMS (JCL)

Number of programs that are to be executed are after the other can also be submitted as a batch in order to get them executed without human intervention (Job control language).

12.12 PRINCIPLES OF GOOD PROGRAMMING

Programming is a highly skilled and creative activity involving intellect, time and cost. Hence, programs are to be written right, at first instance since subsequent modifications are costly, time-consuming and error-prone.

Bad programming would disrupt or delay the business processes, feed wrong information to the managers and result in losses.

Principles of good programming, in order to deliver quality software, minimal programming efforts and costs are discussed below. Subsequent modifications to the programs also need to be simple and easy.

1. **No redundancy of program codes/programs:** Programs (application software) are intellectual assets of the business involving costs and time. Hence business process automation requirements of the business need to be met through minimum

programming efforts. How this could be achieved? To perform a specific business function/task, only one set of instructions (program) need to be written and the same be used across all applications performing the function/task.

For example, there are a number of instances in business, where interests are to be computed. There should be only one program module for computing the interest for the entire organization and the deciding factors like the amount, rate of interest and time periods are to be passed on to this module by the calling programs in order to compute actual interest. This module should return the end result, namely 'interest' to calling programs. This will eliminate redundancy in program codes.

2. **Minimum processing time (efficiency):** Programs need to utilize the computer resources effectively and complete the business processes/tasks with minimum time. In achieving this, the programs need to be written with efficient logic (algorithm) including data handling techniques.

Programming is an intellectual activity and there is no automated mechanism to check the efficiency of the programs. Even if the efficiency of the programs are to be tested by other programmers (intellects), it is more time-consuming and cumbersome.

3. **All conditions incorporated in the programs/programmed decisions are to be tested thoroughly:** Programs need to be tested hundred percent, for all conditions incorporated in them. Since all conditions programmed may not be encountered in real life business situations, exhaustive test data need to be created for testing purposes. All programmed decisions/business rules incorporated in the software need to be tested fully with the test data prepared very exhaustively for this purpose.

4. **Changes in business rules should not impact existing programs:** When the business rules/decision parameters change, they should not warrant any modifications to the programs, e.g. changes in interest rates need to be picked up by the program from the decision table (data) without modifying the programs (which means the interest rates should not be coded in the programs directly).

5. **Program partitioning/modularity objects:** Programs need to be partitioned into a number of logical modules, each module performing a specific task or set of logically related functions (object programming). And any given business function/ task needs to be performed only by one unique/single program module in the entire organization. Program hierarchy under modular programming will consist of main program and number of sub programs or sub routines called in by the main program. The sub programs are executed by instructions like, Perform, Do, Go sub, and so on.

Program partitioning (objects) allows number of programmers to develop independent program modules concurrently so that the programming phase can be completed fast. This also enables simpler modules to be given to novice programmers and more complex modules to experienced programmers.

6. **Passing of data:** When a main program is calling a sub module, certain values/ parameters are passed from the 'calling program' to 'called program'. The 'called program' returns the results of the task executed by it, to the 'calling program' on return. This is called the passing of data/parameters. This general practice need to be followed in modular programming.

7. **Coupling:** Sub routines/program modules need to independently perform a logical activity/task without having to depend on other module/modules. In other words, sub routines/program modules should not be coupled together to perform one logical activity/task.

8. **Span of control:** To have good control over the main program and understanding of the sub modules, it is better that a main program or a 'calling program' calls not more than 10 to 12 sub programs (called programs). It is also possible that a 'called program' may in turn call another sub program (nesting). It is better to restrict the nesting to less than three levels of smaller modules, else the program flow/algorithm would look too complicated.

9. **Module size:** The functions or processes to be performed by a given module decides the module size. There may not be a restriction on how small a module needs to be. But where the modules are very big, it is advisable to split them if there are no other adverse consequences.

10. **Sharing of modules:** The program modules need to be in sharable mode so that main programs can call these modules (objects) to perform the preassigned tasks or program functions.

The advantages of modular programming are as follows:

- Simplifies the programming efforts.
- Simplifies system/program maintenance.
- Helps eliminating redundancy in program codes.
- Eliminates different modules performing the same function/task on different logic and hence producing different results.

12.13 COMPUTER AIDED SOFTWARE ENGINEERING (CASE)

Whereas IBASP automates the business processes, CASE tools automate SDLC processes resulting in IBASP.

CASE automates most of software engineering life cycle (SDLC) activities that are discussed in Chapter 8 and enables completion of the SW project faster. CASE also reduces the manual efforts of the software engineers involved in SDLC activities.

To understand CASE better, the readers are advised to be familiar with the SDLC activities discussed in Chapter 8. The readers should be aware that the software like IBASP is associated with:

- Thousands of data elements, automated processes and programmed decisions
- Hundreds of input, output and MIS formats
- Hundreds of application programs
- Very extensive documentation including diagrams.

- Number of software engineers with different technical skills leaving and joining the project
- Huge amount of highly skilled and time-consuming human efforts

Hence, automation of SDLC activities is an obvious requirement and CASE tools precisely fill this gap.

12.13.1 Advantages of CASE

1. **Enhance software engineers productivity/efficiency:** By using CASE tools, SDLC activities are speeded up. Software engineers are able to spend more time on creative thinking and conceptualizing a fully working business system and less time on documentation and drawing the charts. Design concepts which are in electronic mediums can easily be updated and shared as the designers come up with better alternatives/improved ideas.

2. **Improve effectiveness:** CASE tools incorporate best methods of performing all SDLC activities and enable uniformity in software (IBASP) design by all members in the team. Software engineers are also able to collaborate and brainstorm very closely. All SDLC activities get closely integrated.

3. **Improve quality of information systems/application software:** Software developed using CASE tools, result in better design. Developers are able to visualize the business processes and application programs in a better perspective. CASE allows system walk-through in HLD activities and allows improvements to be made to the design before actual programming works/LLD activities commence.

4. **Reduce the period time for implementation:** For software projects, time is the most important criteria. Since the design is done faster and the programs are tested thoroughly, the project gets completed early.

5. **Monotony of charting activities is eliminated:** Data dictionary, data flow diagrams, system flow chart, formatting of input and outputs, documentation of decision rules, etc. involve repetitive charting/documenting cycles until best solutions are reached. Monotony associated with such activities is eliminated.

6. **Ensures consistency and standards:** Standards and consistency of software engineering activities are ensured in all lifecycle activities. Program partitioning, sub modules and library functions are easily identified and catalogued for common use.

7. **SDLC related data in electronic form integrates all SW engineering activities:** Flexibility in capturing 'as is' processes, 'to be' processes, documentation of requirements and system specifications, programming and documentation standards, software quality assurance, etc. enable software engineers to get good exposure to the application requirements and encourage them to come up with better ideas in the initial stages of life cycle activities. CASE tools integrate all efforts associated with SDLC activities

8. **Excellent documentation:** CASE tools facilitate excellent documentation and communication both at project and post implementation stages.

12.13.2 CASE Tools

A tool is a device, when used, properly improves the performance (quality and quantity) of the task on hand. There are variety of tools and techniques developed to aid the software engineers in all SDLC activities. Some tools guide HLD and others LLD activities. CASE tools are to be read in conjunction with SDLC activities discussed in Chapter 8.

1. **Data collection/requirement analysis tools:** Data collection tools are used in the requirement analysis and 'as is' processes study phase which subsequently leads to requirement specifications and system design. It allows capture of all details required without exception including the description of current systems and business procedures. It documents the business processes including the decisions and flow of information/commands. This enables the requirement analysis to be performed in a more systematic way and reduces the possibility of missing out important issues at this stage.

2. **Diagramming tools/charting tools:** These tools create graphic representations of high level design activities involving data flow diagrams, system flowcharts, formatting of all system inputs and outputs and so on. At low levels, it allows drawing program structure diagram (macro program flowchart) and program flow charts. Powerful graphics capabilities enhance the quality of all SDLC activities.

3. **Dictionary tools:** Data dictionary (centralized data repository) and logical data base are created with the help of these tools which capture the data structures related to all data elements in terms of their names, description, size in bytes, data type, validation rules, decisions taken based on the data element, where used, where stored, what all the programs where it is used (cross reference) and so on.

4. **SDLC project database:** Project database is a software tool that manages a dedicated database to store all of the analysis and design specifications generated through various CASE tools. The database helps to ensure consistency and compatibility in the design of the:

   • Data elements
   • Computer processes (algorithm, decision tables, programmed decisions, etc.)
   • The user interfaces (screen layouts, print/MIS formats, access rights, passwords etc.)
   • Other aspects of IBASP being developed.

5. **Specification tools:** These tools assist in creating the specifications for input, output, processing and data integrity controls. This also includes tools for creating the data structures/specifications.

6. **Layout tools:** These tools help to describe the position of data, messages and headings on display screens, reports, queries and other input and output formats.

7. **Interface generators:** For screen inputs, it can design buttons, list of variables for data, colour schemes, scrolls, various types of GUI, icons, on screen help, and so on.

8. **Code generators:** From program structure diagram or from well written functional specifications, the program code generators generate source programs. However,

these programs need to be checked by the programmers for its accuracy, consistency and completeness. The code generators are generally not used for process intensive programs.

9. **Testing tools:** There are the tools that aid in evaluating the software package against specifications. They also generate test database and test transactions for the programs to be tested thoroughly.

10. **Decision table generators:** Generation of decision tables are also automated for all programmable decisions. Table processors are computer programs that handle actual table creation on the basis of input provided by the analyst. These tools convert set of conditions and decisions into actual computer instructions.

11. **Non procedural languages:** These types of languages allow the end users to easily learn programming through natural language like commands and make inquiries into the data base (extracting business information). One form of non procedural language is called SQL. These tools are aimed at end users who can develop simple applications without depending on the software engineers.

12. **Report generators:** Report generators also permit users to easily extract information from existing files or data base and put them in appropriate reports. This tool is useful for taking reports which are required once in a while and non repetitive in nature (ad hoc reports).

13. **Management tools:** Project management and allocation of resources for the project are done through project management tools.

12.14   COMPUTER VIRUS

Computer virus is the villainous software created with destructive intentions. It infects the computer systems electronically. After the virus code (program) is written, it is buried inside other genuine programs. Once the main program is executed, the virus code (villain program) also gets executed and it attaches itself to other programs in the system. Thus, the infected programs infect the other programs. Virus software is not detected by the operating system. Virus programs can corrupt both the programs and data. They do not damage the hardware.

Virus programs have become a nuisance more particularly in computer networks and Internet. It is always necessary to use licensed and authenticated software to avoid this problem. Files received over Internet need to be scanned for the presence of virus carried in them. Proprietary computers and operating systems are safer against virus attacks.

The impact of the virus may be a simple warning that pops up a message on screen out of the blue or it may destroy programs and data right away or on a given date. It can lie undetected for long and cause damages once in a while.

Anti virus software: As there are hundreds of computer viruses already active and more viruses are added every day, there are vendors who supply anti virus software (vaccines) to protect the computer systems and applications from the onslaughts of computer virus. An anti virus software can detect and eliminate number of computer viruses transmitted and resident in the computer systems. As new and more viruses are detected, new and more anti virus software are also being developed.

In business organizations the computer virus has become a big nuisance. Business organizations have been made to spend money in acquiring anti virus software like any other computer resources. There are software vendors who specialize only in developing anti virus software.

Prevention of virus attacks: Business organizations need to take certain precautions to safeguard the computer applications and the data resources against virus attacks. After all, prevention is better than cure.

- All software used in business need to be from authenticated sources and only licensed software need to procured and used. No copyrights violations with respect to software are to be encouraged by the management.
- No one in the organization is to be allowed to bring any type of software from outside and use them in the computers.
- E-mail users need to be careful when suspicious mails are received by them through Internet.
- When the business organizations send and receive data or programs, they need to scan those files and ensure that no virus is carried in them.
- All software and data need to be backed up regularly so that when the computer systems are infected with virus, it is possible to clear all the data storage areas (reformatting) and restore authenticated software and valid data back to the computers.
- Appropriate anti virus software needs to be bought and installed in the computer systems. Anti virus software also needs to be upgraded with newer versions which carry vaccines for newer virus.
- Proprietary hardware and operating systems supplied by vendors like IBM, HP, SUN Microsystems, etc. are safer against computer virus attacks.

12.15 SOFTWARE AND HARDWARE INTERFACE

Interface means either mechanical or electric or electronic interaction between various functionally independent entities like computer processor, memory, input/output devices, operating system, application software, communication devices, the users, and so on.

Interface is also the logical link between one entity to the other so that one understands the other, performs intended functions, "talks to" one another and passes on the results/controls back to other entities.

Examples of interface are:

- Mechanical/physical interface between the computer and input/output devices are called the adopters/ports (parallel, serial and USB) and electronic interface between them are called device controllers. Physical interface also consist of plugs, sockets, wires, etc.

- Software interface between the operating system and device controllers are device drivers.

- Electronic interface between the computers and communication devices are called protocols (e.g., OSI—open systems interconnect protocols).

- Logical interface between the programs and the sub modules within a program are called Application Program Interface (API). Software interface also consists of languages, codes, parameters and messages.

- Logical interface between the O/S and application programs are called system commands.

- Human interface between the application programs and the users are called graphical user interface, commands, menus, and so on.

- Network interface cards (NIC) and the modems are the electronic interface between the computers and the network.

- Routers, switches, hubs, etc. are the electronic interfaces between various segments of the networks.

- Internet/communication protocols consist of standards in terms of rules, functions and formats for data communication,

- The operating systems nowadays enable all devices (pen drives, printers, camera, mobile phones, hard disks, etc.) to be connected to the computers through USB ports. All these devices are automatically identified by the OS through corresponding device drivers and become operational instantly (plug and play devices).

Well established standards, protocols and various types of 'interfaces' are being precisely followed in the computer world.

12.16 PROCUREMENT OF SOFTWARE—CRITERIA FOR THE SELECTION OF SOFTWARE

Software could be in the form of operating systems, IBASP, RDBMS, programming languages, CASE tools, ERP, office automation software, application specific software, and so on.

All types of software need careful evaluation and the factors discussed below need to be taken into consideration.

1. **Quality of software:** The software needs to perform the stated functions reliably and accurately with no programming errors (program bugs). The software should have a track record of trouble-free working at least for a year or two in comparable business environments.

2. **Functionality:** Software needs to cover the requirements of business process automation, OLTPS, MIS, etc. of all business functions at optimal levels and integrate all business functions. Periodic updates and upgrades are to be made available to the software to enhance its functionality.

3. **Efficiency of software:** The software needs to make use of the resources like CPU, memory, disk space, networking infrastructure and communication bandwidths efficiently and complete the business processes in shortest time.

4. **Flexibility:** The software needs to be flexible to handle the changes arising out of the dynamic business environments. The source programs which are needed for this purpose need to be made available by the vendors to make such modifications. If the source programs are not offered, software vendors need to be bound by an escrow agreement through third party vendors in supplying the upgrades/updates on regular basis.

5. **Interface to other applications:** The application packages offered by the vendors need to provide interface to other programs and applications already in operation.

6. **Security:** Application programs, operating systems and RDBMS need to provide data security at data element, record and file levels through appropriate password management systems. It should also provide security to the computers such that no unauthorized people can have access to the computer resources, application software and the data. For data sent on communication mediums, the software needs to provide secured data encryption and decryption techniques.

7. **Connectivity:** The application software should enable all business users to get connected through Internet. The browser should become the 'front end' interface to the users.

8. **Integration:** The software needs to integrate all business functions through a common database and provide consistent MIS across all functions. The application software should enable close collaboration among all business functions and the managers.

9. **Programming language used:** The software needs to have been developed using efficient programming languages. Such programming skills need to be available locally at affordable costs for subsequent upgrades and modifications.

10. **Documentation:** The software functions and processes need to be well documented. User manuals need to be exhaustive and need to have self learning tutorials. The documentation needs to be available on line to offer contextual help to the users.

11. **User-friendly interface:** Software needs to provide simple user interface (GUI) and be highly user friendly. People with a little business domain knowledge and least computer skills should be able to use the software at ease.

12. **Compatibility:** The software package, the hardware and the O/S need to have perfect compatibility to one another. When one entity undergoes modification/upgrade, other entities need to be backward/forward compatibility with one another (configuration management).

13. **Software support:** Local support needs to be available for training, clarifications, bug fixing, fine tuning, etc. at short notice.

14. **Cost:** The cost needs to be commensurate with its functionality/capabilities and comparable to similar other products. The software needs to be evaluated based on

the costs and benefits. One time cost for the procurement of the software and the recurring costs for software upgrades and maintenance are to be taken into consideration.

15. **Reliability:** The software needs to perform reliably and be available to the business all the time. Peak business volumes also need to be handled by the software with no constraints.

16. **System response time:** All online tasks/business processes need to be completed within a few seconds. The batch jobs need to be completed in a short duration as expected by the users.

Successful implementation of IT applications in business depends mainly on the selection of right software. Since too many vendors are offering variety of software products, very careful evaluation needs to be made before any software is procured.

It is to be noted that customized IBASP developed from scratch can inherit all good features discussed above (please refer Section 8.13).

12.17 APPLICATION ARCHITECTURE/Platforms

Computer/hardware architectures have already been discussed in Section 11.11. IT applications also fall under different architectures. Some of the application architectures are discussed below to enable readers in understanding the relevance of various architectures to their respective business environments.

1. **Central or distributed computing:** Central computing, as the name implies, has a central computer (mainframe/server), integrated business application software (IBASP) and a common database wherefrom the business processes of entire organization are automated. All business functions and users stationed across wide geographic locations are connected to this central/only computer.

The advantages of central computing are:

1. Entire business gets seamlessly integrated and results in better management and control of the business and the automated processes.
2. Managing IT resources is also easy as all central resources are held in one location.

The drawbacks of central computing are:

1. Since transactions pertaining to entire business converge in to one single point (main computer), the main computer needs to be of very high capacity and fast (speed).
2. The network infrastructure needs to be highly reliable with sufficient bandwidths. Heavy data traffic through the networks would also involve higher communication costs.

Distributed computing, as the name implies, has number of computers (servers) each having their own database and integrated application software (IBASP) wherefrom the business processes of respective regions/zones are automated independently. The business functions/users stationed in a particular zone/region are connected to the servers of their respective regions.

However, all distributed computers are also networked with the central computer and the transactions for a day are updated on to the central computer in the evening (or specified intervals) such that consolidated MIS of the entire business is available at the central place. A case study related to the distributed computing is discussed in Section 12.18.

The advantages and the drawbacks of central computing are reversed in distributed computing.

2. **Integrated business applications (IBASP)/ERP and stand alone application:** IBASP has been discussed in Sections 1.13 and 5.1. Prior to IBASP, individual business functions used to have stand alone application software specific to their business functions. Such applications could not integrate the business functions as a whole and also created islands of information. One function's business information was not easily shareable by other functions. Individual functions claimed ownership for respective business information which defeated the very purpose of business process automation.

3. **Real time applications or batch applications:** There are two main characteristics for real time applications, viz.

   ● All business processes and the transactions are completed using the computer resources online all the time. In other words, no business activity is performed without the computers.

   ● The physical status of the business gets truly reflected in the computer database in electronic form in real time. This enables managers in obtaining information from the database that reflects true status of the business any moment.

In batch applications (batch processing systems has been discussed in Section 4.2) the transactions are gathered over a period of time and periodically processed using the computers. Such applications are used in select applications like employee payroll, dividend payment to shareholders, processing of books of accounts, and so on.

4. **Internet/Intranet/Extranet enabled application architecture:** Any business process performed/completed using Internet leads to this architecture. Depending on the extent of the users connected, these architectures are classified as Internet, Extranet and Intranet. This architecture totally removes the constraints posed by geographical, political and time zone boundaries. Any person anywhere in the globe can transact the business and obtain required MIS. This architecture shrinks the multinational business into a local business.

   ● Internet architecture is accessible by any person around the globe.

   ● Intranet architecture is accessible only by the employees of the same organization wherever they are stationed.

   ● Extranet architecture is accessible by all business associates of the business including the supply chain.

5. **Cloud computing:** Cloud computing is new and evolving application architecture made possible by high communication bandwidths (like 3G technology) and made

available to Internet users. The computer resources and variety of application software (like IBASP/ERP) are connected to the Internet all the time/continuously (by cloud computing service providers).

Business organizations can have access to these resources and use such applications on pay per usage basis. The business processes get automated for any business organization even though they do not own these resources. The applications are available as part of ready to use services. It is too early to say how far this architecture will be successful in Indian environments.

The advantages of cloud computing are:

- Business organizations need not make huge investments on computer infrastructure before they are sure of the advantages these applications could bring to their business. They also need not manage the computer resources. They can simply concentrate on running the business and not on the technology.

- There is no need for developing the application software (IBASP), nor do customization of ERP software.

- They could see and understand the prototypes of the IT applications working in similar industries, before making decisions in favour of this architecture.

- Pay per usage concept is an ideal revenue model for start up companies.

The drawbacks of cloud computing are:

- Reliability of IT applications offered on the cloud, data security, continued support from the cloud service providers, system response time, data security, etc. need to be evaluated very closely.

- A non disclosure agreement needs to be signed with the vendors assuring that the business processes/trade secrets of the clients are not disclosed to anyone else.

6. **Mobile computing:** IBASP/ERP applications implemented over Internet can also be extended to include the mobile/wireless devices like smart phones, i-pads, notebook computers and other portable devices. This enables the business users in performing/completing the computer processes and accessing MIS from anywhere and even while travelling. The managers on the move could still manage the business as if they are present at their workplace.

7. **Other possible architectures/platforms:** In addition to the application architectures discussed above, the application architectures are also identified by virtue of entities/names of the entities used in the business like,

- Operating systems
- RDBMS
- ERP packages
- Application/programming environments and so on.

12.18   CASE STUDY—DISTRIBUTED COMPUTING

Chemicals manufacturing and marketing organization headquartered at Chennai is selling a number of industrial and agro chemicals across entire India. The marketing is done by 15 regional offices situated at various cities and towns distributed across the country. They have implemented decentralized organization structure, where the regional heads are fully responsible (with delegation of power) for all the operations of their respective regions (profit centers). They need not look for any decisions to come from the corporate office at Chennai for day to day business operations. They are given all resources to manage by themselves and are accountable for the overall performance of respective regional business.

At each regional office, a LAN is installed with IBASP handling sales, marketing, warehousing and stock management, finance, logistics, and sales force automation functions. All business transactions are processed online (OLTPS) at the respective regional offices and no transactions are communicated to the corporate office at Chennai during the day. This saved enormous computing power at the corporate office and also communication bandwidths and costs required for centralized architecture. The LANs at respective regions worked very reliably and efficiently (fast).

The computer resources at the corporate office are used only for consolidating the business performance of all 15 regional offices including their stocks. The data from all 15 regional offices are uploaded on to the computer at the corporate office during nights which took only a few minutes for each region. At the end of the day, the corporate office still has all advantages of fully integrated business environments. The application software has been developed in-house by the company for this purpose. No main frame computer and no ERP were required for this distributed architecture.

SUM UP

In this chapter, the readers would have clearly understood software, types of software and how it interfaces between the users and the computer hardware.

The operating system, the functions of the operating system and other system software are explained in simple terms.

The application software, need for user-friendly GUI and integrated application software are discussed explicitly.

The principles of good programming are explained so as to enable programmers in producing quality programs.

The roles and advantages of CASE tools, problems caused by computer virus, precautions to be taken to be free of computer virus and various types of interfaces are explained.

The factors that need to be taken into consideration while procuring any type of software are outlined in detail.

Various types of application architectures and their relevance to business are elicited.

A case study has also been presented to enable readers in appreciating how the application architecture is dependant on the type of the business.

13

DATA AND DATABASE MANAGEMENT SYSTEMS

The following questions would guide the readers in navigating through this chapter:

1. How would you define data and information and what are their relevance to business and management?
2. What are data processing/information systems?
3. What are the components of DBMS?
4. What are the serial and direct access devices and what are their relative merits?
5. How the data files are organized and accessed in business applications?
6. What are the steps involved in the creation of the computer database?
7. What are entity/event relationship diagrams?
8. What are the rules to be followed in creating record structures?
9. What are the functions of the database management systems?
10. What are the advantages of RDBMS?
11. What are the three DBMS models and their relative merits/demerits?
12. What is data administration and what are the roles and responsibilities of database administrators?
13. What is SQL and how it is useful to the business managers?
14. What is the need for data and software backup and what are the procedures to be followed in back up and restoration?
15. What are the uses of data warehouse and data mining in business?

16. How the data is collected and fed into the computers in business organizations?
17. What is meant by data concurrency and how this is resolved by DBMS?
18. What is data independence and why the data need to be independent of other entities associated with IT application?
19. A case study is illustrated at the end of the chapter to show how relationships are established between different files.

After finishing this chapter, the readers would have clear answers to these questions.

13.1 INTRODUCTION

By virtue of extensive business process automation, large volumes of business data get captured through computers. We have discussed in Chapter 2 that the data and management information are the organizational resources that help managing other resources effectively. Hence business data need to be rightly identified, collected, processed and used in getting right information leading to better perception of the overall business, both of internal operations and external environments including supply chain and competition.

We need to understand data, the organization of data into records, files and database, operational use of data, management information, data warehouse, data mining, and so on.

Data: Data (plural of datum) are the facts from which information could be obtained and the same be used in drawing conclusions and inferences.

1. Data are the representation of facts, suitable for communication, identification, interpretation or processing by people/computers.
2. Data in business could be in the form of quantities, values, descriptions, date, time etc. to which meaning is or can be assigned. Generally, we perform operations on business data to supply some information about a business entity or event.

Business data are raw facts pertaining to business entities or events. More specifically, data are objective representation of the attributes or characteristics of business entities (such as customers, products, suppliers, etc.) and events (such as purchases, sales, payments, collections and so on).

Data may not convey a meaning until they are processed and converted into appropriate formats (information). These issues have been discussed in detail in Chapter 2.

Information: Information is the meaning that a human assigns to data by means of his perception and its context.

Information is the presentation of appropriately selected and processed data arranged in right formats such that it conveys a definite meaning to a person. It enables the person to perceive the situation better and make him knowledgeable in the process.

13.2 DATA PROCESSING

Data processing (also discussed in Section 2.2.1) would involve one or more of the activities such as:

- Summation, classification, sequencing, and grouping
- Storing, accessing and comparing
- Application of rules or formulae and doing computations
- Editing, formatting, graphical conversion and other forms of representation to improve human perception
- Programmed decisions, identification of exceptions, communication, data manipulation (add/modify/delete/edit) and so on.

Information systems can be defined as a set of entities that collect, store, access, process and distribute information to aid decision making and other management functions in an organization.

In the present context, information system or management information system (IS or MIS) is the management solution based on information technology, in solving business and management problems. Information systems that are aimed at the business managers (at all levels) are called MIS.

13.3 DATABASE, DATA DICTIONARY AND DATA STRUCTURES

A computer database is a computerized, well-defined and centrally managed collection of data elements (data store or data warehouse) shared by all in an organization.

A computer database can also be defined as a set of electronic files, each file containing number of records and each record storing logically related data elements pertaining to a business entity or event.

The data stored in a database is independent of application programs using them and the data storage devices.

Data dictionary is a database of all data (metadata) elements themselves. It is a 'Repository' of all data elements used in the organization (of all IT applications). It describes the data elements in terms of their individual name, description, size (width in bytes), data type (descriptive, quantitative, time, etc.), record key, its usage, associated decisions, file where it is residing, programs or applications using the data element, its source, the range of acceptable values, access rights, and so on.

Entity files (masters) and event (transactions) files: We have already discussed the business entities and events in Chapter 2. Accordingly, the business data could be classified as master and transaction files.

Master files/tables: Business data associated with the entities like employees, vendors, customers, dealers, investors, raw materials, machinery, buildings, finished products and so on are stored in master files. The data pertaining to the entities do not undergo changes very often.

Transaction files/tables: Purchase orders, material receipts, payments, sales invoices, sales collection, salary payments, borrowings, investments, etc. are the examples of business events. The events are captured in the transaction files. Transaction files pertaining to each event grow in volume every day. Sales invoices file, for example, is a transaction file and each sale as a record is added to this file.

File: File is a collection of records having the same record structure (layout) and length all pertaining to one entity (or event). Individual entity or event contained in a file is uniquely identified by a key data element (called key or index), which is part of the record itself. File organization is an important attribute of a file.

Record/record structure: Record (also referred as row) is a collection of all data elements pertaining to one entity (or event) arranged as per the record structure or layout. Record structure means the order in which individual data elements are placed in a record (in a definite order with respect to the first data element) and its fixed length (record length in bytes is equal to sum total of widths of all the data elements placed in a record).

Data element or field: Data element or a field is a single or group of characters. Each data element has definite structure (data type) and width (in bytes).

Most basic form of data element is a character (a byte), which may consist of an alphabet, integer, or any of the special characters.

Data structure describes the data element as:

- Descriptive (alphabets, numerals and symbols)
- Numeric (Integer, decimal and floating point)
- Money value
- Date and time
- Logical

Key field: A record pertaining to one unique entity/event in a file is identified by its key data element called index or key field. The key field uniquely identifies each record within a file. There are two types of keys—primary key and secondary key. The primary key controls the current processing order of a file. Secondary key is not used to control the current processing order of the file. Each file in the database needs to contain a unique primary key.

Example of record structure: Employee data file would consist of records of all employees in the organization. Record structure layout for the employee record would be like as given below:

Data name	Data type	Data width	Record structure	Key field
Employee number	Numeric	5	1–5	Primary
Department number	Numeric	3	6–8	Secondary
Name	Description	35	9–43	
Date of birth	Date	8	44–51	
Designation	Description	25	52–76	
Cadre code	Numeric	1	77	
Date of joining	Date	8	78–85	
Years of experience	Numeric	2	86–87	
Basic salary	Numeric decimal	8, 2	88–95	... and so on

13.4 DATA STORAGE DEVICES, FILE ORGANIZATION AND ACCESS METHODS

1. **Serial access device:** Magnetic tape, digital audio tape (DAT) and cassette tapes are serial recording and serial access devices. Data is recorded in a serial order and accessed in the same order. For example, if employees' data pertaining to 1000 employees are stored in serial access devices, employee data are stored one after the other for all 1000 employees. If the record pertaining to 501st employee is to be processed, the preceding 500 records need to be accessed. These devices are obsolete now.

   Direct access device. Hard disks, compact disks (CD), DVD, etc. are called direct access devices. CD and DVD consist of single recording platter. Hard disk consists of multiple recording platters mounted one over the above over a common spindle.

Data on direct access devices are stored on virtual circular tracks on each surface of the platter and each track is divided into number of virtual sectors. Since the hard disk consists of multiple platters, virtual tracks of same radius found on all platters are called virtual cylinders.

Data storage location on these devices is identified in terms of cylinder number, track number and sector number (storage address). The read/write arm which flies over these platters (without touching the platters) can be positioned directly on any cylinder, track or sector and hence the name direct access device (already discussed in Section 11.6). Data processing invariably involves direct access devices (hard disks).

2. **File organization:** It means how the records in a file are organized while creating the file. File organization decides the type of file access.

The three ways in which the files could be organized are discussed below.

   (i) *Serial/sequential organization.* In serial organization, the records in a file are stored in a serial order one after the other starting from the first. If the record keys are in sequence, the organization is called sequential. Such file organization is ideal for applications like employee payroll, investors' database, depositors' database, etc. as all records in a file need to be processed at a specific instance. The main drawback of this organization is that even for accessing one record, all records in the file need to be accessed and even if one record is to be updated, those entire file needs to be rewritten. This organization is generally not used in business applications.

   (ii) *Indexed sequential organization.* In indexed sequential organization, the records in the main file can be placed in any order. But a second file, called the index file, is created which has only the key data elements (of all the records of the main file) arranged in a sequence along with the location address of the respective record in hard disk.

Any record in the main file can be located with the help of the index file and can be accessed without disturbing other records in it. This file access is also called indexed sequential access method (ISAM). Most of the applications today use this type of file organization.

(iii) *Random organization (hashed file organization).* In random organization, the records are placed at random on the hard disk and their location address is arrived through an algorithm or mathematical formula (hashing) which converts key data element itself into respective storage location address in the hard disk. For example, when a record pertaining to a particular product is to be stored in the disk, the location address is computed through such algorithm using the product number itself. The record of a particular product number is accessed by converting the product number into the storage location address by the same algorithm. No separate index files are involved in random organization. This method is not used today.

3. **File access methods:** The ways by which the records in a file could be accessed are called access methods. The access method is decided based on how the file is organized.

(i) *Sequential access.* The files organized sequentially can only be accessed sequentially. This type of access is limited to a few applications only.

(ii) *Indexed sequential access method (ISAM)/Random access.* The records in the file can be accessed at random using the index file. ISAM files can also be accessed sequentially.

4. **File management activities—Case studies:** Two case studies discussed here relate to file management activities, viz. file organization and access. These case studies would also help in understanding the programming efforts involved in file management activities under each program (in order to appreciate how DBMS helps reducing the programming efforts).

CASE STUDY A: Processing of customer orders and invoicing.

Flowchart (flowchart symbols have been discussed in Section 4.1)
File management activities associated with order processing is shown in **Figure 13.1**.

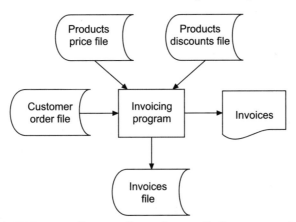

FIGURE 13.1 System flow chart—Order processing.

(a) **Customers order file:** This file needs to be accessed sequentially from the first record to the last since all customer orders need to be invoiced without exception. This file also needs to be accessed at random as and when individual customers want to know the status of their orders. Hence, this file needs to be indexed on customer order number.

Index file, as already discussed, is another physical file created by file management systems (FMS).

This file contains multiple events (orders) and multiple entities (products) under each event, with many to many relationships (entity/event relationships are discussed in Section 13.7).

(b) **Products file:** This contains the product number, description and selling price for each product. This file will be accessed at random depending on which product is invoiced. This file needs to be indexed on part number. This file is a unique entity file, as it contains one record for each product, with one to one relationship (entity/ events relationships are discussed in Section 13.7).

(c) **Products discounts file:** This file would contain only those products, for which discounts are offered. For the same product, there could be multiple discounts based on sales volumes. This file is also indexed on product number. This file will have multiple entries for the same product, (one to many relationships) and hence is kept as a separate file.

All files mentioned above are input files. Orders file though an input file is also updated to indicate that an order has been invoiced.

(d) **Invoices file:** This file is created afresh by the program. For each product ordered, (as contained in customers orders file) a separate record is created in this file. This file is a sequential file as all invoices are to be processed subsequently in MIS, financial accounting and so on. Invoice documents are also printed through this program.

The program processing these business tasks needs to perform the following file/data management activities:

- Open 3 input files and 1 output file.
- Access each record from customers orders file and based on the product contained in it, access products price file and discounts file at random.
- For each product invoiced, it has to create a record in the output file.
- Close all files at the completion of the process.

All instructions to perform such file/data management activities are to be programmed by the programmers. However, index files are created by file management software (FMS), which is a utility program and not by the application programs.

CASE STUDY B: Accessing employee data from the database.

All files in this case are indexed on employee number. All are input files and are related to one another by employee number (relational database).

File management activities associated with employee information system is shown in **Figure 13.2**.

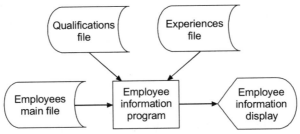

FIGURE 13.2 System flow chart—Employee information system.

(a) **Employee main file:** This file contains all data elements pertaining to one employee which have one to one relationship like name, date of birth, address, father's name, basic salary, designation, and so on.

(b) **Qualifications files:** This file is maintained separately since one employee can have one or any number of qualifications (one entity with many events).

(c) **Experiences file:** This file is also maintained separately since one employee can have one or more experience (one entity with many events).

Employee data contained in these three files are accessed together and displayed on the monitor by this program.

This program needs to perform the following file/data management activities:

● Open all input files.

● Based on the employee number contained in the main file, access other two files based on their index, viz. employee number.

● Assemble all data pertaining to an employee from all these files and display the same on the monitor (output).

Necessary instructions are to be programmed for these file/data management activities under this program.

5. **Logical database:** It is a repository of all data elements pertaining to all business entities and events. Logical database has been discussed in detail in Section 2.14. The data dictionary (already discussed in Section 13.3) and the physical database are built based on the logical database.

6. **Physical database:** It consists of number of files, each file corresponding to a business entity or an event, and each file having unique record structure. For example, employees' database would consist of employees' main data file, qualifications file, experiences file, performance ratings file and promotions file.

7. **DBMS:** It allows creation, accessing and management of all files in business and also the records contained in it. It manipulates the data elements contained in the records. It also establishes the relationship among logically related files. DBMS is discussed in detail in Section 13.9.

8. **Data access time:** The data access time (from the hard disk) would involve

   - *Seek time.* Time required for the read/write arm to position itself over a logical cylinder,

   - *Rotational delay.* Time required for the sector to pass through the read/write head,

   - *Data transfer speed.* Rate at which the data is transferred from the hard disk to the computer memory.

9. **File update:** File update means adding or deleting a record in a file or adding, deleting or modifying one or more data elements in a record (data manipulation).

10. **Programming efforts:** The file organization and data accessing activities discussed above are performed by the programs written using the programming languages (like COBOL, PL/1), without using DBMS.

The programmers under such environments need to write necessary instructions (codes) in the application programs to perform these file/data management functions in each of the programs they write. When a business organization needs to write about 500 application programs, all 500 programs need to have such instructions (involving enormous programming efforts).

The database management systems (DBMS) save programming efforts required for file management activities very appreciably.

13.5 LOGICAL STRUCTURE OF DATABASE

Logical structure of DBMS is shown in **Figure 13.3**.

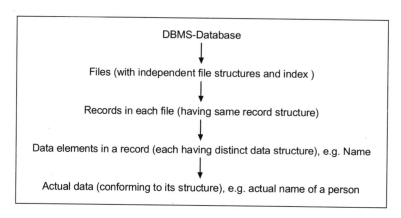

FIGURE 13.3

DBMS is the software package that permits the business to centralize the data resources, manage them efficiently and provide access to all application programs used in business.

13.6 STEPS INVOLVED IN THE CREATION OF DBMS

1. **Creation of logical database:** The logical database has been discussed in Section 2.14. The process of identifying the data elements pertaining to various business entities and events have also been discussed in Section 7.3. It is the responsibility of the business managers to create right logical database for the business.

2. **Creation of data dictionary (meta-data):** The data dictionary, as discussed in Section 13.3, needs to be created by the software engineers as part of SDLC activities. It would have an entry for each data element describing its structure. Data dictionary is created as part of the DBMS design. Redundancy in data elements is filtered by the DBMS.

3. **Design of physical database:** The physical database is created as part of the system design activity under SDLC. The physical database is created by logically grouping the data elements into respective entity/event files (master/transaction files). Record layouts are finalized for all entity/event files. Key data by which the records are to be organized/accessed are finalized. The entity/event relationship diagrams and the rules for creation record structures which are discussed in Sections 13.7 and 13.8 are useful for this activity.

Relations between the logically related files are to be established such that complete data pertaining to a business entity or an event could be assembled/accessed from all logically related files (relational database).

Four logical steps involved in the creation of DBMS is illustrated in **Figure 13.4**.

4. **Creation of DBMS:** The data is then loaded in to the DBMS.

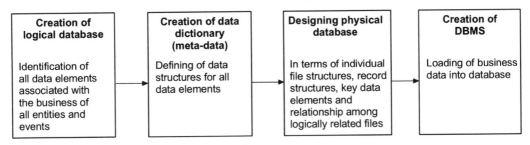

FIGURE 13.4 Logical steps involved in the creation of DBMS.

13.7 ENTITY/EVENT RELATIONSHIP DIAGRAMS

Entity/event relationship diagrams help in understanding the relationship among business entities and events by their relationships with one another as well as the extent of such relationship. This is illustrated through **Figure 13.5** as a case study (some examples of entity/event relationships have already been seen in Section 13.4.4. through two case studies).

Let us consider a case involving

- Number of suppliers
- Number of raw materials supplied by each supplier (one to many relationship)

- Number of purchase orders (placed with various suppliers) and each having number of raw materials (many to many relationship).

1. Unique dependency means that one entity cannot exist without the other.
2. Dual dependency means one to many relationships.
3. Multi dependency means many to many relationships.

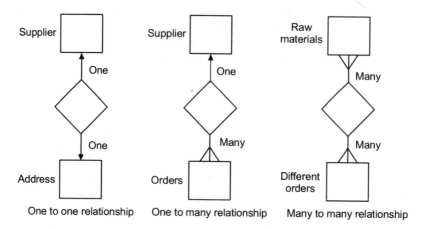

FIGURE 13.5 Entity/event relationship diagram.

In the first case, the supplier and his address have one to one relationship.

In the second case, the supplier and the orders have one to many relationships.

In the third case, the raw materials and the orders have many to many relationships.

13.8 RULES FOR DECIDING RECORD STRUCTURES

Certain rules discussed in this section and Figure 13.5 are useful in understanding the relationship between the business entities and the events, so that the data storage and access methods are designed efficiently. By these rules, placing of all data elements in a single file is avoided and also simpler and easily manageable file structures (with logical relationship to one another) are identified.

The objectives of these rules are:

- To structure the data with no redundancy, e.g. purchase order data and the materials purchased through them are kept as two separate files because one order will have more than one material purchased and the purchase order data are not repeated in all material purchase records.

- To save data storage space and speed up data access and update (for query and reporting).

- To eliminate the need to restructure or reorganize the database when new data elements are added or deleted or new applications are developed.

In other words, creating small, flexible and non redundant data structures from the data dictionary are made possible through these rules.

Three rules generally to be followed are discussed below.

1. **First rule:** All records in a file need to be of same record structure and length.

For example, say the employee name, designation, department code, department name, employee address, educational qualifications and the previous experiences are the data elements to be stored in an employee record.

It is not possible to fix the record length for the employee record, because the number of qualifications and previous experiences would vary for individual employees. If maximum number of qualifications and the experiences are assigned in the record structure, the record space would be wasted for the employees with just one experience/one qualification.

In such situations, the repeating data elements whose number of occurrences cannot be stated are removed and put in other files after establishing the relation with the first file. The employee number serves as relationship for all such files.

Hence we need to have

- Employee personal file (master file)
- Employee qualifications file
- Employee experiences file.

2. **Second rule:** This is achieved when a record satisfies first rule and when each data element in a record is only dependent on the record key (employee number in the above example). In the above example, department name is not dependent on employee number and hence department name is to be removed from the employee record. Another file needs to be created with department code and department name and the department code as the key.

3. **Third rule:** This can be understood with the following illustration.

Let us consider a file structure with the following data elements:

Finished product XXX
    Raw material 1
    Supplier of raw material 1
        Raw material 2
        Supplier of raw material 2
            Raw material 3
            Supplier of raw material 3
                ... ...
                And so on'

Raw material 1, 2 and 3 are identified with the finished product XXX which is fine. But the suppliers of raw materials 1, 2 and 3 also get dependant on the finished product XXX. This is not correct since we may have to buy raw materials 1, 2 and 3 from different suppliers at different times. Suppliers have no dependency on finished product.

So, the record structures need to be split and put into two different files as shown below.

File 1	**File 2**
Finished product XXX	Raw material 1
Raw material 1	Supplier of raw material 1
Raw material 2	Raw material 2
Raw material 3	Supplier of raw material 2
	Raw material 3
	Supplier of raw material 3

Thus, the finished products' file does not become dependant on suppliers. Good understanding of the business entities and the events and relationship between them are essential while designing physical database.

13.9   DBMS: FILES/RECORDS/DATA MANAGEMENT FUNCTIONS

1. **File management:**
   - Allows new files to be added to the database.
   - Organizes and accesses each file based on its key (a key may consist of one or more data elements).
   - Establishes logical relationship among a set of (logically related) files and makes it look like a single virtual file for the users.

2. **Record management:**
   - Allows records to be added or deleted to a file.
   - Maintains a uniform record structure for each file.
   - Accesses a record by its key data element.

3. **Data elements management:**
   - Maintains data structure for all data elements.
   - Data elements can be added or deleted but the application programs are to be modified accordingly.
   - Identifies redundancy and helps eliminating them at the design stage itself.

4. **Data management (data manipulation):**
   - Data can be added, modified or deleted.
   - Data can be accessed by application software.

13.10   FUNCTIONS AND ADVANTAGES OF DBMS/RDBMS

Database management systems enable thousands of data elements (of all entities and events) to be stored, organized, updated and accessed by the business applications very efficiently.

It helps delivering the most important resource, viz. the 'information' to the management fast.

1. **Data definition:** As the business commences the operations every day, large volumes of business data (of all business events and entities, consisting of thousands of data elements) get created. All these data elements need to be captured and processed. It is necessary to define all data elements. The DBMS performs this task.

   ● It enables all data elements to be defined without exception. Data elements are defined in terms of the data structures discussed earlier.

   ● Allows data from different files to be logically related to one another.

2. **Data manipulation:**

   ● Enables users to get business information/MIS from the database using English like commands called SQL (structured query language).

   ● Business functions are allowed to add/modify/delete/access any data stored in any file within the database.

   ● Makes it possible to manipulate (assemble, punctuate, edit, compute, format, highlight, etc.) business data.

3. **Data integrity/consistency/redundancy:**

   ● DBMS allows users to define various rules/controls for individual data elements and based on that it maintains data integrity/consistency.

   ● Performs various data validation checks/controls to filter erroneous data entering the database.

   ● Ensures no redundant data element within the database.

4. **Database access controls:**

   ● Enables only authorized users to access the data elements/records/files based on the access rights defined by the database administrators.

   ● Tracks and maintains audit trails for the data accessed/modified by the users.

5. **Concurrency control:**

   ● Locks the data at data element/record/file levels when more than one user is trying to manipulate the same data concurrently (discussed in Section 13.17).

   ● Entire database is locked when the database as a whole is backed up.

6. **Transaction recovery:** Records the transactions/changes to the database individually, so that the database can be rolled back to earlier status in the event of hard disk or any other failure.

7. **Establishes logical relationship:** Even when logically related data are stored in different files, DBMS enable logical relationship to be established among different files and the data stored therein (as seen in the second case study in Section 13.4.4).

8. **Save programming efforts:** Saves considerable programming efforts otherwise to be spent in managing the files through individual programs (as explained through the case studies in Section 13.4.4).

9. **Database backup and restoration:** Database backup and restoration is a cumbersome job and still needs to be performed very often. Back up and restoration are made more efficient and simpler.

10. **Additional functions:**

- Provide central control for data creation and definition by maintaining the data dictionaries for entire business.
- Complexity of the information systems environments is reduced by centralized management of data, access methods and security.
- Database modifications and restructuring is made simpler.
- Access speeds (data retrieval speeds) are increased because these packages use complex algorithm in such processes.
- Programs (SW) to data dependence is eliminated (discussed in Section 13.19)

13.11   DBMS IMPLEMENTATION METHODOLOGIES

Though three alternative models of DBMS have emerged, Relational Database Management Systems (RDBMS) has become a clear winner in the race.

Let us discuss these models with reference to a case involving four different files, viz.

1. Supplier file (Key: supplier name)
2. Sources for materials file (suppliers and the raw materials supplied by them (Key: supplier name and raw material name)
3. Purchase orders placed with the suppliers for the purchase of raw materials (Key: supplier name, raw material name and purchase (event) order number)
4. Raw materials received from suppliers based on the purchase orders (Key: supplier name, raw material name, purchase order number and material delivery note number).

Hierarchical database management system

The hierarchical data management system divides the database into root segment and number of subordinate segments. The supplier file is placed in the root segment. This root segment will have three subordinate segments, viz. the materials sources file, the purchase orders and the materials received as shown in **Figure 13.6**.

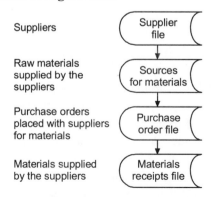

FIGURE 13.6   Logical structure of hierarchical data management system.

The supplier record of the root segment will have pointer to the subordinate segment, viz. the source of supplies to identify all the materials supplied by a supplier. If a supplier does not supply any materials, the corresponding pointer will be empty. Pointers are the data elements in the root segment that direct the system to the respective storage location (address) of the hard disk. The subordinate segments in turn will have pointers to the respective higher segments also, for DBMS to return back.

File at each level will have pointers to the respective subordinate segments and vice versa. This method of organization and establishing links back and forth are more cumbersome, time-consuming and generally not used now.

Networked database management system

The networked model treats data consisting of number of segments but not with one to many relationships but with many to many relationships. All segments will have pointers to other segments (if present) for the same supplier. For a given supplier the first pointer will lead to one segment of data related to the supplier and subsequently to the other pointers as indicated in the respective segments. Though redundancy is reduced in this method and the processing time is improved, more number of pointers would make file maintenance more complicated. This concept is also not generally used now.

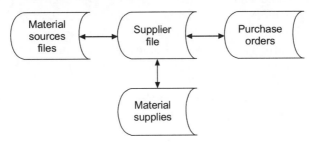

FIGURE 13.7 Logical structure of networked database management system.

Relational database management systems (RDBMS)

Files linked by the relations, in terms of the key data elements of each file are given below.

1. Supplier file (Key/Index: supplier name),
2. Source of supplies file (Key/Index: supplier name and raw material name),
3. Purchase orders placed with the suppliers (Key/Index: supplier name, material name and order number).
4. Materials supplied by the suppliers (Key/Index: supplier name, material name, order number and delivery document number).

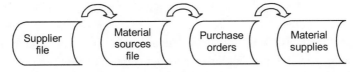

FIGURE 13.8 Logical structure of relational database management system.

Any file can access any other file through relations established through the above keys. Most of the present DBMS adopt relational models which have become de facto standard for DBMS. This database model overcomes the drawbacks of the other two models discussed above. The relational model represents all data in the database as simple two dimensional tables called the 'relations'. The files appear similar to flat files, but the information in more than one file can be easily extracted and combined. All four files share key data elements as indicated above in simple relationship to one another.

All functions/advantages discussed under DBMS in Section 13.10 are applicable to RDBMS as well.

The strength of the relational data model is that it can relate data in one file to data in another file as long as both files share a common key (relations). RDBMS models are highly flexible and are user-friendly. Programming complexity is reduced in RDBMS.

13.12   DATA ADMINISTRATION/DATABASE ADMINISTRATOR

Data administration is a business function which needs to identify the data requirements of entire business. Data administrators assess information needs of all the functions internal to the business and to interact with external entities. The data could be MIS oriented or operations oriented or interaction oriented as discussed in Section 5.9.2. The data administrators could be functional heads or system managers with good business domain knowledge.

The fundamental principle of data administration is that the data/information is an organizational asset and no individual function can claim exclusive rights to it. They need to ensure that data and information flow freely across all business functions, link all business processes and enable people in taking right decisions.

The data administrator is responsible for:

- The policies and procedures for managing data as an organizational resource
- Design of logical database
- Monitoring the usage of data by business functions
- Fixing responsibilities for entering/capturing data and establishing procedures in ensuring data integrity at all stages
- Framing information policy that specifies rules for sharing the data, confidentiality, access rights
- Systems and procedures related to creation of data warehouse.

Database administration refers to technical and operational aspects of managing business data including data dictionary, physical database design, database maintenance and monitoring the performance of database. Database administrator has the following responsibilities:

- Conversion of the logical database into physical database, creation of data structures and record layouts
- Defining file access keys and logical relations among other files
- Developing security procedures to safeguard the database
- Database design and documentation

- Maintenance of DBMS software and fine tuning the application programs to optimize access time
- Selection of right type of RDBMS and servers
- Setting all system parameters such that all computer resources are utilized to the optimum level
- Establishing backup and restoration procedures for the database and so on.

13.13 STRUCTURED QUERY LANGUAGE (SQL)

User-friendly language being used by the managers to make enquiries into the database is called structured query language (SQL). Though complex programming tasks cannot be handled by SQL, they are proving to be very effective with the end users who can access the database interactively for day-to-day business decisions. SQL commands can also be embedded in application programs written in any programming languages.

Various RDBMS vendors adopt certain standards in its structure so that people are comfortable with different RDBMS.

SELECT, FROM, WHERE, etc. are some of the command words in SQL which are easy for the people to know what actually is done by these commands.

13.14 DATA BACKUP AND RESTORATION

Data, operating systems, RDBMS and application software stored in the hard disks, on-line could get corrupted or destroyed due to the following reasons:

- Power surges which would damage the read/write heads of the direct access devices and hence the mediums
- Sudden power failures could damage data definition tables and the index files
- Mechanical failure of the disk drives due to fatigue in the long run
- Application programs which could wrongly modify/delete the data or records or files
- Computer virus
- Human negligence or sabotage or fraud

Hence, anything that is stored on the online devices needs to be backed up and preserved as off line data/software. The O/S, RDBMS and other software packages which are bought from the external vendors would be available in the original mediums as supplied by the vendors and they could be used for restoring them. The data and application programs developed in-house need to be backed up regularly.

The data backup though takes time and efforts, it needs to be done on regular basis without fail. Some critical business applications need to be backed up continuously. Data backup and restoration procedures need to be well documented and implemented without exception. Backed up mediums need to be stored away from the computer centers.

Incremental backup: There are facilities in the RDBMS packages to take the incremental backup of those files or records which have changed since the earlier full backup. Restoration needs to be done with both original and current incremental backup data. Since only those data that have undergone changes are backed up, it would take lesser time for the backup.

Data backup is also discussed in Section 8.7.5.

13.15   DATA WAREHOUSE AND DATA MINING

Data warehouse and data mining have already been discussed in detail in Section 5.9.

13.16   ADVANTAGES OF DATABASE TO THE BUSINESS

Database offers the following benefits to the business:

- Maintains the data records of all business entities and events in electronic form where-from the business performance, exceptions, action items, etc. could be extracted by the business users anytime.
- Allows extraction of right MIS for managerial action and decision making.
- Allows building of decision support systems and data warehouse based on the historic data.
- Enables business organizations to meet statutory requirements of financial accounting and profit reporting in time.
- Allows people of all business functions to collaborate on common organizational data in achieving business objectives.
- Integrates all business functions and operations through a common database.
- Enables capture of data in real time so that real status of the business gets truly reflected as MIS.
- Helps all levels and functions of management to effectively and efficiently manage the business resources.

(Advantages of database has also been highlighted in Section 1.1.3.2)

13.17   DATA CONCURRENCY

More than one user accessing the same file or data in the database at any given moment is called concurrent users.

When many users are trying to update and access same data element at the same time, data concurrency occurs. For example, when a sales clerk is updating the selling price of the product, another person could be creating a sales invoice for the same product. The sales invoice could pick up wrong price in the process.

Concurrency control is the ability of the application software or the RDBMS, which ensures that when one user is using the data, there is no interference from other users.

To achieve concurrency control, either the entire file or a record or a data element is locked by the first user so that the second user waits until the activity is completed by the first user. However, this will not be noticed by the users since such locking gets removed in micro seconds.

When an entire file is locked (coarse granularity), more users or processes get locked out. When a record or a data element is locked (fine granularity), only one or two users are locked out. Entire database also could be locked during data back up.

13.18 METHODS OF COLLECTING DATA

Business data can be entered into the computer either offline or online. Data entry is a time-consuming and error-prone manual activity. Hence, necessary precautions are to be taken to identify and rectify all errors at the data entry stage. Data also need to be complete with respect to an entity or an event.

There are many ways of entering the data into the computer systems depending on the type of applications and availability of computer resources.

- *Direct entry into the computer.* The data could be directly entered into the computer database. OLTPS, IBA and Internet based applications use this method in capturing the data. This is the most predominant method of data capture today.
- *Bar codes/QR codes readers.* These readers have been discussed in Section 11.7.
- *Optical character recognition (OCR).* Text/data in printed forms can be read by the computers directly using OCR technology and convert the data in to ASCII format (already discussed in Section 4.5.3).
- *Electronic data interchange (EDI).* When data is communicated from one computer to other, they can be sent using the mediums like CDs and pen drives, which can directly feed such data into the destination computers. For example, buyers can send the purchase orders data through CD to the suppliers when such data are large in volumes.
- *File transfers.* The data in electronic mediums can be sent from one computer to the other through e-mail. This method is very popular nowadays and it reduces manual data entry efforts considerably.
- *Mouse.* Data can be entered into the computer by choosing a data element from the list of variables displayed on the computer screen, by a click of the mouse button or using the touch screen.
- *Off line data entry.* The data can also be entered on to the CDs/pen drives using stand alone PCs first and such data can be fed as inputs to other business applications like batch processing, OLTPS, IBA, and so on.

13.19 DATA INDEPENDENCE

IT applications are associated with five entities, viz. people, application software/operating systems, DBMS, computers and the business processes. As the technology evolves/progresses, the computer resources, application programs, operating systems and the DBMS undergo changes/upgrades and such changes do occur frequently.

Data independence means that the business data need to remain the same and unaltered, independent of the changes encountered in other entities.

Why data independence?

- Business users should be able to add new data and files and access information out of them without being affected by other IT entities.
- No business data or parameters associated with decision rules (like interest, and discount percentages, tax rates, etc.) are to be incorporated in the software (programs). Else the programs are to be modified when such data undergo frequent revisions. Instead, they need to be stored in separate files and the business users should be able to modify such data in those files.
- Historic data of the previous years stored in the computers should be usable by the business irrespective of the changes taking place with respect to other IT entities.
- It is not possible to re-enact the business events/transactions and the data captured once need to remain the same for ever.
- Data is an organizational resource and need to be protected from other entities associated with IT applications.

13.20 CASE STUDY—DATA MANAGEMENT

This case study would enable readers in understanding file and record structures, file organization and access, entity/event relationships, and the rules for deciding file and record structures.

File A: Suppliers master (entity) file

A1. File structure

Supplier file contains data related to the suppliers. Each supplier is uniquely identified by a supplier code. Since this file is to be accessed at random, this file is indexed and accessed on supplier code. Index file is yet another file created by the system.

This entity file has one-to-one relationship with all the data elements contained in it, i.e., all data elements shown are uniquely identified with a supplier.

A2. Record structure

Sl. No.	Data element description	Data Short name	Data type	Data width	Record structure	Comments
1	Supplier code	Suplr.code	Num	5	1–5	Key data/Index
2	Supplier name	Suplr.name	Desc	35	6–40	
3	Supplier address	Suplr.add	Desc	50	41–90	
4	Supplier town	Suplr.town	Desc	15	91–105	
5	Supplier state	Suplr.state	Desc	15	106–130	
6	Supplier country	Suplr.contry	Desc	15	131–150	
7	Supplier pincode	Suplr.pin	Num	6	151–156	
8	Supplied value	Supld.value	Amt	8+2	157–166	Value of materials supplied
9	Supplier appointment	Suplr.date	Date	8	167-174	

Desc = Descriptive data (alpha numeric), Num = Number data, Date = date field

Amt = Amount field with decimals (rupees and paise)

The above table shows data structures of nine data elements identified with each supplier (record) file. Each supplier will have a record in this file and, if there are 500 suppliers, this file will have 500 records.

It also shows the record structure, viz., relative location of the data elements within the record, data width in bytes of each data element and the record length (which is equal to 174 bytes).

It is now possible to understand the concept of a file, records contained in a file and the data elements contained in a record. This file is organized as indexed sequential on suplr.code and hence can only be accessed by feeding valid suplr.code to the system. All the programs accessing this file should use the 'Data element short name' only as indicated in column number 3 (Mnemonic name).

Nine data elements shown in the above file are for the case study purpose only, but in real business, there could be many more data elements associated with the suppliers like phone numbers, e-mail address, website address (URL), name of the contact person, VAT registration number, PAN number and so on.

File B: Material sources file

B1. File structure

Since one supplier can supply any number of materials, it is not possible to include such uncertainty in File A. Separate file is created with the supplier code and the material code as data elements. This file will have only one record if a supplier is supplying only one material. If a supplier is supplying more than one material, the supplier will have as many records in this file. This file is an example for one to many relationships.

This file is indexed both on the supplier and the material codes. These codes are assigned to uniquely identify these entities without ambiguity.

B2. Record structure

Sl. No.	Data element description	Data short name	Data type	Data width	Record structure	Comments
1	Supplier code	Suplr.code	Num	5	1–5	Key data/Index–1
2	Material code	Matl.code	Desc	12	6–17	Key data/Index–2

This file is indexed both on suplr.code and matl.code and valid suplr.code or matl.code need to be furnished to the system to access this file. This file just establishes the relationship between two entities viz., suppliers and the materials with one to many relationships (one supplier could supply more than one materials).

This file is related to File A through supplier code and is also related to File C through material code.

File C: Materials file (entity file/stock master file)

C1. File structure

Material file contains data related to the materials. Each material is identified by unique material code. Since this file is to be accessed at random, it is indexed and accessed on material code. This entity file has one-to-one relationship with all the data elements contained in it, i.e. all data elements shown are uniquely identified with respective material.

C2. Record structure

Sl. No.	Data element description	Data short name	Data type	Data width	Record structure	Comments
1	Material code	Matl.code	Desc	12	1–12	Key data/Index
2	Material name	Matl.desc	Desc	25	13–38	
3	Unit of measure	Matl.uom	Desc	4	39–42	e.g., no. set, kg,
4	Stock quantity	Matl.stoc.qty	Num	6+2	43–50	With 2 decimals
5	Average cost	Matl.wa.cost	Amt	6+2	51–58	
6	Highest cost/uom	Matl.hi.cost	Amt	6+2	58–65	
7	Purchases for year	Matl.pur.yr	Num	6+2	66–73	
8	Consumption for year	Matl.con.yr	Num	6+2	74–81	

The above table shows structures for all eight data elements accommodated in this file. It also shows the record structure (relative location of the data elements within the record and the record length which is equal to 81 bytes). Each material will have a record in this file. If there are 2400 materials, this file will have 2400 records.

This entity file has one-to-one relationship, i.e. each data element associated with a material is unique. This file is indexed on matl.code and hence can only be accessed by feeding valid matl.code to the system. All the programs accessing this file should use the 'Data element short name' only to access respective data element.

Eight data elements shown in the above file are for the case study purpose only but in real business, there could be many more data elements associated with the material like last receipt date, last issue date, previous year purchases and consumption and so on.

File D: Materials-purchase orders file (events file)

D1. File structure

Materials-purchase orders file contains data related to the purchase of materials. Each purchase order is identified by a purchase order number (events are identified by mere serial numbers). Each purchase is identified by unique purchase order number.

Since this file is to be accessed at random, based either on purchase order number or supplier code or material code, this file is indexed separately on all three data elements (there will be three index files for this file).

D2. Record structure

Sl. No.	Data element Description	Data short name	Data type	Data width	Record structure	Comments
1	Purchase order no	Pur.ord.no	Num	6	1–6	Key data/index
2	Purchase order dt	Pur.ord.dt	Date	8	7–14	
3	Purchase supplier code	Pur.suplr.cd	Num	5	15–19	Secondary key 1
4	Purchase material code	Pur.matl.cd	Desc	12	20–31	Secondary key 2
5	Purchase order quantity	Pur.ord.qty	Num	6+2	32–39	
6	Purchase order Unit of measure	Pur.ord.uom	Desc	4	40–43	
7	Purchase rate/cost	Pur.ord.rate	Amt	6+2	44–51	
8	MaerialDelivery date	Pur.dely.date	Date	8	52–59	
9	Value added tax%	Pur.tax	Amt	2+2	60-63	

The above table shows structures for all nine data elements contained in this file. It also shows the record structure. Each purchase order will have a record in this file. If there are 850 purchase orders, this file will have 850 records. It is assumed that only one material is bought through each purchase order for this illustration.

Nine data elements shown in the above file are for the case study purpose only and in real business, there could be many more data elements associated with the purchase orders like packing, freight and handling charges, mode of transport, etc.

In real life, the materials, suppliers and purchase orders will have many-to-many entity/event relationships.

SUM UP

In this chapter, the readers would have clearly understood data, information and information processing systems and their usefulness to business and managers.

The components of the DBMS have been explained in simple terms.

Serial and direct access devices, how the data files are organized and accessed in the computer (hard disk) and the process of creation of database are explained in a logical order. Three case studies have also been discussed to make the readers understand the file management activities better.

Entity/event relationship diagrams and the rules for deciding record structures are explained with business examples.

Three DBMS models and relative merits and demerits of these models are explained with reference to a business example. The functions and advantages of DBMS and RDBMS are explained in great detail.

The activities associated with data and database administration are explained clearly.

Data associative activities like, data backup and restoration, data concurrency and data independence are explained in detail so that the readers can easily understand what, why and how these activities are to be performed in business.

14

SYSTEM THEORY AND INFORMATION SYSTEMS

The following questions would guide the readers in navigating through this chapter:

1. What is a system and what does in essence the systems theory advocate?
2. How do the business and IT applications relate to systems theory?
3. What are the concepts stipulated by systems theory?
4. What are the logical components of information systems?

After finishing this chapter, the readers would have clear answers for these questions.

14.1 INTRODUCTION

A system is a group of interrelated components working together toward a common goal by accepting inputs and producing outputs in an organized transformation process.

A system can also be described as a set of elements or functions or operations or entities and events joined together in achieving common objectives. A business is a system and all its functions like materials management, production, marketing, finance, HR, etc. are its sub systems. All sub systems need to function in synchronization with one another so that the business becomes an integrated entity in tackling business challenges, exploiting the oppor-tunities and reaching the business goals.

Often, we find various business functions working on different paths and in contra-diction to one another due to their own functional or self-interests. The business thus gets disintegrated. Such organizations also tend to create conflicts of interest leading to unproductive tasks. People tend to rule by the power of knowledge/information possessed by them.

We have seen that IBA help business organizations to be more cohesive by way of sharing common business information among all functions. This eventually helps achieving the unity of purpose among all business functions and helps in optimizing the business output. Inadequate information exchange between the functions leads to fault finding.

Systems theory gets better treatment through IT since

1. Information technology is capable of linking all functions of the business that facilitate organizational integration.
2. The increased complexity of the business and its management due to fierce competition, shorter product life cycles, knowledgeable customers and globalization of the business demand, close interaction and quick decisions by managers. IT makes managers highly knowledgeable of the business, thereby helping in taking quicker and informed decisions.

14.2 COMPARISONS OF THREE KNOWN SYSTEMS

If we look around us we will notice we are part of number of systems like political system, education system, health care system and so on and each system having number of sub systems under them. All systems and sub systems under them exist for a purpose/achieving certain objectives. Three systems that we know are compared in the table given below to understand the key attributes of these three systems.

	Human body	*Business*	*Information systems*
Objectives	Self support, support family, and so on	Serve customers, serve society, and so on	Business effectiveness, business efficiency and so on
Components	Body and soul	Owners, suppliers, business functions, customers, channels	Hardware, software, data, business processes and people
Functions	Physical/Mental activities	Produce and sell	Automation, integration, knowledge creation
Sub systems	Nerve system, blood circulation, digestive system, etc.	Buy, store, produce, finance, HR, logistics, marketing, etc.	Input, process, output, functional sub systems, etc.

14.3 WHAT THE SYSTEMS THEORY ADVOCATES?

Systems theory stipulates that a system is far more superior in performance than the sum total of its sub components. In other words, a system possesses synergy. Synergy is the outcome from individual but interrelated sub systems that act together to produce a total effect greater than the sum of all its parts.

Systems theory guides the systems analysts in effectively performing requirement analysis and systems analysis and in understanding the business as a total system with the objective of bringing synergy in to the business.

IT applications need to be designed for the business as a whole and need to address the objectives, functions, interconnections, flow of data/information, delegation of power, organizational authority and command, knowledge acquisition of the managers, and so on related to all business functions.

For example, the marketing function needs to be integrated with product design, production, costing and logistic functions. Production function needs to be integrated with personnel, procurement, marketing, logistics and finance functions.

14.4 TWO WAY APPROACH LEADING TO BETTER UNDERSTANDING OF A SYSTEM

1. **Top down approach:**   Top down approach has been discussed in Chapter 7. This also needs to consider coordination, collaboration, decision making, flow of decisions, authority levels, delegation of power, knowledge acquisition and dissemination, etc. among all business functions. The free flow of business information should seamlessly integrate all business functions like that of the blood flow across the human body.

2. **Bottom up approach:**   This also has been discussed in Chapter 7. In addition, the working of all business functions (departments) in isolation, the interactions with other departments and other external entities also need to be understood. The processes between all departments need to be integrated in order to gain synergy.

14.5 HOW IT APPLICATIONS RELATE TO SYSTEMS THEORY

System characteristics	*IT applications*
System implies structure and order	Computers automate the business processes incorporating the business rules, procedures, policies and best practices
Interaction among all system components	Integrated information systems allow interaction among all business functions at operational and strategic levels, by virtue of free flow of business information among them.
Interdependence and integration	Integrated systems allow close co-ordination, collaboration and communications among all business entities so as to make any operation dependant on other operations

14.6   SYSTEMS THEORY CONCEPTS

1.   A system is designed to achieve a set of objectives.
2.   Interrelationships and interdependence exist among all components or subsystems of the system.
3.   Objectives of the system as a whole have higher priorities over that of sub systems.
4.   The capabilities of a system far exceeds the sum total capabilities of individual subsystems.
5.   A system functions according to some common principles.

14.7   LOGICAL COMPONENTS OF INFORMATION SYSTEMS

1.   Input
2.   Process
3.   Output
4.   Control
5.   Feedback
6.   Environment
7.   Boundaries and interface

These elements have been discussed in detail in Chapters 1 and 2.

SUM UP

In this chapter the readers would have got an insight into systems theory and how the business and IT applications relate to systems theory.

15

INFORMATION TECHNOLOGY SERVICES DIVISION (ITSD)
Functions and Responsibilities

The following questions will guide the readers in navigating through this chapter:

1. What needs to be the mission and focus of the ITSD in business organizations?
2. What are the roles and responsibilities of ITSD in a competitive and knowledge based economy?
3. What is a typical business organization and what are the line and support functions?
4. What are the roles and responsibilities of the head of the ITSD?
5. What are the roles and responsibilities of the technical functions in ITSD?

   - Project leaders/systems managers
   - Functional consultants
   - Systems analysts
   - Programmers
   - Quality engineers/analysts
   - Systems auditors
   - Network support/infrastructure maintenance engineers
   - Computer operators
   - Data entry operators

6. What are the ISO standards for Software Engineering?
7. What is ITIL?
8. What are the responsibilities of Chief Digital Officer?

After finishing this chapter, the readers would have clear answers for these questions and appreciate the quantum of technical efforts/expertise involved in successful implementation of IT applications in business.

15.1   INTRODUCTION

Information Technology Services Division (ITSD), also called by other names such as, MIS/IT/Information Systems/Computer/Knowledge management division, is sitting in a driver's seat of many businesses today, since it brings strategic and competitive advantages to the business. In this context it is also evolving as 'Business technology management' division.

15.2   MISSION

The mission for ITSD is to:

1. Map right and emerging IT solutions on to business operations and management functions in order to gain competitive edge.
2. Integrate the business functions both within and with supply chain entities.
3. Derive maximum leverage from IT and make managers highly knowledgeable to enable taking the right decisions fast.
4. Establish close customer relations and make the organization highly responsive to customer and market expectations.
5. Exploit the technology and strategic advantages it could bring to the business.

15.3   FOCUS

The IT initiatives need to be focused on the organizational objectives both long and short terms. IT applications need to integrate all business functions and make it a virtual monolith in responding to external environments and the customer needs, more efficiently.

IT applications should enable close collaboration, co-ordination, and communication among all human entities both within and outside the organization. The technology needs to make business processes more effective and efficient.

The managers should be able to take decisions collectively and willingly in achieving organizational goals and collaborate effectively in solving business problems.

The attributes of ideal IT applications in business discussed under Section 9.2 needs to be the focus for entire ITSD.

IT needs to bring in strategic/competitive benefits to business.

15.4 ROLE/FUNCTIONS OF ITSD

The following are the roles and functions of ITSD:

1. Business processes are to be automated in real-time. The managers should be able to get true status of the physical business from the computer database in real time.

2. Right and accurate MIS needs to be designed for all managers at operational, middle (tactical) and top management (strategic) levels based on the needs of the decision situations and the same need to reach them at right time and place.

3. Integrate business operations of all functions through a central and shareable database such that the business information flows freely across all functions (not to allow individual functions to create their own islands of information and claim exclusive ownership for the same). At the same time, confidential and sensitive information needs to be made available only to the authorized people.

4. Installation of reliable and sufficient IT infrastructure across entire organization and make the same available to business on 24×7 basis across all geographic locations.

5. Implementation of tactical and strategic IT applications discussed in Chapters 4, 5 and 6, based on the type of the business.

6. Establish right organization structure for ITSD division and recruit and manage IT professionals effectively.

7. Implement right quality assurance procedures in all SDLC activities to ensure that quality application software is delivered to the business in short time.

8. Create awareness among the business managers including the top management of the emerging trends in IT and their benefits to the business and be the catalysts/change agents in deriving such benefits.

9. Convince top management of the benefits and merits of IT and gain their commitments to all IT initiatives.

10. Conduct periodic survey among the user functions with an objective of obtaining right feedback in enhancing the effectiveness of IT applications in business.

11. Establish necessary systems audit and control procedures to ensure that the business interests are taken care and the assets committed through IT applications are safeguarded.

12. Information technology needs to be strategically integrated with business.

15.5 BUSINESS ORGANIZATION

A typical organization is constituted by the following entities:

- Stakeholders (Shareholders/promoters/investors)
- Board of directors
- Chairman
- Company secretary

- Managing director/CEO/presidents
- Heads of various functional divisions like
  - ◆ Procurement
  - ◆ Materials management
  - ◆ Production
  - ◆ Quality control
  - ◆ Maintenance
  - ◆ Logistics
  - ◆ Marketing
  - ◆ Product development and R & D
- Heads of various support divisions like
  - ◆ Finance
  - ◆ Human resources management
  - ◆ ITSD, and so on.

And hierarchy consisting of general managers, managers, assistant managers, senior executives, executives and so on under each such division.

15.6 ITSD—TYPICAL ORGANIZATION STRUCTURE

1. Head—ITSD
2. Project leaders/systems managers
3. Database administrators
4. Functional consultants
5. System analysts
6. Programmers
7. Quality engineers/analysts
8. Systems auditors
9. Network support/maintenance engineers
10. Computer operators
11. Data entry operators

15.7 ITSD—RESPONSIBILITIES OF TECHNICAL FUNCTIONS

The responsibilities and functions of technical personnel are explained under respective technical functions.

1. Head—ITSD division (CIO, GM, VP, executive director, and so on)
   - Sets the goals for ITSD division in line with the organizational objectives and the IT objectives stated in Section 15.4 of this chapter.

- Possess thorough business domain knowledge and looks at the technology from the business perspective in order to map right IT solutions.
- Selection and implementation of right tactical and strategic applications (discussed in Chapters 4, 5 and 6) based on the requirements of the business.
- Ability to implement integrated business applications including the supply chain over Internet.
- Has capabilities in convincing the management and make them committed to all IT initiatives in the business.
- All functional heads need to have confidence in his capabilities in implementing perfectly tailored business applications for their respective functions.
- Able to make right investment decisions (of IT resources) and capable of assessing both tangible and intangible benefits of all such investments.
- Expertise in business process re-engineering and change management.
- Identify the information needs of the managers at different levels and functions and design appropriate MIS/EIS/BI/DSS/KMS for them.
- Ensure that necessary and sufficient controls are built into the application software to ensure data quality, reliability and accuracy and integrity of all IT applications.
- Establish necessary software quality assurance and documentation standards for the SDLC activities.
- Identify appropriate organization structure for the ITSD and recruit and manage required skills effectively. Be a good leader and motivator for entire technical team.
- Possesses good marketing and communication skills in selling new and beneficial IT concepts to the business managers.

2. Project leader/systems manager
   - He is responsible for the successful implementation of IBASP within the estimated costs and time.
   - He needs to possess excellent business domain knowledge for which the IBASP is designed.
   - He is the main link between the user functions and the IT professionals engaged in the project.
   - He organizes and manages the project team and possesses good project management skills.
   - He works out the time frame for IBASP implementation, installation of infrastructure required for software development and testing, the cost of development, IT infrastructure, investments required, user training, etc. fairly accurately.
   - He gets the approvals from the user functions for the requirement specifications, infrastructure investments, implementation schedules and user training programs.
   - He is responsible for the quality and completeness of all the life cycle activities of the software project.

- He establishes the metrics for IT infrastructure, SDLC activities and IBASP performance beforehand and ensures that the same are achieved.
- He needs to have thorough understanding of the systems audit and data integrity controls, software testing methods, user-friendly GUI, system documentation standards, and so on and implement the same in all project activities.

3. Database administrators

This is already discussed in Section 13.12.

4. Functional consultants

- Functional consultants decide the 'to-be processes'/requirement specifications for ERP packages.
- They need to have thorough understanding of the ERP packages so that such packages are exploited to the maximum.
- The heads of the business functions concerned are trained in the respective functional modules of ERP so that they can become functional consultants.
- They need to have good experience in customizing the ERP package in respective functional modules.

5. System analysts

- Need to analyse all business functions and their processes in order to improve the same and accordingly design the most appropriate IT applications for the business.
- Design the system and prepare system flowchart indicating the processes to be carried out by individual programs and the data files accessed/updated by them.
- Design the physical RDBMS consisting of files/tables, key data element for each file and logical relationship among them.
- Prepare the program specifications for individual programs and assign them to individual programmers.
- Prepare the standards for programming activities like screen formats, print layouts, file access techniques, programming, technical documentation, and so on and ensure its compliance throughout the project.
- Prepare the norms and extent of testing to be done for individual programs and unit testing to ensure that all programs are tested thoroughly.

6. Programmers

- Programmers write the programs based on the program specifications.
- Decide the program logic/efficient algorithm and draw program flowcharts for individual programs.
- They fully understand the functions of the program, all data files to be accessed, processes to be completed, decision parameters, decisions to be programmed, outputs to be created, and so on.
- After writing the programs, they go through the programs to check the program logic and all functions coded in the program are correct (program walk through).

- Test the programs thoroughly using carefully designed test data which simulates the business environments fully.
- Program bugs noted during the testing are rectified immediately. The testing is repeated until the program is found to be error (bug) free.
- Prepare complete documentation for all programs consisting program listing, test data, test results, program flowcharts, and so on.

7. Quality analysts (software testing)

- Quality analysts are responsible for quality assurance and quality control of all software engineering life cycle activities including documentation and testing.
- Ensure that the standard procedures including the documentation are followed in all SDLC activities.
- Evaluate the documentation created during the project and certify their sufficiency and the accuracy.
- Create the test data (test database) and specify testing norms for all the programs involved in the project.
- Certify individual programs and also the entire package as 'ready for implementation', after performing integration testing.

8. Systems auditors

- Systems auditors check whether the application software package implemented has brought in all benefits to business as envisaged at the initiation of the project.
- Check whether organizational resources (like materials, fixed assets, money, etc.) committed through the automated systems are adequately controlled and safe.
- Ensure that the applications implemented are safeguarded against misuse, fraud or human errors.
- Ensure that all computer resources are fully utilized and the data back up and restoration procedures are being done without fail.
- Prepare hypothetical test cases (with extreme data values) and test all application programs for their reliability.
- Ensure the availability of fault tolerant/back up systems so that business does not face any interruption when the system failures occur.
- Check whether the users are performing computer operations as stipulated in the user manuals including system controls.
- Certify the sufficiency of the integrity controls built into the computer systems that ensure data integrity, accuracy, quality and consistency.

9. Network support/maintenance engineers

- Network support engineers are responsible for the procurement and maintenance of all computer resources, viz. hardware, operating systems, RDBMS, networking resources and the support infrastructure like power supply and A/C.
- In case of computer networks/Internet, they ensure that the organizational data is secured against internal/external hacking.

- Interact with vendors in getting their services as and when required.
- Ensure that the computer systems are available to all users all the time.

10. Computer operators

- In business organizations, all business operations are performed by the business functions concerned using computer resources. However, computer operators need to perform certain tasks common for the entire business.
- Responsible for starting the main computer and load all necessary applications and database for the users to perform the business processes on line.
- Back up the database and the application software regularly.
- Manage all IT resources at the computer centre.
- Perform bulk printing jobs using the heavy duty printers.

11. Data entry operators

These jobs generally are not encouraged in the business organizations today. Data entry operators key-in the data off-line on to CDs/DVDs. For example, the data acquired through market survey are entered into the computer in this process (off-line data entry). This is done when large volumes of data are to be entered into the computers.

15.8 ISO STANDARDS FOR SOFTWARE ENGINEERING

ISO/IEC 12207 standards for software development life cycle (SDLC) is an international standard for software life cycle processes. It is the standard that defines all the tasks required for developing and maintaining the software.

The ISO/IEC 12207 standard establishes a process for SDLC, including the processes and activities applied during the acquisition and configuration of the services of the system. ISO/IEC 12207:2008 defines 43 systems and software processes.

The standard has the main objective of supplying a common structure so that the buyers, suppliers, developers, maintainers, operators, managers and technicians involved with the software development use a common language. This common language is established in the form of well-defined processes. The structure of the standard was intended to be conceived in a flexible, modular way so as to be adaptable to whoever uses it. The standard is based on two basic principles, modularity and responsibility. Modularity means processes with minimum coupling and maximum cohesion. Responsibility means establishing responsibility for each process.

The set of processes, activities and tasks can be adapted according to the software project. These processes are classified in three types—basic, for support and organizational. The support and organizational processes must exist independent of the organization and the project being executed. The basic processes are set according to the situation.

15.9 INFORMATION TECHNOLOGY INFRASTRUCTURE LIBRARY (ITIL)

ITIL stipulates set of practices for IT service management (ITSM) that focusses on aligning IT services with the needs of the business. ITIL has series of five core publications, each of which covers an ITSM life cycle stage.

ITIL describes procedures, tasks and checklists that are to be used by business organizations for establishing a minimum level of IT competency. It allows the organization to establish a baseline from which it can plan, implement and measure IT competence levels. It is used to demonstrate compliance and to measure improvement.

Practices stipulated under ITIL are very exhaustive and they stress the IT practices discussed throughout this book.

These documents are not discussed in this book because they carry copyrights. Software engineers who are interested in learning them could refer to the sources which are available in public domain.

15.10 CHIEF DIGITAL OFFICER (CDO)

The challenges and opportunities for business in the digital age are enormous. Companies need to focus on the web, social networks, wireless technology, digital devices (camera, camcoders, tablets, i-pads etc.) and smart phones (android, apple and windows) because millions of younger generations with enormous buying power are roaming there digitally. In addition, the business strategies need to include local and new innovations that are occurring everyday.

Customers are demanding fresh information and new products all the time and have the ability to buy whenever, wherever and however (credit, EMI etc.) of what they want. They are leveraging their digital resources to download information, compare features and prices, find best products and search for deals. Digital devices are reshaping consumer behaviour.

Smarter, faster and advanced digital devices bring in new opportunities for the business.

This has necessitated creating new breed of managers called **Chief digital** officers, in customer, retail, entertainment and leisure focussed business organizations. CDO oversees the full range of digital strategies and drive growth and change across the enterprise.

15.10.1 What CDOs need to be?

CDOs must have the following skills and expertise.

- Ability to plan and execute long-term strategies revolving around driving customer awareness, engagement and monetization.
- E-commerce and transactional expertise in driving traffic, conversion and revenue generation.
- Online marketing, e-tailing and social media expertise.

- Drive brand awareness, brand activation and consumer engagement.
- Ability to develop new channels, business models, innovative products and services.
- Skills related to personalized and localized communication as opposed to mass communication.
- Transform product and technology capabilities to match the digital world.
- Familiarity with web, mobile technologies and social networks and all at local levels.
- Technology savvy and if not, capable of asking technical people right questions.
- Setting right digital strategies.
- Orientation, execution and ability to deliver results despite of complex and fluid environments.
- Leading requisite talents across the organization, building relationships and conflict resolution.
- Demonstrate cultural sensitivity in seeing the digital world differently and distinctly.

SUM UP

In this chapter, the readers would have understood the organization structure of a typical business.

The mission and focus of ITSD have been explained in order to enable readers in understanding the need for ITSD in a business organization.

The roles and responsibilities of all technical positions in ITSD have also been discussed in great detail. The readers now would appreciate how these responsibilities align with the attributes of ideal applications discussed in Section 9.2.

16

IT APPLICATIONS IN SELECT
SERVICE INDUSTRIES
(Banks, Hospitals and Hotels)
AND E-GOVERNANCE

Chapter Quest

Chapter Quest

The following questions will guide the readers in navigating through this chapter:

1. What are various IT enabled services being offered by the banks to their customers and more specifically under branchless banking?
2. What are various IT enabled services that could provide better services to the patients at the hospitals?
3. How IT makes the hotel/resorts/property management more effective and efficient?
4. What is e-governance and what are the objectives set by GOI and for example, Government of Tamil Nadu in this regard and what are the benefits the citizens of this country derive through e-governance?

After finishing this chapter, the readers will have clear answers to these questions.

16.1 BANKS

Discussing the gamut of IT applications in the banks is beyond the scope of this book. However, IT enabled services (ITES) being offered to their customers in India are highlighted in this section.

The objectives of IT enabled banking services to the customers are to:

- Offer efficient (quicker) and customer-responsive banking services, meeting their needs and expectations.
- Extend banking services to rural areas leading to financial outreach/inclusion.
- Reduce transaction/banking costs.
- Make public beware of all banking products and services.
- Build customer loyalty through ease of use, trust and financial security.
- Make customer interactions with the banks pleasant experience for them.
- Provide secured communication links and reliable computer resources.
- Ensure customer privacy, security and safeguard customer interests.
- Integrate all customer touch points to have unified approach and personalized service delivery for each customer.
- Advice customers on managing their investments, borrowings and wealth management

IT enabled services can broadly be grouped into **eight** distinct services discussed below.

16.1.1 Core Banking Solutions (CBS)

Banks have networked the computer resources at most of their branches into virtual private network (VPN) at the national level. All customers' accounts and bank branches are also being identified through unique numbers across the country. This enables customers of one branch to perform banking transactions through any other branch. Isolated 'Branch' customers are now virtually converted into national 'Bank' level customers. This results in instant debit/credit to be accounted in any branch from any other branch. This has made the banking operations highly efficient because the efforts involved in creating mammoth banking instruments (documents) and clearing/forwarding of them are saved.

Through CBS, customers of one branch can perform various activities mentioned below through any other branch of the same bank.

- Enquire bank balances or the status of any particular debit/credit transaction.
- Get statement of account.
- Receive cash payments.
- Deposit cash/cheque.
- Deposit cash/cheque into any other person's account.
- Get DD/banker's cheque of any branch, and so on.

Since the transaction processing and database update take place at distant sites, the customers are served faster (front desk operations) and hence gain delightful banking experience. This is indeed a banking revolution caused by IT in India.

Core banking has also helped corporate and retail customers in availing the services in the form of:

- RTGS (Real time gross settlement), which refers to electronic intimation given by banks to other banks to transfer funds from one account to the other of any bank and branch.

- NEFT (National electronic fund transfer) which refers to electronic payment from one account to other of any bank and branch
- ECS (electronic clearing service) refers to accounting of bulk payments/receipts into individual bank accounts, e.g. salary/pension/dividend payments by various organizations to their beneficiary accounts and issuance of standing instructions to the banks by its customers to pay the bills on periodic basis.

These services save lot of time and efforts and make the banking operations of the retail and business customers more efficient.

16.1.2   Internet Banking (Online Banking)

Internet banking forms part of branchless banking. It allows customers to accomplish many banking activities very conveniently sitting in the comforts of their home. It saves lot of human resources at bank branches and associative manpower costs otherwise needed at the branches. Customers can:

- View all their transactions and bank balances.
- Print statement of accounts.
- Apply for bank loans and repay loan installments.
- Pay their bills for various services rendered by third parties.
- Pay taxes to various statutory bodies.
- Transfer funds to other accounts of the same bank.
- Send requests for cheque books.
- Import data into personal accounting software (electronic data transfer).
- Buy products and services online by availing payment gateway services.
- Get on line decision support from banks for managing personal finances.
- Avail quick and cheap clearing services.
- Get support for account aggregation to monitor all their accounts in one place, whether they are with the bank or with other financial institutions and so on.

16.1.3   POS (Point of Sales) Devices—ATM/Debit Cards/ Credit Cards/E-Wallet

These services also fall under branchless banking. ATM/debit cards issued by banks offer two facilities for their customers.

They could draw cash (subject to certain limits) any time, anywhere through ATM kiosks. The amount drawn gets immediately debited to the customer's accounts.

Same cards can also be used by the customers for making payments towards the purchase of goods and services. These cards are backed by worldwide card service providers like VISA and Mastercard, who maintain a central database of all their customers across the country/world. As the sales clerk at the retail outlets swipes the card on the electronic reader (POS device), the details related to the customer like name, account number, the bank, etc. stored in the card, electronically get transmitted to the central database. If the data is found to be correct, the computer allows the transaction to proceed and the amount gets credited to the seller account. The buyer's bank accounts get debited accordingly through VISA/Mastercard networks.

Credit cards

The functioning of credit cards is the same as debit cards. But the bank customer need not have any bank balances and the amount is treated as short time loan and the customer has to pay back the amount with interest at a later date. Since banks charge high interest rates on such amounts and the customers are tempted to buy beyond their means, banks push this service with great force on to their customers.

Debit and credit cards are also called EFTPOS (electronic fund transfer/POS devices).

Electronic wallet (e-wallet)

Some retailers (oil companies, food courts, etc.) sell smart cards (which electronically stores value of money in it) with definite money value to their customers so that they can use such cards (instead of paying cash) while buying the products/services offered by them. These cards are called e-wallets. On actual purchases made, the money value stored in e-valet is reduced to the extent of purchase value. Such cards, however, are not accepted by other retailers.

Mobile phones would become e-wallets of individuals soon. GOI has brought in necessary regulations to enable creation of mobile payment gateways by banks and the TELCOs (Telephone companies like Airtel, Reliance, etc.) for this purpose. When any money value is bought by people from the banks or TELCOs, such values get added to their respective mobile phones. Mobile phones would become a POS device/e-wallets acceptable by all commercial establishments. Users need not have bank accounts for this purpose. The money value for which the purchase has been made would get deducted from the balance stored in the mobile phones. Through this process, it is always possible to carry e-money in the mobile phones (e-wallets). This mode of payment would be accepted by all shop owners and the service providers.

16.1.4   ATM Services

ATMs are also considered to be part of branchless banking operations. ATMs are local computer controlled mechanical devices, connected to the banks' computer networks. ATMs are capable of stacking and disbursing small amounts of money (currencies of denominations ₹ 100 or 500) to the bank customers. Customers need to use debit/credit cards which electronically store customers' banking information in them and provide PIN (personal identification number) for authentication of the banking activity. In addition to withdrawal of money, certain other banking activities like enquiring bank balances, request for cheque books, changing PIN numbers, depositing of cheques, etc. can also be performed through ATMs.

Since ATMs are installed at convenient locations, they offer 24 hrs × 7 days continuous service to the bank customers. At the same time, ATMs also save lot of time, efforts and costs for the bank branches as well because of such automation.

However, ATMs are to be fully secured and guarded all the time against theft or misuse or fraud. ATM customers also need to be very careful and exercise enough precautions in safeguarding their accounts and PIN numbers while availing such services. It is necessary for the bank customers to get printed statement accounts every month and check all the transactions very judiciously.

16.1.5 Mobile Banking

Mobile banking also forms part of branchless banking. Mobile banking refers to the banking transactions that can be performed by the bank customers using their mobile phones or any other smart devices. The following services could be availed by the customers through mobile banking:

- Mini statement of accounts
- Getting account balances
- Alerts on accounting activities
- Requesting new cheque book
- Stop payment advices
- PIN management
- Fund transfers
- Recharge of talk times
- Commercial POS payment
- Bills payment
- Electronic wallet
- Peer to peer payment
- Blocking of lost/stolen card
- Making micro payments, and so on.

16.1.6 Branchless Banking (Bank and Non Bank Based)

India has vast rural population who still do not (more than 50% of its population) have access to banks/banking services. GOI has enacted various bills that will facilitate financial inclusion for such vast populace. At the same time, more than 75% of Indians have access to mobile phones, thanks to wireless communication technologies.

Branchless banking makes use of mobile phones and the services offered by mobile telecommunication companies (TELCOs). TELCOs, by virtue of their rural presence, act as agents in offering limited banking services beyond bank branches. GOI is in the process of enabling mobile payment switches/inter bank mobile payment services for this purpose.

Branchless banking primarily involves appointment of agents/business correspondents/intermediaries by the banks (e.g., TELCOs, post offices, local retailers, etc.) who will perform small value banking transactions like collections and payments on behalf of the banks at rural locations and earn some commissions for themselves.

There are three models of branchless banking.

1. **Agentless model:** This model covers ATMs, Internet banking, mobile phone banking and POS devices like debit/credit cards, e-wallets and so on which we have discussed already. There are no agents/intermediaries (since all processes are carried out electronically) in the process.

2. **Bank account model:** Under this model, the customers perform micro level banking transactions through business correspondents/agents appointed/authorized by the banks. They could be retail shop owners, TELCOs, post offices, schools, etc. who enter into some agreement with the banks in offering select services to the customers on commission basis. The customers are bank account holders. Banks are able to outreach rural population in offering financial services (financial inclusion as contemplated by GOI) using different delivery channels which are cheaper than branch bank operations.

This makes use of the computer resources made available to the agents which are connected to the banks' computer networks. All processes are carried out by the agents through their computers.

3. **Non-bank account model:** Under this model, customers need not be bank account holders. Agents/business correspondents perform all banking operations of the customers including account management on prescribed fees chargeable by them for each service. Banking transactions are at micro levels. Banks merely act as safe keeper or custodians of funds. This model also makes use of the computer resources made available to the agents which are connected to the banks' computer networks.

16.1.7   Payment Services/ECS

Banks allow their customers to give standing instructions to the banks to pay their bills regularly to third parties through ECS (electronic clearing system) facility. This saves lot of efforts for the customers in following up and payment of bills every month. ECS has also been discussed under CBS.

Many business organizations today sell their products and services through Internet (e-commerce). Internet based consumers can make payments to the sellers through secured payment gateway services offered by the banks.

16.1.8   Online Trading

Many banks and non-banking financial institutions offer their customers facilities to trade on-line at various stock exchanges of India. Customers need to enter into a separate agreement with the banks for this purpose (separate account number) and buy and sell shares availing the funds they hold or availing credits offered by the banks. Banks charge certain commission on the values of the shares bought or sold (on traded values). This facility has made on-line trading an easy task for retail investors and has drawn millions of them to trading of shares/equities.

Customers can manage their shareholdings (portfolio management) of all the shares bought and their purchase prices, know current market values and so on from the computer database maintained by respective banks. These computers, in turn, process trading transactions and access required information from respective stock exchanges. The banks also enable their customers to view fluctuating share prices of all stocks being traded in real time. Trading in share markets today is hassle-free and very convenient.

Portfolio management, real time stock quotes, personalized alerts/notifications on security prices and lot more facilities are also part of such services.

16.1.9   Impact of Information Technology on Banking Services

- Results in increased efficiency (faster services) and effectiveness (lesser resources, cost reduction, etc.) of banking services.
- Greater convenience and ease of availing banking services by the customers any time/anywhere.
- Enhanced geographic reach and wider customer base.
- Increased visibility for banking products and services through websites, bank portals and internet banking.
- Complete and integrated support in all banking processes like KYC (know your customer), signature verification, biometric and photo verification, online application retrieval, accepting deposits and issuance of receipts for the same, periodic interest payments, loan application processing, sanctioning and disbursements of loans, and so on.

16.1.10   Other IT Applications at Banks

Other IT applications at banks (and branches) like financial accounting systems, books of accounts, front desk transaction processing, the systems for the management of equity, term deposits, short-term and long-term loans, assets, debtors, creditors, HR, materials/consumables inventories, fixed assets and maintenance of plant/equipment/machinery are similar to the applications discussed under Chapters 4 and 5.

In view of distinctively different products and services offered by individual banks (to attract new customers and to excel against competition), data security requirements and distinctly different banking procedures being adopted, the banks generally develop and implement fully customized application software at their banks/branches.

16.2   HOSPITALS

IT applications associated with the hospitals and health care organizations are highlighted in this section. Hospitals in India are yet to exploit information technology fully in order to offer more efficient health care to the Indian population.

16.2.1 Websites

Most of the private hospitals in India have their websites to describe the facilities and various health care services offered by them. They also need to furnish the names, qualifications and clinical specialization of all the doctors who are offering their services under various medical disciplines, their contact phone numbers, e-mail addresses and so on. The 'website address' (URL) needs to be made known/popular to the public and the same needs to be linked to popular search engines under various medical disciplines.

16.2.2 Hospital Portals

Hospital portals are interactive websites where the public can interact with the doctors and health care professional to fix up appointments, make payments for selective services, and so on. Some hospitals offer telemedicine facility for select customer groups who register themselves for such services. Hospitals also need to get feedback from the patients and general public about the quality and extent of services offered by the hospitals through such portals.

16.2.3 Patients' Clinical Information System

Technically speaking, this application is similar to KMS discussed in Section 4.7. But this system stores each patient's physical, medical and clinical history in various formats in terms of:

- Patient's ailments past and present (clinical history)
- Doctors' diagnosis/assessments of each ailment as text or audio
- Treatments/surgeries intended and underwent
- Medical prescriptions past and present
- Test results of all clinical tests performed like blood tests, BP, ECG, ultrasound, X-ray, CT/MRI scans, endoscope, etc. in digital/multimedia formats
- Clinical variations observed in all such test results over the period of time
- Various surgeries/clinical procedures performed, doctors' observations in the process, video recordings in electronic media and so on
- Discharge summary issued by hospitals
- Patients' personal data like name, address, age, qualification, family details, life style activities and so on
- All other relevant data as decided by the doctors and health care professionals necessary for managing the health care of individual patients.

However, this system is made to be accessible only by the doctor concerned and the patient. Such systems are not used in Indian hospitals. Hospitals in US and many European countries use these systems more predominantly. Given a patient's name or unique identification number, clinical/health history in its entirety pertaining to a patient is made known to the doctors from the computer database. It results in more efficient diagnostics, treatment and patient care.

This is the greatest facility the technology could offer to patients. Fortunately, most of the clinical tests and procedures (x-rays, CT/MRI scans, clinical laboratory reports, angiograms, endoscope procedures and so on) are performed by computer controlled devices which automatically store such data in electronic/digital formats today. Doctors' diagnosis dictated orally is also converted into electronic media by a process known as medical transcription. Such systems store the patients' clinical information in various media and still it is only the doctors who can interpret such data and make diagnosis before treating the patients.

16.2.4   In-patients Billing Systems

This system is being used by most of the big hospitals in India today. All in-patients are assigned unique in-patient identification numbers while getting admitted into the hospital. All costs associated with a patient as listed below are updated in the computer.

- Advance amounts paid
- Bed charges
- Doctors' fees
- Costs of medicines and other hospital consumables
- Food charges
- Nursing costs
- Costs related to various clinical tests and diagnosis
- Operation theatre and ICU costs and so on.

In addition to such costs, ailments of the patients, diagnosis, treatments, recovery details, date and time of admission and discharge and so on are also updated on to computers.

This is a simple system which makes in-patient billing hassle-free, efficient and transparent. This will also enable preparation of prompt and accurate discharge summary for each patient when they get discharged from the hospital. All these data need also to be added to patient's clinical information system discussed earlier.

16.2.5   Hospital Beds and Operation Theatres Allocation/ Occupancy Monitoring Systems

There is always a great demand for hospital beds and operation theatres in Indian hospitals. These resources need to be allocated very judiciously based on each patient's ailment, medical emergencies and doctors' recommendations. These resources need to be optimally utilized and at the same the needy patients' accommodation requirements should always be met. These systems need to be incorporated with certain decision rules (decision support systems) related to normal/priority allocation of these resources.

This system would yield management information related to capacity utilization of available resources and the quantum of resources to be added based on actual shortfall of such resources.

16.2.6   Hospital Pharmacy Management Systems

Hospital pharmacy though is like any other pharmacy, it has to ensure availability of medicines all the time anticipating doctors' prescriptions. The pharmacy needs to get suggestions from the doctors during procurement planning. Procurement planning, actual purchase, stock accounting, selling, billing, charging respective in-patients, monitoring medicines expiry dates, etc. need to be incorporated in such application software.

Availability of medicines, their stocks, consumption pattern, physical locations where the medicines are stored, alternate brand names for a given generic medicine name, etc. are also to be made available to the pharmacists online always.

16.2.7   Medical Insurance Claims for In-patients

Many patients today take medical insurance cover and settle their medical bills through insurance companies. Insurance companies specify certain procedures to be followed while settling the claims of their clients. These procedures mostly involve activities to be certified by the hospitals and the doctors. The hospitals need to have efficient systems in informing and submitting all details along with certified statements to the insurance companies and getting the patients' bills settled by the insurance companies directly. Entire process/workflow associated with these activities needs to be automated.

Hospitals also need to have good 'insurance claims tracking systems' to inform the patients of the status of their claims and the bottlenecks, if any, in getting the claims settled through insurance companies.

16.2.8   Issue of Discharge Summaries for In-patients

Since most of the information related to in-patients is available in the computer database, doctors should have on line facility to issue discharge certificates from the computer. If so required, the discharge summary should also be sent by e-mail to outstation patients. Discharge summaries need also to be updated on to patient's clinical information systems discussed earlier.

16.2.9   Quality Rating for the Hospitals

Many Indian hospitals get ISO certification for the patient care/hospital management processes and make it known to the public. However, ISO certification alone would not guarantee quality services/treatments to the patients.

The hospitals need to collect exhaustive data from the patients and the doctors of the ailments, treatments, effectiveness of hospital care/cure, recurrences and remissions, accuracy of diagnosis, effectiveness of treatments and medicines and so on and convert such data into hospital/doctors' performance rating in terms of:

- Risk adjusted mortality rate
- Readmission rates

- Infection rates including hospital acquired infections
- Attainment ratios in serious ailments like heart attacks, strokes, etc.
- Patient's safety indicators and so on.

Necessary application software for processing such data and obtaining the information are already available and are being used in many hospitals in USA and Europe. However, no hospital in India is doing this as of this day.

16.2.10 Other IT Applications

Other IT applications at the hospitals like financial accounting systems, books of accounts, front desk transactions processing, the systems for the management of equity, fixed deposits, loans, assets, debtors, creditors, HR, inventories, consumables, emergency supplies, fixed assets and maintenance of plant/machinery/equipment are similar to the applications discussed under Chapters 4 and 5.

There are many ready to use application software available for hospital/health care organizations. They need to be evaluated based on the functional requirements of individual hospitals, ease of use by doctors and hospital staff, installation base of such software packages, reliability of software vendor and so on. Big hospitals can also develop and implement customized application software as discussed in Chapter 8.

16.3 HOTELS AND RESORTS (Property Management)

IT enabled services used by hotels/hospitality industries (property management) are highlighted in this section.

Since all customers/guests have personal mobile phone numbers, it should be used to identify individual guests uniquely. It will help knowing customers' preferences and frequently visiting customers and so on based on such identity.

16.3.1 Hotels and Resorts—Internet Portal

Hotels need to have their own portals (interactive websites) or can be part of other popular/tourism oriented portals. The portals need to be user-friendly and interesting to the guests and inform them all the facilities available at the hotel, tariffs, process of making reservations and so on. If so required, the guests should be able to make firm booking of the rooms and other tour and travel requirements on line. The portal has to have secured payment gateway to enable the guests to pay on line for the services intended/availed.

The portals need to be made popular through other media including search engines and attract guests by informing various entertainment facilities available at the hotel and other local attractions/leisure time activities. The portals need to play video recording of its facilities and other attractions. If so required, the portals need to offer total solution to prospective clients from the stage of picking up the guests at their residences, travel by air/train/bus and similar arrangements for the guests until they are back home. Designing an effective portal itself is a big subject which cannot be discussed in this book.

The portals information also needs to be submitted to various search engine service providers for inclusion of the URL in such search engines. Most of the hotels and resorts in India are available on the Internet and can be located through popular search engines today.

16.3.2   Guest Billing Systems

Guests need to be identified by unique names or mobile phone numbers along with their addresses, duration of their stay, room numbers of their stay and so on. There needs to be a front desk system to receive advance amounts from the guests and issuance of receipts for the same. Many hotels offer electronic keys to the rooms wherein data related to the room number and duration of their stay are encoded on to electronic keys by the computer. The electronic data contained in such keys are recognized by electro mechanical locks provided in the doors of the respective rooms. Entry into wrong rooms and stay beyond allocated days are automatically stopped by such devices.

All food, beverages and other room services availed by the guests are to be automatically booked under respective room number/mobile number/name of the guest staying there. The billing information needs to be made known to the customers on line any time. While the guests are checking out, the computer should print an integrated bill, showing details of all costs, advances paid by them and the balance amounts to be settled. Such activities need to be completed fast as any number of guests would be checking out at a given time.

All data captured through billing systems need to be taken to guests' data warehouse to manage customer (guests) relations (like identifying guests' food preferences, periods of their stay and so on) better.

16.3.3   Guests Tour and Travel Planning System

Hotels and resorts need to assess guests' requirements for tours and travels (from picking up from their residences and dropping them back) and direct their requests to reliable travel agents who are linked to variety of such service providers. Travel agents services are too complex to be managed by small and medium hotels and resorts individually.

16.3.4   Restaurant Reservation, Ordering of Food and Billing

Restaurant management involves many modules. The reservation module needs to keep track of table reservations in terms of table number, number of guests, arrival time, food preferences and so on for breakfast, lunch and dinner. Hotel call centre needs to be linked to restaurant reservation module so that fresh reservations are made efficiently. Feedback on the quality of food, cleanliness, service, etc. is to be obtained from the guests and summed up against each parameter so as to make improvements all the time. This module will help knowing table capacity utilization, planning additional capacities and offering discounts during lean days/times.

Guests' orders for food and beverages, guest name, table number, etc. need to be communicated to the kitchen through handheld electronic devices with wireless communication facilities to make the whole process more efficient. This also needs to be linked to the billing system wherein the final bill is issued by the computer automatically. Guests should be allowed to make payments either by cash or debit/credit cards or any other electronic payment systems.

These systems would help identifying fast moving food and beverages, timely procurement of various food ingredients, restaurant peak times and days, average time taken in serving the customers, etc. which would eventually lead to better utilization and management of customer relations and restaurant resources.

16.3.5 Hotel Room Reservation and Occupancy Monitoring Systems

Hotel rooms and beds are profit centres which need to be managed profitably. Hotel call centres need to have room reservation system on line to confirm the bookings made by the guests through telephone, e-mail, SMS and so on. Based on the reservations and expected time of arrivals (of the guests), housekeeping functions need to keep the rooms ready for occupation, neat and clean.

The room services functions also need to be automated as it has to perform large number of activities each day before, after and during the stay of guests at all rooms. A checklist of activities to be performed including the working conditions of all equipment and devices every day by various service personnel and its compliance with respect to individual rooms need to be monitored through the computers.

16.3.6 CRM for Hotels and Resorts

CRM principles discussed in Section 5.5 are more appropriate for hotel industries and property management. Certain characteristics of regular guests would enable the hotels to focus their marketing efforts on specific target groups having matching attributes.

16.3.7 Other IT Applications

Other IT applications at hotels/resorts (property management) like financial accounting systems, books of accounts, front desk transactions processing, management of equity, fixed deposits, loans, assets, debtors, creditors, HR, inventories, maintenance of plant/machinery/equipment, consumables management, fixed assets and so on are similar to the applications discussed under Chapters 4 and 5.

16.4 E-GOVERNANCE IN INDIA

16.4.1 Introduction

Government of India (GOI) has evolved 'National e-governance plan' (NeGP) with an objective of providing hassle free, transparent and efficient services to common man/every citizen living in urban and rural areas across the country.

GOI is planning to create about hundred thousand 'Common Service Centers' (CSC) across the country for this purpose, on a public/private enterprises partnership. GOI has nominated 'National level service agency' (NLSA) for this purpose. Infrastructure Leasing and Financial Services (IL&FS) company is nominated as NLSA for entire country.

Access and delivery of Government services and information under e-governance are classified into four broad categories, viz.

- G2C (Government to citizens)
- G2B (Government to business)
- G2E (Government to its employees)
- G2G (Government to government)

We are discussing some of the services being offered by the Government of Tamil Nadu under its e-governance initiatives in this section.

16.4.2 Tamil Nadu State Government (TNSG)

TNSG has created an e-governance, Government agency to offer policy level support to Service Centre Agencies (SCAs). TNSG has nominated 3i-Infotech and Srei-Sahaj e-village Ltd., as SCA's who are conducting e-governance training programs across the state now.

SCAs manage and control Common Service Centers (CSCs). TNSG is planning to have about 5,440 CSCs (Common Service Centers) in Tamil Nadu, of which 2,500 CSCs are already operational now.

SCAs oversee the operations of CSCs at the village level. Village level CSCs are run by entrepreneurs being nominated to run the business at village level/cluster of three villages.

16.4.3 E-governance Infrastructure

TNSG infrastructure to support e-governance in the state are:

- State data centers (SDC) offering 'back end' computerization
- State-wide area network with sufficient bandwidth (TNSWAN)
- Common service centers (CSCs)
- Support infrastructures like, State service delivery gateway, Tamil Nadu state portal, etc.

E-governance initiatives are being implemented through Mission Mode Projects (MMPs) across various line departments of TNSG.

16.4.4 TNSG E-governance Mission

- To harness IT in order to offer services to common man/citizens in a convenient and easily accessible delivery channels to make all citizens an integral part of the ever growing knowledge society and in accomplishing quality living.
- To effectively make use of web enabled media in offering efficient, transparent and reliable services at affordable costs.

16.4.5 E-governance Objectives

- Build services around citizens' choices and needs
- Make Government easily accessible
- Make information transparent
- Use Government resources more effectively
- Reduce Government spending
- Deliver online services
- Involve citizens in governing processes
- Uniquely identify every citizen of state and the immigrants
- All departments to focus on development to specific segments of the society and have information on all individuals of their target, online
- All departments to know the status of deliveries across the state any time.

16.4.6 Services Offered by ALL Government Departments (of TNSG)

- Citizens charter indicating the mission of each department in serving the citizens
- Downloading applications forms/formats required by concerned departments
- Frequently asked questions (FAQ) and answers to them
- Obtaining information as per RTI (right to information) Act
- Officials to be contacted
- Feedback from the public
- Circulars, GOs, Notifications, Acts, rules and so on involving the public
- Tenders notifications, and so on.

16.4.7 Department SPECIFIC E-governance Services (Select Departments)

The departments listed below offer services/information related to their respective functions:

1. District administration/social welfare departments make crucial information be made known to the public such as
   - Information related to scholarships and educational assistance to students
   - Issuance of community, nativity, income certificates, etc.
   - Assistance schemes to non graduate families
   - Deserted women assistance schemes
   - Marriage assistance schemes
   - Widow daughter marriage assistance schemes
   - Orphan girls' marriage assistance schemes and so on.
2. Commercial taxes department
   - VAT (value added taxes) clarifications to business organizations
   - Commodity search and rates of taxes

- Dealer registration procedures
- E-payments
- Registering grievances and reporting their status and so on.

3. Education department

- List of approved books for all classes
- Fee structures for private schools
- Online textbooks
- Rights of children to free education
- 'Samacheer kalvi' schemes and so on.

4. Health and family welfare

- Health education and lists of institutions in Tamil Nadu
- Health care facilities
- Home remedies
- Public immunization schemes and programmes
- CT scan and MRI facilities
- Health guidelines to the public and so on.

5. Industries departments

- Functions of industries departments
- Information on support schemes
- District industrial profiles
- Industrial policies, rules, regulations and so on.

6. Municipal administration departments

- Online citizen services
- Issuance of birth and death certificates
- Collection of property tax through Internet
- Information on fund releases and so on.

7. Revenue department

- Survey map books and survey numbers
- Property ownership
- Information related to Pattas and issuance of the same.

8. Rural development department

- Development schemes
- Maps
- Databases and so on.

9. Registration (land and buildings)

- Guideline values
- How to register properties

- Property valuation norms
- Fee structures for property registration
- Copies of registered documents
- Encumbrance certificates and so on.

10. Treasury and accounts
   - Functions and locations of treasuries
   - Compilation of accounts
   - ECS
   - Pension payments
   - Procurement and disbursement of high value stamps
   - Group insurance schemes and so on.

E-governance initiatives of TNSG are having very good impact on all citizens of the state and more so in rural areas.

11. Police
   - Tamil Nadu police provides varieties of options, links, and interaction for the people to get connected with law enforcing agencies
   - Complaints other than murder can be lodged with police using Internet
   - Women's helpline links are available round the clock across the state
   - Applications for obtaining police licenses and permissions can be down loaded and applied on-line.

SUM UP

The readers would have understood the impact IT has on the banking industry and the tremendous benefits it has brought to banks' customers. Branchless banking which would take banking services to rural India, has been discussed very briefly but clearly.

The readers would now be aware how IT could benefit the patients and the hospitals in offering better health care services to the former. Patients' clinical information system, if implemented in Indian hospitals, would bring immense benefits to the patients and make clinical management of the patients far more effective for the doctors.

The benefits the technology brings to the hotel industry have been discussed such that the readers could appreciate how easy it is for the people to avail hospitality services across the world and how efficiently the hotels and resorts could be managed.

The readers would have got an insight into what the technology could offer to Indian citizens in the form of e-governance initiatives of GOI and the Government of Tamil Nadu.

CHAPTER

17

INFORMATION TECHNOLOGY
Genuine Concerns for Humanity

The following premises would guide the readers in navigating through this chapter:

1. The social concerns of IT, both favourable and adverse, and how the favourable things outweigh the adverse ones.
2. Issues concerned with human privacy and rights of expression and how they are impacted by the technology.
3. The health and occupational hazards facing the IT professionals and how they are to be managed.
4. The ethical issues that are of concern to people and how such aspects are to be addressed by the IT professionals and other users of technology.
5. Some more aspects of e-fraud, cyber crimes and wireless worries.
6. Cyber terrorism which still eludes solutions to humanity in spite of all advancements in technology and even though it offers a variety of solutions in countering them.

After finishing this chapter, readers would be aware of how such issues are to be taken care and managed, while exploiting IT discussed all through this book.

17.1 INTRODUCTION

Like any other technology, IT, offering tremendous benefits to business, its customers, managers and general public, also carries certain risks/threats/social concerns which need to be taken care by business, IT professionals, users and also the society in general.

Certain important aspects of these issues are discussed in this chapter. If issues related to all IT entities in their entirety and the business in general are to be discussed, a separate book needs to be written for the purpose. However, the readers will be able to understand certain key issues through this chapter.

What is unique to this technology is that all processes performed under it cannot be subjected to human scrutiny because of huge volumes and all the activities happening in electronic form. And the activities are happening so fast that it is not possible to stop them in time.

17.2 SOCIAL CONCERNS—FAVOURABLE CONTRIBUTIONS

1. **IT boon to India:** For India, IT has been a boon since the country is considered to be super (brain) power in software engineering and other IT enabled services. India got world recognition in this aspect. For Indians, particularly young Indians in the age group of 20 to 40, IT had made their lives more prosperous and more so the girls and women, who got greatly empowered in the process. They lead a more comfortable and respectable lives in India and in developed countries. However, Indian contributions are mostly in low level design (LLD) activities discussed in Chapter 8. Probably in the years to come, India would go up in the value chain to high level design (HLD) activities (requiring more intellect). India's capabilities in HLD need to be recognized by developed countries.

2. **Boon to Indian citizens:** India is a unique country with a very large population and majority of them living in villages and still dependent on welfare, social support and subsidy schemes offered by state and union governments. IT applications like mobile phones (wireless communication), branchless banking, Internet and e-governance are great boon to Indian citizens. It enables them finding out various avenues that could improve and enrich their lives.

3. **Loss of jobs/unemployment:** There was a general fear that computerization would lead to unemployment. Trade unions were also resisting computerization in many industries for this reason. But in reality, computers relieve people of mundane, repetitive, monotonous and error-prone activities and in turn entrust them with more creative and productive works. This has actually led to higher productivity, job satisfaction and job enrichment among the employees. Moreover no business today can be run without computers.

4. **Knowledge society:** Thanks to Internet and mobile communications, people around the world are becoming highly knowledgeable of all products, services and facilities that could make their lives better. They are aware of wide choices of products and services available to them and their costs. Be it better opportunities of employment, selecting one's life partner, avenues for better education and so on, the human race is being continuously exposed to tremendous knowledge capable of improving their life styles and well being.

Relative merits and demerits of number of products available in the market get compared and evaluated in social networking sites.

There are a number of knowledge based applications which bring huge benefits to people. For example, patients clinical information systems (discussed in Section 16.2.3) are very useful for the doctors and the patients. Police database consisting of all crimes, criminals, their fingerprints, biometrics, photographs and the modus operandi of the crimes help police personnel in preempting the crimes.

5. **Stay in touch with families and relatives:** People, wherever they are or on the move, are able to stay in touch with their families, relatives and friends all the time through Internet and mobile phones. Seventy five percent of Indian population is covered by mobile communications today and no other technology had penetrated to this level in such a short time. This has made the society more cohesive than what we had been accustomed to earlier. Because of this, people do not hesitate to go far away places in search of jobs and better opportunities.

6. **Convenience of homes:** People are able to buy tickets and a number of products and services, pay for various services availed by them, and perform banking operations sitting in the convenience of their homes. Branchless banking is of great use for people not covered by bank branch networks. All such services so far being availed by people, who possessed computers, can now be performed by all people who possess mobile phones.

7. **Right to information (RTI) Act:** Governments are taking a number of initiatives in putting certain information in public governance domain to be made known to the people and the society. If this is to happen, Internet would become much more useful and more popular medium for the society in learning such critical information.

8. **Social networking:** There are many social networking sites where people can exchange their personal information and photo albums, post their views and opinions related to public interests, find out career opportunities, share their experiences both good and bad with the rest of their communities, and so on. Some networking sites adopt 'crowd sourcing model' where everyone can contribute their knowledge to already existing knowledge base of such websites.

17.3 SOCIAL CONCERNS—ADVERSE CONTRIBUTIONS

1. **Censoring internet contents:** The human race, on the one hand, argues in favour of human rights, freedom of speech and expressions. On the other hand, lot of contents hurting the people/countries' beliefs, sentiments and feelings are being published through Internet. A search engine shows a wrong map of Kashmir belonging to India as part of a neighbouring country, which is not acceptable to India and Indians. China censors all Internet contents going in and out of China. There are big discussions going on in India whether to do the same or not. After all, one's freedom stops once it encroaches upon others' freedom/rights.

2. **Obscenity:** Obscene pictures and video themselves were the driving forces for the growth of Internet in its initial stages. As long as they remain in adult domain, there is not much concern for the society. But as it can reach the children and youngsters very easily and traumatize such young minds, it should be stopped by all means. Parents and elders need to be present when the children are accessing Internet. Various facilities are also available for this purpose. It is of serious concern to the society because the students at schools and colleges extensively access Internet for their academic work now.

3. **Interruption to IT enabled services/denial of services to the public:** This is more prevalent in India. The banks, insurance companies, public enterprises offering services like water, power supplies, and so on, often tell the customers that the computers are not working and ask their customers to come next day. This is not right for whatever reasons, as customers and the general public experience terrific inconvenience and hardships in the process. Other instances belonging to this category are the ATMs being out of service, ATM's not having cash stock, inordinate delay in buying train tickets using Internet, and so on.

4. **Dot com (.com) bubble:** Having witnessed the success of companies like Amazon and DELL in e-commerce, supported by highly reliable logistic providers like FEDEX, world economies thought that conventional commerce would be replaced by e-commerce. Dot com companies came into existence in large numbers and their share prices soared to high levels. But the dot com bubbles got burst very soon and the physical business fuelled by Internet and powerful IT applications emerged much stronger.

In India, it did not take off at all, since the consumers here did not trust the sellers and there were no reliable logistics service providers here.

5. **Loss of human touch and warmth:** Since all business activities are performed electronically, there is loss of human touch and warmth in all business interactions with the customers and other supply chain entities. Sellers do not know their customers. However, this is bound to happen because the business volumes are growing and the customer base is also increasing around the world.

17.4 PRIVACY CONCERNS

1. **Customer privacy:** By virtue of extensive business process automation including sales and marketing, sensitive customer data like name, address, phone numbers, e-mail address, financial status, buying patterns, photographs, and so on reside in corporate databases. It is necessary that customer privacy be respected by business organizations and such data be kept confidential all the time. If such data are to be used in other applications or business entities, customers consent needs to be obtained without fail.

Today, e-marketing and e-advertisements have become so powerful and cheaper that the business organizations indulge in acquiring such confidential data from other sources through fraudulent means and encroach upon people's privacy to highly deplorable levels. Various laws and rules enacted by the Governments are still of no use in this regard.

2. **Trade secrets:** Business organizations entrust software development and various other IT enabled services to third parties and also interact with supply chain entities in doing the business. Certain trade secrets, confidential/sensitive business information and process methodologies are shared with the external entities in the process. All entities involved in such interactions need to respect others' secrets, privacy and should not disclose them to anyone else. Generally, non disclosure agreements (agreeing not to disclose confidential and sensitive information) are signed between the parties concerned for this purpose. Some business organizations do get such agreements signed by their managers and employees also.

3. **Others' e-mails, movements and whereabouts:** Accessing others' e-mails, amounts to encroaching others' privacy. And trying to know others' whereabouts through GPS and 3G devices are also encroachments to others' privacy. Though Internet and mobile devices make people believe that their actions are discreet and confidential, it is not so. Electronic devices used in the process are capable of tracing peoples' locations and such methods are used by enforcement agencies in detecting cyber crimes. And anyone could experience such encroachments.

4. **Customer profiles:** Business organizations do create the profiles of their customers so as to have closer interaction with them. This would also amount to encroaching upon their privacy. At the same time, certain customers would get preferential treatment amounting to definite social injustice to others.

17.5   HEALTH CONCERNS

1. **Impractical targets and long hours of work:** Fuelled by tough competition among Indian IT companies and different time zones of their clients in USA and Europe, IT personnel are given impractical targets/dead lines and 12 hours work schedules mostly extending to nights. Families also get physically separated for various reasons and live in different countries and cultures. This leads to mental stress and psychological problems.

2. **Physical ailments:** A number of IT professionals and computer users work for long hours staring at the computer monitors with their hands and fingers constantly flying on the key boards. Their sitting postures and such work environments spell great burden on their eyes, wrists, hands, backs and the legs. People have to abide by the doctors' advice related to such work environments. They need to take frequent breaks from their work and do some simple exercises as part of their job.

3. **Microwaves:** Lot many things are being discussed and published in public domain of all possible harm that could be caused by microwave devices like mobile phones which are not yet proved either way. But what needs to concern us more are the air pollution, dust, noise, depleting ozone and so on more than microwave transmissions.

4. **Addiction to internet and social sites:** Some people, more particularly the college students and young employees, get addicted to websites and more so to social networking sites detrimental to their studies and career growth, though technology cannot be blamed for this. Children are deprived of physical activities and play times in the process.

5. **Ergonomics:** People need to use right chairs, tables, keyboards, monitor positions, sitting postures and so on, which would reduce bodily strains. People need to take frequent walking breaks and do some exercises to get rid of fatigue.

17.6 ETHICAL ISSUES

Ethics related to IT would mean a lot of things and it is so vast that it is not possible to discuss all of them here. However, some important ethical issues are discussed here.

1. **Truthful to customers:** Companies selling their products and services should tell their customers the truth of the products being sold and should not make false claims of their products. The pricing needs to be transparent and the deliveries are to be prompt.

2. **Software piracy:** Computer software are intellectual properties and the companies should not allow anyone to use pirated software since it is not legal.

3. **Misleading customers:** Software vendors should not make unrealistic promises of their products or services to their clients. Internet service providers (ISPs) should not promise, for example, one MBPS speeds in order to trap unsuspecting customers when they could offer only 10 or 20 KBPS speeds.

4. **Information overload:** IT and high speed communications involving multimedia should not be used to send unsolicited contents or overload others of all unwanted and unnecessary information just because they are easily available (forwards) and communicated through Internet.

5. **Truthful reporting of financial results:** Since all financial transactions are held in electronic mediums, it is susceptible to manipulation by a select few in an organization without being noticed by others. Such practices should never be allowed and the business organizations need to report true financial performance of the business to regulating agencies, general public and the stakeholders.

6. **IT professionals:** IT professionals need to contribute their professional efficiency to the benefit of the business and ensure that the business gets maximum leverage from IT.

They need to take the responsibility and be accountable for all their deeds affecting others' privacy and welfare of other employees and the general public.

They should not use confidential/sensitive information passing through them for personal gains. Any shortfalls in the systems need to be reported to the authorities concerned without fail.

17.7 E-FRAUD/CYBER CRIMES

Some aspects of cyber crimes have already been discussed in Chapter 10.

1. **Bank frauds:** Ever since Internet/branchless banking (discussed in Section 16.1) came into operation, bank frauds have increased exponentially. In branch banking, as the person needs to be physically present at the branch, the very fear of being caught (due to face-to-face familiarity with bank staff) did not encourage bank frauds to large extent.

   With Internet/branchless banking, which makes use of electronic cards, user ids, PIN numbers and passwords which can more discreetly or easily be stolen or copied by bank fraudsters (using high tech gadgets which even the banks are not aware of), bank frauds have increased very appreciably now. Stealing money electronically is very discreet unless the bank customers are watching their bank transactions every day. Tracing the fraudsters is also a very difficult job.

   Bank customers need to be careful with respect to their bank accounts and their transactions. They need to be very careful while availing such services and abide by the advice given by the banks and the police in this regard. They need to maintain recorded evidences (like pass book entries) of all their interactions with the banks performed through branchless banking and verify the same frequently.

2. **Business frauds:** People who are interacting with business applications (operational users) are entrusted with the responsibility of handling various business resources including money. Such users could feed unauthorized data with the intention of making personal gains or favouring external entities. It is a business fraud and very difficult to trace some times. Elaborate systems, controls and accountability need to be established in preventing such frauds (discussed in Chapter 9). Change in employees lifestyles also needs to be watched by the managers. Employees revealing their user ids and passwords to others is also a crime. One such fraud is discussed in Section 9.7.2.

3. **Programming frauds:** Software engineers, by virtue of their specialized skills and knowledge which are not easily understandable by others in the business organizations, should not use such knowledge in creating fraudulent software with the intention of defrauding their employer organizations.

4. **Impersonation/blackmail:** In many Internet crimes, men impersonate as women and vice versa and old people impersonate as young ones to lure unsuspecting Internet users. Though people are to be careful, such acts are crimes. Using discreet/personal contents known only to two persons, one person can blackmail other by exposing it to others through Internet. This is a very difficult crime to be detected.

5. **Unauthorized access to computer resources and data:** In business environments, unauthorized access of any of the computer resources like data, copying of programs, revealing sensitive information to others, obtaining information illegally, denying others accessing their computer resources, and so on are also considered as crimes.

Withholding important information meant for others, using such information for personal gains, taking business data/software out of the organizations are also cyber crimes.

6. **E-mail:** Accessing others' e-mails, stealing and using others e-mail addresses and passwords, sending vulgar messages, derogatory remarks and obscene pictures through e-mail or other means are also cyber crimes.

7. **Wireless worries:** Wireless communication is a boon to humanity. However, it brings in worries along with the benefits.

   - People nowadays use wireless keys to lock and open their car doors. There are electronic devices both in the key and the door lock to transmit and accept microwave signals. The device in the door activates physical locking mechanism based on the signals received from the car owner. It was found that a fraudster staying near the car was able to intercept the signals (after all signals travel in air in all directions) with another electronic device in his possession and used the same signals to steal the car itself.

   - Another instance relates to ATM frauds where the fraudsters insert thin film like cheap electronics called 'skimmer' into the ATM debit card slots to steal the electronic codes inscribed on the customers cards like the bank, account number etc., and the PIN number entered by regular ATM users. Skimmer cards can also be inserted into card slots fitted on the doors of the ATM kiosks which also open using the ATM cards. The skimmer card in turn is connected to another small electronic device kept inside the kiosk which can transmit wireless signals through Bluetooth to the device handheld by the fraudsters standing somewhere outside the ATM kiosk. Then, it becomes easy to create duplicate ATM cards and PIN numbers and draw money as if a regular customer does.

   - People around the world now use mobile phones along with 3G wireless communication links to send and receive multimedia contents very fast. They also get connected to a number of networking sites and reputed vendors' sites for downloading number mobile applications. Many people are not aware all personal details and address book stored in their mobile devices are auto-matically picked up by such sites and reveal the same to others (virtually to the world). There is also the possibility of viruses being transmitted to the mobile phones, which can erase all its contents including the software and make the devices non-functional. All this happens in flip of a second unnoticed by the mobile users.

17.8   CYBER TERRORISM

It is an irony that the computers themselves were invented during World War II (1940s) to intercept secret messages/codes sent by enemy nations and to decrypt the same to know the enemy's plans and movements in advance. Secret (analog) computers, viz., ENIAC and COLLOSUS built with thousands of valves were used for this purpose (I generation computers). Actually, this is the first activity of the human race that later on led to the creation of stored instruction digital computers. This was the threshold event, which led to the present day IT as being discussed in this book.

Terrorist groups today have become high tech entities having the same knowledge as college professors of communication technology. The attack on twin towers, New York, USA was backed by discreet communication systems not traced by security agencies in that country.

Powerful explosives attached to mobile phones could be activated and made to explode through microwave signals sent by the terrorists sitting at unknown locations. Though there are number of pre-emptive actions being taken by various governments and surveillance agencies around the world, solutions to such terrorism are still evading. One can ask that wireless communications have been in use for many decades and why it needs to be of concern now. It is because the wireless technologies have become powerful with longer reach, affordable and easily available today.

Today, the mobile phones come with Windows, Apple and Android capabilities and also the wireless communications are becoming powerful through 3G technologies. In India, it is possible to acquire such facilities discreetly in spite of strict rules and laws of the country. Any crime committed with such resources is extremely difficult to trace and more so in catching such terrorists who use Internet for committing crimes.

USA has very powerful encryption technologies to make the messages highly secured, but is not selling to anybody because of the fear that it will land in the hands of the terrorists/ perpetrators of various crimes.

Today, all countries are engaging powerful computers and electronic devices to scan and filter all wired and wireless communications taking place around the world and sniff for doubtful words, languages, contents, etc. which could be traced to terrorist outfits.

There are sophisticated electronic devices capable of capturing large volumes of data/ voice traffic from mobile phones and satellite networks and subjecting them to extensive scrutiny. The activities of terrorist groups and the countries from where they are operating are continuously being watched by satellites and listening posts stationed around the globe at close ranges.

17.9 DOS' AND DON'TS FOR INFORMATION TECHNOLOGY/ INTERNET USERS

1. People should not disclose their personal details and particularly bank related details and the photographs to anyone else. Under no circumstances the photos and other personal information should be posted on to any Internet resources.

2. People should not allow others to take their photos unless it is done by family members and close relatives. If the photos are taken by friends, they should allow it only when it is necessitated by the circumstances. People need to be careful in public places like wash rooms, change rooms and trial rooms and look for doubtful devices in such places (pen like cameras are available today). They need to be highly suspicious of doubtful behaviours of others whoever he or she may be.

3. Basic philosophy each individual needs to do or follow in this regard is simple: to do to others what you expect them to do to you.

Note: Though this is too vast to be covered in this book, some more dos' and don'ts were also discussed in Chapter 10.

SUM UP

The readers would now be in a position to understand why humanity is so much concerned about IT and its applications. They would now be in a position to appreciate:

◆ Both favourable and adverse contributions of IT to society
◆ Issues concerned with human privacy and rights of expression
◆ Health and occupational hazards facing the IT professionals
◆ Ethical issues to be taken care by people associated with the technology
◆ Fraud committed using IT resources and cyber crimes and
◆ Cyber terrorism.

18

BUSINESS TECHNOLOGY MANAGEMENT

Chapter Quest

The following questions would guide the readers in navigating through this chapter.

1. What are the twelve distinctive perspectives of Business Strategy today?
2. What is meant by Business Technology and its Management?
3. What is CMM and how this is adopted in BTM?
4. How IT applications are mapped on to Business Strategies?

18.1 INTRODUCTION

Until year 2000, due to their own limitations, IT applications were generally used in tactical management of the business (in the form of tactical applications discussed in Chapter 4).

At the dawn of new millennium, the exponential growth of the Internet, smart mobile phones and social networking and the birth of 3G and 4G wireless technologies have brought in newer capabilities, which could be exploited in strategic management of the business.

Today the technology is looked at as bringing strategic advantages to business in addition to tactical advantages derived through it in the second half the previous century. Technology today needs to be exploited by the business to derive its strategic advantages. The concept of strategically exploiting IT in business is termed Business Technology. Business Technology needs to be understood in terms of twelve perspectives of business strategy and

IT applications that could be mapped on to them in gaining competitive edge. However, readers need to understand that there are still some shortfalls of the technology as of today, in this regard.

This chapter aims at integrating twelve perspectives of business strategies, BTM concepts and various strategic applications discussed in Chapters 5 and 6 so that the readers and managers could be able to map right strategic IT applications on to their business in gaining competitive advantage.

18.2   TWELVE PERSPECTIVES OF BUSINESS STRATEGY

Business strategy refers to pursuit of competitive edge in the market place. Strategic management refers to the strategic processes of planning, organizing, value additions, collaborating, controlling, leading, innovating, profit making and developing business policies leading to competitive edge. Competitive edge is attained when a business generates good return of investment (ROI), by offering products or services which add definite value to its customers and by using cost effective processes and right technology.

Business policy refers to set of rules, procedures, statements and decisions aimed at enhancing and retaining its competitive advantages based on certain extrinsic and intrinsic values. Extrinsic values refer to what the business delivers to its owners equity owners, employees, investors, suppliers, market channels, customers and the society in general. Intrinsic values refer to transparency in business operations, truthful reporting of financial results, ethics, credibility, responsiveness to the customers and commitment to environments and general public.

In this chapter we will discuss twelve distinctive perspectives of business strategy, to understand the enormity of business strategies in total and will clearly analyse each such perspective. This would help readers in mapping right IT applications discussed so far in the book.

18.2.1   Business as a Battlefield

The word strategy is derived from a Greek word 'strategos' which means art of winning over an enemy in war or a plan of action or policies to stay ahead of competition in business.

In business, strategy means mobilizing and engaging necessary and sufficient resources to gain competitive advantage. It is like establishing preemptive dominance through effective use of business resources and logistical capabilities.

Perspective of battlefield strategy includes logistical capabilities, coordinated efforts, integrated value addition processes involving seven business resources (men, materials, machinery, money, managers, minutes (time) and management information), customers and competition and establishing a winning position in terms of measurable and time bound targets. This would also include market intelligence and assessing competitors' strategies and plans.

In simple terms, this perspective covers future oriented preparedness of the business, winning mindset of the managers, motivation to grab opportunities for growth, developing special expertise where the competition is weak, and not to loose the market share. It means not only winning the competition but also staying there forever and looking beyond the boundaries of business objectives, deadlines, processes and existing markets and developing an overall winning business situation all the time.

18.2.2 Business as a Chain of Marketing Operations

Business strategy is influenced by the market structures such as new markets, fierceness of the competition, niche markets, oligopoly, monopoly, level playing fields of the markets and so on and the operational aspects of the business like product differentiation, economies of scale, investment outlays, market leadership, entry or exit barriers, products' pricing, cost advanatges and so on.

Businesses with homogenous and identical structures are said to be in perfect competition or having level playing fields.

On the contrary, business having unique assets and rich capabilities in terms of technical know-how, reputation, brand image and loyalty, collective decision making, patents and trade marks, well integrated processes and so on is said to be in imperfect competition (non-level playing field) and they tend to generate higher ROI.

In yet another concept, a business is said to possess distinctive competence (what a company is good at when others are not), when all its managers, departments, business functions and the business as a whole have clearly stated objectives and all of them work in unison in achieving those objectives without deviating from them. Quality and commitment of its managers, readyness to adapt to external environments (responsiveness), well engineered processes and products also add distinctive quality and identity to the business.

Business organizations need to evaluate their strengths and weaknesses in terms of their capabilities, reputation, responsiveness, past performance and so on, with the opportunities and threats of the market place (SWOT analysis). Mission focussed pursuit of opportunities enhance the competitiveness of the business. Since strategic decisions are taken with long-term perspective, distinctive competence needs to be looked at longer time spans instead of short-term gains or losses.

Business needs to build the following capabilities under this perspective:

- Adopting right marketing strategies based on the competition, dependence and reliability of its suppliers, customers' expectations, and assessing the impact of substitute and complimentary products.
- Gaining good knowledge of the markets while releasing new products.
- Generating suffcient cash profits to fund attacks on competitors.
- Developing strategic alliances including cooperative competition (co-opetition) with competitors and with other market channels to gain marketing leverage.
- Achieving excellence in marketing in terms of low cost of production, right product differentiation, clear market focus, flexibility and speed of business processes, and continuous innovation in restricting or staying ahead of the competition (High Performance Organization).
- Responding to and mastering the rules of competitive markets.
- Acquiring and defending market share and building high entry barriers for others.
- Offering only those products or services which fit the businesses' distinctive competence.

18.2.3 Business as a Repository of Resources

A business is a repository of seven resources (discussed in Section 2.16.2) which are either deployed or consumed or utilized in exploiting the opportunities found in the market place. These seven resources could be grouped into following three categories, to enable us to understand their unique characteristics:

- Tangible resources or assets such as plant and machinery, land and buildings, information technology infrastructure, suppliers and so on, which can be replicated by the competitors.
- Intangible resources or assets such as patents, intellectual assets, best business practices, brand image, information systems, business technology, supply chain integration and customer relationship management and so on.
- Competitive capabilities such as managerial excellence, organization culture, team work, innovation, learning, networking, responsiveness and abilities to identify, develop, retain and deploy right and sufficient resources aimed at gaining distinctive competitive edge.

Competitive advantages are to be gained by adopting following strategies using all three types of resources:

- Resources need to add definite value to the customers (consumer surplus) for which they would be willing to pay. Such value additions need to result in profits. Right strategies need to be conceived and implemented in using the resources very effectively (minimum) and efficiently (quick) so that the customers needs are satisfied at right time.
- Capabilities need to be built in acquiring and deploying unique and distinctive resources. to enhance the value of business. Accumulated resources also need to be exploited and conserved very judiciously.
- Resources need to be protected by their inimitability and non-substitutability so as not to allow the competitors to duplicate them easily.
- Customers should not be able to claim most of the value additions made by the company from other sources. For example, Apple has positioned its i-phones, i-pads and i-pods, virtually closing down the opportunities for all other vendors to encroach into their markets.
- Needs to possess in-depth understanding and capabilities, of what resources need to be acquired, developed, protected and deployed and how to develop such understanding and capabilities.
- Needs to enlarge its learning abilities or knowledge base dynamically, so as to build newer capabilities in handling the organizational resources innovatively.
- Needs to have the ability to adapt business resources to newer markets and customer expectations through innovative combination of internal resources and establishing the linkage with external resources by striking appropriate strategic alliances (core competency).
- Accumulated resources and the capabilities arising out of them are to be constantly reviewed, renewed and adapted to changing business environments.

18.2.4 Business as a Series of Decision Making Processes

Business is managed by way of deployment, utilization and consumption of heterogeneous resources, based on series of managerial decisions.

Business involves decision making at all levels of management, both simple or rule based and complex. Decisions at operational levels are structured and rule based with definite actions prestated. Since such decisions are automated by computer programs, people at operational levels are relieved from the responsibilities of taking such decisions (programmable decisions).

Some decisions are complex, unstructured and at the most probabilistic. Though technology aids managers in such situations, they can only support or reinforce the decisions taken by them using their cognitive skills. Business strategy in this context means a set of consistent decision behaviours, cognitive capabilities and support systems through which business establishes distinctive competitive edge.

Business decisions include the following characteristics:

- Managers' decision making is influenced by their psychology, confidence, cognitive skills, knowledge, information systems and time span by which decisions are taken.
- Uncertain and turbulent environments demand newer strategies supported by cognitive skills, thorough knowledge of the business situations, risk assessment and support from statistical and mathematical models.
- Business organizations cannot resort to systematic decision-making when operating under too many uncertainties because of the lack of right information. Such decisions are also subject to cognitive limitations of the managers (bounded rationality).
- A set of consistent decisions are to be taken before the business commits its resources in order to retain its markets.
- Small changes can be made over the set of historically proven decisions.
- Futuristic, imaginative and complex decisions are to be taken in managing major changes happening in the business environments.
- High performance can be achieved in number of ways and each way cannot be effective under all conditions (principle of equifinality).

18.2.5 Business as a System Influenced by its Environments

Competitive strategy also refers to how the business manages its environments, internal environments involving its own employees, trade unions and the managers and external environments involving the suppliers, customers, wholesalers, dealers, investors, debtors, creditors, competitors and general public in resolving uncertainties arising out of them (relationship management).

The business processes such as procurement, materials management, production, quality assurance, logistics, marketing, finance and so on need to be compatible to the business environments which change dynamically.

In order to tackle business uncertainties arising out of its environments, the organization needs to establish following preparedness:

- Situational preparedness means the business needs to align its business strategies, technology used, products offered, channels of marketing, pricing etc. with its environments. For example, the business needs to adapt e-marketing and e-advertisement, as the world business is greatly influenced by the Internet, e-business, smart phones and social networks.
- Organizational preparedness means aligning the organization, its structure, reporting relationships, organizational culture and leadership styles, integration of the business processes, networking of human resources etc. in line with dynamically changing/ global business practices.

The situational preparedness and organizational preparedness should compliment one another.

18.2.6 Business as a Continually Learning Organization

When managers are engaged in managing internal and external business environments, they learn something new every time and become more knowledgeable in the process. Such learning plays an important role in subsequent decisions involving mobilising and deployment of all business resources. These learning experiences of managers need to be pooled into an organizational knowledge so that others can learn from them.

Based on the decision outcomes (feedback), managers also alter their practices and actions in short term. In long terms the organizations are able to alter their values and beliefs matching the business environments or situations.

Business organizations need to facilitate such learning and create physical structures to share and accumulate such learning into organizational knowledge. Such knowledge (operating procedures, routine's to be followed, simple do's and don'ts, fixes for the problems etc.) needs to be used by other managers of the organization subsequently. The organizational learning enhances its capabilities in achieving the business objectives.

Readers are to be aware of the following four types of knowledge that could be accumulated by business organizations:

1. **Migratory knowledge:** Migratory knowledge is easily transferable and they can be converted into documents, statements, procedures and so on, so that others can pursue them easily, e.g., business process manuals incorporating best business practices, work flow diagrams, etc.

2. **Explicit knowledge:** Explicit knowledge is easy to express and communicate and can be stored in the computer database, e.g., product design, patents, production processes, quality assurance techniques, cost saving methods and so on.

3. **Embedded knowledge:** Embedded knowledge is not transferable as they are embedded in social relations, cultures and decision-making styles of the organization.

4. **Tacit knowledge:** Tacit knowledge is highly personal, hard to formalize and to express. Tacit knowledge again has two types viz.,

1. Technical knowledge, e.g., craftmanship and physical skills developed over years through constant practice and specialization

2. Cognitive knowledge, e.g., mental maps, decision-making wisdom, gut feeling, risk averting abilities and so on.

Knowledge creation in business is not simply a process of accumulating objective information. Instead it involves a challenging task of mobilization and conversion of tacit, embedded and subjective insights of the managers into organizational knowledge base.

All the above types of knowledge are to be combined and acquired by the business through the processes of:

- *Socialization:* It is the process of sharing the experiences with one another through social and informal interactions.

- *Externalization:* The process of articulation of tacit knowledge into explicit concepts which can be done using the aids like naming, describing, documenting, drawing, charting, using symbols, diagrams, vague descriptions and so on.

- *Combination:* It is the process of combining different types and forms of explicit and tacit knowledge into new knowledge.

- *Internalization:* It is the process of learning by doing and thus creating new tacit knowledge.

Business needs to build following capabilities under this perspective:

- Business organizations need to create a right policies, procedures, cultures and structures for creation, retention and transfer of business knowledge for use by others in the organization and for further enhancement of its quantum and quality in future.

- Organizations would turn more innovative, if they develop the capabilities to create new knowledge based on internal knowledge and enable sharing of such knowledge across the organization. Such knowledgebase needs to be exploited in creating commercial and competitive advantages.

- Managers need to be trained and motivated to enhance their absorptive capacities.

- A user friendly Knowledge Management Systems should be set up to transfer all types of knowledge, in all forms, formats and media so that the managers can use it with least efforts.

- The organization must have rewards and incentive system for the managers to compensate for such efforts.

- Business needs to create social cohesion among the managers to freely interact and exchange their knowledge with each other without hesitation. Physical and psychological barriers, if any, need to be removed by fostering informal networks.

- People need to be moved or transferred across different locations and functions to gain newer knowledge.

- Managers need to be encouraged to examine, correct and reformulate their existing and newer knowledge.

- Barriers and misfits, if any, in the process of transfer of knowledge intra- or inter-organization, among the learning units, their social contexts, manager relations etc. need to be eliminated.

- Managers' efforts need to be appreciated and they are to be made to believe that by sharing their knowledge, they actually are transforming the business and creating a great future.
- Managers need to look at the entire process as an opportunity for learning and knowledge creation for themselves and for the organization.
- Knowledge management systems are discussed in section 4.7.

18.2.7 Business as Creating Win-Win Relationship with Diverse Human Entities

Business is an active interaction among diverse human entities such as the owners, employees, managers, suppliers, investors, wholesalers, retailers, customers, Governments and general public, each wanting their own interests to be taken care or safeguarded at the most. While owners expect best ROI and capital appreciation, employees expect higher salaries and stock options. Suppliers expect higher turnover and more profits from their client companies. Wholesalers and retailers expect higher commission, least investments and faster sales. Customers expect high quality products at cheaper rates.

Business organizations need to aim forging win-win situation among all human entities associated with the business, because it is not possible to replace or acquire these entities at will. Replacing these entities would involve search and information costs, negotiating costs, policing and disciplining costs and reorientation costs. It is also better to retain those activities whose costs are high, within the organization.

Business organizations need to do value engineering and costing for all the materials being bought from the suppliers, if they want to enter into effective and meaningful negotiations. Employees and managers' salaries and other earnings need to be benchmarked with the industry or local norms, cost of living, inflation and so on. Wholesalers and retailers investments, costs of their services, fair return on their investments, etc. are to be taken into consideration while fixing their commission. Modern management theory advocates that all the business entities should be looked at as extended profit centres of the business. No entity should be allowed to gain undue advantage from the main business.

Asset specificity refers to the extent to which the present assets cannot be redeployed to alternative uses without sacrificing its present values, e.g., ROI. Higher the asset specificity, higher would be the lock-in periods among the above business entities.

18.2.8 Business as a Conglomeration of Management Functions

In this section we will discuss management perspectives with respect to top, middle and operational level managers.

Four Distinctive Views of Management Strategies

- Entrepreneurial and innovative CEOs would believe in innovative product lines and designs and would be the initiators of future oriented innovation and change.

- Conservative and cost conscious CEOs would view innovations as costly and disrupting the production and efficiency of the business. Their behaviour would be compatible to past performance and tradition and would manage based on the requirements of the current business.
- Analysis oriented CEOs would show less acceptance to innovative and unproven ideas. They would be focussing on efficiency rather than the flexibility.
- Renewing strategy oriented CEOs would compete based on efficiency of business operations and would create competitive environments. They will exploit strategic opportunities to lower costs or bringing out innovative products.

Strategies associated with CEOs are highlighted below:

- Some CEOs would reduce uncertainties in business by adopting central organization structure with high levels of control, direct supervision and conservative decision making.
- Some CEOs would depend on business analytics to dominate in their business environments and would use formal processes for decision making and control.
- Some CEOs would reduce the complexity and sophistication of the business, engage in fuller and more explicit analysis of various alternate courses of action and efficiently reach the best course of action and reduce organizational politics to minimal levels.
- Creative and competitive CEOs would go for explosive growth and expansion plans.
- Bureaucratic and conservative CEOs would go for continuous growth combined with business consolidation.
- Brave CEOs would adopt turnaround strategies.
- CEOs styles and behaviours would vary depending on the life cycles through which the products are passing through, viz., emerging phase (prospector style), growth phase (analyzer style) and matured phase (defender style).
- Innovation, new and better resources and processes could happen only with the vision and the will of the top management.
- A heterogeneous management team with multiple skill sets, diverse educational backgrounds, rich experience and different age groups would lead to improved competitive strategies, decision making and cognitive skills, mastery on business information and knowledge and innovative capabilities. However, this would result in more scrutiny, criticism and questioning of underlying assumptions and decisions.
- A homogenous management team on the contrary would only be conservative as everyone carries same values and assumptions.

Roles of Middle Level Managers

- Pursuit of excellence in terms of labour productivity, effective management structure, exploitation of technology and so on requires strong top and middle level managers.

- Information based organizations could replace middle level managers with the result oriented task force or team of managers with requisite skills who can work as a network while completing a given task.

- Middle level managers need to be radical innovators of new products and efficient processes and adopters of right and emerging technologies. They would identify opportunities for new products because of their long exposure to the markets, customers, product designers and R&D functions. They possess knowledge-based capabilities in integrating various business functions in delivering value to the customers.

- They would handle internal politics very tactfully in getting new projects started and getting the support of the people for the projects. They need to interact with the functional heads and the top management in order to facilitate new ventures and initiatives. They are aware of how the system operates, distinctive elements in it, potential for implementing better business practices and the ways of convincing the employees that the change is essential for the business.

- Top management as facilitators need to clarify strategies and make middle level managers to take initiatives in implementing strategies through bargaining and negotiation. Increased strategic consensus resulting from middle managers involvement would smoothen implementation of newer strategies. However, middle management could only fine tune existing resources and processes which do not require additional investments. Middle management would become ineffective if top management becomes bureaucratic, dictatorial and rule base.

- Middle level managers are vanguards of innovation and change. They need to be empowered to stimulate entrepreneurship. They need to use their political skills to change and channelize organizational energies in implementing new strategies, discovering newer markets and products, improving the business processes, adopting newer technology and creating new organization structures or networks who can accomplish the above.

- Managers at operational levels need to focus on efficiency of business operations, quality of products and services, events management and transaction processing.

General Organizational Strategies

- In addition to vertical communication along the line of control, a free formal and informal communication horizontally across all business functions and departments is required. Each employee or a manager should have only one boss in the organization.

- Managers' personal interests and ambitions need to be subordinate to organizational objectives.

- Managers need to willingly participate and play active roles in all the management functions.

18.2.9   Business as Value Creation for Customers

The success of business ultimately depends on how much value it adds to the products or services offered to its customers or as economic theory suggest, the consumer surplus of its products. Another important aspect is the costs of its products, i.e., at what costs the products are offered for sale. It should be reckoned that value delivered to the customers would either be in the form of enhanced performance and utility or reduced costs.

The factors that contribute to reach these objectives are scales of economy, organizational learning of what values are expected by its customers, innovative use of technologies, manufacturing processes, logistics, marketing and post-sales services and how effectively these functions are managed.

The following strategies need careful evaluation and implementation in order to gain competitive advantage in this context.

- Organizations need to know what the customers expect from the products and services, what values are required to be added, how the values are to be added and what profits such value additions would yield.

- The value addition costs are to be measured at micro levels by doing value chain analysis of all activities involved in the process and establishing the customers' willingness or preparedness to pay for each such value addition. Costs, which the customers are not willing to pay, need to be eliminated.

- The short-term cost reduction should be weighed with innovation costs and costs of long-term development of technological competitiveness. By understanding the customer needs better, the business needs to offer differentiated value to the customers while aiming enhanced profitability rather than just satisfying the customer needs. Product differentiation needs to be done within the target cost parameters.

- Cost drivers in business are structural costs or fixed costs associated with the structure of the industry, organization structure, technologies used and so on and the operating costs involving material costs, conversion costs, marketing costs and so on.

- Business organizations need to focus customer retention strategies since acquiring new customers are costly. Moreover, only a small percentage of customers would be contributing to major profits. Such customers are to be managed more profitably.

- Organizations need to reach the levels of competition at which the customers are even willing to pay more, reduced cost structure supported by low cost and continuous improvement practices and cost and quality conscious work culture.

- IT needs to be deployed to radically redesign the business processes in order to achieve dramatic improvements rather than just automating outdated processes. Product life cycles and lapsed time between procurement of raw materials to realization of sale proceeds need to be reduced to bear minimum.

- Customer service and support centres need to be established across all geographic locations either independently or with collaborative business associates. Customers are to be supported upto the life-span of its products.

- Knowledge and experience are to be used to lower the costs and for enhancing the profits rather than beating the competitors just on the costs.

- Businesses need to build agility aimed at quicker decisions and rapid response by building efficient information systems and other IT applications rather than just trying quick fixes.

18.2.10 Business as an Adopter of Right IT Strategies

IT in the form of computers, integrated business applications, e-business, Internet, smart mobile phones, social networks and so on, drives most of the businesses today. This chapter emphasizes how business strategies and IT are to be managed in combination in the form of Business Technology. Entire book is aimed at educating the managers at all levels to formulate right IT strategies for their businesses.

All IT applications that could leverage modern business are discussed in Chapters 4, 5 and 6. Key factors by which the technology leverages the business and make it more competitive are discussed in Chapter 1. Information as an important organizational resource and how it helps managing other business resources and make the business more competitive are discussed in Chapter 2.

18.2.11 Business as an Establishment Focussing on Risks

Any business is exposed to number of risks, some being very serious. Business organizations need to have right strategies in place that would enable identification of all types of risks, procedures to be followed in mitigating the risks, management of risks when they occur, employees and managers responsible for risk associative activities and so on. A business's competitiveness is also decided by its preparedness in managing and withstanding the risks.

All information about the risks and their management ought to be documented and made known to all employees and the managers. Much more awareness needs to be created when the risks are associated with external entities, general public and the environments. Risk management systems are discussed in Section 6.11.

18.2.12 Business as System Involving Measures, Metrics and Analytics

Business strategies need to reckon that for anything to be managed effectively, the outcomes from them need to be measured. Thanks to computers and business process automation, all business resources and their performance could be measured effectively. Right business strategies should also include setting performance yardsticks, targets, or budgets for all resources so as to ensure how the business resources perform against such targets. Throughout this book various systems have been discussed to enable the readers to clearly understand how measures and metrics are established and managed in a business. Unless right measures and metrics are established, it is very difficult to control the business.

Today information explosion is taking place in all types of business organizations whether small or big. Enormous volumes of data related to materials, products, processes, markets and customers are stored in the computer databases. Such data also store very useful information that could yield valuable information to the business. For this to happen, various modelling techniques using statistical, mathematical and financial models need to be built by the specialists in such areas. Business organizations need to have right strategies that would enable discovering hidden, newer and more useful information. These aspects have been discussed in Sections 5.9 and 5.10.

18.3 BUSINESS TECHNOLOGY (BT)

Business technology (BT) refers to convergence of customer and ROI focussed business strategies and IT capabilities including Internet, e-business and mobile technologies. BT looks at the technology beyond management information systems and business process automation. It is clearly a shift from tactical applications (discussed in Chapter 4) to strategic applications (discussed in Chapters 5 and 6).

We are living in a digital world where humanity is ruled by the computers, Internet and numerous digital devices (using 0's and 1's only). Technology undoubtedly has become a strategic business tool.

Business technologists need to have a clear grasp of the winning strategies for the business and the capabilities of current and emerging technologies that would support such strategies. They need to spearhead all their efforts in implementing profitable strategies using the technology. Business organizations today need to establish business technology leadership.

18.4 BUSINESS TECHNOLOGY MANAGEMENT (BTM)

Business Technology Management (BTM) is an emerging management science that seeks to unify business and technology decision making by the managers at all levels, thereby enhancing BTM capabilities of entire organization. Consequently, all business practices and processes are organized and improved around BTM solutions.

BTM strategically combines operational and infrastructural aspects of BT in realizing strategic advantages. Such structured approach is used by the business organizations in deploying right technology in delivering best business practices, risk control and improved profitability. BTM needs to support, enable and leverage company's current and evolving business strategies continuously. BT needs to offer solutions in facing the competition, tackling threats and exploiting business opportunities. When the priorities, investments and capabilities of the business match with that of the technology, BTM can be considered having reached a maturity level. BTM needs to take cognizance of twelve perspectives of business strategy discussed in Section 18.2 and support the business initiatives in all those perspectives.

18.5 BUILDING BLOCKS OF BTM

Key building blocks which could enable business organizations achieve BTM maturity level are Business processes, Organizational resources (people), Information (business knowledge) and Technology (hardware and software). These issues (five entities that constitute IT applications in business) have been discussed throughout this book.

18.5.1 Business Processes

BTM needs to implement robust, flexible and responsive business processes incorporating best business practices. In addition to implementing such processes, BTM needs to clearly define all such processes, make them work optimally and continuously evaluate them to ensure,

- Right things are done at right time (quality of business processes).
- Doing things quickly with no redundancy (efficiency).
- Doing things in right ways (effectiveness).

Readers need to keep in mind the enormity of the business processes discussed in Chapter 1 and all such processes are to meet these expectations.

18.5.2 Organization

For BT initiatives to succeed, the businesses need to have supporting organizational structure with a clear understanding of roles, responsibilities and reporting relationships with decision-making capabilities. An ideal organizational structure means,

- **Participative management:** Top management needs to understand the strategic benefits the technology brings to the business and support all technology initiatives. They need to empower a senior management position to spearhead BT initiatives with right support from technical teams. Business managers need to be tech savvy business strategists.
- **Technical team:** There need to be a right technical team well-versed with current technologies and business domain involving all twelve perspectives of business strategies and their objectives.
- **Networked organizational structure:** Top and middle level managers capable of formulating right business strategies and managers with right technology skills need to be networked together and given time bound BT targets or goals. Similarly, networked organizational structures need to be created for all projects by combining requisite skills. Networked organizational structure is discussed in Section 6.7.3.

The organizational structures may vary, depending on the type of the business, markets, customers, competition and maturity levels of BTM.

18.5.3 Information

Information which is made available to management functions needs to meet the following criteria. Attributes of an ideal MIS have also been discussed in Chapter 2.

- Right information need to be made available in real time.
- The format and the contents need to comprehensible even for novice managers.
- Enable informed decisions.
- Useful information does not happen by chance. It depends on three related elements viz., right data, managers perception and metrics.
- Relevant data must be available and reliable metrics should distil useful information from them.

18.5.4 Technology

- Technology needs to seamlessly connect all business functions and processes leading to business process automation, information sharing, coordination, communication, collaborative decision making and business integration.
- The focus should not be just automating existing processes, but to derive strategic advantages.
- New tools like data mining, modelling, business analytics and so on need to be exploited all the time.

18.6 BTM CAPABILITIES

Right BTM capabilities would lead to:

- Competitiveness
- Automation of well-defined business processes
- Right organization structure
- Effective information architecture
- Reliable technology infrastructure and so on.

18.7 BTM MATURITY MODEL

A maturity model in business describes how well an organization performs a set of activities compared to prescribed standards or benchmarks.

BTM maturity model defines five levels of maturity (rating) scored against four critical success areas discussed earlier viz., process, organization, information and technology. Rating is done based on the levels of (bad to best) achievements in each area. BTM maturity model makes it possible for the business to isolate the shortfalls in its performance when it is benchmarked across other similar businesses.

18.8 CAPABILITY MATURITY MODEL (CMM)

CMM relates to the degree of structure and optimization of processes, compared to ad-hoc practices, to formally structured steps, to managed result metrics, to realistic optimization of the processes.The model's aim is to improve software development processes. However, it is also used as a general model to aid in business processes generally.

The CMM model's application in software development has been problematic because applying multiple models that are not integrated across an organization, created problems in training, appraisals and improvement activities. The Capability Maturity Model Integration (CMMI) project was formed to sort out the problem of using multiple models for software development processes, thus the CMMI model has superseded the CMM model.

A maturity model can be viewed as a set of structured levels that describe how well the people, practices and processes of an organization can reliably and sustainably produce good results.

A maturity model can be used as a benchmark for comparison and assessing the degree of maturity.

1. The maturity model involves five attributes:

- *Maturity Levels:* In a 5-level process maturity continuum, the uppermost (5th) level is a notional ideal state where processes would be systematically managed by a combination of process optimization and continuous process improvement.
- *Key Result Areas:* Key Result Area (critical success factors) identifies a cluster of associative activities that, when performed together, achieve right goals.
- *Goals:* Goals of a key result area summarize the states that must exist for that key result area to have been implemented in an effective and lasting way. The extent to which the goals have been accomplished is an indicator of how much capability the organization has established at that maturity level.
- *Common Features:* Common features include practices that implement and institutionalize a key result area. There are five types of common features— commitment to perform, ability to perform, activities performed, measurement and analysis, and bench marking the performance.
- *Key Practices:* The key practices describe the elements of infrastructure and practice that contribute most effectively to the implementation and institutionalization of the area.

2. Levels

There are five levels defined along the continuum of the model and, according to the 'Software Engineering Institute' (who spearheaded CMM concepts), "Predictability, effectiveness, and control of an organization's software processes are believed to improve as the organization moves up these five levels. An empirical evidence to date supports this belief".

1. Initial (chaotic, ad hoc, individual based): It is the starting point for use of a new or undocumented repeat process.
2. Repeatable: It is the process which at least is documented sufficiently such that repeating the same steps are attempted.
3. Defined: The process is defined/confirmed as a standard business process, e.g., Work Instructions.
4. Managed: The process is quantitatively managed in accordance with agreed metrics.
5. Optimizing: The process management includes deliberate process optimization/ improvement.

Within each of these maturity levels are Key Result Areas which characterise that level, and for each such area there are five factors—goals, commitment, ability, measurement and verification. These are not necessarily unique to CMM, as they are the stages that organizations must go through on the way to becoming mature.

SUM UP

The readers now would be aware of twelve perspectives of business strategy which are to be addressed while IT solutions are mapped on to the business. IT applications need to support business strategies.

The readers would also have understood how Business Technology, Business Technology Management and BTM and CMM maturity levels would guide the business in becoming 'High Performance Organization'.

INDEX

3G, 281

Access controls, 250
Accessing employee data from the database, 312
ACID test, 128
Activity based costing, 53
Advantages of IBA/ERP, 27
Advertising network, 134
After-sales service/customer support, 12
Analog computing, 91
Analytical applications, 109
Application architecture, 302
Application packages, 223, 292
Application service providers, 59
Application software, 291
Application specific software packages, 292
'As is' study, 187
Assembler language, 290
Assets safeguard, 233
Asymmetric cryptography, 252
ATM services, 347
Audit trails, 239
Authentication, 250

B2B model, 126
B2C, 127
Back office, 60
Banking services, 350
Banks, 344
Banner advertisement, 132
Bar code readers, 269
Bargaining power, 31

Base line, 211
Batch data processing, 34, 69
Batching of programs, 293
Benefits of IT, 178
Best business practices, 15, 38
BIT, 264
Blog, 133
Bluetooth, 281
Bookkeeping, 4, 35
Books of accounts, 70
Bottom up approach, 178, 332
Branchless banking, 348
Browser, 117
BTM maturity model, 385
Budget control, 171
Business, 179
Business (operations) planning, 165
Business communication, 35, 113
Business computations, 4
Business data management, 34
Business decisions, 55
Business documents, 34
Business effectiveness, 232
Business entities and events, 50
Business expectations, 230
Business functions, 7
Business intelligence, 80, 82
Business knowledge, 5, 179
Business objectives, 163
Business organization, 336
Business perception, 35
Business perspective, 191
Business plans, 16
Business policies, 15

Business process automation, 3, 36, 179, 189
Business process engineering, 190
Business process integration, 113
Business process manuals, 15, 164
Business process outsourcing, 60
Business processes, 23
Business relationship, 233
Business strategy, 372
Business technology, 383
Business technology management, 383
Business users, 61, 62, 232
Buying power, 31
BYTE, 264

CACHE memory, 264
Call centre, 112
Capability maturity model, 385
Capacity planning, 166
CASE Tools, 297
Central computing, 302
Central processing, 261
Checklist, 239
Chief digital officer, 342
CISC processor, 262
Classification of data, 149
Classification of software, 285
Client, 116
Client server, 277
Clinical information system, 351
Cloud computing, 303
Code generators, 297
Cognitive skills, 49
Collaboration, 17, 169
Collecting data, 325
Commitment accounting, 171
Commitment accounting systems, 54
Common user interface, 28
Communication, 170
Communication systems technology, 21
Compact disks, 266
Company law, 13
Competitors, 31
Compilers, 290
Complementary products, 32
Complex instruction set, 262
Compliance, 233
Compliance management, 172
Compliance to rules, 39
Compliance with statutory rules and regulations, 19

Comprehension, 45
Computer aided software engineering, 295
Computer architecture, 276
Computer instructions, 263
Computer operators, 212
Computer resources, 189, 213
Computer time share, 61
Computer virus, 298
Computer-based/aided learning, 40
Concurrency control, 319
Confidentiality, 38, 250
Configuration management, 220
Content management, 122
Contributions of IT, 3
Control, 171
Controlling, 18
Convergence, 83, 113
Convergence/multimedia, 6
Coordination, 17, 169
Coordination and collaboration, 28, 38
Core banking solutions, 345
Corporate-social responsibility, 14
Cost estimation, 200
Coupling, 295
Creative thinking, 39
Credit cards, 347
Critical success factors, 63
Customer complaints, 32
Customer database, 110
Customer feedback, 110
Customer interactive applications, 109
Customer loyalty, 32
Customer orders and invoicing, 311
Customer privacy, 364
Customer relationship management, 36, 108
Customer response, 114
Customer support, 102
Customer touch-points, 111
Customers, 11, 105
Customization, 223
Customized IBASP, 225
Cyber crimes, 257, 367
Cyber theft, 258

Data, 43, 307, 319
Data accuracy, 231
Data administration, 322
Data backup, 219, 323
Data concurrency, 324

Data conversion, 213
Data element, 309
Data elements management, 318
Data flow diagram, 203
Data Independence, 325
Data integrity, 319
Data management, 287, 318, 326
Data manipulation, 319
Data migration, 213
Data mining, 36, 110, 148, 151
Data processing, 43, 307
Data processing system, 68
Data security, 38, 249
Data storage, 265
Data types, 52
Data warehouse, 36, 110, 148
Database access controls, 319
Database administrator, 322
Dataflow diagram, 89
DBMS, 313
Debit cards, 346
Decision making, 18, 173
Decision support systems, 35, 153
Decision tables, 205
Decisions, 49
Delegation of power, 15
Departmental heads, 64
Desktop publishing, 79
Device controllers, 265
Device drivers, 265, 288
Device management, 288
Devices, 267, 270
Diagramming tools, 297
Dictionary tools, 297
Digital (PowerPoint) presentation, 78
Digital audio tapes, 267
Digital certificate, 255
Digital envelope, 254
Digital signature, 254
Digital stenography, 79
Digital still camera, 269
Digital video camera, 269
Digitizer, 268
Disintegrated information systems, 26
Display advertising, 132
Distributed computing, 302, 305
Distributors, 11
Document management system, 77
Document repository, 77
Documentation, 216
Domain name system, 143

Dot matrix printer, 270
DRAM, 264
Drip Marketing, 136
DSS database, 153
Dumb terminals, 70
DVD, 266

E-business, 12, 35
e-business infrastructure, 115
E-commerce, 113, 122
E-fraud, 367
E-governance, 356
E-mail, 77
E-mail marketing, 135
E-mail spam, 136
E-marketing, 130
e-wallet, 347
Ease of management, 36
Effective management, 2, 34
Efficiency of business, 232
Efficient business operations, 2
Efforts estimation, 197
Electronic data processing, 68
Electronic diary, 78
Electronic pen, 268
Electronic relations, 112
Electronic relationships, 6, 179
Electronic spreadsheets, 78
Electronic wallet, 347
Employee fraud, 246
Employees, 64
Encryption, 251
End user computing, 39
End user methodology, 222
Enterprise information system, 80
Entity files, 308
Entity/Event relationship, 315
Environmental responsibilities, 8
ERP, 223
Establishes logical relationship, 319
Ethical issues, 366
Evolution of IT applications, 91
Executive information systems (EIS), 80, 160
Expert system, 155
Exports and imports, 12
Extension of vehicles warranty period, 158

Facilities management, 59
Feasibility analysis, 193

Feedback, 49, 216
File, 309
File access methods, 311
File management, 288, 318
File organization, 310
File update, 314
Finance, 12, 102, 182
Financial, 167
Finished stock inventory, 11
Firewalls, 256
Firmware, 289
Floppy disks, 266
Flowchart symbols, 68
Focus of IT, 3
Format, 45
Fourth generation languages, 291
Front desk, 60
Front end, 116
Front end tools, 293
FTP, 143
Function points, 200
Functional consultants, 339
Functional managers, 63

Generations of computers, 282
Geographic information system, 85
Global exposure, 113
Global positioning system, 147
Global reach, 6, 179
Goal seeking analysis, 86
Good programming, 293
Goods in transit, 147
Group decision support systems, 38, 88, 169
Group decisions, 88
Groupware applications, 88

Hacking, 118, 258
Hard disk, 265
Head—ITSD division, 337
Health concerns, 365
Hierarchical database management system, 320
High, 290
High performance organization, 37, 39
Hospitals, 350
Hotels and resorts, 354
HTML, 143
HTTP, 143
Human resources management, 13, 102

Human warmth, 118
Hyperstitials, 134

IBA server, 117
Ideal IT applications, 230
Impact printers, 271
Inbound marketing, 131
Indexed sequential access, 311
Indexed sequential organization, 310
Information, 307
Information contents, 45
information dash board, 80
Information drilldown, 48
Information overload, 118
Information security, 231
Information systems, 21, 111
Information Technology, 20
Information technology services division, 13, 237, 335
Infrastructure design, 196
Infrastructure maintenance, 59
Ink-jet printer, 271
Innovation, 20, 173
Innovative business processes, 8
Input, 267
input data, 189
Integrated business applications, 26, 27, 98, 303
Integration of business, 5, 35, 179, 232
Integration of business functions, 159
Integration testing, 211
Integrity controls, 238
Integrity of application software, 234
Integrity of business processes, 234
Integrity of computer infrastructure, 234
Integrity of people, 233
Interactive applications, 111
Interactive media, 133
Internet, 114, 278
Internet banking, 346
Internet portals, 114
Internet service providers, 59, 117
Interpreters, 291
Interstitials, 134
Investor management, 13
Islands of information, 27
ISO standards, 341
IT applications, 64
IT assets aafeguarding, 241
IT leveraging the business, 33

IT strategy, 8, 20, 174
ITIL, 342

Job management, 287
John von Neumann, 261
Joint application development, 226
Junk e-mail, 136

Key field, 309
Key pairs, 253
Key result areas, 63
Keyboard, 267
Knowledge, 48
Knowledge base, 48
Knowledge based management, 28, 85
Knowledge economy, 2, 109
Knowledge management, 20, 175
Knowledge management system, 38, 82

Large scale printing, 35
Laser printer, 271
Last mile connectvity, 116
Layout tools, 297
LCD projector, 271
Lean advertisement, 134
Learning organization, 8, 37
Ledgers, 35
Legal proceedings, 13
Limiting perception, 46
Line and support functions, 9
Line printer, 270
Local area network, 278
Logical database, 52, 194, 313
Logical structure of computer, 261
Logical structure of database, 314
Logistics, 11, 101, 147
Low level languages, 290

Machine language, 290
Magnetic tapes, 267
Main frame computers, 276
Main memory, 263
Maintenance engineers, 340
Malware, 140
Management by exception, 37
Management by objectives, 37

Management control, 37, 236
Management functions, 7
Management information system, 37, 75
Management support systems, 15
Management's responsibilities, 62
Managerial effectiveness, 39
Managers, 65
Manager's unethical practice, 247
Manpower planning, 166
Marketing, 180
Marketing planning, 165
Marketing transactions, 109
Master data, 52
Master files, 308
Material requirement planning, 166
Materials management, 10, 100, 181
Materials purchase, 156, 244
Medium business, 227
Mega tags, 130
Memory management, 287
Message integrity, 250
Metrics and measures, 201
Metropolitan area network, 278
Microphone, 269
Middle level management, 14
Miniaturization, 6
MIS contents, 188
MIS format, 44, 47
Mission, 14
Mobile banking, 348
Mobile computing, 304
Mobile devices, 274
Model base management system, 154
Models, 152
Models base, 154
Modems, 272
Modern managerial functions, 15
Mouse, 268
Multi-terminal systems, 70
Multidimensional MIS, 47
Multimedia, 83

Network architecture, 278
Network file system, 144
Network interface cards, 272
Network service providers, 59
Network support, 221, 340
Network—mediums, 273
Networked database management system, 321

Networked organization structure, 38, 170
Networking hardware, 272
Networking operating system, 289
New products, 32
Non-procedural languages, 298
Non-repudiation, 250

O&M, 164
Objectives, 15
Office automation, 36
Office automation systems, 76
Office data, 79
Office management, 13
Online analytical processing system, 86
Online banking, 346
Online complex processing system, 87
Online help, 215
Online trading, 349
Online transaction processing system, 34, 54, 70
Open systems, 277
Operating systems, 286
Operational plans, 16
Operational users, 65, 212
Operations management, 14
Optical character recognition, 77
Optimization analysis, 87
Organization structure, 17, 167
Organizing, 16, 167
OSI model, 145
Outbound marketing, 131
Output, 270
Outsourcing, 224

Paperless business, 114
Paperless office, 38, 77
Passing of data, 295
Payment gateway, 60, 122
Payment services, 349
Payroll, 69
Pen drive, 266
Perception, 45
Performance appraisal, 175
Personalization, 139
Personnel, 183
Pervasive computing, 36
Physical database, 313
Physical processes, 32
Planning, 16, 167

Plant and machinery, 101
Plotter, 271
Point of sales, 109, 346
Positioning, 30
Post office protocol, 144
Post-sales services, 110
Price, 30
Principles of good programming, 293
Privacy, 106, 118, 140
Privacy concerns, 364
Privacy issues, 259
Process metrics, 201
Procurement, 100
Procurement of software, 300
Product development, 12
Product development life cycle, 148
Product packaging, 11
Product presentation, 31
Production, 101, 181
Production and production control, 11
Production planning and scheduling, 10
Products, 29
Profiling, 138
Program flowcharts, 209
Program partitioning, 294
Program specifications, 208
Programmable decisions, 4
Programmed decisions, 34
Programmers, 339
Programming, 208, 209, 290
Programming efforts estimation, 198
Programming languages, 289
Project approval, 202
Project leader, 338
Project management, 79
Project planning, 165
Promotion, 30
Property management, 354
Proprietary programming, 224
Proprietary systems, 276
'Pull market' strategy, 8
Purchasing, 10

QR code readers, 269
Quality analysts, 340
Quality assurance, 11, 208, 244
Quality control, 101
Quality control of inputs, 10

Random organization, 311
Rapid application development, 226
Real time information, 28, 34, 231
Real time MIS, 74
Real time systems, 73
Record management, 318
Record structure, 309
Reduced instruction set, 262
Redundancy of program codes, 293
Relational database management systems, 321
Relationship management, 20, 174
Repairs and maintenance, 12
Report generators, 298
Requirement analysis, 187
Requirement specifications, 187, 195
Responsibility, 54
Restoration, 323
Retailers, 11, 105
Retrospective price increases, 157
Retrospective revision of taxes, 158
Right MIS, 64
RISC processor, 262
Risk management, 13, 19, 172
Routers, 273

Sales and marketing, 12, 99
Sales force automation, 107
Sales forecast, 165
Scalability of business processes, 39
Scanners, 268
Search engine listing, 132
Search engines, 39, 113
Secured file transfer protocol, 143
Secured socket layer, 142
Security, 118
Selection of computer, 274
Self diagnostics, 288
Semi structured information, 81
Sensitive analysis, 86
Sequential access, 311
Serial access device, 310
Service providers, 59
Seven resources, 9
Sharing of modules, 295
Shrinking, 179
Simple message transfer protocol, 144
Sincerity of sellers, 118
Social, 8
Social concerns, 362

Social network advertising, 133
Software and hardware interface, 299
Software development service, 60
Software engineering, 201
Software piracy, 257
Software updates, 219
Source programs, 289
Sourcing of inputs, 10
Span of control, 295
Speaker, 271
Speeds up the business, 33
Staff functions, 12
Staffing, 17, 168
Statutory compliances, 13
Strategic plans, 16
Strategy, 15
Structure of business processes, 33
Structured cabling, 272
Structured decisions, 4
Structured information, 80
Structured query language, 323
Substitute, 32
Super resources, 53
Supplier bills payable system, 244
Suppliers, 104
Suppliers bills payables, 156
Switches, 273
Symmetric cryptography, 251
Symmetric encryption, 252
System analysts, 339
System availability, 231
System bus, 263
System controls, 243
System design, 203
System documentation, 217
System flowchart, 71, 204
System response time, 232
System specifications, 204
Systems analysis, 187
Systems audit, 207, 233, 236
Systems audit and control, 235
Systems auditors, 340
Systems manager, 338
Systems theory, 331

Tactical IT applications in business, 21
Tactical plans, 16
Task management, 287
Technical functions, 337

Technical people, 61
Technology perspective, 191
Three dimensions of modern business, 9
Three levels of management, 14
Three tier system, 277
To Be processes, 194
Top down approach, 178, 332
Top management, 14
Touch screen, 268
Transaction data, 52
Transaction files, 308
Transaction processing, 4
Transaction processors, 65
Transaction recovery, 319
Transparency in business, 8
Transport layer security, 142
Transporters, 106
Two tier system, 277

Unit testing, 210
Unstructured information, 80
UPS, 274
User-friendly interface/GUI, 7, 40
User interface, 232
User interview, 189
User manuals, 215
User training, 211
Utility software, 291

Value chain costing, 30

Value for the customers, 52
VDU, 270
Vehicles to reach the markets quicker, 159
Video conferencing, 78
Vision, 14
Voice mail, 77

Warehouses, 11, 105
Waterfall method, 226
Web publishing, 88
Web server, 117
Website, 39, 88
Website hosting, 122
What if analysis, 86
Wholesalers, 11, 105
Wi-fi, 281
Wide area network, 278
WiMax, 281
Wireless LANs, 274
Wireless worries, 368
Wireless/3G technologies, 279
Wisdom, 49
Word processing, 76
Work groups applications, 169
Workflow management, 169
Workflow management systems, 87

ZIP disk, 267